FOR THE RECORD

FROM WALL STREET
TO WASHINGTON

ALSO BY DONALD T. REGAN

A View from the Street

FOR THE RECORD

FROM WALL STREET TO WASHINGTON

DONALD T. REGAN

HUTCHINSON

LONDON MELBOURNE AUCKLAND JOHANNESBURG

First published in Great Britain in 1988 by Hutchinson,
an imprint of Century Hutchinson Ltd, 62–65 Chandos Place,
London WC2N 4NW

Century Hutchinson Australia Pty Ltd
PO Box 496, 16–22 Church Street, Hawthorn, Victoria 3122,
Australia

Century Hutchinson New Zealand Limited,
PO Box 40–086, Glenfield, Auckland 10, New Zealand

Century Hutchinson South Africa (Pty) Ltd
PO Box 337, Bergvlei 2012, South Africa

British Library Cataloguing in Publication Data
Regan, Donald T.
For the record: from Wall Street to Washington.
1. United States. Politics—Biographies
I. Title
973.927′092′4

ISBN 0–09–173622–6
Printed and bound in Great Britain by
Butler & Tanner Ltd, Frome and London

TO ANN

—and all the others who stood by me

Contents

CONTENTS

Acknowledgments

Many people helped me in the writing of this book, and they deserve credit for whatever virtues it may be judged to have. Its flaws are my responsibility.

In particular, I wish to thank my wife, Ann, for her patience, devotion, and help all during our life together and especially in my final weeks at the White House, when it looked as though I was the condemned man and every meal she set before me might be my last.

When, only weeks after I left the White House, Charles McCarry agreed to help me organize my experiences and materials into a book, he stipulated that he wanted no credit or acknowledgment of any kind in return for his efforts. I am overruling his wishes in saying that no finer person could have been found for this exercise. In the face of my enthusiasms and occasional doubts he remained calm, cool, and professional. It was a great relationship.

My associate, Tom Dawson, has been a tower of strength and an inexhaustible source of energy during the seven eventful years we have been together. Tom's gift of almost total recall for persons, places, names, and dates is nothing short of phenomenal. Two other associates from government days, Bruce Thompson from Treasury and Bill Henkel from the White House, have been helpful in furnishing details and confirming recollection. Peter Wallison, who also was with me at Treasury, and was Counsel to the President during part of my time at the White House, has provided invaluable insight and excellent advice. Peter's associate, John Mintz, was with me during the Iran-Contra hearings and afterward.

Larry Speakes also provided wise counsel. John Kelly, Lee Roselle, and Betty Lehrman, my very efficient secretary for many years, refreshed my memory of people and events at Merrill Lynch.

Norman Brokaw of the William Morris Agency is the godfather of this book and of many other aspects of the new career I have undertaken since leaving the Reagan Administration. Norman's colleagues in New York, Robert Gottlieb and Owen Laster, handled the negotiations with skill and sensitivity.

At Harcourt Brace Jovanovich, Bill and Peter Jovanovich had faith in this project from the start, my editor, Daphne Merkin, kept the faith from first to last, and Claire Wachtel coordinated a hectic production process with steady efficiency.

My assistant at the White House, Brooke Vosburgh, gave up her White House position to accompany me to private life, where she worked tirelessly to make the transition smooth and my surroundings comfortable so I could write. Brooke dedicated the better part of a year to organizing hundreds of pages of notes and manuscript while keeping the daily routine of the office running without a hitch. Kathleen McCloskey spent so many hours at the word processor that I'm sure she must have seen my scrawls in her sleep. Another colleague from West Wing days, Kathy Reid, helped check the manuscript for accuracy, and her bubbly personality, levelheaded judgment, and excellent memory kept us all on the straight and narrow.

To all these, and to others whom I have not mentioned, I am deeply grateful.

D. T. R.

Alexandria, Virginia
March 1988

Foreword

"The most glorious exploits do not always furnish us with the clearest discoveries of vice or virtue in men," wrote Plutarch in his *Life* of Alexander. "Sometimes a matter of less moment, an expression or a jest, informs us better of their characters and inclinations than the most famous sieges, the greatest armaments, or the bloodiest battles."

I have kept Plutarch's observation in mind while writing this memoir of my more than six years of public service as the Secretary of the Treasury and as Chief of Staff in the White House under President Reagan, and have attempted to describe the President I served, the people I encountered in the course of that service, and the events in which I participated, exactly as I remember them.

Although I have consulted some of my own unclassified memoranda in order to verify dates and facts, I have not based this narrative on classified documents. Nothing is quoted or paraphrased from unpublished or non-public Presidential papers or other confidential White House documents. All my life I have kept detailed notes of my workaday actions and conversations, and I did the same while I worked for the President. Those contemporaneous notes, and the press, constituted my basic source material. Journalists and historians may be disappointed to hear it, but there is really no need to consult secret documents in describing the fortieth Presidency because, as a practical matter, it kept no official secrets. In the Reagan Administration the leak was raised to the status of an art form. Everything, or nearly everything, the President and his close associates did or knew appeared in the newspapers and on the networks with the least possible delay.

Except where press reports are quoted, this book is free of hearsay. In all but a very few cases I have reported only what I observed with my own eyes or heard with my own ears. Where it has been necessary to describe an offstage event in order to make sense of the author's direct experience, I have always quoted or paraphrased the account of an eyewitness as the eyewitness himself narrated it to me personally. Direct quotations of individuals are based on my notes or my clear recollection of words spoken. Out of deference to the office and the man, I have not enclosed language attributed to the President in quotation marks except in cases where his words have already appeared in print elsewhere.

Because actions that would otherwise bewilder the reader cannot be understood in its absence, I have revealed in this book what was probably the most closely guarded domestic secret of the Reagan White House. In any other household in America, this would have been a harmless, even charming, secret; and so far as I know it did the country no irreparable damage during the eight years in which it was a dominating factor in White House business. The reader will be shocked or amused by it according to the way he already feels about a President who has inspired more affection in his admirers, and more bafflement in his adversaries, than almost any other in our history.

Between the graffito and the whitewash lies the brushstroke, and it is the brushstroke that I have striven to employ in rendering this portrait of one of the most interesting and maddening experiences of my life. The main topics—the Iran-Contra affair; the President's convictions, style, and economic philosophy; the negotiations with Mikhail S. Gorbachev; and my differences with Nancy Reagan, among others—had already been systematically salted into the press by persons acting on behalf of the President and his wife.

I was not one of those people. In writing what I myself observed and did as the President's principal assistant, I have introduced no new subjects, but rather have aimed to provide footnotes, a glossary, and alternative explanations to the extensive but deeply flawed narrative that already exists in the public press. Culpability for error and irresponsibility in that untidy journalistic record certainly does not fall primarily on the press; reporters write and broadcast what they are told, and they are often told lies. Those who know the truth have some obligation to prevent lies from entering unchallenged into history.

Throughout this narrative I have been as frank as I know how to be. That, too, is the habit of a lifetime. I have described things as I observed and understood them; otherwise there would have been little purpose in writing this book. Others will no doubt remember what happened from somewhat different perspectives. They will have the opportunity to say so in their own memoirs. I hope that they, too, will be candid. The question of whether everything about the Reagan years should be on the public record was settled long ago by the President's most intimate advisers, and we must all be content to let the public and history decide where truth and justice lie.

In my opinion, this much is incontestable: the Reagan Administration, in its extraordinary accomplishments as in its apparently incurable compulsion to talk about itself through the media, has been one of the wonders of our history and a most illuminating case study of populism in action.

PART ONE

A Case of Poison

· 1 ·

The End of the Beginning

Nancy Reagan stammers slightly when she is upset, and her voice was unsteady when she called me from Bethesda Naval Hospital on Friday afternoon, July 12, 1985, to tell me that her husband, the President of the United States, would require surgery for the removal of a large polyp in his intestinal tract. In illnesses of this kind speedy treatment is essential, and so I was concerned—apprehensive would be a better word—when she told me that the operation might be delayed for a day and a half.

"I'm reading something into this," I said, speaking cautiously because we were on the telephone. "Am I on firm ground in doing it?"

"Yes, possibly," the First Lady replied.

Her answer worried me. I feared two things—first, that President Reagan's condition was more serious than his wife had been able to tell me over the telephone, and second, that the First Lady was choosing the date for surgery in consultation with her astrologer. Of the two possibilities the second seemed the more likely. Virtually every major move and decision the Reagans made during my time as White House Chief of Staff was cleared in advance with a woman in San Francisco who drew up horoscopes to make certain that the planets were in a favorable alignment for the enterprise.

Nancy Reagan seemed to have absolute faith in the clairvoyant powers of this woman, who had predicted that "something bad" was going to happen to the President shortly before he was wounded in an assassination attempt in 1981. Before that, Mrs. Reagan had consulted a different astrologer, but now believed that this person had lost her powers. The First Lady referred to the woman in San Francisco as "My Friend."

Although I never met this seer—Mrs. Reagan passed along her prognostications to me after conferring with her on the telephone—she had become such a factor in my work, and in the highest affairs of the nation, that at one point I kept a color-coded calendar on my desk (numerals highlighted in green ink for "good" days, red for "bad" days, yellow for "iffy" days) as an aid to remembering when it was propitious to move the President of the United States from one place to another, or schedule him to speak in public, or commence negotiations with a foreign power.

On the telephone from Bethesda, Mrs. Reagan continued to suggest that the removal of the polyp would be delayed. "Tell Larry [Speakes, the White House spokesman] to say that the President will have surgery next week," she said. It was now Friday afternoon. "Larry can say that the polyp was larger than expected, but he mustn't say a word more than that."

Her tone was insistent and tinged with anxiety. This was not the moment to dispute the wishes of a worried wife. But I did not altogether agree with the advice she was giving me. The risks of withholding the smallest part of this story from the media and thereby creating the suspicion of a cover-up were obvious. So was the danger of making a statement about the timing of the operation that might later have to be withdrawn.

After the First Lady hung up, I called Speakes, who was already at the hospital, and told him to be very careful to tell the whole truth, or as much as we knew, but not to go beyond it.

"No dissimulation," I said. "And no alarms."

Minutes later Dr. Burton Smith, the senior White House physician, gave me the first professional report on the results of the examination of the President. He said that the growth was not malignant but could become so. My notes of this conversation describe the growth—or "mass" or "polyp" or "lesion": the terminology varied from doctor to doctor—as being "the size of a golf ball." The President would probably remain in the hospital for seven to ten days after surgery.

Dr. Kenneth Lee, a Navy doctor detailed to the White House, confirmed these general observations and told me that Mrs. Reagan had been discussing the timing of the operation with the Presidential physicians. So far she had told the President only that a polyp had been found and that it must be removed.

When the matter of timing was raised with the President himself, he settled the issue. He had already prepared for the colonoscopic examination, and the preliminaries for major surgery included measures, such as fasting and the cleansing of the bowel, that had just been completed for the less serious procedure. There was no point in going through them a second time, as he would have to do if he delayed.

Why wait? the President asked the doctors. Do the tests and go ahead with the operation. I can function just as well in the hospital as at home.

When the President said this it was Friday, July 12, 1985. That night he would undergo a CAT scan and other tests, and the results of a preliminary biopsy of the growth would become available. The surgery would be performed on Saturday.

In his dealings with the doctors, Ronald Reagan was cheerful, optimistic, considerate, courteous—himself. Although he would sometimes remind me, when I suggested a change in plans, that certain days were not good days for a speech or a public appearance, I never knew for sure whether he was aware of the role played by the First Lady's astrologer in the making of his schedule. But on this occasion, if the Friend's powers were in fact invoked, the Chief Executive apparently decided to ignore them. I later learned that the Friend had failed to predict the discovery of a malignant growth in the President's bowel.

All Presidential decisions create work on a grand scale. Obviously a decision to undergo surgery magnifies the urgency and complexity of these labors. The President had said that he could function just as well in the hospital as in the White House; it was up to his staff to make sure that he could in fact do so. In the

White House, I turned to first things first. How long would the President be under the effects of anesthesia and therefore unable to exercise his office? What were the procedures for a temporary transfer of power under the Twenty-fifth Amendment? Vice President George Bush was vacationing with his family at their summer place in Kennebunkport, Maine. On the secure telephone, I told him that the news about the President was not good. We agreed that he would stay where he was, go on with what he was doing, and await further word.

No government in history can have been more sensitive to the media, or more driven by the printed word and the television image, than the Reagan Administration. The way in which the news of the President's illness was given to the press was vitally important—not only because the people of the United States had a right to know the facts, but also in terms of the President's peace of mind. I knew that he would be deeply concerned that the episode be handled in a way that served the truth without creating undue excitement.

Mrs. Reagan, whose own skills as a manager of the media are formidable, had already told Larry Speakes that he must avoid the use of the words "cancer" and "massive." I asked Speakes, though he hardly needed such guidance, to be sure to discuss the case in detail with the doctors so that he would be able to describe the President's condition fully and accurately with reporters.

Meanwhile the Cabinet and the leaders of the Senate and the House of Representatives were informed of the situation. I spoke to some of these men and women myself. Among them was Robert C. ("Bud") McFarlane, the National Security Advisor, who told me that he had an urgent need to report to the President on a matter of great importance.

"I've just got to see the President," McFarlane said, using a phrase that would become familiar to me over the next hours and days.

His sense of urgency was obvious. At the time I had no idea that McFarlane's matter of great importance was, as he later testified, a verbal message from the prime minister of Israel raising the possibility of a political dialogue between U.S. officials and members of the government of Iran. I told McFarlane I would do my best for him.

While these things happened, I had been trying to get through to Mrs. Reagan, who was with the President. At 5:50 P.M. she called me back to say that the doctors had told her that the growth in the President's bowel was a large flat mass that had all the earmarks of being malignant. She had not confided this information to her husband or to Speakes. My earlier fears notwithstanding, this came as very sad news to me.

It was important to maintain an atmosphere of calm. For the sake of appearances—that is, to avoid speculation by the media—the First Lady had decided not to spend the night at the hospital. When I spoke to George Bush later that evening, he told me that he was anxious to return to Washington. The press was already at his gate in Kennebunkport. But after we discussed the impression a Vice Presidential night flight to the capital might create, he decided to remain in Maine until morning.

At Bethesda, the President's CAT scan was interrupted twice by power surges caused by electrical storms. Around 11 P.M. Dr. Smith told me some excellent news.

"The liver's okay—and that's vital," he said.

Later I was informed that the first biopsy had revealed no cancerous cells, but I was less cheered by this news than I might have been: Mrs. Reagan, who often described herself as the daughter and the sister of physicians (her late stepfather and her stepbrother were medical doctors), had warned me that the mass was so large that the preliminary biopsy, based on a sliver of tissue, might not produce an accurate result.

Surgery was scheduled for 11 A.M. on Saturday, July 13. When I saw the President shortly after nine o'clock, he was lying in his hospital bed with books all around him. Oddly enough, the fact that he was dressed in a green hospital nightgown did not make him seem any the less Presidential. He was the same bright-eyed, apple-cheeked, shaved and combed Ronald Reagan as the man I saw every day in a business suit.

"Are you ready for the operation, Mr. President?"

Sure, he said. I'm not worried. I told 'em, Let's get it over with.

At 10:25, I returned to the President's suite. He was sitting up in bed with the First Lady by his side. After a moment or two of small talk, Mrs. Reagan withdrew to the small private waiting room that adjoined the President's bedroom.

Fred Fielding, the White House Counsel, was with me. He had prepared a number of versions of a letter for the President's signature temporarily transferring his powers to the Vice President during the period of his incapacity. We showed the President the long and short forms of this document, and recommended that he sign the longer one. As is his habit, he did so without question or demur. According to my watch, the time was 10:32 A.M.; the whole process of placing the Presidency of the most powerful nation in history into the hands of a constitutional caretaker had consumed seven minutes.

As he put down his pen, the President surprised me by leaping to a new subject. The annual battle of the budget was going on, with the President's opponents on Capitol Hill in full cry. In that morning's *Washington Post*, Senator Robert Dole, the chairman of the Senate Budget Committee and a member of the President's own party, had accused the White House of "surrendering to the deficit."

Even after a lifetime in the public eye the President is easily stung by printed criticism, especially when it comes from someone he thinks ought to be on his side. He was upset over Dole's remarks and in a feisty mood.

What's Bob Dole think he's up to? he asked. What's he doing to get this budget moving? I'll never raise taxes—those people on the Hill are going to have to cut spending. You tell Bob that!

I promised that I would.

Not many subjects have the power to bring out the battler in this most affable and passive of Presidents. The contest between the spenders and the fiscal conservatives is one of them. Reagan's eyes shone with conviction and with the pleasure of argument on a favorite subject.

His wife took things more personally. "When you call Bob

Dole," she said in a tone of deep sarcasm, "be sure to thank him for his remarks about this President just before he went into surgery."

It was time to go. Fielding and I wished the President well; I made some lame joke about everything coming out all right. The President laughed and gave us a cheery wave as we went out the door.

As the world knows, the President's surgery was successful. A growth five centimeters in extent was removed by the surgeons, together with two smaller polyps and a section of the large intestine. No other tumors were found anywhere else in the body. The fact that the growth had been detected and excised early was a favorable augury.

As they emerged from the operating room with the happy news, the doctors commented on the President's remarkable physique. He was seventy-four at the time and already the oldest man ever to serve in his office. One of the surgeons, his professional tact perhaps overcome by a sense of wonder, exclaimed, "This man has the insides of a forty-year-old!"

The President slept or dozed from 11:28 A.M. until about 7 P.M. under the influence of the anesthetics. All the while, of course, George Bush was acting President of the United States under the terms of the letter the President had signed before entering the operating room. I asked the doctors if they believed that the President was now able to resume the powers of his office. They saw no reason why he should not do so.

These small moments of history are to me very affecting. At 7:10 P.M., when Fred Fielding and I entered the recovery room bearing the letter by which he would reclaim his powers, we must have worn very solemn expressions, because the President was ready with a mordant joke.

The Russians have dropped the bomb! he cried jovially, but in a voice slightly strangled by the tubes in his throat and nose.

"No, no, no," I replied. "We just wanted to see how you are."

Despite his good humor, the President was pale and drawn. Another tube and needle in his arm were connected to a bottle of intravenous solution. His hair was neatly combed, and contrary to later rumors, it had not turned gray during the operation but remained its natural dark brown.

The recovery room looked something like a Presidential recovery room in a motion picture. It was vast and every bed but one had been moved out. A team of grave-faced doctors and Navy nurses hovered over the patient. Secret Service men guarded the door and other agents stood watch inside the room, including at least one armed with an Uzi submachine gun. White House communications specialists stood by in case of need. The "football"—the briefcase containing the codes for use in case of nuclear attack—was not far away.

The President took all this for granted; it was the apparatus of his everyday life.

The President's reading glasses were not in evidence. Holding up the letter, I said, "Can you read?"

Let me see that thing, said the President.

He held the letter at arm's length, head thrown back to focus on the typewritten page.

"Do you understand it?" I asked.

Yup, I'll sign it now, said the President.

I gave him a pen from my coat pocket. It was the kind he liked, a dark blue plastic souvenir pen with his signature embossed in gold on the barrel. Maneuvering the pen around the tubes and other hospital apparatus, he signed (black ink—it shows up better when photocopied), capped the pen, and gave it back to me. It was 7:22 P.M.

Then, in an impressive display of alertness, he took up where he had left off before he went under the anesthetic—with Senator Dole and his public criticism of the White House.

What's the matter with Bob Dole? the President said. He's got to be a leader on this budget.

He made some joke from his enormous fund of stories on human foibles. He seemed so strong and clear-minded that I took another minute or two to tell him that all was calm on the international scene. He listened, then thought of something that made his cheerful expression change.

Any word on the hostages? he asked.

I said that there was nothing new on the Americans held by

terrorists in the Middle East. It was a subject that had long preoccupied the President, and I was not surprised that it was very
nearly the first thing that came into his mind when he regained
consciousness after the ordeal of surgery. Ronald Reagan is a
deeply compassionate and patriotic man. The thought of kidnapped American citizens being held in makeshift jails for the
"crime" of being Americans preyed on his mind. The scenes he
had seen on television showing the hostages in captivity and his
talks with their agonized families had affected him profoundly.
On July 2, he had visited the grave of Robert Dean Stetham, a
young American sailor murdered by terrorists aboard the hijacked TWA Flight 847. Later, at Andrews Air Force Base, he
had talked to the young man's family, and to the TWA hostages
and their families. He wanted the remaining hostages back.

The President would not drop the subject. For longer than I
would have thought wise, we talked about the hostages—how to
get them back, how to get our hands on the terrorists who were
responsible for crimes against American citizens and bring them
to justice.

At last he turned to another topic.

How long do I have to stay here? the President wanted to
know.

He was anxious to get back to work. His brother Neil, two
years older than himself, had been released from the hospital
only four or five days after an operation that was similar to the
President's.

I want to get out of here soon, Don, the President said. See
what you can do.

"Mr. President," I replied, "forget it. Just follow your doctors'
orders."

He frowned in displeasure. Such expressions never linger long
on the Presidential features. In a moment he recovered his good
nature and smiled.

But Ronald Reagan was very unhappy to be where he was.

The urge to call on a hospitalized President is almost irresistible.
The President himself asked that visitors be kept to a minimum.

Members of the Cabinet will want to come and see me, he said. But unless they have something urgent to talk about, say no.

He told me a Hollywood story. Years before, when he was still a movie star, he had spent eighty days in traction and had got into such a routine of reading, thinking, doing his exercises, and planning his meals that he came to resent the well-meaning people who interrupted him by coming to call. The President, who does not like to think ill of his fellow men, seemed to be as worried about resenting his visitors as about his own comfort.

We took the necessary measures to protect his privacy inside the hospital, posting Secret Service men and other White House personnel to divert the curious. In earlier episodes of sickness and injury, I was told, the President had been the subject of sightseeing by hospital staff, who found excuses to putter around his bed; some had even asked him for autographs and he had good-naturedly acquiesced. This time we found ways to protect him from his own geniality by strictly limiting access to his sickroom.

But I never imagined that the President would refuse to see anybody at all. Vice President Bush, who had returned to Washington during the crisis and had comported himself with his usual flawless tact and loyalty, wanted to come to the hospital and pay his respects. Bud McFarlane, too, continued to press for a meeting with the President. Even if Bud had had nothing out of the ordinary to tell the President, it would have been a good thing for the President to be briefed on national security matters; he loved to read the daily intelligence summary and hear the news and gossip of the international scene. I scheduled both men for 9 A.M. Monday.

The First Lady objected. "Why are you doing this?" she asked over the telephone on Sunday evening. "It's too much. He needs rest."

I explained my reasoning. It did not impress her. She was adamant, distraught. The day before, while removing a picture of herself and the President from the wall in order to hang it in his hospital room (in a spot, she said, that would ensure that the picture was the first thing he saw when he opened his eyes), she had fallen off a chair and knocked the wind out of herself. That day, Chris Wallace, the NBC White House correspondent, had seen her stumble as she got out of the car at the hospital. This had seemed a small matter to me, but she was afraid that Wallace might report the incident on national television, and that the media might somehow learn that she had fallen off the chair.

Our conversations since the President's operation had been devoted almost entirely to the media. Mrs. Reagan had designed a number of photo opportunities for the White House photographer, always insisting that the camera angle be such that the tubes in the President's nose and mouth did not show, and that she and the President be shown together. The photographs included one as she greeted her husband on her arrival at the hospital, and another the scene as the two held hands on his first day out of bed. Tomorrow they would visit the children's ward together in the company of photographers. Mrs. Reagan believed that these pictures ought to be released to the media as soon as possible as a means of "humanizing" the President's experience in the hospital. I agreed that this would be done, but also spoke about the necessity of making a full and frank statement of the facts should the biopsy show that the growth removed from the President was cancerous. This was, naturally, a more difficult subject. "All that," she said, "has to be downplayed."

Mrs. Reagan's voice was angry. She had heard that Vice President Bush and I might go to Bethesda by helicopter. This was true. The round trip by car took an hour and a half, and I was anxious to conserve time in my schedule, which was divided into fifteen-minute segments, beginning at 7:15 A.M. and ending well into the evening. The First Lady objected vehemently to my travel by helicopter—a Presidential form of transportation. Listening to her voice, I jotted down the words "*very* mad."

In the end—the conversation had lasted for twenty minutes—I agreed that I would check with the doctors in the morning as to whether the President was really up to receiving Bush and McFarlane, and that I would reconsider the helicopter.

I had hardly hung up the phone when I received a call from Edward Hickey, an old friend of the Reagans who was in charge of scheduling White House transportation. Ed, who died in 1988, was a good friend of mine, too.

"I'd cancel the helicopter if I were you, Don," he said. "The First Lady's staff are talking about it."

"Why should they talk about it?" I asked. "I'm just trying to save time. I've got to go out there seven days a week and it's forty minutes by car each way—that's more than ten hours down the drain in a single week."

"That would be a good reason to fly instead of drive under normal circumstances," Ed replied. "But right now circumstances are not normal. The buzzards are out, Don. Be very careful what you're doing."

His choice of language took me aback. So did the realization that my actions were being monitored by the First Lady's staff and turned into a subject for gossip. This was something new in my life and I did not welcome it.

"Okay," I said. "Cancel the damn helicopter."

That night, the second after his operation, the President stayed up late, reading. He finished a novel before dozing off. He was experiencing a little pain now because the effects of the inter-thekal morphine he had been given had worn off.

On Monday morning I arrived at the White House by 7:15, my usual time. Very soon after that Mrs. Reagan called me again to continue her argument against a hospital visit by George Bush and Bud McFarlane. I explained that McFarlane had an urgent reason to see the President; after all, he was the National Security Advisor.

"Whatever it is, Bud can put it in writing," she said. "Ronnie can read. But talking to visitors will tire him out. Besides, it would be very bad for anybody to see him while he still has tubes in his nose."

I told McFarlane that he would probably have to wait a little before meeting with the President. His disappointment was obvious; his tone of voice was insistent.

"Look, Don," he said once again, "I've just got to see the President."

I did not ask him why; I was not even curious. McFarlane was his own man with his own job and his own reasons for talking to the Chief Executive. Ordinarily he reported to the President every day, delivering the national security briefing at 9:30 A.M. My job was to make such meetings possible, not put myself between the two men. I promised McFarlane that I would arrange a meeting as soon as possible, but I am not sure that McFarlane believed that I meant it. Bud is a man who smarts when slighted, and he may well have thought, as was later said and written, that I was blocking his access to the President for reasons of my own. That was not the case, but I was not at liberty to explain the real reason why he was being shut out.

On Monday afternoon the doctors reported that the biopsy showed the presence of a malignancy. The cancer had penetrated the wall of the intestine, but it did not appear to have spread further before it was removed. There was at least a fifty-fifty chance that it would not recur. No chemotherapy or radiation would be necessary. The President would require chest X rays and CAT scans at regular intervals, but he should be back to normal in a matter of weeks.

At 3:20 P.M. Mrs. Reagan and the doctors gave the President the news. He told them that he was relieved to hear that the cancer had been removed. Apparently his cheerful mind did not dwell on a recurrence of the malignancy, for he asked few if any questions on this subject.

That's the end of that, the President seemed to be saying. Let's talk about something else.

"It was as though he had had a wart removed from his finger," said someone who had been present. "His attitude was, Well, that trifle is taken care of, let's forget about it."

That morning I had tiptoed into the President's room to find him asleep in a chair with a biography of Calvin Coolidge open on his lap. When I saw him the next morning, Tuesday, at eleven o'clock, he told me he had finished the book, and he chatted for a moment about Coolidge, a President he admires for his warnings against speculation and greed, his decision to keep the government out of the marketplace, and his successful foreign policy, especially the 1928 Kellogg-Briand Pact renouncing aggressive war. Except for the pursuit of the bandit Sandino in Nicaragua by the U.S. Marines, the Coolidge Administration had engaged in no military action. I listened with interest. My wife's father, a Marine captain, had been killed on active service in Nicaragua in 1927.

The President looked strong and alert. Evidently he had put the biopsy report out of his mind; the subject did not arise. I told him that Prime Minister Margaret Thatcher had phoned from London the afternoon before to ask about his condition. She told me that she had been dining with Chief Justice Warren Burger and others and had decided to get up from the table and call because they were all worried about the President. Was he really all right? Mrs. Thatcher asked. I told the President I had assured her that the media reports were correct; we were hiding nothing, holding nothing back. Mrs. Thatcher's thoughtful gesture pleased Reagan; he and the Prime Minister, both conservatives and both political dark horses who have won office and the grudging respect of their enemies against the odds, truly like and admire each other.

Earlier that day I had chaired a Cabinet breakfast to discuss the budget. Afterward, carrying out the President's instructions to talk about the budget with Senator Dole and the rest of the Republican leadership of the House and Senate, I went up to Capitol Hill. The senators and congressmen assembled in House Minority Leader Bob Michel's office gave me a report from the trenches. I delivered the President's message: There would be no tax increase. He would go along with the Senate budget bill if additional savings could be found to make up for the $28 billion shortfall created by preserving COLAs.

Dole wanted to know why David Stockman, the Director of the Office of Management and Budget, had been quoted as saying that the budget cuts made by the Senate did not matter. Earlier, on the telephone, Dole had been sharp-tongued and unrepentant when I told him that the President and his wife had been upset by his remarks in the *Post*. A story in the *Washington Times* had claimed that I was going to support Congressman Jack

Kemp of New York for the Republican nomination for President four years hence. Dole, himself an undeclared candidate for the nomination, was upset about *that;* I told him there was no truth in the report, and that as far as the budget was concerned, his fight should be with the Democrats in the House of Representatives, not with his own President. I did not deliver the First Lady's more sardonic message.

At the hospital, I told the President that I had delivered his message to the Hill, and to Dole.

Stay tough, he said. Tell them I'm not going to raise taxes, no matter what. And I'm not going to go back on my campaign promises.

Then, once again, he raised the subject of the hostages, asking whether I thought Syria and Iran might be helpful. Ali Akbar Rafsanjani, the Speaker of the Iranian parliament, had been helpful in persuading the Shiite terrorists who hijacked TWA Flight 847 to release their hostages, including 134 Americans. The President, in a secret message, had thanked Rafsanjani for his actions and had expressed the hope for better U.S.-Iranian relations.

On Tuesday evening I mentioned to McFarlane the President's question, and we discussed Syria, Iran, and the possible role of Israel in any plan to release the hostages. We spoke in generalities; McFarlane did not tell me about the secret message from Prime Minister Peres of Israel—the message that started the Iran ball rolling.

Once again McFarlane asked when he could see the President. His words were the same as before: "I've just got to see him."

I told him that as soon as the doctors would permit it, I'd get him in.

That evening Mrs. Reagan, in the course of a forty-minute telephone conversation, came down hard against a visit by the Vice President.

I said, "Come on, Nancy. This is the third day. I wouldn't blame George Bush if he was very upset about this. Why can't he go out there for just a few minutes?"

Her answer was an adamant no.

"What about Bud McFarlane?"

Her voice rose. "No, no, no," she replied. "Absolutely, this President cannot be put through all these visits. Don, he's got to be kept quiet. He's getting better, but having all these visitors will wear him out."

At ten o'clock or so Mrs. Reagan called me back and said that she had changed her mind. George Bush could visit the President after all. I called up the Vice President and told him that the President would be happy to see him the next morning.

But McFarlane was still excluded. When I gave him this news he said that he would put something in an envelope for the President and for me. Knowing what I know now, I am astonished that he even suggested putting his message in writing. In fact, he never did.

"All right," I said. "But stand by. If I can possibly get you in to see him tomorrow morning, I'll do it."

When I was ushered into the President's hospital suite on Wednesday morning, I was startled to find him perched on a chair in the sitting room, chatting with George Bush.

I spoke before I thought, blurting out these words: "What the hell are *you* doing here?"

The President gave me a broad grin. The tubes had been removed from his nose and he looked as if he'd just had a shave and a shower. George Bush's face was wreathed in that smile of affectionate wonder that Americans reserve for precocious children and for the Commander-in-Chief.

Well, the President replied, George was coming so I came out here to see him. When I heard the sirens I said to the nurse, 'Get me out of bed.' I walked down to the sitting room, and by the time George arrived, here I was.

If the President was tired out by Bush's company or mine, he showed no sign of it. We talked for forty-five minutes about the budget, the tax reform bill, and the future of Social Security. He told California stories and cracked a couple of jokes. We called in the photographer while he signed some bills and then an extradition treaty with Great Britain that would make it more difficult for those who had committed acts of terror in the United

Kingdom to find refuge in the United States. He was in high spirits from beginning to end, and as gleeful as Huck Finn for having pulled a good one on Bush and me by turning up in the sitting room.

I asked him what time he had gone to bed the night before.

Oh, I stayed up late and watched Bogart and Bacall, the President said. You know, it's amazing, the difference between movies today and the classics of yesteryear. We had much better writers in those days, and better directors. They knew how to imply things, how to leave something to the imagination. There was no filth, no sleaze.

This was one of the President's favorite subjects: very few R-rated movies were shown at the White House or at Camp David. It could only be a very good sign, that he was back on the old subjects as if indeed nothing had happened.

Finally, on Thursday, July 18, Mrs. Reagan gave permission for Bud McFarlane to visit the President. Even then, on the sixth day of his hospitalization, she was reluctant. But the situation could not continue; the White House was abuzz with happy gossip about the President's high spirits and remarkable recovery, and stories were beginning to appear in the media suggesting that I was freezing out McFarlane and feuding with Bush.

"Regan appeared to be the single assistant carrying information to the President," said the *Washington Post*. George Bush was quoted in the same paper as saying that I was "doing a darn good job of running the White House in the President's absence," adding, "it is just as if the President is on vacation." Speakes attempted to clarify matters as follows: "The Chief of Staff is not making any decisions that the President doesn't want him to make."

The press corps may have thought that Bush and Speakes were protesting too much. The drama surrounding the President's surgery was beginning to subside and the correspondents on the Presidential beat, marooned outside the windows of a recuperating President, were looking for a new story. Reporters were asking members of the staff if I had become some sort of

Prime Minister or acting President. Nancy Reagan and I were the only people they ever saw going in and out of the hospital. A rumor was abroad that I would only approve pictures of the President in which I, too, appeared.

Later on I complained to Mrs. Reagan about the unfairness of this press campaign. She did not sympathize. "Pull back," she said. "Keep a low profile. Don't be seen out too much; people are talking."

I did my best to dampen the speculation by avoiding television appearances and keeping contacts with the press to a minimum, but it was a losing battle. In obedience to the First Lady's wishes, I was the only one besides herself who was seeing the President. Because he is news incarnate, that made me news.

When I spoke to Mrs. Reagan about McFarlane's need to see the President, I was already exasperated by the situation.

"It's unconscionable," I told her, "and damn curious to the press and foreign governments that the President isn't seeing anyone from his National Security Council staff."

At last she relented.

Bud came into the room at 10:22 A.M. and spoke to the President for the next twenty-three minutes. This meeting which was to have such fateful consequences seemed routine at the time, and it seems routine in memory.

I was present throughout. My notes say, "Middle East/Hostage Release/problem," then "Soviet/Geneva arms talks."

McFarlane has testified that he mentioned to the President the possibility of establishing a political dialogue with Iranians through Israeli contacts before he entered the hospital. I don't remember his having done so, and if he had I don't know why he would have felt such a sense of urgency ("I've just got to see the President") to tell him the same thing a second time.

In any case I do not remember that the hospital meeting was marked by a sense of drama. McFarlane asked the President if he was interested in talking to the Iranians, reasoning that this was a good idea because the United States ought to be talking to the Iranians about the future so as to have established contacts if and when a new government came into being in Tehran. The hostages were discussed in a general way. The sense of this part of the conversation, as well as I can remember it, was that the Iranians, who had already been helpful in connection with the TWA hijacking, might be disposed to be helpful in other situations if we were more friendly to them.

There is nothing in my notes or in my memory to suggest that the idea of swapping arms for hostages was mentioned by either man on this occasion. As I write, more than two years afterward, I am sure that any mention of such a scheme would have made me prick up my ears. Any suggestion to do such a thing would have been such a departure from established policy, and such a departure from the President's instincts, that it would have been noted by everyone present—including, I am sure, the President himself. He was discussing a subject that was of the deepest interest to him, and he was certainly in full possession of his faculties.

The question of Iran took up no more than ten or twelve minutes. McFarlane spent at least half of his time before he left at 10:45 talking about the Geneva arms negotiations, another subject close to the President's heart. It hardly seems likely that an entirely new policy, involving a brusque departure from past practices and established principle—and bringing in a third country, Israel, as a middleman in a secret arms sale—could have been decided on in such a brief encounter. The President said later that he had no recollection of this meeting. That did not surprise me. I wonder if I would have remembered it if I hadn't had such a difficult time persuading his wife to let it take place.

After leaving the President I went back to the White House and worked at my desk until early evening. In the six days since the President entered the hospital, I had worked eighty-seven hours, including many hours on the telephone with the First Lady.

At 5:20 a happy Nancy Reagan called. The day before she had flown out to the carrier *America* off the coast of Virginia and had an enjoyable visit with the crew. She had arranged a very successful photo opportunity at the hospital, with the President waving to the press from a window with her at his side, and he had looked happy and vigorous. The President was coming home on Saturday and she wanted the two of them to be photographed waving from the balcony of the White House.

"That would make a great picture!" she said enthusiastically.

The next day Mrs. Reagan would be more matter-of-fact, giving emphatic advice on Presidential appointments and asking what kind of a house had been found as a Presidential residence during the Geneva summit in November.

But today she was elated. She and the President were going to leave for the ranch on August 10 to complete his convalescence. Insofar as it is possible for the most famous man in the world to be alone, he would be alone with his wife. Ronald Reagan loves the ranch, largely built with his own hands, and guards its privacy jealously. Invitations to outsiders—even to his closest friends and aides—are very rare, and almost never involve an overnight stay.

There was, however, one cloud in an otherwise blue sky. The press was reporting that the President hadn't talked to his children since his operation. Mrs. Reagan wanted that impression corrected.

"How could he talk to them?" she asked. "There was a tube in his nose, in his mouth, in his arm. There was no way he could have talked to them."

All her husband could do was nod and mumble, she said, and only she could understand what he was saying.

· 2 ·

In the Kingdom of the Blind

The meeting at Bethesda Naval Hospital between the President and Bud McFarlane was, of course, the first in a sequence of events that very nearly led to the fall of one of the most popular Presidencies in the history of the United States. That is clear to everyone now. But at the time the matter seemed so unremarkable, so low in the President's order of priorities, that far less time and thought were devoted to it than to the discussion of an acerbic remark made in the heat of an interview by Senator Dole, a man who is justly celebrated for his sarcasm.

The McFarlane meeting passed out of the President's memory. The President's state of mind with regard to the hostages did not, however, change. He knew that he had defeated Jimmy Carter in large measure because the Iranians were holding forty-four American hostages in our embassy in Tehran during the 1980 Presidential campaign and Carter seemed weak and ineffectual in the face of this humiliation.

You're an ex-Marine, the President said to me. Do you know what the first line of the "Marine Hymn" is about? Thomas Jefferson sent the Marines to the shores of Tripoli to rescue Americans who were being held for ransom by Barbary pirates.

The President's old friend William Casey, Director of Central Intelligence, had informed him that William Buckley, one of the hostages, was a CIA officer and that he was undoubtedly being tortured by his captors. The President knew what the released hostages had said about the conditions of their captivity, and of course he had met with the families of hostages.

"Every day we are tortured in our own minds," one of them told him, "wondering, Are our loved ones being tortured? Are they getting any kind of decent food? Are they locked up in a filthy cell?"

They spoke to the President as they might have spoken to a father. He knew that they thought he had the power to help them. The men would shake his hands; the tearful mothers and wives and sisters would embrace him. He left those meetings in a sorrowful mood.

I wish I could tell these people something more than just that we're doing all we can, he said one day.

Once or twice I gripped his arm or laid a hand on his shoulder and said, "Buck up, Mr. President." He would square his shoulders and go on to the next event, but the frustration was immense. He was accused in the media of not doing enough to free the hostages. He was the Commander-in-Chief of more than two million soldiers, sailors, airmen, and Marines, and of thousands of intelligence and law-enforcement agents—yet he could not act.

He would say, Why can't we just get somebody to lead a group in there and storm their installation and take them?

And Shultz or Secretary of Defense Caspar Weinberger or Vice Admiral John M. Poindexter would reply, "We don't know where they are, Mr. President."

The reader should understand that these meetings and conversations concerning the hostages took up very little time. The daily national security briefing lasted only fifteen minutes. In a typical quarter-hour session, McFarlane—and later Poindexter—would also discuss the arms negotiations, Nicaragua, the war in Afghanistan, the fall of Marcos and the rise of Mrs. Aquino in the Philippines, and half a dozen other subjects. The President was deeply concerned about the hostages, but an inventory of the time he spent on this problem in a given month would undoubtedly show a very low total—minutes rather than hours.

Like that first meeting with McFarlane at Bethesda, the events that snowballed into the catastrophe that came to be known as the Iran-Contra affair made little impression at the time that they happened. Much of what happened was hidden from the President (and incidentally from me) by McFarlane and his successor as National Security Advisor, Admiral Poindexter, and by that remarkable young Marine who was a virtual stranger to both of us, Lieutenant Colonel Oliver L. North. According to White House records, North never saw the President alone; when he did see him, he was always accompanied by other people. In my two years as Chief of Staff I talked to North once on the telephone. There is no record that he ever saw me alone; although it is possible that he may have visited me as part of a group, I have no recollection of any such encounter.

Even if this had not been the case, the question exists as to how much attention any President, or any Presidential staff, would have been likely to devote to any single question involving the fate of a very few American citizens during a sixteen-month period in which the Administration was winning the adoption of the most far-reaching tax reform bill in history; fighting two budgets through the Congress; participating in two summit meetings with a new leader of the Soviet Union; and campaigning to maintain a precarious majority in the Senate and a viable minority in the House in a midterm election. At the same time they were carrying on the day-to-day business of a government whose every move produces incalculable consequences all around the earth.

In the eyes of public opinion and in the judgment of history, all that is no excuse. On Tuesday, November 4, 1986, the day of the congressional elections, the wire services reported that *Al Shiraa,* an Arabic-language magazine published in Lebanon, had stated in its issue of November 3 that the United States had been supplying military spare parts to Iran, and that McFarlane and four other Americans had visited Tehran in September to negotiate the release of hostages held by terrorists in Lebanon.

The date was wrong—McFarlane had been in Iran in May

not September. But there was enough truth in the rest of the report to make it plain that an informed source was doing the leaking. Experts in the subtleties of Iranian politics speculated that the story had been planted by agents of Ayatollah Hussein Ali Montazeri, a rival of McFarlane's principal contact, Speaker Rafsanjani.

I thought that it was inevitable that the story would metastasize and advised the President to respond to it at once. Poindexter pooh-poohed the danger from the start. "It will blow over," he told the President, urging him not to go public with the details. Poindexter quoted warnings by Terry Waite, the negotiator associated with the Church of England, that disclosure would endanger the hostages.

In my opinion, the damage had already been done. The story was out, and if the experts were right in thinking that the bitterly anti-American Ayatollah Montazeri was the source, then it was being put out by our enemies. There was no hope of containing it.

"I don't believe we can stonewall," I told the President. "We've got to come out with some sort of explanation. People are going to wonder what Bud was doing in Tehran."

The President shook his head no. In no way, he said in the adamant tone that is so unusual for him, would we discuss publicly any of the methods we used to gain the release of the hostages, or comment on whether Bud McFarlane had gone to Tehran or not.

Poindexter, sphinx-like, nodded his approval. His objective, I gathered, was to keep the secret at all costs; I did not understand how any secret could be more valuable than the credibility of the Presidency, or how we expected to keep this one for more than a few more hours. I did not at this point speak my mind fully: it was obvious that the President wanted to move on to another subject. His resolve was soon reinforced by a dramatic encounter that showed how strong an influence a chance event can have on history.

On November 2, the day before the story broke in *Al Shiraa*, one of the American hostages, David Jacobsen, had been released by his captors, a terrorist group called Jihad Islami ("Islamic Holy War"). These terrorists announced that they had acted in response to overtures from the U.S. government.

Jacobsen visited the White House on November 7 and, while cameras whirred, was welcomed home by the President in a ceremony in the Rose Garden. As the two men, accompanied by Mrs. Reagan, turned away from the podium, some of the stronger-voiced reporters shouted questions about negotiations with terrorists at the President. He responded with nothing more than his familiar grimace and a wave of the arm, but Jacobsen wheeled on the newsmen.

"In the name of God, would you please just be responsible and back off!" he cried, wagging his finger at the questioners from the steps of the colonnade.

Although the President certainly did not expect Jacobsen to say what he did, the tongue-lashing that he gave the press had the flavor of ventriloquism. Jacobsen was saying exactly what the President himself would have said if he had been able to afford the luxury of losing his temper.

Moments later, inside the Oval Office, Jacobsen was still overcome with emotion—and, no doubt, with the memory of his own captivity and worry for the friends he had left behind in the hands of the terrorists. "My God, Mr. President," he cried, "these people are savages! Don't they realize what they're doing?" The President listened sympathetically.

Later that afternoon, when emotions had cooled, I went in to see the President. I found him more determined than ever to avoid any step that might lead the hostages' excitable captors to change their minds about releasing them. On the basis of what Poindexter had been telling him, he believed that Jacobsen was just the first to be released. The rest would be coming out soon.

It was impossible not to sympathize with his concern. Nevertheless I said again that he should preempt the inevitable disclosure by putting the facts on the record.

He said, Don, you heard what Jacobsen said, what John keeps saying. I *can't* talk.

I took my courage in my hands. "Mr. President, I don't care,"

I replied. "We're between the devil and the deep and it's not going to help things to maintain silence. If these hostages don't materialize soon, you're going to have to speak up. You're going to be ripped apart on the weekend talk shows. The Monday morning papers will pick it up. The American people are going to start demanding to know what's going on here."

In moments of stress, the President sometimes leans forward in his chair and lets his arms dangle loosely between his knees. He did that now, fixing his eyes on a point in space.

Well, all right, he said at last. Let's get together Monday and see where we stand. We have to give these people the weekend.

At the end of the day, after the President had gone upstairs to the family quarters, the First Lady phoned me. "He's not going to talk to the press," she said. "My Friend says it's, you know, it's just *wrong* for him to talk right now."

"My God, Nancy," I replied. "He's going to go down in flames if he doesn't speak up."

But she insisted that the timing was wrong, and glancing down at the red days and yellow days marked off on my desk calendar, I saw that from her point of view she was correct.

That same day the *New York Times* ran the first of many stories to quote State Department sources to the effect that Secretary of State George M. Shultz was opposed to shipping arms to Iran because such action was contradictory to the U.S. policy of not negotiating with terrorists. The story went on to say that a secret operation to supply Iran with military hardware had been under way for a year and a half.

There were a few grumbles about this leak, but the attention of the Administration was focused elsewhere. The Republicans had just lost control of the Senate while suffering a net loss of seven seats in the House. These midterm losses were remarkably small by historical standards, but in the media, inevitably, they raised the specter of a lame-duck Presidency. The President had campaigned vigorously for Republican candidates, the commentators said, but he had not saved the day for his party. His program, his popularity, his leadership were all in jeopardy because fewer than twenty seats had changed hands on Capitol Hill. These were moot points; Reagan had done well enough in his first term with a Congress controlled by Democrats, and his advisers believed that he was anything but a lame duck now.

Post-mortems by the Cabinet and the senior White House staff concentrated on methods of completing the Reagan revolution. Reform of the budget, arms control, prolonging the economic recovery—these were the topics of the day. No one questioned the President's ability to complete his agenda. He had tremendous assets. After six years in office, he was at a high point in his popularity, with 70 percent or more of those polled approving of the way he was handling his job.

The paramount fact was this: more than any Chief Executive since Eisenhower, Ronald Reagan enjoyed the trust of the American people. Baffled though they might be by this phenomenon, even his enemies admitted that his credibility was beyond question.

That would not last much longer. I had appeared on ABC's "This Week with David Brinkley." The discussion was devoted entirely to the election and its meaning. Not a single question was asked about Iran.

One week later, the Sunday talk shows resounded with the issue. The *New York Times* reported that an outraged George Shultz, despite speculation to the contrary, was not going to resign in protest over the secret initiative to Iran. The role of Israel was beginning to break to the surface, and questions were sure to be raised about this when Prime Minister Peres visited Washington in the coming week. Congressional sources told the media that there might very well be investigations in the House and Senate of the Iran situation, and of alleged disinformation campaigns by the NSC staff in regard to Libya and the Reykjavík summit.

On November 12, Patrick J. Buchanan, the White House Communications Director, sent me a memorandum telling me bluntly that "the best response . . . would be earliest and fullest disclosure of what we did, what we attempted, [and] why."

Exasperated, I scrawled my reply across the face of Pat's memo: "I agree, and have so advocated for a week. We are going to do something on Thurs (tmrw), finally. It's late but I hope not too late."

Bud McFarlane, pursued by the media and loath to evade the questions of his many journalist friends, urged a public explanation of his role in the affair and an explanation of its purposes. Larry Speakes and the rest of the staff were being bombarded with questions by a hostile and suspicious press corps. I told the President that we had no choice but to go public with an explanation of our actions and our motives. But Admiral Poindexter continued to argue against disclosure. The truth would endanger the hostages, he said; it would bring the hope of rescue to an end.

"The Iranians are interested in more meetings," he told the President. "They haven't broken off contact."

Neither had the American media. The newspapers and the networks smelled a big story. It appeared that the Reagan Administration, which had insisted that it would never deal with terrorists under any circumstances, had swapped arms for hostages held by terrorists. Naturally editors were eager to confirm this. It is no business of the media to give the U.S. government the benefit of the doubt when a scandal appears to be brewing. Reporters scurried from source to source, producing a blizzard of speculation and a few solid leads. Nobody outside the NSC staff really knew what was going on, but few wanted to admit that. In Washington, where information is power, nothing is more maddening than the absence of information. The State Department, largely ignored by McFarlane and then by Poindexter in the planning and execution of what seemed to be a daring foreign policy initiative, was a particularly productive source of leaks and analysis.

Senators and congressmen, particularly the party leaders, who had also been left out in the cold, were resentful and curious. It was obvious that some explanation had to be made to them, but Poindexter resisted even that. His standard advice to the President when the subject arose in morning briefings was that it would be best not to talk to anyone—and especially not to senators and congressmen because they would almost certainly leak it to the press.

On November 12, only nine days after the story broke, the pressure from the Hill was so great that the President had no choice but to talk to a congressional delegation. The leaders of both parties on Capitol Hill—Bob Dole and Robert Byrd from the Senate and Speaker Jim Wright and Representative Dick Cheney from the House—gathered in the Situation Room, the basement room equipped with communications and other gear in which crises are sometimes managed. The President told them that we had, in fact, supplied arms to Iran, but it was only a small amount and we had not swapped arms for hostages.

Some of those men were skeptical—you could see it in their faces, hear it in their voices. But they had no choice but to accept what the President told them. Ronald Reagan had never lied to them (or in my experience, to anyone). And there is no question in my mind that he believed that he was telling the truth.

He knew, of course, that the United States had shipped anti-tank and anti-aircraft missiles to Tehran and that certain Iranians had exerted influence over terrorists in Lebanon to facilitate the release of American hostages. But in Ronald Reagan's own mind that did not constitute a swap of arms for hostages.

You should never deal with kidnappers, the President said over and over again in connection with the dealings with Iran. He reasoned this way: If there is a kidnapping, and if one of the kidnapped person's relatives—say a father or husband or wife— is contacted by an intermediary who says that he might be able to contact the kidnappers, and if the relative is then able to secure the release of the victim through that intermediary, and if in the end the intermediary is rewarded for his services, then you haven't dealt with the kidnappers or paid them ransom.

In Ronald Reagan's mind, that was what we were doing with Iran. Greater events have no doubt been founded on shakier analogies.

At the time, I myself believed that the potential benefits— not only the return of the hostages, but also the opening of a dialogue with a faction that might one day come to power in one of the most strategically important countries in the world—outweighed the risk. Of course I did not at that time know all the secrets. Neither did the President.

Politicians, like actors, live and die by the public's favor. Ronald Reagan, who has practiced both crafts, understands this in his bones. In the end, the pressure of the media's curiosity and speculation was too great for the President to bear. The President decided that he must explain matters to the American people and scheduled a nationwide television address for November 13.

It was his intention to tell the whole truth and clear the air once and for all. Unfortunately, the raw material for the speech came from people on the NSC staff who were not prepared to tell the President the truth. John Poindexter permitted the President of the United States to say the following to the American people: "I authorized the transfer of small amounts of defensive weapons and spare parts for defensive systems to Iran. . . . These modest deliveries, taken together, could easily fit into a single cargo plane. We did not, repeat not, trade weapons or anything else for hostages, nor will we."

Many concluded that the President was lying. The *Los Angeles Times* published a poll indicating that only 14 percent of the American people believed the President when he said that he had not traded arms for hostages. The White House polls obtained similar results. He was shaken by this development.

The President was baffled by his loss of credibility. He flushed and pursed his lips when he talked about it, a sure sign of dismay. He thought that he was telling the truth in his television address. Why didn't the people believe him? In fact he was not telling the whole truth. He could not because he did not know the whole truth. Nobody had told him the facts—that his subordinates had been trading arms for hostages with the Iranians through some very dubious middlemen, that Israel was deeply involved in these transactions for purposes of its own, and that millions of dollars in unsavory profits had been diverted to the Nicaraguan Contras.

His National Security Advisors, first McFarlane and then Poindexter, had reported to him in generalities. They told him that they were dealing with Israelis who had put them in touch with certain Iranians. But we don't know the extent of their influence, they said, and they're very suspicious of us. The name [Manuchehr] Ghorbanifar came up but never, in my hearing, the fact that he was an arms dealer with an ambiguous reputation who had in 1984 reported that a Middle East assassination team had infiltrated the United States with orders to murder President Reagan. On the basis of this fanciful incident his word was gravely doubted by the CIA.

Other names that later became familiar to television audiences—Ledeen, Nir, Secord, Hakim, Nimrodi—were never mentioned to the President in my presence. So far as I know, no briefing book with pictures of these men and descriptions of their backgrounds and estimates of their reputations was ever shown to the President. If he had seen them for what they were, the President might have made a different decision. Certainly I and others would have urged him to do so.

After McFarlane met Ghorbanifar in London in December 1985 he realized that he had got involved with some dubious types and recommended having nothing further to do with them.

But then McFarlane resigned, Poindexter with his love of secrecy took over, and as we now know, Oliver North found a way to prolong the relationship.

John, tell me, the President asked Poindexter at a morning briefing when the crisis was new. Just how many arms did we ship?

"Oh, I think they could all be carried in the cargo bay of one plane," Poindexter had replied through a wreath of pipe smoke.

The President believed that. When I asked Poindexter to check it out, he came back to me and sheepishly said, "Make that a C5A. It's more like two planeloads." But it was the one planeload that stuck in the President's mind and stuck in the media's craw.

Whatever may have been said afterward in attempts to rationalize this appalling sabotage of the Presidency, the fact remains that people Ronald Reagan trusted put lies in his mouth and very nearly destroyed him as a result.

The media wanted to talk about little besides Iran, but there were other things to do in the White House. While the controversy rattled the windows, we compiled the first trillion-dollar budget in history, with every department of the Executive Branch meeting the goal of restraining spending growth to a level below growth in anticipated revenues. This encapsulated the Administration's philosophy on budget management: don't stop growing, but spend less than you take in. We worked on reports on the family, on federalism, on welfare reform, on catastrophic illness insurance, on the competitiveness of American industry, and on international trade. Arms-reduction talks continued with the Soviets, and we began to see an avenue opening toward the day, which now seems to have arrived, when nuclear arms would be significantly reduced. Prime Minister Thatcher came to the United States and met with the President at Camp David. As usual they met alone, without aides, for several hours of intensive conversation.

The uproar continued. The *Washington Post* reported rumors that an Israeli arms dealer had brokered the first deal and that the shipments had included parts for antiaircraft missiles. A former White House political director, Edward J. Rollins, was quoted in the *Christian Science Monitor* as saying that the White House was in the grip of a siege mentality. If so, we were defending a fortress of glass. Arrows continued to fly over the battlements, sometimes from unexpected quarters. George Shultz appeared on television to state that he had thought all along that the Iran initiative was wrong and had told the President so. Cap Weinberger let it be known that he, too, had advised against dealing with Iran.

The President shook his head in disappointment. George and Cap *were* against it all along, he said, but I wish they could find a way to stay with me on this one.

Shultz came in and asked the President to give him a firm commitment that the U.S. would provide no more military equipment to Iran and that all future diplomatic contacts with Tehran would be handled by the State Department. The President said mildly that he would take that under advisement. Afterward he expressed stronger feelings, but evidently he was not angry enough at Shultz to fire him.

The media were clamoring for a news conference. Larry

Speakes and I urged the President to hold one. After Mrs. Reagan cleared the date with her Friend, the President decided to hold one at 8 P.M. on Wednesday, November 19. Over the weekend we gave him the usual thick briefing books on domestic and foreign issues, and as usual he read them religiously. I remarked that he'd have to answer very few questions on domestic issues. The onslaught would come on Iran, and he could expect harsh questions from a hostile press corps. He shook his head impatiently; better than anyone else, he already knew this, but he thought that he would win in the end because he believed that he was, after all, telling the truth.

The prebriefing took place on the day before the news conference in the family theater off the corridor to the East Wing of the White House. The domestic briefing went off without a hitch. Then came the foreign-policy part of it, with Poindexter in charge. Three staffers, playing the roles of reporters, sat on one side of a long table, firing questions, and the President stood at a podium, trying to answer them.

The President kept making mistakes; he did not seem to have the situation clearly in mind. He could not keep the sequence of events straight or remember exactly what he had approved or what he had been told. This was because he was being told that he had been told things that he had not in fact been told. Poindexter was withholding the whole story from him.

Foreign affairs may not have been my province, but the way in which the President was served was. I took Poindexter aside. "If this goes on," I said, "we'll have a disaster on our hands. He must be briefed in a way that will get him ready for what he's going to be up against."

Poindexter, puffing on his pipe and peering at me through his round glasses, seemed to be genuinely embarrassed. But he was still keeping secrets, and I think that his anxiety had an effect on the President's state of mind. Ronald Reagan went before the press on November 19 possessed of the idea that he must not reveal Israel's role in the Iran affair.

As a result he made a serious misstep, stating that "we did not condone, and do not condone, the shipment of arms from other countries." A written clarification had to be issued twenty minutes after he had left the podium, admitting that a third country was involved in our secret project in Iran.

The news conference did not clear the air and it certainly did not put the arms-for-hostages issue to rest. The President, over-briefed but underinformed, uncertain of the facts, concerned with keeping secrets that were already bubbling up onto front pages all over the world, lacked his usual cheery demeanor and trans-parent candor.

Nevertheless, he had carried off a difficult news conference better than his enemies wished to concede. On November 20 Dick Wirthlin, the White House pollster, told the President that the news conference had not affected his popularity one way or the other. But his approval rating had slipped well below 60 per-cent—a euphoric high for most sixth-year Presidents but a dis-turbing low point for Ronald Reagan.

Only 38 percent of those polled thought that the President could handle foreign policy well. Events buffet perceptions, and Wirthlin, a canny judge of public moods, was not unduly wor-ried. "If there are no new revelations," he said, "Iran will burn off."

If there was as yet no siege mentality within the White House, there was a certain atmosphere of exasperation. As the week ended I blurted out an opinion that found its way into the newspapers. At a senior staff meeting someone reported that McFarlane was suggesting that Shultz knew more than he was saying about the Iran affair. In the course of the discussion, before the sound of McFarlane's name had dissipated, someone else remarked that the results of the policy were lousy. I said, "You give lousy ad-vice, you get lousy results." I stand by the aphorism, but I don't think that I was just talking about McFarlane.

Meanwhile the intelligence committees of both houses of Congress announced that they would hold hearings on the arms sales to Iran. Poindexter was designated to brief both committees in private, and Bill Casey would give formal testimony on the Hill.

In an exercise that demonstrated the independence of action

enjoyed by the National Security Advisor, Poindexter excluded Peter Wallison, the White House Counsel, from giving advice with regard to the contents of his statement or Casey's testimony, or even reading these texts, which were being coordinated by the NSC staff. Arrangements had been made, however, for lawyers from the Justice and State departments to review the material.

On the afternoon of Thursday, November 20, the day before Casey was scheduled to testify before the Senate Intelligence Committee, Shultz telephoned and requested an immediate meeting with the President. Shultz told me that State Department lawyers reported that Casey's proposed testimony contained "outrageous" statements, and also asserted that the President had made five errors of fact in his remarks during his press conference.

I set up a meeting for 5 P.M. in the family quarters; Poindexter and I were also present. Shultz repeated his statements to the President. His manner was heated. The President seemed puzzled. As far as he knew, he had stated the facts exactly as they were. Poindexter defended the information he had provided to the President and offered no new data.

In light of this serious disagreement over the facts, I suggested to the President that the Attorney General, Edwin Meese, be asked to verify all the facts in Casey's testimony before it was delivered. Since Justice was already involved, the President agreed to this.

I urged Meese to try to complete his full inquiry in time for the Monday meeting of the National Security Council, at which the President intended to review the whole Iran situation.

Very early on Monday morning, November 24, Meese called and said that he wanted to see me. Shortly after eleven he came to my office. Meese told me that he had to see the President at once: his investigation had discovered, in his words, "things the President did not know"—including a possible diversion of funds from the Iran arms sale.

A diversion of funds? The phrase made my blood run cold; I had had thirty-five years' experience in handling other people's money, and I knew what lay ahead for the President and the country.

"Ah, —!" I said. "Damn it all! Well, we'd better go see the President."

The two of us went into the Oval Office at 11:13. The meeting was hurried because the President was expecting Zulu Chief Mangosuthu Gatsha Buthelezi at 11:30 and a foreign leader could not be kept waiting.

In his report to the President, Meese did not mention the possible diversion of funds. He told him that he wanted to forewarn him that something was very wrong in regard to the arms transaction. "It's a terrible mess, Mr. President," he said. "I have a few things to button up and then I'll give you a full report. But it's going to be bad news."

We left the President at 11:32 after agreeing to meet again that afternoon at 4:15, following the National Security Council meeting.

Meese was late. He arrived at the Oval Office at 4:22. There were just the three of us present.

Without preamble, Meese said that his investigation had revealed that the Iranians appeared to have paid $30 million for the equipment we had sold them. But the U.S. government had only received $12 million. Where the other $18 million had gone and what had been done with it, nobody seemed to know. But Lieutenant Colonel Oliver North had admitted to Meese over the weekend that he had diverted some of these funds to the Nicaraguan Contras.

The President, in person, is a ruddy man, with bright red cheeks. He blanched when he heard Meese's words. The color drained from his face, leaving his skin pasty white.

The President wore a stern, drawn expression that was new to me—and just as new, I suspect, to Meese, who has known him for more than twenty years. Nobody who saw the President's reaction that afternoon could believe for a moment that he knew about the diversion of funds before Meese told him about it. He was the picture of a man to whom the inconceivable had happened.

Get to the bottom of this, Ed, the President said again. We have to go public with what we already know as soon as we can.

The three of us spoke for sixteen minutes. I made two main suggestions:

First, that the leaders of Congress should be told the next morning what Meese had discovered, and then the President and Meese should appear together in the press room and state the facts. The President should make a statement, then leave Meese to take reporters' questions.

Second, the President should forthwith appoint a bipartisan commission, similar to the Rogers Commission that investigated the *Challenger* space shuttle disaster, to look into the situation, establish the facts, and make recommendations.

Meese said that in his judgment an independent counsel might have to be appointed.

The President, as usual listening more than he talked, accepted all these recommendations and told Meese and me to get to work on them. He paused for a moment.

What does John Poindexter say about this? the President asked.

Meese replied that he had asked John for an explanation— that was why he was late. John had said that he knew something about North's activities, but he hadn't wanted to investigate too deeply for fear of what might turn up.

The President looked at Ed Meese in disbelief.

Meese left. The President stood in the middle of the Oval Office.

"This is a bitter blow, Mr. President," I said.

He shook his head in bewilderment. He was pale and unsmiling.

What went on in their minds? he asked. Do you understand it, Don?

I did not know how to answer his question. It was well past the hour when he usually left the office and went home.

"Why don't you go on upstairs, Mr. President?" I suggested. "There's nothing more you can do today."

Earlier in the day Bill Casey had wanted to see me, and when I had been unable to find time, he had asked me to drop into his office at CIA Headquarters in Langley, Virginia, on my way home.

Casey wanted to talk to me about his testimony on Iran. Before he did I told him the gist of what Ed Meese had reported to the President. Casey asked no questions and, after a moment, he itemized the possible consequences of the scandal—a cutoff of funds to the Contras, the unopposed Sandinistas poisoning the rest of Central America with their revolution, outrage in the Middle East over the Israeli role in the affair, the predictable wrath of the Iranians when they discovered that they had been overcharged for their missiles.

Casey asked if I realized that disclosure would have these consequences. I said that I did, but we had to get the story out. It had been a long day, and the day wasn't over yet. I cut the meeting short and went home.

That evening I received a phone call from the First Lady. The President had briefed her on Meese's discoveries, and she had many questions, and many suggestions, about the management of the crisis. Her mood was furious, and there was no mistaking her message: Heads would roll. I had the impression that mine might very well be among them.

Before going to bed I drafted a plan of action on the handling of the crisis, and it was this handwritten document that provided the basis for nearly everything we did in the troubled weeks ahead to get out the facts about the Iran-Contra affair to the American people and contain, as best we could, the massive damage that had been inflicted on the Presidency.

· 3 ·

Blood in the Water

The next morning I could not find John Poindexter. I was told that he had an early dental appointment, an explanation that struck me as bizarre under the circumstances. I later learned that the admiral had canceled the dentist when he was summoned to the Attorney General's office, where Ed Meese had delivered the same message that I was carrying: the President wanted Poindexter's immediate resignation.

I did not know this when, at 7:40 A.M., I finally found Poindexter in his office in the northwest corner of the West Wing. He sat at the end of a polished conference table, eating breakfast alone, as was his habit. In retrospect I marvel at his calm self-control. Not every man would sit down to a plate of ham and eggs half an hour after being told that he was being fired under circumstances of public disgrace.

We did not say good morning to each other. He looked up in his unblinking way as I entered and politely offered me a cup of coffee.

I refused the coffee, but sat down at the table. Poindexter, waiting for me to speak, went on eating his eggs and toast.

I said, "John, what the hell happened? What went on here? What did you know about all this?"

The unflappability for which Poindexter was admired did not desert him now. He put down his knife and fork, dabbed at his mouth with his napkin, and repeated what he had told Ed Meese the afternoon before.

"I had a feeling that something bad was going on, but I didn't investigate it and I didn't do a thing about it," he said. "I really didn't want to know."

I asked him why not.

Poindexter did not grope for an answer. "I felt sorry for the Contras," he said. "I was so damned mad at Tip O'Neill for the way he was dragging the Contras around that I didn't want to know what, if anything, was going on. I should have, but I didn't."

Poindexter spoke in his usual reasonable tone of voice. I got the impression, though he did not say so outright, that he had felt that interfering with North would, somehow, have been a form of giving aid and comfort to the enemy. If Poindexter saw how astounded I was by his words, he was too polite to say so.

I asked him no more questions. It seemed to me that he had said everything that it was necessary for him to say. His sincerity was obvious, but sincerity was not the issue.

The day before, I had advised the President that Poindexter must go, and Reagan had tacitly agreed.

Now I said, "I'm sorry, John, but I think you'd better have your resignation ready when you come in to see the President at nine-thirty."

Poindexter sighed, the first sign he had given that anything out of the ordinary had been happening. "I think you're right," he replied. Discreet to the last, he did not tell me that Meese had already given him this word, even though Meese and I had agreed that I would be the one to deliver it. Meese did not mention it, either, when he and I met at 8 A.M. to discuss the plans for disclosure.

At nine-thirty, when Poindexter, unblinking and ramrod-straight, came into the Oval Office at his usual time, there were no grand gestures, no recriminations. He simply handed the President an envelope containing a letter of resignation; the President, tight-lipped and sorrowful, accepted it and held it unopened in his hand.

Poindexter said, "I'm sorry it's come to this, Mr. President."

So am I, John, the President replied.

Poindexter, speaking in a firm voice, told the President what he had told me, in essentially the same words: He should have investigated North's activities, but had not done so. He accepted responsibility for the consequences. Later, in his public testimony before the select committees on Capitol Hill, Poindexter said that he did have knowledge of North's activities and had approved them without the President's knowledge.

The President said nothing in reply to the words that he heard that morning in the Oval Office. After an awkward moment, Poindexter departed. The two men did not shake hands or say good-bye.

Ed Meese witnessed this scene, along with the Vice President and myself. Poindexter left at 9:35. The four of us then discussed the details of the President's public disclosure of the facts, confirming that the President would accompany Meese into the press room to break the story of the diversion of funds. Meanwhile he would brief the Cabinet and Congressional leaders. I set up the necessary meetings.

As arranged, the President took no questions after he spoke at the news briefing, but left that task to Ed Meese. The President described the actions he had taken and conceded that "in one aspect, implementation of that [Iran] policy was seriously flawed."

In answer to questions, Meese said, "The only person in the United States government who knew precisely about this [the diversion of funds to the Contras] was Lieutenant Colonel North. Admiral Poindexter did know that something of this nature was occurring, but he did not look into it further. . . . He did not try to stop it."

As revelation followed revelation and the reporters, shouting and leaping and gesticulating, began to understand the magnitude of the event, their excitement created an atmosphere that can only be described as primal. Fundamental emotions came into play. The many minds in the briefing room seemed to be thinking a single thought: another Presidency was about to destroy itself. The blood was in the water.

Earlier, at a meeting of the National Security Planning Group (NSPG), Meese had briefed the President, the Secretaries of State,

Defense, and the Treasury, and the Director of the CIA on what he had discovered so far. There had been four shipments to Iran in 1986—one each in February, May, July, and October. Matériel had been shipped to Iran from Israel after Iran had paid for it by depositing money in a Swiss bank account. The amounts involved were not precisely known. It appeared that the Iranians had been overcharged, and that Israeli agents had placed some or all of this money into three separate Swiss accounts. Adolfo Calero, a Contra leader, had drawn funds from these accounts.

It was now clear to everyone that all the facts must be discovered and made public as quickly as possible. There was a clamor in the NSPG meeting for fast action in putting together the Presidential commission to investigate the episode. Several members favored the appointment of William P. Rogers, the former Secretary of State and Attorney General of the United States, to head the panel because of his distinguished work as chairman of the Presidential commission that investigated the *Challenger* disaster. I opposed this because Rogers's work on the *Challenger* investigation had already required him to spend an inordinate amount of time away from his law practice. Besides, he had begged me to stay away from him for a while so that he could catch up on work and play.

At about 4 P.M. I assembled a group of Presidential assistants to discuss the makeup of the board. I suggested that the chairmanship be offered to John Tower of Texas, the former chairman of the Senate Armed Services Committee, who was just completing a tour as the chief U.S. negotiator at the Geneva arms-reduction talks. Tower's credibility on Capitol Hill, and with the media and the public, was beyond question. Brent Scowcroft, a retired Air Force general who had served as President Ford's National Security Advisor, was a natural choice as one of the members because the commission would be charged with recommending ways of improving NSC procedures with the idea of preventing what had happened from happening again. Both these men were Republicans. I wanted to keep the board small so that it could work quickly and report decisively. As the commission's third member I recommended Edmund Muskie, the Democrat from Maine, a former Senator and Secretary of State.

That afternoon I phoned these names to the President and he approved them. I then began calling the candidates. None leapt at the chance to undertake this difficult assignment. All three, and especially John Tower, wanted strong assurances that they would have a free hand in the investigation and proper facilities to carry it out. I told them that the President wanted to discover the truth and assured them that the commission could have any document in the files and could question anybody in the Executive Branch, from the President on down. All the President was asking for was a report, delivered within sixty days, telling him and the American people what had happened, who was responsible, and what should be done to prevent it from happening again. Although Muskie took a few hours to accept—he wanted to be sure that the others would take the job—all three men agreed to serve.

Before the scandal broke, the Reagans had made plans to spend Thanksgiving on the ranch. On November 26, the day before the holiday, the Presidency moved to California.

While the Reagans retired to the privacy of the ranch, the Presidential staff put up, as usual, in Santa Barbara hotels, cheek by jowl with network correspondents and print journalists. By now the White House press corps was in a prosecutorial fever. Given the circumstances, this was not surprising. The time when Presidents and their aides were regarded as upright citizens devoted to the service of the nation had long since passed. Since Vietnam and Watergate much of the big-time media have tended to regard every public official, elected or appointed, as a suspect from the day he takes office, and public service as a crime waiting to happen. With the Iran-Contra affair, the maddening six-year vigil in anticipation of the moment when Ronald Reagan would have to face his accusers seemed finally to have ended.

But this was not an unmixed blessing for correspondents; each was expected by his editors or producers to scoop his colleagues every day with a new and startling revelation, so stress reigned along with joy. The tension showed.

Because of my position, and because in a sense I was the only game in town, I was sought after by these excited men and women. The President was inaccessible on his mountaintop. Poindexter and North had gone into seclusion on the advice of their lawyers. It was useless to explain that these two men were the only authentic sources on the scandal. I doubt that there existed a single reporter who believed in his or her heart that Oliver North, a mere lieutenant colonel, had done what he had done without the approval of higher—much higher—authority. My office was inundated with requests for interviews from newspeople who wanted me to address this point.

I tried to relieve the pressure by arranging for interviews to discuss the budget, the deficit, and other topics. The reporters were not interested. Even when I could not be communicative I tried to be affable, and I listened to the excellent advice of knowledgeable people who told me that I must always smile in the presence of cameras—otherwise I risked looking tough, or worried, or angry. But I discovered that it is not always possible to be cheerful when the media are taking your picture.

On Thanksgiving Day my wife, Ann, and I invited the rest of the Presidential staff, about forty people, to be our guests at a turkey dinner in a private dining room at the hotel. The correspondents got wind of this, and when we emerged from the little cottage in which we were staying on the hotel grounds to go to the dining room, a phalanx of journalists and photographers awaited us.

As we made our way across the lawn, photographers danced backward through the flower beds, shooting. Famous faces from the evening news scowled and reddened as their owners, tethered by microphone cords to television cameras, shouted for my attention. Newspapermen, dodging and stooping in an attempt to stay out of camera range, held up their tape recorders in the hope of capturing any words I might utter in response to the babble of questions that were being shouted at me: What did I know and when did I know it? What did the President know? What were we going to do about this situation? How well did I know Ollie North? Had I known that money was being diverted to the Contras?

When we emerged after dinner two and a half hours later, the same group awaited us, and the performance was repeated.

The television footage and the still pictures of this episode showed me scowling and looking cross. I was worried about Ann, who walks with difficulty owing to a severe case of arthritis, and I was concerned that some of the scrambling journalists were going to trip over those cables and break their necks or destroy the hotel's flowers.

In the days that followed, the frenzy did not abate. We were searching for a new National Security Advisor. This appointment was a matter of desperate interest to the press, and members of the staff were pressed to reveal them. If Ann and I went for a walk in the evening, we encountered reporters. If we went to the hotel dining room or out to a restaurant for dinner, somebody from a newspaper, a network, or a newsmagazine was likely to arrive soon afterward and sit at the next table. If I went to the lobby to buy a paper or a roll of mints, a journalist was sure to materialize as I paid the cashier and invite me to luncheon or, if I was not free for the midday meal (as I never was—I ate soup at my desk), suggest a chat about the diversion of funds over breakfast the next day. Even if I said nothing, my picture would make the front page and the evening television news. Remembering the distress my overexposure in the press had caused the First Lady when the President was in the hospital, I knew that difficulties lay ahead.

Somehow the press had got the idea that Poindexter, and McFarlane before him, had reported to me and I was therefore responsible for their performance. I explained that neither man had ever worked for me, but there was no dispelling this mistaken idea.

In fact the independence of the National Security Advisor is enshrined in precedent and practice; he is exclusively the creature of the President and is freer of supervision than any other appointed official in the U.S. government. All National Security Advisors except one since Henry Kissinger have reported directly to the President. The exception was Richard V. Allen, President Reagan's first Advisor, who reported through Meese. His successor, William Clark, insisted on reporting directly to the President. Clark's successor, McFarlane, operated under the same

arrangement. I did not even think about changing these arrangements when I took over from James A. Baker III as Chief of
Staff at the beginning of Ronald Reagan's second term.

From first to last, McFarlane and Poindexter ran the NSC
staff as they saw fit. Though I tried, as a matter of administrative
tidiness, I could never even find out what their budget was or
how many people they had working for them. Most senior NSC
staff worked along what was called "Secrecy Row" on the third
floor of the Executive Office Building, next door to the White
House, but others were winnowed away in other buildings and
were paid from other budgets. The Office of Administration, which
reported to the Chief of Staff, issued White House passes to NSC
employees and provided office space and parking and other
housekeeping amenities. There its authority ended.

My nonadministrative contacts with Bud McFarlane were casual. I attended the national security briefing at 9:30 A.M. every
weekday and listened to what McFarlane, and Poindexter after
him, told the President in the fifteen minutes allotted to him. But
the Advisor carried the russet leather folder containing the daily
intelligence material and occasionally documents for signature into
the Oval Office himself and handed it directly to the President.
The papers it contained did not pass through my hands or under
my eyes, and after the President was finished with the folder and
its contents, he sent it back to the Advisor through his secretary.
The documents in this folder did not form a part of the central
White House files; they were kept, instead, in NSC safes on Secrecy Row.

Reporters were not prepared to believe this. They had heard
that I was an autocrat who knew, in the fanciful phrase attributed to me by the *Washington Post*'s Mary McGrory, when every
sparrow fell on the White House lawn. This misconception solid-
ified during the four days we spent in Santa Barbara. I could
only reply with the truth—that I did not control the National
Security Advisor. That was not what the media wanted to hear.

The media blitz in Santa Barbara put me squarely into the
middle of the scandal. The impression this position created would
intensify in the few months I had left as Chief of Staff, with sus-

picion, accusation, and gossip crisscrossing Washington. By the time we got back to town on November 30 I was firmly locked into the consciousness of the media—and therefore into the minds of politicians who live and die by the media—as a cause of the problem, as a liability to the President, as a man who must go.

Ironically, I would have been gone already except for the scandal. I had never intended to stay in the job for more than two years, and as I later told the President, I had it in mind to leave after the 1986 elections. But when we left for Santa Barbara I told myself and my wife that I could not desert the President in the middle of a crisis. By the time we got back to Washington I realized that resignation was unthinkable for another reason: it would look like an admission of guilt.

If at this stage the President wanted me to go, he gave no sign of it. Our day-to-day relations did not change. Every morning at a few minutes before nine Vice President Bush and I stationed ourselves in the office of Kathy Osborne, the President's secretary, and watched for his arrival. Promptly at 8:59 we would see him through the French doors, striding along the colonnade from the family quarters with Jim Kuhn, his personal assistant, at his side. As soon as he glimpsed her through the windows, the President would give Kathy a grin and a big wave—he never passed her by without making these gestures—and then go into the Oval Office. Sometimes he would open the bottom drawer of his desk, extract a big plastic bag filled with acorns gathered at Camp David, and feed the squirrels that waited for him outside the glass door. Grinning, he would take a moment to watch the little animals scamper away with the acorns. Then he would sit down at his desk and begin the day. This routine rarely varied, and he was never so much as a minute late or early except when the First Lady was out of town. On such occasions he came in a few minutes early, catching us all by surprise. Once I asked him what had thrown him off schedule.

I couldn't sleep with Nancy away, he confessed.

After his return from the Thanksgiving holiday in California, the President was troubled over the Iran-Contra affair. Not once in my hearing did he complain about the damage the scandal was doing to him personally. His consistent concern, as his actions clearly show, was to get to the bottom of the affair and make all the circumstances public. Ronald Reagan's instincts are sunny. He thinks well of people in general, and especially well of those who have gone into battle in defense of the United States. He simply did not want to believe that he had been betrayed by an admiral and by a Marine who had been wounded in combat and decorated for gallantry. These were the considerations that led him to tell *Time* magazine that North was a "national hero."

The President had made great efforts to discover and publish the facts and reassure the nation. He was puzzled and frustrated that his efforts had not succeeded. He was exasperated with the press.

It was important that he be seen to be taking action. On the basis of staff work carried out in Santa Barbara, the President decided to appoint Frank Carlucci, who had widespread support for the job in the Administration and in Congress, as his new National Security Advisor.

Nevertheless, it was evident that the situation was coming unglued in ways that would soon put it out of control. Senator Richard G. Lugar, Republican of Indiana, called for a wholesale shake-up of the President's staff and Cabinet. His voice was one among many on Capitol Hill and elsewhere, and my name nearly always led the list of those recommended for the sack. The other candidates usually included Bill Casey, Weinberger, and sometimes Shultz.

Shultz's State Department was still in a state of territorial dudgeon. On November 24 Deputy Secretary of State John Whitehead, in an appearance before the House Foreign Affairs Committee, had contradicted the President's contention that Iran was not directly engaged in terrorism and called for an investigation of the NSC staff.

The investigations of the intelligence committees were, for the moment, moving slowly. North appeared in his Marine uniform before the House Foreign Affairs Committee and took the Fifth Amendment. "I don't think there's another person in America that wants to tell this story as much as I do, sir," he said to Chairman Dante Fascell, Democrat of Florida. It was expected that John Poindexter's lawyer would be just as scrupulous as North's in protecting his client's constitutional rights. Finding a way to induce North and Poindexter to tell their stories without giving them the Presidential pardons that the wily future Speaker of the House, Jim Wright, among others, later suggested, would consume much time and thought in weeks to come.

Bill Casey thought that the President ought to announce that North had violated the law by failing to report his activities.

"Then you can put Ollie and Poindexter on TV and let them tell the whole story," Casey said. "After that the President can pardon them."

Bob Dole, among others, suggested a similar scenario to me; but it was clear to me that a Presidential pardon in these cases would be the worst possible course of action.

Besides awakening memories of Gerald Ford's pardon of Richard M. Nixon, it would certainly be interpreted as condoning whatever offenses might be revealed—and no one except North and Poindexter knew what these might be. Peter Wallison and I began to discuss alternatives, including the waiver of executive privilege and the possibility that the Senate Intelligence Committee might grant limited-use immunity, a legal formula under which a witness cannot be charged with crimes he admits to in the course of his testimony.

In theory, testimony before the committees was secret. In practice, the media knew most of what the witnesses had said almost as soon as they said it. The *New York Times* reported that several senators, after listening to Bud McFarlane's testimony in closed session, were convinced that knowledge of the Contra transaction went beyond McFarlane, Poindexter, and North. In a separate story, the *Los Angeles Times* stated that North had briefed me; this was false. The *Washington Post* reported that profits from the sale of arms to Iran had been traced to a CIA account used to channel arms to the Angolan rebels, and elsewhere quoted sources as saying that the Justice Department investigation had found at least a dozen violations of law. Meanwhile Senator Ernest Hollings, Democrat of South Carolina, said that the President should "come clean" and admit that he knew about the diversion of funds. "No one in the country believes that either Colonel North or Admiral Poindexter acted without authority," Hollings said.

On December 2 the President heard from the leaders of the Republican party in Congress when he met in the Oval Office with Senator Bob Dole, Senator Alan K. Simpson of Wyoming and Representatives Bob Michel, Trent Lott of Mississippi, and Dick Cheney of Wyoming.

The President read aloud from a press statement he was going to deliver later that day concerning the naming of an Independent Counsel and the appointment of Frank Carlucci. His visitors listened politely, and politely congratulated him on both actions. A rambling conversation ensued about how Congress should handle its investigations. The President was not volunteering strong opinions or sharing information. His visitors seemed restive.

Interrupting, I made a point-blank suggestion to him. "Mr. President, what happened?" I said. "What did you know and when did you know it? Those are the questions on these fellows' minds. Tell them what you know."

The President, responding to the prompt, launched into a clear, orderly summary that lasted for at least ten minutes and covered the ground as far as his own knowledge of the case would take him. His guests, wide-awake now, asked a lot of questions.

I knew nothing about the diversion of funds to the Contras, the President said. And as far as I know, neither did anyone else except Poindexter and North.

Toward the end of the meeting, talk turned to the media. Republicans know that most reporters do not like their policies or their party, and living with this fact of life has given them a healthy respect for the power of the press. To the President they counseled caution: Don't beat up on the press, they advised. Of course the media is in full cry, of course the coverage is unfair— but counterattacking the media will only make things worse.

Our adversaries in the press are after the Presidency itself, one of them said; others agreed. Maybe the President should appease the press and his other critics by making a public apology. Again heads nodded.

I'll have to think about that one, the President said.

Sweeping changes must be made, the visitors insisted. Carlucci is not enough.

This meeting took place on a Tuesday. In the days that followed, the press grew shriller. On Wednesday, December 3, to take a typical day, on the "NBC Nightly News," Senator Lugar again advised the President to fire me. Chris Wallace reported that the appointment of Carlucci, whom I had recommended to the President, "may be a sign that Regan is losing power." On ABC, Sam Donaldson reported that my "scalp was being called for in many quarters." On the "CBS Evening News," Bill Plante said that "a lot of people around the President . . . insist that before this is all over Donald Regan will have to go." The Associated Press reported that "Nancy Reagan declined today to express a view on how Donald Regan is serving her husband . . . saying that 'has nothing to do with me whatsoever.' " Dick Cheney, who had been President Ford's Chief of Staff told the *Washington Times* that he had "enormous sympathy" for me. The Associated Press quoted me as saying, "After a guy's been on Wall Street for thirty years, he doesn't jump out the window every time the market goes down."

On December 6, the *Washington Post* reported that McFarlane had told the Senate Intelligence Committee that the President had given his approval in August 1985 to an Israeli arms shipment to Iran. This was one of many leaks of McFarlane's testimony that tended to shift blame and responsibility away from Bud and onto others, including the President. In a process peculiar to Washington, a public relations defense was being mounted for a man who was passing through a legal process that everyone knew could lead to criminal indictment. It could only be assumed that whoever was doing the leaking had McFarlane's interests at heart.

On Friday, December 5, a larger group of Republicans came down from Capitol Hill to talk to the President about his troubles. These men took the McFarlane defense very seriously. I was present, but the participants spoke about me as if I were not. Several of them said that I should be fired forthwith.

"Don Regan may think that this is some kind of bank, but he's wrong," said Representative Silvio O. Conte of Massachusetts. "This is big-time stuff, this is big money." Senator John H. Chafee of Rhode Island told the President that he should fire the entire White House senior staff, including me, and start over again with a clean slate. "I'd rather have an exposure of Don Regan and what he knows [than an attack on the President]," said Senator Phil Gramm of Texas.

So far, said the President in his soft voice, only two have been named, and those two have been let go. If others are named I'll take action, but I'm not going to change my team.

Senator Mark O. Hatfield of Oregon agreed. "Don't throw anyone to the wolves yet, Mr. President," he said. "Wait till the facts are known."

Nobody will be thrown to the wolves, the President said.

I wondered.

The President stoutly defended the Iran initiative and the Contras. If you're not for the Contras, you're for communism, he told the group. The enemy is Managua.

"People aren't listening to what you're saying, Mr. President," said Conte. "If anybody goes to jail, make sure it's your client—not you. That's what lawyers say."

The President smiled at this joke. Well, he said, I guess we'd better conclude this meeting, but before we do, let's all say happy birthday to Strom Thurmond.

The senior senator from South Carolina was eighty-four that day. A cake was brought in and Thurmond blew out the candles.

· 4 ·

The Beginning of the End

When, in Robert Graves's novel *I, Claudius*, the inquisitive Claudius asks his grandmother, Livia, whether she prefers slow poisons or quick ones, she replies that when she wanted to dispose of a rival she preferred "repeated doses of slow tasteless poisons which gave the effect of consumption." In the novel, Livia is portrayed as a clever but ruthless woman who ruled the Roman Empire from behind the scenes through the manipulation of her much older husband, Augustus Caesar.

Without stretching things too far, it can be suggested that the most popular poison in twentieth-century Washington is bad publicity. In massive doses it can destroy a reputation outright. When leaked slowly into the veins of the victim it kills his public persona just as certainly, but the symptoms—anger, suspicion, frustration, the loss of friends and influence—are often mistaken for the malady. The victim may realize that he is being poisoned; he may even have a very good idea who the poisoners are. But he cannot talk about his suspicions without adding a persecution complex to the list of his faults that is daily being compiled in the newspapers. A good many people—National Security Advisor Richard Allen, former Secretary of the Interior James Watt, and former Secretary of State Alexander M. Haig, Jr., come to mind—have left the Reagan Administration after whispering campaigns broke into the press and destroyed their dignity and, with it, their effectiveness.

On Thanksgiving Day in Santa Barbara, I had discussed my own burgeoning troubles with the press in a telephone conversation with Nancy Reagan. I was still fuming as a result of the media mob scene outside the hotel.

"Obviously I'm becoming the center of attention for the press, and I don't understand it," I said. "If this keeps up it will be a major problem by next week."

The White House staff had picked up many signs of a campaign of leaks designed, as they thought, to undermine my position as Chief of Staff and destroy the President's confidence in me. I mentioned this to the First Lady and asked whether she thought that this theory was paranoia or reality. Instead of answering my question she lapsed into a silence. After exchanging a few holiday pleasantries, I hung up the phone.

I turned to my wife, who had heard my end of the conversation, and told her about Mrs. Reagan's curious loss of voice.

It was not until later that I realized the full significance of the First Lady's stony response.

In early November Dick Wirthlin's polls showed that 70 percent of the American people approved of the way the President was doing his job. A month later a poll commissioned by the *New York Times* and CBS found that the President's job-approval rating had dropped below 50 percent. Fifty-seven percent of the sample polled thought that the Iran crisis was as bad as Watergate.

Given the storm in the media, this drop in popularity was not surprising, and it would almost certainly be temporary, but it produced deep anxiety among some in the White House. The First Lady's staff and her confidants from outside the government, known collectively as "the East Wing" in White House jargon, were especially worried. Reports of their gossip filtered into my office, and I knew that this was a sign that it would soon start pouring into the press.

That occurred on December 11 when the *New York Times*, citing "sources close to the President," printed a front-page story stating that two "key personal advisers, Michael Deaver and Stu Spencer, are scheduled to meet with President Reagan next week in what could be the climax of a campaign by some longtime Reagan confidants to oust Donald T. Regan as the President's Chief of Staff."

Mike Deaver, of course, is the longtime Reagan assistant and public relations expert who was the third member of the triumvirate that ran the White House during the first Reagan term. At the time of these events Deaver was under investigation in connection with his lobbying activities since resigning as White House Deputy Chief of Staff, and was subsequently convicted of perjury. He has appealed his conviction.

Stu Spencer is a California publicist and lobbyist whose broad, feet-on-the-other-fellow's-desk manner conceals a shrewd political aptitude. Though Spencer is little known to the public, he has been an intimate Reagan adviser since the President's earliest campaigns and was a carpenter of the famous Kitchen Cabinet of California insiders. Spencer is a ruthless pragmatist, and although he has never held any official position in the Administration, he is one of the few people who is licensed to speak his mind to the President and his wife on all subjects and has the audacity to do so. The Reagans have formed the habit, over many years, of listening very carefully to what he says.

A *Los Angeles Times* article dated December 13 pointed out accurately that Nancy Reagan, Deaver, and Spencer had "collaborated in the past on crucial personnel problems facing the President." The three of them "hoped to work out a scenario whereby Regan will take himself out during the [Christmas] holidays or right after."

The article continued: " 'He's got to go,' one source said, 'because absolutely nobody's for him. Even some of his own staff would like to tell him to go but they don't dare. Everybody's on board except the Old Man [Reagan].' "

This planted version of events, appearing in an out-of-town newspaper that the President reads religiously, was a message to Ronald Reagan from his advisers. It told him that the gloves were off in the East Wing where I was concerned. Mrs. Reagan and her advisers, having failed to convince him in private that he must get rid of me, were going public. ("Get off my goddamn back!" the President is reported to have told his wife during a discussion about me. According to one source—if I may lapse into media*ese* for the sake of protecting that source—it was this outburst that inspired the *Los Angeles Times* article. "Some Reagan associates say that the President is so angry and frustrated by the pressure to oust Regan," the *Times* had reported, "that he's digging in his heels. . . . One thing is clear . . . he isn't going to fire Don Regan based on what's been disclosed to date.")

It will no doubt seem incredible to the reader that people close to the President of the United States would send him warnings through the newspapers. Before I learned that this was a common practice, and a very effective one—at heart, Ronald Reagan is an old-fashioned, small-town American who believes what he reads in the papers—I, too, found it hard to believe.

The campaign to get the "Old Man" on board was intensifying. On December 12 the *Washington Post* reported that the President had visited with Bill Rogers and Robert Strauss, the former chairman of the Democratic National Committee about Iran. Ostensibly the meeting had been convened because, like some of the senators and congressmen the President had heard from, Mrs. Reagan believed that her husband's staff was too closely involved with the crisis to see it objectively and he should have the benefit of outside advice. Why Bob Strauss, a Democrat whose party had everything to gain from the mistakes of a Republican President, should have been regarded as a probable source of objective advice was an interesting question whose answer apparently was known only to Deaver and Strauss.

The meeting with Bill Rogers and Bob Strauss was conducted in great secrecy. I learned the details later. In order to shield the two visitors from the eyes of the press and the staff, they were brought into the White House by Deaver and whisked upstairs to the family quarters.

Soon the conversation came around to me. The First Lady felt that I had become a liability to the President and should go. Strauss agreed that there were strong arguments for getting rid of me.

Read the newspapers, the President was told. The press hates and mistrusts Regan and believes that he has mishandled the crisis. The impression was being created that I bore major responsibility for the disaster that was engulfing the Presidency. Whether this was true or not was irrelevant—in politics, appearance is reality, and the momentum of the press campaign was so great that matters could only get worse. I was going down fast and the President's friends were afraid I would drag him down with me. If his popularity was destroyed, his ability to govern would be destroyed, too. The President's place in history was at stake.

Ronald Reagan had to get rid of me. Everyone except Bill Rogers was saying so. "You don't have to do it yourself," he was told, in effect. "Someone else can approach Don and appeal to his loyalty."

The President indicated that the meeting was over. The participants went away with the knowledge that the President, if he had not accepted their advice, had at least heard them out. One of them immediately leaked a report of the meeting to the *Washington Post*.

Meanwhile John Poindexter and Oliver North, very properly instructed by their lawyers to avoid talking to the press, had moved to the edge of the media radar screen. Most Senate Republicans hoped to get the investigations over with while their party still controlled the Senate. The Democrats, naturally, hoped to delay until after the New Year, when the 100th Congress would convene and all committee chairmen in both houses would be Democrats. Robert Byrd of West Virginia, the Democratic leader in the Senate, wanted a full-scale televised hearing by a select committee.

Senator David Durenberger, Republican of Minnesota, the outgoing chairman of the Senate Intelligence Committee, had told the President that he could not control the votes of the Republicans on his committee; consequently the committee would not vote to grant limited-use immunity to Poindexter and North. Because the President was not foolish enough to pardon these key witnesses, and because there was no reason to think that they would give up their constitutional right to remain silent unless they got something valuable in return, it was possible that they might never testify. Their silence, combined with the shifting hints of higher culpability in what purported to be Bud McFarlane's testimony before Durenberger's committee, created a dark impression. Many believed, and some wrote and said, that Poindexter and North were keeping silent not to protect themselves, but to protect higher-ups. The White House regarded limited-use immunity as a device to smoke North and Poindexter out; the Democrats, understanding our tactic perfectly, were reluctant to let it succeed.

The intelligence committees were interested in hearing from me and I was determined to testify to the full extent of my knowledge. Through Peter Wallison, I had communicated my willingess to testify without conditions, assuming that the President would authorize me to do so. Finally the Senate committee asked if I could appear before it on Tuesday, December 16.

The President had already waived executive privilege for McFarlane, Shultz, Weinberger, Meese, Casey, and anyone else the committees wanted to hear from. Under this doctrine, which has routinely been resorted to by past Presidents as a means of preserving the constitutional separation of powers, members of the Presidential staff cannot be compelled to testify before Congress. The President (who, it is fair to say, was as curious about the true facts of the case as anyone in the country) had refrained from cloaking Poindexter and North in the doctrine because, again, he wanted them to tell the whole truth as quickly as possible.

At our morning meeting on Monday, December 15, I told the President that Durenberger's committee wanted to hear my testimony the next day, but I could not give them an answer until he made a decision on the question of executive privilege. As I spoke, the President's lips began to purse in disapproval and there was a question in his eyes. I could not read his thoughts, so I blurted out my own.

"Please, Mr. President, don't say no," I said. "I *want* to testify. This is the time to take Nancy's slogan and turn it around—just say yes."

The President grinned at the joke and let out a relieved breath.

You really are making my day, he said. I was afraid for a

minute that you were going to ask me to invoke executive privilege on your behalf.

That was the last thing I wanted him to do. The town was buzzing with false rumor as to what I knew about the Iran-Contra affair. Testifying under oath in closed session before a Senate investigating committee was a heaven-sent opportunity to get everything I knew said for the record—and, Washington being Washington, it was also an absolutely certain means of having the highlights of this secret testimony published in the newspapers and broadcast over the networks with a minimum of delay.

I appeared before the Senate Intelligence Committee without counsel or aides at the witness table and testified without referring to notes. The hearing room is windowless and protected by elaborate security devices. Although, as I have said, the media are usually present in spirit in this inner sanctum, they are barred from entering it in person. This produces a somewhat more relaxed atmosphere than a public session, and is supposed to stimulate frankness. Certainly Senator Durenberger and his colleagues in both parties were cordial to me in a guarded way, and this created the impression, which I believe to be correct, that committee and witness were engaged in a mutual search for the truth. I had had less than twenty-four hours to prepare for this testimony, but I tried in my opening statement to assure the senators that I would do my best to answer their questions candidly, forthrightly, and completely.

The committee operated under a rule that permitted each of its fifteen members to question a witness for ten minutes before passing him on to the next senator in line. If all members were present, therefore, it took a minimum of two and a half hours to go around the table. In practice it took much longer because the Senate committee's counsels also put questions to the witness and because of interruptions for votes on the Senate floor and other necessary business.

There is no guarantee that the right questions will be asked during the round robin. That is not a problem about which witnesses ordinarily complain. But I was determined to make a full statement of the facts for the record, and after Durenberger, the chairman, had asked the first two questions, I interrupted. "Perhaps I should just give you the narrative that's in my own mind about what happened in this affair," I said, "and then, when you've heard my story, you can ask me questions."

The committee, nodding their assent to the chairman, agreed to this suggestion. For the next three-quarters of an hour or so I testified without interruption about the events of the sixteen months that had passed between the time McFarlane made his initial report to the President at Bethesda Naval Hospital and the time Meese discovered the diversion of funds to the Contras and the President told the world about it. The senators, one after the other, then questioned me sharply and at length; the session lasted for about five hours.

"Today was cooperation," said Senator Patrick Leahy, the ranking Democrat on the Senate Intelligence Committee and a tough opponent of the Administration. I am prevented by the committee's rules from describing my testimony, but it was essentially the same, except for classified matters that involve the security of intelligence operations, as that which I gave on July 30–31, 1987, during the televised public hearings of the Joint Select Committees investigating the affair.

After my appearance, Senator Durenberger said that he was convinced that North had acted without authority from President Reagan in diverting funds to the Contras. The Associated Press reported that my testimony contradicted McFarlane's public testimony before the House Committee on Foreign Affairs that the President had authorized the indirect shipment [that is, shipment via Israel] of small amounts of arms to Iran. Copley News stated that "Regan testified under oath that neither he nor President Reagan had any knowledge about the diversion."

"[Regan] told an unbelievable story in a believable way," said Senator Dennis DeConcini, Democrat of Arizona. I don't know what he meant by that. Possibly I had not told him what he wanted to hear. Certainly that was the case where some of the press was concerned. From my point of view, newspaper and broadcast coverage and commentary was fragmented and grudging. I knew better than to expect exoneration, but I thought I had at least raised a reasonable doubt as to the plausibility of the media's wilder suspicions.

But all that was by the way. Two days later I testified again, this time before the House Intelligence Committee. Back at my desk in the West Wing, I felt a tremendous sense of relief in having stated the truth as I knew it for the record. A poll taken by Dick Wirthlin on December 17, the day after my Senate testimony, showed that the President's approval rating had gone up from 52 percent to 56 percent. Forty-two percent of those sampled now answered yes to the question "Are we getting the truth from Ronald Reagan?" That was an increase of 7 percent over the week before.

It seems naïve now, but I thought in the afterglow of my testimony that the worst was behind me and I could go back to doing my job in relative peace. The facts were coming out in a way that would have to reassure all but the truly irrational, and Wirthlin's polls were not the only signs that this was true. The press apparently decided, in the mysterious way in which journalists all seem to get the same idea at the same time, that the Regan story was over for the time being. The *Washington Post* reported on January 14 that "Regan is now secure in his position." Said *The New Republic*, traditionally a cue sheet for neo-liberal Washington journalists, "For good or bad [Regan]'s in charge again at the White House."

Frank Carlucci had taken a firm grip on the NSC staff and was instituting reforms, including many changes in personnel. The Tower Board was going about its work and would probably report on schedule. It was even possible that an Intelligence Committee controlled by the Democrats would be so eager to expose the mistakes of the Administration on national television that it would buy the testimony of North and Poindexter with an offer of immunity. The President, who was without sin in the matter of the diversion of funds and had already confessed his mistakes, had everything to gain by this—and so, in my less significant way, did I.

For the past month the staff and I had been consumed by the

distraction created by Iran, and I had been telling the President that he must put one man in charge of the crisis. In the latter part of December the First Lady suggested that Herbert ("Jack") Miller, a well-known criminal lawyer who was representing Mike Deaver, would be a good choice for the job.

I did not act on her suggestion; appointing a famous defense attorney to defend an innocent President seemed unwise from every point of view. But a day or two later, the President himself raised Miller's name.

I said, "Mr. President, what are you guilty of?"

He was startled by my question. Well, he said, Miller seems to know a lot about this kind of stuff.

"You bet he does," I replied. "That's because he defends people who are charged with felonies. Giving him the job would send all the wrong signals. Imagine what the press would do with an appointment like that."

The President saw my point. I wouldn't mind Fred Fielding, he said.

My own first choice was Fielding, who had resigned as Counsel to the President before the scandal broke in order to return to the private practice of law. But Fred declined the job when I offered it to him on grounds that he could not abandon his law partners. I knew that his decision was influenced by the fact that the First Lady had acquiesced in his earlier return to the White House with great reluctance.

On Christmas Eve, at my suggestion, the President decided to appoint David Abshire, the retiring ambassador to NATO, as Special Counsel to the President in charge of the day-to-day details of the crisis. At Abshire's insistence—and after much dickering—he was invested with Cabinet rank and broad authority.

On Monday, December 15, Bill Casey had collapsed in his office at the CIA. Not long before that, Bill Rogers and I had played a round of golf with Casey at Burning Tree Country Club. At his best, Casey was an inept golfer, but on this particular day his score would probably have exceeded two hundred if we had been keeping count. Neither Rogers nor I had ever seen him play so poorly. Casey didn't seem to be aware that anything was wrong. I thought that he was overworked or preoccupied.

An examination by doctors at Georgetown University Hospital revealed the presence of a growth on the brain, and on Thursday the eighteenth an operation was performed to remove it. The growth proved to be cancerous. Nevertheless, Casey's doctors inexplicably gave it as their opinion that he would be able to resume normal activities after a period of recuperation.

In fact, although he seemed to understand what was said to him and would make wordless responses to questions, Casey had lost the power of speech. The right side of his body was also affected. Casey, whom I had known on Wall Street before we both joined the Administration, was a remarkable figure. Rising from a modest neighborhood on Long Island, he finished college and law school. When he was barely out of his twenties he became the trusted assistant of Major General William J. ("Wild Bill") Donovan, head of the Office of Strategic Services (OSS) in World War II. After the war Casey made a fortune from investments, and was chairman of the Securities and Exchange Commission in the Nixon Administration. He managed Ronald Reagan's triumphant Presidential campaign in 1980. It was said that Casey wanted to be Ronald Reagan's first Secretary of State, but he was born in the wrong age and was serving the wrong Administration for that to be possible. Casey, who in his maturity looked like an old polar bear, was not telegenic. His New York speech, throaty and rapid, was difficult to understand. He suffered reporters impatiently and fools not at all. Ronald Reagan, who understood how brilliant and loyal and curmudgeonly Casey was, sent him across the Potomac to Langley, Virginia, as Director of Central Intelligence. Casey was as well qualified for this job by experience and temperament as any man who had ever held it.

I liked and admired Casey, whose Irish origins and Wall Street career were in some respects very much like my own. The President had genuine affection for him and, when Casey fell ill, was deeply worried about his prospects for recovery. At seventy-three he was the President's junior by a couple of years, and in Ronald Reagan's view he had been cut down in the prime of life while many accomplishments still lay before him.

After talking to Robert M. Gates, Casey's deputy, and doctors at CIA and Georgetown Hospital, I realized that the prognosis was bleak. As the Iran-Contra scandal unfolded, Casey had been severely roughed up in the media and on Capitol Hill when it appeared that the CIA had participated in some aspects of North's covert action operations without reporting what they had done to the oversight committees of the Congress. No culpability on Casey's part in this affair had been proved, and I certainly knew of none.

When at last Oliver North testified before the select committees in July, 1987, he stated that he had had the guidance and support of Casey in the diversion of funds to the Contras. By that time Casey was dead and no record of his alleged participation in the affair has been discovered, so the question remains unanswered. Probably that would not bother Bill Casey; he is no doubt just as ready to serve his country in the next world as he had always been in this one.

As a result of the uproar over Casey in the press and on Capitol Hill, Nancy Reagan came to regard him, too, as a political millstone. While he was alive and well, his friendship with the President protected him. After he was incapacitated by illness, however, the First Lady urged me, in a series of candid telephone calls, to seize the opportunity and find a replacement for the Director of Central Intelligence. I resisted this advice. It seemed unwise as well as inhumane, I told Mrs. Reagan, for the President to fire a man who was known to be one of his closest friends while the man was lying on what was almost certainly his deathbed. Besides, the President had given me no sign that he would even think of doing such a thing. He frequently raised the question of Casey's health and had called Sophia Casey to make inquiries and offer comfort.

Just before Christmas the First Lady rang to ask, for the third or fourth time since Casey's surgery on December 18, what I was doing to get rid of him.

"Nothing," I said.

"Why not?" Mrs. Reagan asked in her familiar stammer. "He's got to go. He can't do his job; he's an embarrassment to Ronnie. He should be out."

"But, Nancy, the man had brain surgery less than a week ago. He was under fire before he got sick. This is no time to pull the rug out from under him."

Mrs. Reagan said that Casey would never be able to work again; her stepbrother, who is a neurosurgeon, had assured her that this was so.

"That may well be," I said. "But I don't think anyone has told Bill Casey that. Sophia and the family are taking the illness very hard. It's Christmastime. It wouldn't be seemly for Ronald Reagan to 'fire anybody under these circumstances, much less Bill Casey. We're not going to do it."

Mrs. Reagan, who had already shown signs of irritability, now became angry.

"You're more interested in protecting Bill Casey than in protecting Ronnie!" she cried. "He's dragging Ronnie down! Nobody believes what Casey says, his credibility is gone on the Hill."

"All that may be true," I replied, knowing that some of it was. "But Bill Casey got your husband elected, and he's done a lot of other things for him, too. He deserves some gratitude and a better break than you're giving him, Nancy. The time will come when he can bow out gracefully. Please be patient."

But the First Lady was tired of waiting. She was still angry at me when she said good-bye and hung up the phone.

Mrs. Reagan stayed angry and insistent on the Casey matter through the Christmas holiday. Under the circumstances, Ann and I decided not to join the Reagans and the others who had been invited by Walter Annenberg and his wife, Lee, to spend New Year's Eve with them at their place in Palm Desert, California. Besides, I was tired. The wear and tear of the crisis, added to my normal workload, had left me fatigued. My grandchildren were complaining that I never came to see them anymore. We got out of Washington for the holiday and found that people beyond the Capitol Beltway had other things to think about and talk about than Iran and the Contras.

Early in November, just as the Iran-Contra scandal broke out, the First Lady had informed me that doctors had discovered that the President had an enlarged prostate, a common condition in men of his age. The condition would be relieved by transurethral resection, a technique that eliminated the need for incision of the skin, on Monday, January 5, at Bethesda Naval Hospital; it was expected that the President would be in the hospital for about four days and that he would have a rapid recovery.

Before the surgery, Mrs. Reagan phoned me from the Annenbergs' to talk about the President's schedule. She said that her husband should be seen to be active and capable of carrying on the normal routine of the Presidency after he left the hospital. I agreed, suggesting that the President make some one-day trips on *Air Force One* after February 1 to deliver speeches around the country, and reminding her that he was scheduled to visit Canada in early April for the annual summit with the Canadian Prime Minister.

"He hasn't had a press conference since November nineteenth," I said. "What about having one on January twentieth?"

The First Lady's voice rose. "No," she said. "No press conferences for at least three months."

"Nancy, he has to talk to the press or it will look like he's hiding. We've penciled in a press conference every four to six weeks after the one on January twentieth."

"No," Mrs. Reagan repeated. "Absolutely not."

I did not ask the reason for this decision. It was obvious that Mrs. Reagan's protective instincts were fully aroused, and I assumed, too, that she had been talking to her Friend, the astrologer.

The staff and I had worked diligently over the holidays to produce a tentative schedule for the President covering his activities for the next six months. So far we had only settled on the events, not the dates. Mrs. Reagan's Friend had provided a list of good, bad, and iffy days for 1988 that eliminated many key events. Discreetly, because we were talking over an open telephone line, I hinted at the problem.

"We have press conferences, speeches, activities all lined up," I said. "But I need your help on the actual dates."

Mrs. Reagan stammered, as she often did when her secret Friend came into the conversation.

"I'll, uh, uh, uh, have a discussion about that and get back to you," she said.

This conversation was, for the most part, friendly and devoid of her usual references ("Are you still here, Don?") to resignation.

The President's operation went well. Having learned from experience, I remained out of the press's sight, communicating with the President by telephone and sending members of the staff to him with paperwork. During his previous hospital stay he had asked for more documents to read, complaining that he was bored by the reduction in his routine.

On Tuesday, January 6, the President's third day at Bethesda, Mrs. Reagan told me that I should visit him in the hospital.

In my two years in the White House the First Lady was a constant telephone presence in my work. But I seldom encountered her in person, and when I did, it was usually at a public function in the presence of many other people. At Bethesda that day we were alone for a few moments in the waiting room next to the President's room.

We exchanged a few words about the President's health and spirits, and then the First Lady said, "What are you going to do about Casey?"

"Bill's partially paralyzed," I said. "He can't speak. Nobody knows if he understands what is said to him or what would happen if we asked for his resignation. There's not much you can do in all decency when a fellow is in that condition."

"Oh, yes there is," Mrs. Reagan replied. "Ronnie could just send him a letter telling him that since he can't perform his duties we're sorry, but that's it."

"I don't think that would sit very well with anybody," I said. "Really, this is something we have to think through very carefully."

It was clear to me that Mrs. Reagan had not said her last word on this subject, but she quickly turned to another—that of Pat Buchanan, the White House Director of Communications. Pat is a man of strong conservative views, and during the height of the crisis he had made a number of emphatic public statements in support of the President and his policy. Pat had spoken out with my prior approval of his action if not of his exact words, and if I was a little surprised when he gave a speech at a rally in Lafayette Park in which he called the President's critics in the media "a liberal lynch mob," I could hardly claim that I did not know what his views were before he expressed them—or that I thought his description was altogether wrong. His similar defense of North ("If Ollie North ripped off the Ayatollah and sent thirty million dollars to the Contras, then I say, God bless Colonel North.") amused me less, but it had produced an unexpected result. Pat was being mentioned by some right-wing Republicans as a possible candidate for President. He had not said no to these overtures. The First Lady found a Buchanan candidacy ludicrous, and she had told me more than once that she wanted Pat to resign. I had told her previously that Pat had told me that he wanted to leave soon, and he and I had agreed that he would depart by February 1.

"What about Pat Buchanan?" she said now. "When is he going?"

I told her again what the plan was. The First Lady said she hoped that Buchanan would go even sooner than that. In the meantime he should be watched very closely to make sure that his conservative pronouncements did not harm the President.

"Don't you let Pat have a single thing to do with writing Ronnie's State of the Union speech," she said. "His ideas aren't Ronald Reagan's ideas."

She wanted Ken Khachigian, a skillful writer who had worked on the President's Bergen-Belsen speech, to ghost the State of the Union address, scheduled for delivery on January 27.

We had not been so lucky in regard to other engagements. Mrs. Reagan's Friend had told her that January was a bad month for the President—any activity might produce unhappy results. This prognostication had the effect of immobilizing the President. His schedule was in a state of chaos. Mrs. Reagan had canceled or refused to approve a number of important appearances. Among these was a speech before the Alfalfa Club. The Alfalfa Club, an informal association of political figures and business leaders, holds only one meeting each year; and the mixture of good fellowship, unabashed patriotism, and humorous oratory provides one of the most enjoyable and relaxing evenings of the Washington winter. President Reagan was a member of the club; no President wants to miss the dinner. Although I understood the reasons only too well, I was astounded that Mrs. Reagan would ask her husband to pass up the fun. A speech to the Alfalfa Club provided a fine opportunity for him to demonstrate, in one of the gentle lampoons of himself that he carries off so brilliantly, that he was in good spirits despite his political troubles and in good health after his operation. He was already working out, in a measured way, in his gym in the family quarters.

His other activities, however, were severely limited. He came to the Oval Office at 9 every morning as usual, but went back to the family quarters immediately after luncheon. He read and signed the papers put before him and listened to his briefings, but he appeared to be in the grip of lassitude. He seldom, if ever, emerged from his office and wandered down the hallway as he had done before. The quick humor, the curiosity about new subjects, and above all, the political combativeness operated at a much lower intensity than usual. He seldom raised the subject of the Iran-Contra affair, and seemed uninterested in the fact that the field had largely been left to his detractors at one of the most critical hours of his career.

I thought that an evening at the Alfalfa Club might be just the medicine he needed to restore his optimism and appealed to Mrs. Reagan to let him attend. On the telephone, she replied that the appearance had been scheduled too soon after the President's surgery—only eleven days after he was released from the hospital. A society reporter from the *Washington Post* had told her that her own husband had gone back to work too soon after a similar operation and had suffered a setback as a result.

"But the doctors have assured us that a man of his age in his physical condition only needs two or three weeks for a complete recovery," I said.

"You're not a doctor," Mrs. Reagan replied.

She disapproved two other important appearances in February—the National Prayer Breakfast on the fifth and the Executive Forum on the sixth, Ronald Reagan's seventy-sixth birthday. The Executive Forum was invented by the Reagan Administration as a once-a-year meeting of political appointees of the Executive Branch; they look forward keenly to what is for most of them their only chance during the year to see the boss in person. The planners had believed that celebrating the President's birthday on this occasion would be a morale-builder for those attending, and would also provide an occasion for the media to observe the oldest Chief Executive in our history at the top of his form. Mrs. Reagan also changed the date of a dinner for freshman congressmen and once again rejected all proposals to hold a press conference or arrange other contacts with the media for the President. She didn't want her husband to undertake any travel or other important outside activity until he went to Canada in April.

These decisions would isolate the President from the American people during the most crucial period of his Presidency. His critics and his troubled former subordinates were filling up the press with leaks and opinions. He was saying nothing in return. The Tower Board report would be out in two weeks and we had no idea what it would say. Public opinion must be prepared for this event. Leaving aside the Iran-Contra affair, the President had a full agenda of foreign and domestic policy to explain to the nation and to defend and enact in Congress.

Mrs. Reagan's concern for her husband's health was understandable, even admirable. But it seemed to me excessive, particularly since the President himself did not seem to think that there was any need for him to slow down to the point where he was lying dead in the water. I pointed out to the First Lady that the restrictions she was laying down left the President with only one important public appearance, the State of the Union address, over a two-month period. Couldn't he make at least one follow-up speech to reinforce his message after the State of the Union address?

"I wish that you were as protective of the President's health as you are of Bill Casey's," Mrs. Reagan replied.

The First Lady's state of mind did not surprise me. I remembered the intensity of her concern when the President had been hospitalized in July. She seemed even more upset this time. Dick Wirthlin, concerned and sympathetic after a prolonged telephone conversation with the First Lady, told me that he was going to change his advice on the President's schedule. Though Wirthlin's polls suggested that the President should make a strong personal effort to bring his case to the people, Dick was prepared to advise the opposite in the hope of soothing Mrs. Reagan's anxieties. He described these as being stronger than any he remembered in the eighteen years of his association with the Reagans. Undoubtedly her fears arose in part from her fear of a relapse, but I think, too, that she was concerned that the President, surrounded by enemies at a time when his medical experiences had left him vulnerable, would make some sort of slip of the tongue or other public mistake and rouse the press to new attacks on him and his policies.

And then there was the question of the astrologer's influence. Before I came to the White House, Mike Deaver had been the man who integrated the horoscopes of Mrs. Reagan's Friend into the Presidential schedule. He did so with the utmost tact, leaving the impression with the dozens of people who wait on any Presidential scheduling decision that he, Deaver, was the ditherer. I found this odd because Deaver was remarkably punctual and efficient in everything else that he did. When, after a few days on the job, I asked Deaver to explain the hesitation, delay, and uncertainty surrounding the schedule, he was plainly uncomfortable.

"Ssshhh," Deaver said, throwing up his hands and casting furtive glances. "Don't bring that up. Leave it be."

The confusion continued even after Deaver left the White House. The President's trip to Bitburg was plagued by inexplicable changes in scheduling that arose, as I subsequently learned, from the astrologer's warnings to Mrs. Reagan concerning possible threats to the President's safety. Naturally I complained to Bill Henkel, the aide in charge of implementing the President's schedule, about this state of affairs. Poor Bill, who had been in on the secret for some time but was not at liberty to disclose it to me, made no excuses.

It was Henkel who finally persuaded Deaver to tell me the

facts. He said I had to know them or the entire scheduling process would collapse. Deaver came to see me and explained the mystery. I thought at first that he was joking, but he made it plain that he was not.

Deaver told me that he had been dealing with astrological input for a long time. Mrs. Reagan's dependence on the occult went back at least as far as her husband's governorship, when she had depended on the advice of the famous Jeane Dixon. Subsequently she had lost confidence in Dixon's powers. But the First Lady seemed to have absolute faith in the clairvoyant talents of the woman in San Francisco.

Apparently Deaver had ceased to think that there was anything remarkable about this long-established floating seance; Mike is a born chamberlain, and to him it was simply one of many little problems in the life of a servant of the great.

"Humor her," Deaver advised. "At least this astrologer is not as kooky as the last one."

As I discovered in my turn, there was no choice *but* to humor the First Lady in this matter. But the President's schedule is the single most potent tool in the White House, because it determines what the most powerful man in the world is going to do and when he is going to do it. By humoring Mrs. Reagan we gave her this tool—or, more accurately, gave it to an unknown woman in San Francisco who believed that the zodiac controls events and human behavior and that she could read the secrets of the future in the movements of the planets.

(Apparently she couldn't always do so. On one occasion the First Lady explained that there would be a longer delay than usual in choosing a date for some Presidential appearance or other. "I can't reach my Friend," Mrs. Reagan said. "Her mother died suddenly." I sympathized, but also wondered why this sad event should have come as a surprise to a clairvoyant.)

Mrs. Reagan talked to her Friend mostly on Saturday afternoons, from Camp David. The First Lady once complained to me in budgetary terms about revisions in the schedule.

"I wish you'd make up your mind," she said testily. "It's costing me a lot of money, calling up my Friend with all these changes."

On weekdays Mrs. Reagan normally called me in the late afternoon, while the President was taking his two hours of daily exercise in the small gym that had been fitted out for him in the family quarters. Sometimes she would cover the mouthpiece and call out an answer to a question he evidently had asked her while using the rowing machine or the stationary bicycle.

Mrs. Reagan's determination to oust Bill Casey had not abated. It was obvious that Casey would not continue as Director, but the question of common decency remained and I temporized. Sophia Casey was fearful that any sudden demand for a resignation might have an impact on her husband's prospects for recovery.

The President was aware of this and instructed me to proceed cautiously in a search for a successor. The favorite candidate to be the next Director of Central Intelligence had been Howard H. Baker, Jr., of Tennessee, the former Republican leader of the Senate. Although Baker was a member of the President's Foreign Intelligence Advisory Board, and as Minority Leader and Majority Leader had been part of the Senate's intelligence oversight apparatus, he had no direct managerial or other experience of intelligence operations. He did possess the inestimable advantage of being trusted absolutely by his former colleagues on Capitol Hill, and of being admired by the press to a degree unusual in a Republican. These qualifications would recommend him for another job—my own—in a shorter time than either of us could have imagined. On January 14, Baker and I met in the office that had belonged to the Secretary of the Navy when the Executive Office Building was known as the State, War, and Navy Building. At the end of our conversation Baker said that he could not accept the post because he had not yet come to grips with his Presidential ambitions. He mentioned that a call from the President of the United States might change his mind, but the President felt, when I mentioned this to him, that no one should be persuaded to accept a job by anything but his own enthusiasm.

Presently Mrs. Reagan phoned me from Camp David to say that she had found an ideal candidate for Director of Central Intelligence—Edward Bennett Williams, the famous Washington lawyer. She had a feeling, she said, that Williams would be interested in the job if we asked him about it; I said that I would be

sure to call him. I supposed that Mrs. Reagan had already discussed the job with Williams or with those close to him—an as-
sumption that was reinforced when, soon afterward, former CIA
Director Richard Helms, a friend of Mrs. Reagan's, phoned with
a list of well-qualified candidates on which Williams's name appeared. (In fact Williams and I did discuss the job on a holiday
when the White House was nearly deserted. After a pleasant chat
he withdrew his name from consideration on personal grounds.)

By now, the middle of January, the First Lady's telephoning
was so frequent that I was spending two or three times as much
time talking to her as to the President. The memory of all these
conversations remains vivid. The Iran-Contra affair had made
her sensitivity to criticism more acute than ever. Even routine
stories in the press upset her. She was disturbed about an article
in the *Washington Post* that was critical of the President on Iran.
A segment of the CBS show "60 Minutes" had also been negative.

"Nobody up on the Hill is defending Ronnie on Iran," she
said. "We have to get somebody in who will defend him. Larry
[Speakes] should defend him more."

I replied that someone else, namely David Abshire, was now
in charge of the Iran-Contra affair, as she had desired; I was
supposed to be doing other things, such as minding the budget
and the business of the Cabinet.

"Tell both of them [Abshire and Speakes] they've got to do
something," Mrs. Reagan said.

"Okay, Nancy, I'll tell them to get moving," I said. "But, really,
you asked me to stay out of the Iran situation. How can I be in
it and still stay out of it?"

As was often the case, the First Lady's instincts were correct
in this matter. The President was taking a public battering and
he was not defending himself. This made others hesitant to defend him because they did not know what his inactivity signified.
Dick Wirthlin told me that his polls showed that the President's
lack of public visibility was creating the risk of a serious loss of
public support. Wirthlin feared, as I did, that a leak from the
Tower Board, whose report was due to be issued at the end of

January, would distort the controversy even further and upstage the President's one major public appearance, the State of the Union Address.

"This inactivity is hurting the President," Dick said.

"I know it," I replied, "but there's nothing we can do about it. Nancy won't let him go outside, and the President is going by what she says."

On Saturday, January 24, Mrs. Reagan rang me from Camp David to tell me that her stepbrother had talked to Casey's doctors and reported that Bill would be incapacitated for the foreseeable future. This inside information had made the First Lady more determined than ever that Casey should be forced out.

"What we're going to have to do," she said, "is prop up our guy here."

The First Lady meant that we must stiffen the President's resolve. I told her that the President was probably going to send Casey a gentle letter soon, asking him to step aside.

"Send it to his lawyer," Mrs. Reagan said, "because Sophia won't let it be delivered to Casey. Do it Monday. Ronnie is ready, so why wait?"

She asked once again if Pat Buchanan was really going to leave on February 1. She said she was glad that Ken Khachigian, not Pat, was writing the State of the Union speech. She liked the second draft, and she and the President had invited Khachigian and his wife to Camp David over the weekend so that they could work on the speech together.

"The parts about abortion have got to come out," she said.

I pointed out that the President had particularly wanted some language on this subject included in his address.

"I don't give a damn about the right-to-lifers," Mrs. Reagan retorted. "I'm cutting back on the Iran stuff, too. It's too long and it's not appropriate. Ronald Reagan's got to be shown to be in charge."

I told Mrs. Reagan that I agreed with this last observation. Did she mean that the President could now be more active? Could we move ahead with the schedule?

"No," she said. "Not for at least three weeks."

"But that takes us to the end of February," I said, dismayed. "We need to get going."

The First Lady was adamant. "We've got to wait," she said. "The surgery requires it."

Later the President himself called me from Camp David and asked if I had arranged a meeting with Sophia Casey to discuss Bill's resignation. I told him that Ed Meese and I would be calling on Casey in his hospital room on Thursday, January 29.

Bill Casey, when Meese and I saw him that day, was devastated physically and intellectually. The change in his appearance was startling. He had lost a great deal of weight and all his hair. The skin on his hands was mottled. He sat up with difficulty in a chair, dressed in a bathrobe. He was incapable of coherent speech. He waved his hands about weakly and made inarticulate sounds in answer to questions.

Sophia interpreted the sounds he made, asking, Bill, did you want to say so-and-so? If Casey gave a sign of assent, then his wife would repeat the sense of what she believed he wished to say to the visitor.

Because of the damage to his brain, Casey was unable to swallow properly. He trembled. His facial expression, before so intensely thoughtful, had become bland. In response to nearly every question he uttered a garbled sound that resembled the word "yeah." That sound constituted his response to contradictory questions coming one right after the other.

In these melancholy circumstances, Ed Meese and I attempted to converse with Casey for a few moments. Then I took Sophia aside and asked if we could talk to her husband now about his job. She nodded. I went back to Bill's chair and, standing beside him, said, "Bill, I'd like to talk to you about the agency and you."

I was carrying a letter, signed by the President, that acceded to the First Lady's wishes by summarily relieving Casey of his duties. Bill may have sensed this.

Casey waved his hands about and uttered a long string of incomprehensible sounds. Interpreting, Sophia said, "He says, 'Get the best man you can.'"

"In other words," I said to Casey, "you're saying you want to be relieved of your task and we should look for someone else."

He seemed to nod.

I said, "All right, Bill, then I'll tell the President about your decision. But there's one condition: when you're ready to come back, the boss wants you next to him as Counselor to the President—Ed Meese's old job."

Tears filled Casey's clouded eyes. He gripped my hand with surprising strength.

Minutes after I returned from the hospital to my office in the West Wing, the telephone rang.

"Well, what's the news on Casey?" Nancy Reagan asked. "What happened?"

I told her that Casey had agreed to be relieved of his duties and the President was signing a letter to that effect.

"Good," the First Lady said. "Now I hope the other guy [Williams] accepts."

· 5 ·

The Conscience of the President

The President had decided that he would make no public statement on the Iran-Contra affair while the Tower Board—properly, the President's Special Review Board—proceeded with its investigation. On January 26, after sixty-four days of operations, the Board first interviewed President Reagan in the Oval Office. I was not present. The Board's report summarized the President's statement as follows:

> The President said that sometime in August he approved the shipment of arms by Israel to Iran. He was uncertain as to the precise date. The President also said he approved replenishment of any arms transferred by Israel to Iran.

> The President said he approved a convoluted plan whereby Israel would free 20 Hizballah prisoners, Israel would sell TOW missiles to Iran, the five U.S. citizens in Beirut would be freed, and the kidnappings would stop. A draft Covert Action Finding had already been signed by the President the day before the meeting on January 6, 1986. Mr. Regan told the Board that the draft finding may have been signed in error. The President did not recall signing the January 6 draft.

[McFarlane] told the Board that he discussed this proposal [that 100 TOW missiles to Iran would establish good faith and result in the release of the hostages] with the President on several occasions and on at least one occasion with the 'full' members of the NSC. Within days after the meeting, the President communicated his decision to Mr. McFarlane by telephone.*

Because he was the only principal who was willing to testify about the events that had been so imperfectly reported to the President, McFarlane had been the Board's primary source of testimony. (Although the testimony of Poindexter and North was still desirable, it ceased to be absolutely indispensable. The two men had attempted to erase their message files from the NSC computer, but the Board's investigators, fortunately, had found a duplicate in the computer's central memory. This provided a set of tracks, if not a historical tour, across the landscape of the conspiracy.)

Not surprisingly, the Board found McFarlane a sympathetic figure. He was a cooperative and penitent witness. Even before his unfortunate attempt to take his own life by swallowing a large number of Valium tablets on February 9, 1987, his anguish over the damage wrought by the Iran initiative was beyond question. So were his patriotism and his record of faithful service as a Marine and a civilian employee of the federal government. McFarlane had been the protégé of a succession of powerful figures, including Henry Kissinger and Alexander Haig. He had worked for John Tower as a member of the staff of the Senate Armed Services Committee.† He and Brent Scowcroft had been colleagues on the NSC staff during the Nixon and Ford Adminis-

*Report of the President's Special Review Board (Washington: Government Printing Office, February 26, 1987). All quotations that follow in this chapter are from the same source unless otherwise noted.
†In its editions of November 27, 1986, the New York Times quoted Senator Daniel Patrick Moynihan, Democrat of New York and a former vice chairman of the Senate Intelligence Committee, as saying that he had "one reservation" about the appointment of John Tower as chairman of the President's Special Review Board: "I hope that Senator Tower will clearly and quickly set out his relationship with Bud McFarlane."

trations. McFarlane was, from his days on the Hill, also a familiar figure to Ed Muskie. His many friends in the press had reason to be grateful to McFarlane for the generosity he had shown them in the past, and in general they were generous in their accounts of his trouble; this was no more than he had coming to him under Washington rules.

Nevertheless, I was and am sure that his recollection of the President's actions was faulty. The Tower Board was confused by what it called "the different histories offered by Mr. McFarlane in three PROF notes [messages or memoranda entered into the NSC computer] . . . and in his several testimonies on the Hill and before the Board. His various positions on the question of Presidential authorization in August and September, 1985, have made this question very difficult to resolve."

In testimony before the Board, McFarlane quotes himself as saying the following words to Attorney General Meese on November 21, 1987, when Meese was engaged in his fact-finding mission on behalf of the President: "I want you to know that from the very beginning of this, Ed, the President was four-square behind it, that he never had any reservations about approving anything the Israelis wanted to do here."

That assertion was the heart of McFarlane's defense. It is seriously at odds with my own recollection of events.

Correcting the record was no simple matter. All the files pertaining to the Iran initiative were in the custody of the NSC staff; no White House file on this matter existed. The Tower Board was relying almost entirely on the testimony of the NSC staff in conducting its *viva voce* inquiry. From the beginning of the Board's work to the end, only one member of the White House staff appeared as a witness before it—me. The President's diary, in which he jotted down random impressions of the events of his day, had been made available to the Tower Board in edited form and, later, to the congressional committees. It shed no light on the issue.

But I had a distinct memory of what had—and had not—been said. And this record, like my own memory of events, directly contradicted McFarlane's version. It was essential that the

President state the facts correctly. In the presence of Vice President Bush, I brought this forcefully to the President's attention soon after his first statement to the board.

"You certainly never approved the transfer of arms before the fact in my presence, Mr. President," I said.

In answer to a question from me, Vice President Bush said that he had no memory of any such action by the President. We went back over the trail step by step.

I told the President that I had no recollection of his authorizing the sale of arms when McFarlane visited him at Bethesda Naval Hospital after his cancer surgery. Had he somehow done so without my knowing it?

The President replied in the negative.

"Then when *could* you have done so, Mr. President?"

The President replied that he had no recollection of ever having given verbal or written authorization for the transfer of arms to Iran.

Neither did the Vice President, who normally was present, as I was, at all meetings between the President and the National Security Advisor.

"That's the way I remember it, too," I said. "I think you should clarify this matter to the Board."

After our discussion, the President met with the Board again, on February 11, and informed its members that "Mr. Regan had a firm recollection that the President had not authorized the August shipment in advance. The President said he did not recall authorizing the August shipment in advance."

On February 20, the President sent a letter to the Board in which he wrote:

I have no personal notes or records to help my recollection in this matter. The only honest answer is to state that try as I might, I cannot recall anything whatsoever about whether I approved an Israeli sale in advance or whether I approved replenishment of Israeli stocks around August of 1985. My answer therefore and the simple truth is, "I don't remember—period."

This statement was greeted by widespread skepticism. Yet I believed it to be the truth then and I believe it to be the truth now. The reader may ask, How could such a thing be? I can only answer that experience has taught me that great events are the product of small details, and that petty motives play a greater role in the affairs of the mighty than is generally supposed.

The President's faulty recollection, the shifting testimony of McFarlane with respect to the sequence and the nature of the President's actions, and the catastrophic misconstruction by North of his superiors' intentions have been matters of puzzlement to the bodies investigating the Iran-Contra affair and to the press and public.

Why was no record kept of what was said and when it was said? The answer is so simple that I have little hope that it will be believed. But the fact is, leaks of sensitive information to the press, even by the President's highest and most trusted advisers (for example, verbatim notes from a meeting of the National Security Planning Group, whose members are the President, the Vice President, the Secretaries of State and Defense, and the National Security Advisor), had achieved such epidemic proportions that the inner circle was afraid to take notes lest they read them next day in the newspapers or hear them broadcast over the networks. In the past, confidential clerks sat in the Oval Office with notebook in hand, recording the exchanges between Presidents and some of their visitors. This provided a record to support or correct the President's memory of events and an aide-mémoire to history. No such record can exist, however, except in conditions of inviolable confidentiality. And no such condition existed or was even imaginable in the White House that I knew.

In fact, that root of the scandal may well lie in the fact that McFarlane and Poindexter and their assistants were, in a sense, driven mad by leaks; certainly the insistence on secrecy long after the secrets were out, and the peculiar belief that some of the most unsavory foreigners ever to sidle into our history were more trustworthy than elected officials who constitutionally must be trusted, suggest that their judgment had been knocked awry. What ought to have been diplomatic objectives and policy objectives became ideological objectives. Supporting the Contras was more important than supporting the Constitution because some people on Capitol Hill seemed to be blind to the real and present danger posed to the United States by an adventurist communist regime in Nicaragua.

Feelings were just as high, and just as skewed, on the other side of the issue. Opponents of the President's policy on Capitol Hill and in the press typically subjected statements of the Administration to courtroom rules of evidence, but were often willing to accept what the Nicaraguan government and its supporters said at face value. In this connection, Speaker O'Neill repeatedly told the President that he was "all wrong on Central America." O'Neill's aunt, a Maryknoll nun who had been posted to the region, had told the Speaker "the real story" and he was uninterested in any information developed by the diplomatic and intelligence services that contradicted it.

What this fracture in democratic trust between two camps of Americans may produce in the future is a question to ponder. But whatever his recollection of events may have been, or whatever the recollections of others may be, the Ronald Reagan I knew and served was no part of this plan to divert funds—in his mind or in his actions. The President's heart was another matter. As I have written, his concern for the safety of the hostages, his frustration in not being able to apply the enormous power of the United States against a weak but hidden adversary, and his firm (and in my view, correct) belief that a communist Nicaragua represents a long-term danger to democracy and peace in the western hemisphere, were genuine and visible.

I offer excuses for Oliver North with great reluctance, but it is possible that he would have acted differently if he had not imagined, as he has testified he did, that it was his mission to relieve the President of burdens that could not be lifted by the usual methods of a democratic government.

Historical forces of great antiquity were also at play. At the National Prayer Breakfast on February 5 (the First Lady had relented and accompanied the President to this event), the main speaker was Elizabeth Dole, the Secretary of Transportation. As her text she took the Book of Esther, which tells the story of the deliverance of the Jews from a plot to destroy them in ancient Persia, a vast kingdom described in Esther 1:1 as containing 127 provinces that stretched from "India even unto Ethiopia." My mind was occupied with questions involving Iran and Israel, but as I listened to Elizabeth Dole's spirited retelling of the story of Esther, a beautiful Jewish maiden who became queen of Persia and persuaded her husband, King Ahasuerus (probably Xerxes I, who lived around 519–465 B.C.) to spare her people, it occurred to me how very long is the history of the Middle East, and how little its fundamental conflicts change.

The Tower Board, unable to publish its report by the original deadline, had asked the President for an extension of time until about February 20. This was granted. The delay was disappointing. Although it never occurred to me in light of the facts as I knew them that the report could have anything but a positive effect in the long run, I understood that the potential for bad press was considerable. That was why it was important that the President prepare public opinion for the facts that the Board would discover and publish.

My own contacts with the Board and its staff had been brief and pleasant. They asked me what I knew about the history of the affair and I told them, as I had told the intelligence committees, everything I knew. The Board's questions to me related exclusively to the history of the affair as I understood it from my own observation of events.

I was not asked what I had done, or what I had recommended, in regard to managing the crisis after it broke. Therefore the Board did not know, in the sense of having taken down testimony for its own records, that I had argued strenuously, but privately and in vain, for full and immediate disclosure of all the facts. My memoranda to the President, my instructions to the staff on this matter—in fact, the entire White House file and staff were available to the Board. Moreover, I had suggested, among other measures designed to get out the facts, that the

Board itself be created in the first place, and had acted for the President in asking all three of its members to serve.

Therefore I was unhappy, if not surprised, to read in the February 16 issue of *Newsweek* that "tough, arrogant . . . assertive . . . Donald T. Regan . . . is now the target of relentless speculation about his potential liability for the Iran arms-sales imbroglio." The story continued:

> *Although no one has yet advanced any evidence of Regan's active participation in Iranscam's covert blunders* [emphasis added], his critics have repeatedly argued that the Chief of Staff must at least be guilty of not protecting Ronald Reagan from error. Some have pointedly suggested that Regan should fall on his sword, while others, including Presidential confidants Michael Deaver and Stuart Spencer, are reliably reported to have joined Nancy Reagan in an unsuccessful attempt to force Regan out in December . . . Once again the smart-money players are betting that Regan will be under increasing pressure to resign.

I will discuss the Washington press corps and its sources and methods in another chapter, but this is a good place to remark that the hectic courtship of journalists and public figures, each by the other, sometimes produces what might be called "dysjournalism." *Webster's* defines the prefix *dys-,* derived from Greek and Latin, as denoting a phenomenon that is "abnormal : diseased . . . faulty : impaired . . . bad : unfavorable."

The *Newsweek* story was a striking example of dysjournalism. If *Newsweek*'s sources said that I would be under increasing pressure to resign, then undoubtedly I would be. The people who planted the story were the same ones who were going to apply the pressure. *Newsweek* had been one of the most important outlets for the December speculation that I was on the way out, and had printed a picture of my troubled face (I seldom looked pleasant and relaxed in *Newsweek*) on the cover of the December 8, 1986, issue next to the boldface question "WHO KNEW?"

The pressure came from the same quarters as before—and,

as before, it was accompanied by a rolling barrage of provocative stories in the press. The *Washington Post*, in an article that captures the flavor of others like it, reported on February 18 that ". . . Regan, under fire for managerial shortcomings by Republican politicans and First Lady Nancy Reagan, is finding it increasingly difficult to fill the growing number of vacancies on the White House staff."

In fact, several important White House aides had planned, like me, to leave after the midterm election. Larry Speakes had resigned to join Merrill Lynch and had been replaced by Marlin Fitzwater, an excellent man who had worked for me at Treasury and had later been Vice President Bush's press secretary. Mitchell E. Daniels, the political director, had decided to return to private law practice in Indiana. And, of course, Pat Buchanan had kept his bargain and resigned (albeit a month later than expected), effective March 1, as Director of Communications.

The First Lady, who always took a close interest in White House staff appointments, called me at home at 9:46 A.M. on February 7, a Saturday, to talk about her candidates for these vacancies. She was in exceptionally good spirits. She recommended Frank Donatelli, who had worked in all three Reagan Presidential campaigns, for political director. Donatelli was a very good choice for this demanding job, which involves working with the Republican party and its elected and appointed officials from the county level on up.

For Pat Buchanan's old job, Mrs. Reagan favored John O. Koehler, a German-born American who had been recommended by the Reagans' good friend, Charles Z. Wick, Director of the United States Information Agency. I knew little about Koehler besides the fact that he had worked for Wick at USIA.

"Charlie Wick says Jack Koehler would be great," Mrs. Reagan said. "Bob Tuttle [the White House Personnel Director] has a lot of information on Koehler, and he thinks we should hire him right away."

I told the First Lady that my own first choice as Director of Communications was Stu Spencer. There was, I admit, an element of mischief in this suggestion: the fact that Spencer had never given up the benefits of the commercial world in order to serve in the Administration had always rankled, and his recent activities had irritated the situation. If he was going to sharpen the knives, I thought, then he might as well come right into the kitchen. But there were also sound managerial reasons for wanting Spencer. He was the sort of big name we needed to replace Buchanan. He knew the Reagans and their public relations requirements better than anybody, and as I had reason to know, he was a gifted handler of the press. Why not get the best? I asked.

"Oh, Stu can't come," Mrs. Reagan said quickly. "He's in the middle of a divorce."

Pointing out that lots of people in the Reagan Administration were divorced, I insisted that we at least offer Spencer the job; if we didn't ask, how could we know whether he would accept?

"He won't accept—it's too much of a sacrifice," Mrs. Reagan replied. It was clear that she wanted to drop the subject.

But I persisted. "All kinds of people have made sacrifices for your husband," I said. "Look at Ed Meese, Bill Clark, Bill Smith, Bill Casey—even me. Why shouldn't Stu Spencer do the same?"

"Well, all right, you can ask him," Mrs. Reagan said. "But I know he won't come."

The First Lady turned to a new topic. She was unhappy over a growing tendency in the press to criticize the President's lack of activity. The day before had been Ronald Reagan's seventy-sixth birthday. Tom Brokaw and Chris Wallace had implied on the "NBC Nightly News" that the President was old, slipping, and that his Administration was in disarray. Mrs. Reagan was dismayed that these two correspondents should misunderstand and misrepresent the state of the President's capacities.

"I'll be darned if I'm going to speak to Chris Wallace anymore," she said tartly.

Striking a familiar theme, I suggested that the way to overcome the media's pent-up hostility to the President and their ill-informed criticism of the way he was doing his job (his job approval rating had dropped by thirteen points, to only 56 percent, up from the lows after the scandal broke but still nowhere near the pre-November levels) was to get the President out into public view. We needed a press conference, public appearances, speeches; the President had been invited to visit Berlin and deliver a speech at the Berlin Wall. A full month after the President's release from the hospital, his schedule was still a dead letter because Mrs. Reagan's Friend had not provided a list of auspicious days. The whole month, it appeared, was inauspicious for the President.

"Please, Nancy," I said, "get us some dates. He didn't even appear in public on his birthday."

The next morning Mrs. Reagan told me that she had gotten the dates and had handed them on to Bill Henkel. The First Lady's Friend had previously looked with favor on Thursday, February 26, as the date for a press conference; this was an essential commitment because it came about a week after the Tower Board planned to issue its report, and it gave the President the long-awaited opportunity to answer the media's questions on the Iran-Contra affair. It was time to get the scandal behind him.

"I hope you haven't discussed that date with anybody," Mrs. Reagan said. "I'm not sure we should have a press conference."

"Why not, Nancy?" I asked. "We need one. February twenty-sixth would represent a period of three months since his last press conference on November nineteenth. We can't have him talking to himself in the West Wing. He's got to answer the questions on Iran. It looks like we're shielding him."

"What do you mean, 'shielding him'?" Mrs. Reagan asked.

Clearly my choice of words had heated up the discussion.

"We're not shielding Ronnie, the press is just writing it that way," Mrs. Reagan went on. "We shouldn't rush this thing. He may not be ready. I wish you'd never said he could have a press conference."

"But I have said it. And there is going to be a press conference."

"Okay!" Mrs. Reagan cried. "Have your damn press conference!"

"You bet I will!" I said.

The press reported soon after this incident that I had hung up on the First Lady. That may be true, but if it is, it is only because I was quicker than Mrs. Reagan. At the time it seemed to me that it was a race between two angry people to slam down the receiver. I really don't know who won.

My wife, who had been reading the Sunday paper while I spoke into the telephone, gave me a quizzical glance. "Was that Nancy Reagan you were talking to in that tone of voice?" she asked.

I confirmed that it was and described some of my recent experiences. I told Ann that I had decided that I must stick it out until after the Tower Board issued its report. If I resigned before that, it would look as though I had been driven out of the White House by fear of what the report was going to say about me.

Ann, who had never understood why I wanted to be Chief of Staff in the first place, rallied to my support as she had done so many times before in the forty-four years of our marriage.

"That's fine by me, honey," she said. "Stay with it as long as you think you have to."

I sincerely hoped that that would not be very much longer.

Five days later the Tower Board asked for yet another postponement in order to give itself time to read and analyze the electronic file that Poindexter and North had inadvertently left behind. Now the Board hoped to issue its report on February 26. Stu Spencer, who had already explained that he could not accept the job of Director of Communications (he, too, was pushing for the appointment of Jack Koehler), phoned to advise me against holding to the scheduled date for the press conference.

I disagreed. At the time I assumed that in the exercise of ordinary official courtesy the President would be given an advance copy of the report, or would at least be briefed in detail on its contents by the Tower Board so that he would be able to meet the press on equal terms.

"How long can this silence last?" I asked Spencer. "Everybody in the press, on TV, on the Hill will be talking about the Tower report except the President. His enemies are already saying that he's lying, and if he keeps quiet that will make things worse."

Spencer tried to soothe my exasperation. "Nobody ever said this town was easy," he said.

"Leaks don't make it any easier," I snapped. "Especially when they come from friends."

That was the day after the *Newsweek* article appeared. (It was entitled "Regan Bashing.")

In the afternoon Marlin Fitzwater, the new White House spokesman, told me that the First Lady had phoned him to say that he didn't have to be quite so firm in defending me before the press. Fitzwater, who had been in his difficult job for only two and a half weeks, was puzzled. He thought that what he had been saying about me was all right. I explained the situation and suggested that he stand back out of the way.

The First Lady had continued to advocate the appointment of Jack Koehler as Director of Communications, telling me that the President was enthusiastic—he had been reminded that he had corresponded with Koehler and had admired an article he had written about Central America. I was still reluctant to act on this appointment until the background investigation was complete. I had no premonition about Koehler, who had done a good job at USIA; I was just exercising routine prudence.

The next morning, Friday, February 13, as I sat in my usual chair beside the President's desk, he pulled a note out of his pocket and read it. Then he said he had been thinking overnight about the staff changes. How were we coming?

I told him we were still looking for a political director and a replacement for Pat Buchanan.

I think Frank Donatelli should be the one for the political job, the President said amiably. And this Jack Koehler ought to be the communications person. And by the way, there's a fellow by the name of Stuart who's our ambassador to Norway. We ought to keep him in Oslo.

If I had ever heard Ambassador Stuart's name before, I didn't remember it. "Fine, Mr. President," I said.

On Monday morning, referring to another scrap of paper, the President raised the subject again.

Let's go ahead and get this guy Jack Koehler in, he said. I like his style; he'll be good. And let's go ahead on Frank Donatelli—he'll be good, too.

Personnel was still checking Koehler's qualifications and background. I told the President that and added, "I don't know much about the man, Mr. President, but if you want him, we'll get him for you."

Good, the President said. I sure hope you'll get to work on this right away.

Following the morning briefing, at which this conversation had taken place, the President attended a meeting of the National Security Council. Afterward, he consulted his scrap of paper again and looked across the desk at me.

You're taking care of Koehler and Donatelli? he asked.

No more than an hour had passed since he had told me to get moving on this matter.

"Yes, sir," I replied. "I'm taking care of that."

The President crumpled up his scrap of paper and threw it into the wastebasket.

On February 10, two days after my heated telephone discussion with Mrs. Reagan, the President had agreed to hold a press conference and deliver a television address on the Iran-Contra affair. After our last squabble, I ceased hearing directly from the First Lady, though several newspapers printed remarkably detailed accounts of our final telephone conversation, always leading with the allegation that I had hung up on her.

USA Today reported on February 19 that Mrs. Reagan had stopped talking to me as a result of this insult. That certainly seemed to be the case. Evidently she had reconsidered sending NBC's Chris Wallace to coventry; on the "NBC Nightly News" he quoted "a source very close to Mrs. Reagan" as saying, "[The First Lady] purposely leaked the story that she is no longer talking to Donald Regan . . . to try to force Regan to step down."

On February 16, after a consultation with her Friend, Mrs. Reagan informed Bill Henkel that there could be no press conference until March 19—four full weeks after the rescheduled appearance of the Tower Board's report. The Friend had approved March 4 or 5 as being auspicious for a Presidential speech.

The official celebration of George Washington's Birthday that year fell on Monday, February 16. I spent the whole day on the telephone seeking the advice of men whose political judgment the President respected—Senator Paul Laxalt; Frank J. Fahrenkopf, chairman of the Republican National Committee; Robert Gray, a well-known Washington lobbyist; Harold Burson, a public relations expert; and Dick Wirthlin. All offered the same advice: Don't wait; get the President out as quickly as possible after the Tower report appears.

The President himself, when I passed on this collective judgment, did not disagree with it. He readily accepted my suggestion that he deliver a televised speech to the nation on February 27, the day after the report appeared, and that he hold a press conference on March 4 or 5. After that, he would follow up by inviting small groups of correspondents into the Oval Office for additional interviews in which he could make his points on Iran, the Contras, and a whole range of other issues on which it was his place to lead public opinion.

The President appeared to look forward to all this. The prospect of taking the offensive against his critics brought out his old combative political self. Let's start the speech off this way, he said. And in a dozen homespun phrases he summed up our intentions, explained our actions, itemized our limited successes, admitted our shortcomings, and defended our policy on practical and humanitarian grounds. Listening to this fluent and persuasive summary, and watching the conviction shining in the President's eyes, I could only wonder how anyone could imagine that it was a good thing to silence this extraordinary man who could speak for himself so much more eloquently than anyone else could speak for him.

All the while, the newspapers and the networks continued to buzz with rumors of dissension between Mrs. Reagan and me. About this time I began to hear about a *Newsweek* cover story that was being prepared for the March 3 issue of the magazine. No one from *Newsweek* had talked to me or anyone close to me in the preparation of the article, but some of the charges it contained leaked out. The charges were scurrilous (*Webster's:* "vulgar and evil . . . containing low obscenities or false abuse"). They were also untrue.

Before publication, three *Newsweek* correspondents and editors visited Peter Wallison, who from his investigation of the facts up to that time knew more than anyone else about what had happened. On hearing the allegations *Newsweek* was planning to publish, Peter denied that they had any basis in fact. The magazine plunged ahead anyway.

The issue appeared with the words "THE IRAN COVERUP" emblazoned on the cover and at the head of the story inside. The first paragraph read, in part:

> The word was out from Donald Regan himself: "Protect the President." So lights burned late in a bustling, paper-strewn office in the White House last Nov. 18 as Oliver North and his colleagues in the Iran arms deal tried to massage the record of the complex weapons-for-hostages negotiations into a chronology that would minimize Ronald Reagan's role. As no fewer than three witnesses described it last week, the challenge was to portray Reagan as not knowing what he had done until five weeks after he had done it.

The reader should not imagine that I was so hardened by my experience of public life that on reading these poisonous lies about the President and myself, I tolerantly smiled and muttered a line from Kipling's "If."

I was furious. After strangling the cover-up in its cradle I was being accused of being the creature's father. Like the originators of this libel, I knew that the memory of it would remain long after its falsity had been proved.

There is no defense for the American public figure against premeditated character assassination. *Newsweek* had not completely made up this story; it had been the gift of sources whom the magazine's editors apparently were prepared to believe and protect.

I knew that I was mortally wounded and that for the sake of the country, the President, and my own reputation and peace of mind I must remove myself from the White House as soon as possible. The *Newsweek* story, of course, destroyed the last vestige of any possibility that I might honorably resign as Chief of Staff before the Tower Board issued its report. If I did that now, my action would be taken as an admission of guilt and my name would be blackened beyond recall.

In the circumstances I paid less attention than I might have to another breaking story. Jack Koehler had been appointed Director of Communications the previous week. On Thursday, February 19, the "NBC Nightly News" reported that Koehler had been a member of the Hitler Youth during his boyhood in Nazi Germany. Somehow this information had never surfaced in the preemployment background checks. Koehler had not mentioned the association to us. When asked for an explanation, Koehler said that he had joined the Hitler Youth when he was ten years old to see whether he liked it. After a short time he found that he did not, and he withdrew. It was difficult for Koehler to understand why he should be pilloried for something he had done when he was a child. The Hitler Youth was in reality a sort of German Boy Scout movement, he explained.

The embarrassment of this revelation was all the more acute because the press already knew, as a result of leaks that had detailed the reasons for the discord between Mrs. Reagan and myself, that Koehler had been the First Lady's candidate. The *Washington Post* reported in its Saturday edition that I had told the staff that "the 'East Wing' was responsible for an oversight in checking [Koehler's] background."

At 10:10 A.M. on Monday, February 23, Vice President Bush called me into his office, which was next to mine.

He said, "Don, why don't you stick your head into the Oval Office and talk to the President about your situation?"

I asked Bush why he was making this suggestion. The President already knew that I planned to leave after the Tower report came out but not before; Ronald Reagan and I had agreed on that.

"Well," Bush replied in his usual courteous tones, "the President asked me [this morning] if I knew what your plans were."

At about 10:15, the time when the President usually finished reading his daily briefing, I went into the Oval Office and took my usual chair at the side of his desk. Strict protocol attaches to these chairs, and where the visitor sits signifies his rank and importance. I felt as I sat down that this seat would not be reserved for me for very much longer. I asked the President if he wanted to talk about my situation and my plans.

I think it's about time, Don, he replied.

I felt drained but combative. "All right, Mr. President," I said. "Why don't you tell me? Where's your head on this? What do *you* think I should do?"

The President leaned back in his chair, a sure sign that he was disturbed.

Well, good Lord, Don, he said. This last weekend the airwaves were filled with all that stuff about Nancy. She's being blamed for Koehler and she's being seen unfairly. I was the one who wanted him. She never met him.

I kept silent. I was determined to do nothing that would make it easy for him to play this scene, to make him talk. The President remained as he was, his face somber, feet planted on the rug, hands gripping the arms of his chair.

He said, I think it's time we do that thing that you said when we talked in November.

In November I had told the President that I would go quietly on a signal from him if at any time he thought that I had become a burden on his Administration.

"I'll stick by that," I said. "I'll go whenever you say."

Well, said the President, since the report is coming out on Thursday, I think it would be appropriate for you to bow out now.

His words shocked me. I said heatedly, "What do you mean, 'now'? This is the Monday before the report. You can't do that to me, Mr. President. If I go before that report is out, you throw me to the wolves. I deserve better treatment than that."

My temper was up; I made no attempt to conceal it but said a great deal more on the subject of loyalty and its rewards. My anger and dismay took the President aback. I could see that he was shaken and not quite sure what to do or say next.

Finally he said, Well, what do you think would be right?

"The first part of next week," I replied. "Let the report come out, let the world see what really happened and where the blame lies. I'm willing to take my chances on that."

The President agreed to this timetable. We talked then for a few more minutes about the Koehler case and the stories in the press. Inevitably the subject of Mrs. Reagan's role in managing the Presidency came up. Again I spoke very frankly. The President seemed surprised at what I had to say. Naturally he defended his wife.

I'll bet all that took place while I was convalescing, he said.

I told him that Mrs. Reagan's activities went far beyond a sincere wifely concern for his health.

"I thought I was Chief of Staff to the President," I said, "not to his wife. I have to tell you, sir, that I'm very bitter about the whole experience. You're allowing the loyal to be punished, and those who have had their own agenda to be rewarded."

The President, who dislikes confrontations more than any man I have ever known, looked at me without anger.

Well, we'll try to make that up by the way we handle this, Ronald Reagan said softly. We'll make sure that you go out in good fashion.

Even as I left the Oval Office, angry and humiliated, yet understanding the rules that Presidents and their servants live by, I believed that this President, genial and kind and good at heart, and surely grateful for the six years of loyal service I had given him, would do me no harm in my last hours at his side.

In that, I was very much mistaken.

PART TWO

An American Life

· 6 ·

Growing Up

My father, William Francis Regan, was a policeman who was fired by Governor Calvin Coolidge during the Boston police strike in September 1919. He was a member of the Metropolitan District Police Force, whose work involved protecting public property in the Boston area. When his unit was ordered into Boston by Coolidge to take over the duties of the striking city police, a majority of my father's fellow officers refused to obey. Coolidge summarily discharged them all. As a result of his resolute actions in breaking the police strike, Coolidge became what would now be called a media hero, and the following year he was nominated by the Republican party as its Vice Presidential candidate on the same ticket with Warren G. Harding; on Harding's death on August 2, 1923, Coolidge became the thirtieth President of the United States. My father, then thirty-three years old, was left jobless with a wife and two small sons—William, Jr., two years old, and myself, aged nine months.

"There is no right to strike against the public safety by anybody, anywhere, anytime," Calvin Coolidge said when he broke the police strike. I believe that my father, in his heart, agreed with this statement. Although he found new employment as a policeman with the New York, New Haven, and Hartford Railroad and eventually rose to the rank of lieutenant, he brooded for many years about his dismissal from the Metropolitan District Police Force. He had been intensely proud of belonging to the force, and his belief in duty was very strong. His friends told him that he had done the right thing to refuse to be a strikebreaker, but I do not recall that he ever said that he agreed with that sentiment. To my father, his dismissal was a dark cloud hanging over his reputation. To this day, although I cast my first vote for Wendell Willkie and spent most of my working life on Wall Street, I have great difficulty in crossing a picket line.

There had been hard times while my father was without a job after the police strike, and even after he found employment there was never any surplus of money. He and my mother, born Kathleen Ahearn, lived with their babies on the ground floor of a three-story wood-frame house in South Boston. Though we moved many times so that my father could be near his work, this is the first home I remember. It stood in a row of others very much like it on Gates Street, near the popular harbor beach called the Strand. There were alleyways behind the houses and tiny backyards for the trash cans; there were horse-drawn delivery wagons in the street, and icemen who lugged big blocks of ice up three flights of stairs in a rubber sling thrown over their shoulders. Sometimes we walked the mile beyond L Street to look at the yachts tied up at the yacht club. The neighbors were mostly Irish, with a few Polish families intermingled, though my best childhood friend was a Portuguese boy whose father was a fish dealer.

Although my mother had some Scottish blood, my family is Irish to the bone on both sides. My father's parents, Thomas and Bridget Flynn Regan, were born in County Cork; my mother's parents, Peter and Margaret Ryan Ahearn, were born of Irish parents in Prince Edward's Island, Canada, but came to the United States as teenagers. My father was one of five children, my mother the eleventh of thirteen. The nuclear family did not exist in our world and time. Grandparents, aunts and uncles, and cousins were always about, and when they weren't present in person, they were being talked about. My Regan grandparents were hardworking, thrifty folk who owned their own home, a rambling, thirteen-room house in Cambridge, where I was born on December 21, 1918. My own family lived in that house for a while during my high-school days, but later we moved to an apartment house near

Harvard Square, where I lived during my college years. I never knew my maternal grandfather, who was the only one of my grandparents to die before the age of seventy-five. My grandmother Ahearn, sunny of countenance and generous of heart, lived in Hingham, on the South Shore. Grandma Ahearn's house was my favorite destination: she placed a kiss on my cheek and a cookie in my hand when I came through the door on arrival, telling me to be sure to ask for another as soon as I felt the need.

In our neighborhood everybody's father went to work every day except Sunday, and the loss of a job through sickness or layoff was, as my own family knew, a disaster. Everybody had food on the table, but nobody had any money to spare. For children, sweat was the only source of spending money. As soon as boys and girls left school and went to work, often at age sixteen, they paid board to their mothers. We boys swam in the harbor and ran races and played baseball in the streets and on the playgrounds in the summertime. In the fall we played football; the ball in those days was a plump, nearly round, leather object that you blew up with your breath and drop-kicked. There was always plenty of snow in Boston for snowball fights in winter. You learned how to use your fists if you wanted to be left in peace and get home to supper on time. There were tough kids and weak kids in our neighborhood in South Boston, and smart ones and slow ones—even a few bad boys who banded together in gangs for purposes of thievery and vandalism. My brother and I and our friends stayed away from the gangs. We all knew that our parents and our teachers would smite us if we strayed from the straight and narrow. We were drilled daily by our parents, by the parish priest, by the nuns who were our teachers, and by the books we read in the difference between right and wrong. We were all Catholics together and that, too, was taken for granted; I knew that Protestants existed during my childhood—Calvin Coolidge, like all American Presidents up to that time and long afterward, was a Protestant—but I didn't meet very many.

Although I didn't realize it at the time, our isolation was a matter of necessity as well as a matter of choice. For the Irish, who had suffered from severe discrimination in Boston and elsewhere only a generation before and who were still scorned and mocked by many earlier immigrants, there were good psychological reasons to live in a world of their own. Nobody dwelled on these difficulties. Many remembered the miseries, economic and political, of the Ireland they had left behind in order to emigrate; few were under the illusion that there was any better place on earth for an Irishman or anyone else than the United States of America. There was little reason, then, to escape from a neighborhood and a life that offered so many satisfactions and so much security. Though the opportunity to improve themselves existed—it was better to be a policeman than, say, a mill worker—poor boys of my father's generation seldom went to college. My father was as intelligent a man as I have ever known, a voracious reader of every kind of book who was possessed of a practically photographic memory, but I don't suppose that he or his parents ever dreamed that he might go to a university; it cost too much. When my time came to go to college on a partial scholarship, it never occurred to anyone in the family that I would do anything but work my way through.

Marriage was the usual feminine destination, and the vocation of motherhood gave women of the time a higher status and more power in things that matter than many executives and lawyers enjoy in the 1980s. My mother, dark haired, fair skinned, pretty, and hardworking like her mother, was at least my father's equal where the management of the house and the rearing of the family were concerned. He gave her his pay envelope and she paid the bills. She also made all the financial decisions; her right to make them was never questioned. Because my father loved to swim, and because he and my mother had met by the seaside, we rented, for a couple of weeks every summer, a small cottage on the beach near Cohasset on the South Shore; the rent on this vacation house was paid with money Mother had saved from the household budget. If the object of life is to raise a family, as my parents believed, then my mother made all the truly important decisions in every aspect of our lives. It was she who decided every detail of her children's upbringing—when we stayed in and when we could go out, what we would wear and eat, who our friends would be, what we would study, where we would live.

She taught us manners and a strict moral code, and insisted that we believe in God, love our country and our family, and show respect to our elders and teachers. She taught us other things as well. When my younger sister, Teresa, called Terry in the family, was diagnosed in early childhood as being afflicted with the diabetes that eventually deprived her of her sight, our mother nursed her, encouraged her to be useful and happy despite her handicap, and by her example inspired the rest of the family to do the same. Our father may have been the symbol of authority, but our mother was its embodiment.

Nevertheless, my father inspired awe in me. He was like a sleeping lion whose anger you hesitated to arouse. He had been an athlete in his youth, a baseball player and an amateur boxer who had won a lot of neighborhood championships. He had the sloping shoulders of a puncher and short, blunt fingers that made a good fist. He cropped his hair short. He had serious brown eyes and there was a mole on his cheek. He seldom smiled and almost never laughed except when he was listening to Jack Benny or Fred Allen on the radio. Allen came from a Boston neighborhood like ours, and his jokes provoked the most belly laughs. Though my father seldom talked about his work, I knew from the stories that others told that he was a clever detective. His powerful memory made it possible for him to put two and two together more effectively than many other policemen, and he brought many crooks to justice on the basis of clues that others had overlooked. I did not doubt that I'd be caught just as quickly as the crooks if I tried to put one over on him.

My father never brought his pistol home or talked about the violent encounters that must have been part of his life on the job. He and my mother did not quarrel. He seldom raised his voice. He may have slapped me on the backside two or three times during my childhood, not more. Instead, he worked on my character and conscience through criticism; even though I usually led my class, he always seemed slightly disappointed that I had not done better than I had done. Above all, he wanted me to be more like my older brother in every way, a transformation that was beyond me then and later.

But my father had reserves of understanding. When I rebelled against my mother's bossiness and ran away from home as a very little fellow, he found me sitting on a bench beside the Strand all by myself and sat down next to me. Was I ready to come home now? he asked in his quiet way. I told him no—not unless he could get his wife to see reason and straighten up. He explained that there wasn't much chance of my winning this unequal contest against Mother and advised me to come back to the house and make my peace with her. Without uttering a disloyal word about my mother he made me feel that I had a good point but I had to surrender to reality like a man, just as he had done. I still remember walking home with him, side by side, in the twilight that day.

It was my mother who told the nuns at Saint Augustine's Parochial School to handle me with strict discipline when I entered the first grade. She thought I needed it. The year before, I had led my kindergarten class in the Back Bay of Boston in bombast and revolutionary ardor and had been thrown out on my ear as a result. According to the story told about this incident in the family, I informed the teacher, a young woman in her first job, that she was doing everything wrong and insisted that she reorganize the class along more sensible lines devised by myself.

Although I never really stopped trying to take over any world I found myself in, I discovered early in my career at Saint Augustine's that these tactics did not work with the Sisters of Notre Dame de Nemours. The nuns of this pious order of teachers knew how to handle obstreperous boys. Their usual punishment consisted of ten or more hard blows on the palm of the hand with a rattan blackboard pointer. If a six-year-old had the right stuff he took his punishment without shedding a tear or even showing a flicker of facial expression. The objective was to get the nun so mad she would break the pointer over your hand. I achieved this reputation-building feat on more than one occasion.

Discipline was only one aspect of parochial school life. Very few students escaped from Saint Augustine's with empty heads. The sisters who taught there were women who knew their subjects, knew the true nature of small boys, and set a standard of achievement for every student that was just slightly beyond his reach. The sisters I knew must all be in heaven now. I remember them with affection and gratitude. The lessons they taught me about reading, writing, and arithmetic, and about myself, have been invaluable to me all my life.

So, in a different and far deeper way, has been the example of my older brother, Billy. William Francis Regan, Jr., born sixteen months before me, was a truly exceptional child. A brilliant student, always at the head of his class and always in the good graces of the nuns, he was a natural athlete who was invariably the first to be named when sides were chosen up, and a born leader. Because of the difference in our ages and the difference in our gifts, I was always a little behind him. If we ran through the back lots after school, Billy would be far ahead, flying over fences while I was still thinking about climbing them.

Billy was named for our father, and he was a joy to him in every way. If I excelled in school, Billy shone. My father loved baseball, and Billy was a precocious ballplayer. I was still playing softball instead of hardball well past the date when my father thought I should have made the change. My father and Billy were avid fans of the Boston Red Sox; their favorite player, not surprisingly, was Bill Regan, the second baseman (lifetime batting average about .267). In the 1920s both Boston teams usually finished in or near the cellar. I followed the ragtag Boston Braves and was a member of the Braves' "Knothole Gang," which entitled me to an occasional free seat in the bleachers.

In spite of the fact that Billy was held up to me daily as an example, my brother and I were close. I admired him as much as my parents did, and with good reason: for all his wonderful gifts, Billy himself never made me feel that I was anything but his equal in every way.

In 1929, when Billy was twelve years old and I was ten, he had an attack of appendicitis. The inflamed appendix was removed at a hospital in Dorchester and after a few days Billy came home to convalesce. He did well enough at first—an appendectomy, in the days before antibiotics, was a serious operation— but then, on Monday, March 11, while I was in school, he took a turn for the worse. My mother called an ambulance and rushed him to the hospital. I knew nothing about this and I do not believe in supernatural events, but the fact is that right on the hour of three that afternoon, while I was sitting at my desk in school, I broke out into a cold sweat and was overcome by nausea. After a few moments the symptoms went away.

Just before the bell for dismissal rang, a nun gave me a message: I was not to go home, but to go instead to the house of some friends of my parents' and wait there for my mother. It was quite a long wait, but finally Mother came. She told me that my brother had died at three o'clock that afternoon. He had developed peritonitis, an infection of the abdominal cavity that resulted from faulty cleansing of the surgical wound, and the doctors had been unable to save him.

My father, who had loved Billy so much, was inconsolable. He wept for days, wandering aimlessly through the house, unable to sleep. "Why?" he would cry, "Why?" After Billy's funeral, when my mother and father and I were all standing together, my parents turned to me and said (I remember the exact words), "You're going to have to take Billy's place. From now on you're going to have to be two sons to us."

I promised that I would try, and I always have. My behavior improved and my father and mother were less critical of my shortcomings and more appreciative of my achievements; there was peace and love between us. But the passage of nearly sixty years has not sufficed to heal the wound inflicted by the death of my brother. My father never recovered from it, and to the end of her life my mother kept Billy's memory ever green, as if she expected that he would come back one day.

In a sense, of course, he never went away, and whatever the psychologists may make of that, it has been a fact and a blessing in the lives of all who survived him. I know that I would not have been half of what I've been except for Billy's example. Nor would I have tried half as hard as I have tried, as the father of four children, to accept each of them for what they are.

In the summer of 1931, when I was twelve years old, we moved back to Cambridge, a few miles up the Charles River from Boston, and took up residence with my Regan grandparents. Cambridge in those days was a far more genteel place than South Boston, and I encountered a different breed of student (but the same order of nuns) in the eighth grade at Saint Mary's School. I worked hard, graduated first in my class, and went on to Cambridge Latin School, the public high school that prepared students for college. Cambridge Latin was a coed school, and the distraction of being with girls for the first time made concentrating on the no-nonsense curriculum (four years each of English, Latin, mathematics, and history, three years of French, and two of science) a considerable challenge. Although I liked arithmetic and have always been able to add up a column of figures and compute interest rates, I discovered at Cambridge Latin that algebra, geometry, and trigonometry did not come naturally to me. The abstract did not interest me then and has never interested me since.

I did well enough at all my subjects, however, to pass the Harvard entrance examination and win one of the Buckley scholarships, named after the late Daniel A. Buckley, a Cambridge newspaperman who had endowed them. The Buckley scholarship covered tuition only—four hundred dollars a year in those days. In 1936 that was a considerable sum; my father's annual salary probably amounted to no more than five thousand dollars, and after working for tips as a caddy at local golf courses during my first two high-school years, I had moved up to thirty-five cents an hour as an usher in the University Theater in Harvard Square. When a hit movie was playing, the money rolled in; in the spring of 1937, my freshman year at Harvard, Walt Disney's *Snow White* was being shown continuously from one in the afternoon until midnight, seven days a week. I usually worked five hours on weekdays and eleven on Saturdays and Sundays for a total wage of $16.45 each and every week. In the summer before my freshman year I dusted books in the airless oven of the Widener Library at Harvard. One summer was enough. The next two summers I worked as an electrician's helper on the university maintenance crew. The electrician ran the wires and I drilled the holes through brick and concrete and stone with a chisel and a mallet and a hand drill, work that made you feel that your arms were going to drop off. But this experience, tedious as it was at the time, later opened an unexpected door for me in life, and may very well have been the fundamental reason why I lived through nearly five years of Marine Corps service in World War II.

Later on I worked as a tourist guide for a student at the Harvard Business School who had set up shop in Harvard Square. When he graduated in 1939 I bought the business, quadrupled the staff to twelve guides, put them all on straight commission, and added new tours and a chauffeuring service ($1 an hour to drive your Ford while describing the sights of Cambridge and Boston; $1.50 for a Buick, $2 for a Cadillac or Pierce Arrow). In the summer of my senior year I cleared more than two thousand 1940 dollars (the equivalent of about $18,000 today) from my share of the business and graduated from Harvard with money in the bank. There's no doubt that this early experience left me with a taste for the entrepreneurial life and a belief that good ideas plus hard work equals profits.

It was a hectic life I led during the academic year—out of bed while it was still dark in winter, study until classes began, go to the library to research and write, work the four-to-nine shift at the theater, have a sandwich and a milkshake for dinner, then go home and study until midnight. On football weekends I worked as a student usher at Harvard Stadium and eventually was put in charge of half the ushers, a paying job. As a high-school student I had sold programs at the stadium, and from 1932 through 1940 I saw every single Harvard home football game, a record I was proud of at the time. There was little time for social life, and I missed a lot that most people go to college mainly to experience. Sometimes I asked a girl from Radcliffe or Wellesley to go out with me (though I seldom suggested a movie). I made a few life-long friends at Harvard, but no wide circle of acquaintances. Occasionally I would pass my classmate, John F. Kennedy, in the Yard, and we would nod to each other; I'd be surprised if he even knew my name.

The education I received at Harvard, and the credential my diploma represented in the minds of others, has been a great asset to me. But I grew up too close to the place and spent too little time in student haunts to be nostalgic about it. I haven't seen a Harvard football game since I worked my last one as an usher in 1940. But I enjoyed the twenty-fifth reunion of my class, the only one that I ever attended, and I plan to show up for my fiftieth in 1990. The old University Theater, unfortunately, has been gone for years, so I will not be able to revisit one of the most important landmarks of my undergraduate career.

There were obvious reasons for working at the jobs—jobs I remember so much better than some of my classes. My parents, who had the extra burden of my sister's medical bills, were unable to give me money, but I was living at home and paying no board, and that was a boon. The generous but stern Mr. Buckley had specified that winners of his scholarship must remain on the dean's list, which meant maintaining a B average, or lose their stipend. One semester my marks fell below that level and my scholarship was suspended. This was a desperate situation. The only way to get the scholarship back was to raise my marks, and the only way to do that was to remain at Harvard. I borrowed money from the university's student loan fund in order to remain in school. In the absence of this financial support I would have been out of Harvard forever. The shame and the loss would have been difficult to overcome. I am still grateful for the godsend of this loan, and many years later, when I became chairman of the Board of Trustees of the University of Pennsylvania, I was able, together with some generous colleagues, to establish a similar low-interest loan fund for financially embarrassed students at Penn.

In the spring of my graduation, 1940, the German armies conquered Denmark, Norway, and the Low Countries. France surrendered in May and the British Expeditionary Force was evacuated from Dunkirk. The Battle of Britain began that summer. In the Pacific, Japan was preparing for aggression. Although the United States was neutral, it was clear even to the pacifists on campus that that condition was unlikely to endure. The Selective Service Act had gone into effect, and every man my age fatalistically awaited the grand lottery in which numbers would be drawn to determine the order in which those registered would be drafted into the Army. Everybody talked about draft numbers—marriages and careers were planned around them, and there were songs and jokes about them on the radio and human interest stories in the newspapers. When the first number was drawn in front of the newsreel cameras, as I remember, a female relation of the poor fellow who owned it screamed and fainted in the audience. My own number was a low one, too, meaning that I would be among the first to go. This gave life a measure of uncertainty, but of one thing I was sure: after going to all the trouble of working my way through Harvard, I didn't want to be a buck private in the Army.

My ambition was to be a lawyer (I'd been an English major because my undergraduate adviser at Harvard believed that I ought to broaden my mind with literature before cluttering it up with torts and precedents) and I had won a scholarship to Harvard Law School. In September 1940 I entered the law school on schedule, but I had already decided that I would volunteer for officer's training in the reserves before my number came up. The Boston quota for the Navy's V-7 program had already been filled, so I applied for admission to a similar Marine Corps program and was accepted. (My father looked on military service as an obligation and considered a commission a wise choice for a Harvard graduate; my mother warned that I would probably never finish law school if I went into the service. How right she was.)

By the end of October I found myself at Quantico, Virginia, as a member of the First Officer Candidates Class of the United States Marine Corps. It was a wonderful experience—good men, hard physical exercise, a sense of belonging to an elite corps that knew exactly how to carry out a mission that was as old as American history itself. After observing the officers and noncommissioned officers who trained us, and getting to know my fellow candidates on and off the training field, I was absolutely sure that the United States would win any war it was forced to fight. In my innocence I did not imagine the cost of victory. History may have known a finer group of men than those who served in the U.S. Marines in 1940 and afterward in World War II, but no one could have convinced me of that at the time. Or now.

We had expected to be commissioned as reserve officers who would return to civilian life and await a call to duty in case of need. But when our colonel, Lemuel H. Shepherd, later Commandant of the Marine Corps, told us that the corps would expect us to remain in uniform "for the duration" if we accepted our commissions, I did not hesitate. If the corps believed that I was needed for the duration, I would stay for the duration. I did not then understand the full meaning of *for the duration*, one of the most meaningful phrases of the war that was about to begin. Neither did my fellow candidates. But as brand-new second lieutenants, we all became members of the Fourth Reserve Officers Course.

While at Quantico I cast my first vote in a Presidential election—for Wendell Willkie, the Wall Street lawyer and corporation president who was opposing Franklin D. Roosevelt's bid for a third term in the White House. I had heard Willkie, tousled and hoarse, speak in Harvard Square. Everyone knew that he was doomed to defeat, but I liked what he said. In fact I would probably have voted for anyone who ran against FDR. Economics was one of my favorite subjects at Harvard, and though Republicans were as rare among the Regans as Presbyterians, I had become a Republican on economic grounds. I thought that Roosevelt had too little faith in the natural energy and resiliency of the marketplace, that he trusted the people too little and bureaucrats and intellectuals too much, and that he was putting too much government into the economy and into too many other aspects of American life and we were going to have a hard time getting it out again. In those days you could get radical ideas like these at Harvard. In my case they have lasted a lifetime.

My future was about to be sealed in another way. A fellow student officer, Fred Ptucha, invited me to ride up to Washington with him to visit a girl he had been dating, Jackie Nicklin. This was in the days before proper young officers invited proper young ladies to go out over the telephone, and the purpose of Fred's thirty-mile drive on a weeknight (reveille at 5:30 next morning) was to ask Jackie to be his date at the Saint Patrick's Day dance the following Saturday night at the Quantico Officers Club. After Jackie accepted, her mother asked me whether I had a date for the dance. I said that I didn't.

"But how can you not have a date for the Saint Patrick's Day dance with a name like Regan?" Mrs. Nicklin said. "What type of girl do you like?"

"I prefer tall blondes," I said.

Both ladies exclaimed, "Ann!"

"Ann who?" I said.

"Ann Buchanan," Mrs. Nicklin said. "She's tall, blonde, and very pretty. And her father was an officer in the Marines."

Ann Buchanan was Jackie Nicklin's best friend, and she agreed to come to the dance on a blind date with me. On Saturday night she arrived, and the moment I saw her I knew that my future was settled. It was love at first sight. Fortunately, Ann felt the same. After that, Ann Buchanan and I dated every weekend, and by the end of May 1941, when the reserve officers course was completed, we knew that we would be married.

Because I had ranked among the top ten in my class (fourth, to be precise), I was offered a regular commission in the Marine Corps instead of a reserve commission. I accepted, expecting to be assigned to the infantry because of my lack of scientific and mathematical qualifications. In the old Corps it was engineers to the artillery, readers to the rifles. To my amazement and delight I was assigned to the antiaircraft artillery school at Quantico. Infantry officers were sent to regiments in Parris Island, South Carolina, or San Diego—a long way from Ann Buchanan's home on Bancroft Place, N.W., in Washington, D.C.

If the assignment amazed me, it must have dumbfounded Master Gunnery Sergeant Thomas, who in my first days in candidates class had watched me as I tried to put a disassembled machine gun back together and exclaimed (not his exact words), "Regan, you look like a monkey kissing a football!"

Discreetly, so as not to raise doubts about the wisdom of the assignment, I made inquiries about its basis. How had I been chosen? The Marine Corps had ordered us to list every single

Ann Gordon Buchanan at about 17 years old.

Wedding picture.
July 11, 1942.

At Guadalcanal, July 1944.

Donald T. Regan, Ann Buchanan Regan, and daughter, Donna. Donna is 27½ months old. July 1945.

Major Donald T. Regan.

Helping Donna hang her stocking on our first Christmas together, December 24, 1945.

Donald T. Regan in New York as head of
Merrill Lynch trading department. 1953.

Donald T. Regan in front of portraits of
Charlie Merrill and Win Smith.

Being sworn in as Secretary of the Treasury by Robert D. Linder, a White House administrative officer. Ann is holding the Bible; looking on, from left, are my son-in-law Peter Doniger, my daughter Diane, my son Richard, my daughter-in-law Ruth, my son Tom, my daughter Donna, and her husband, David Lefeve. January 22, 1981.

Secretary Regan and Mrs. Regan with dog, Impy. 1981.

The Regans and the Reagans. Official White House Photograph, December 18, 1986.

job we had ever held, no matter how irrelevant, no matter how long it lasted. Among my many odd jobs I had listed my two summers as an electrician's helper. Consequently, "knowledge of electricity" was entered into the records among my qualifications. My actual knowledge of electricity begins and ends with the ability to wire a lamp, but I had been in the Marines long enough to resist the temptation to correct the record. By the end of the course, taught in a way that was designed to make it impossible for the dullest student to misunderstand the material, I knew a lot more about the 90-millimeter and 40-millimeter antiaircraft guns than I had ever known before about any other single subject. As with nearly everything else the Marines taught me, the lessons have remained fresh in my mind. Given a crew of Marines to manhandle the shells (which, in the case of the 90-millimeter gun, weighed forty-five pounds each), I think I could set up either of these weapons today and hit a target moving through the sky at World War II speeds and altitudes with it.

My weekends were free; Washington was an hour and a half away. Ann and I had an idyllic summer. In mid-September the Marines sent me to Iceland. We had been invited by the government of Iceland to defend the island in succession to the British, who had occupied it to keep it out of German hands after the fall of Denmark. But the Icelanders, many of whom were pro-German, were not especially happy to see us arrive. We were not the first Marines to find ourselves in this ambiguous position, nor would we be the last. The pan-Germanic sentiments (if that's what they were) of an Icelandic minority were irrelevant to our mission, which was the defense of the United States and its neutrality. We all knew that Iceland was vital to the defense of the North Atlantic, and nobody in the Marine Corps thought that the United States was going to be neutral much longer.

I arrived in October, a bleak month in arctic latitudes. The island was practically treeless, a strange landscape for a boy from Boston who had seen northern Virginia and very little else outside of Massachusetts. The most interesting thing in Iceland (the girls, all beautiful and blond and unfriendly, were of no interest to a man in love) were the horses. These were about the size of

Shetland ponies, and the Marine Corps made sure that we understood that these animals were horses, not ponies, in case we should offend the Icelanders by referring to them by the wrong term.

I was assigned as a gunnery officer to a battery in the rocky hills above Reykjavík. We emplaced the guns and set up defensive positions for our .50-caliber and .30-caliber machine guns. (These activities were to have an archeological interest for me many years afterward, but I'll tell about that experience in a later place.) As it turned out, we had a quiet time in Iceland. The Luftwaffe did not appear during the long hours of autumn daylight, and the noise that drifted down into the city from our position was more likely to be the banging of hammers than the boom of 90-millimeter guns, as we hurried to build huts before winter came down from the North Pole. Word came out from Headquarters to form a battalion boxing team. I was appointed as coach. My father, the old amateur middleweight, had taught me the fundamentals of the sport, and though I never went out for the Harvard team, the boxing coach, Henry Lamar, had sometimes sparred with me after hours. A couple of our men made it into the finals against the Sixth Marine Regiment; we thought it was a pretty good accomplishment for an antiaircraft battery to be fighting an infantry regiment on even terms.

Iceland was tedious duty, with plenty of time to write letters home, but it wasn't completely unpleasant because, as usual in the Marines, the company was so good. While serving in that barren place my outfit learned about the attack on Pearl Harbor, the fall of the Philippines, and the other military disasters and occasional victories of early 1942. No Americans, least of all the supremely confident Marines, were prepared for the defeats. During that long winter in a strange place I began to sense that *the duration* was going to be long—longer than the lives of many of the seasick young Marines who sailed back to the States when the Army relieved us in March 1942.

By now I was a first lieutenant, earning about $275 a month. This was all the money I had in the world except for my modest savings, but it seemed enough under the circumstances. Ann and

I were married on July 11, 1942, in Saint Matthew's Cathedral in Washington. It was a Marine wedding with swords and white uniforms and a bride who was even more beautiful than Marine tradition demanded. My best man was Bill Taft, who had been with me from Officer Candidate Class through Iceland; he survived the war and was a lifelong friend.

After a brief honeymoon I reported back to my battalion in Parris Island. In early September my battalion was ordered to report to San Diego, the port of embarkation for the South Pacific Theater. The Marine Corps advised against bringing wives to San Diego because train travel was difficult and the time before embarkation was likely to be brief. Ann, the daughter of a Marine officer who had lost his life on active service, took the news bravely since we both knew, as the phrase of the day had it, that there was a war on. She and I said a tearful farewell at Camp Lejeune. She was carrying our first child. We did not see each other again until July 4, 1945.

In the thirty-three months that I spent in the Pacific Theater of Operations I took part in five major campaigns, from Guadalcanal to Okinawa. My uppermost memories of the conflict do not generally involve moments of combat, which were brief and filled with fear and confusion, but rather the times in between and just afterward—and most of all, the unimaginable, inescapable discomfort of living outdoors on a coral island in the tropics. Surrounded by tens of thousands of other men, a very high percentage of whom had dysentery, we spent our days sweating inside unwashed clothes, shuddering with the fevers and chills of malaria, treating the suppurating cuts inflicted by coral, eating canned food that did not taste or look like food, and very often being thirsty, with only enough fresh water to keep the body functioning.

Yet we managed, most of the time, to remember that we were human. A good example of that involves a Catholic chaplain named O'Malley stationed on the island of New Georgia in 1943. O'Malley was a real Irishman—born in Ireland, educated in Ireland, ordained in Ireland, and endowed with an Irish tongue. The United States was then regarded by the Roman Catholic church as missionary territory, and Father O'Malley had been sent to Los Angeles as a missionary; he had joined the Army as a missionary and had been sent ashore with an Army hospital unit that had set up its tents next door to our antiaircraft positions. Father O'Malley regarded it as part of God's work always to have a drop of brandy on hand to fortify and uplift the spirits of men tried by danger and privation. And though they knew it was against regulations to consume alcohol in a combat zone, the Marines provided the mixer—usually warm pineapple juice.

O'Malley happened to be with my battery during a Japanese bombing attack on our position in which men were killed by a direct hit on our 40-millimeter battery. Ninety-millimeter guns were single-shell, hand-loaded weapons, but Marine crews were trained, believe it or not, to load the forty-five-pound shells and fire them off at a rate of eighteen rounds per minute. The raid may have lasted two minutes, which meant that the four guns of my battery, urged on by me in a loud voice to *get those* [Marine terminology] *buzzards!*, had fired off at least 144 rounds while Japanese bombs were exploding in and around our position and filling the air with shrapnel.

All this made a hell of a racket, so when it was all over, the silence seemed unreal. The only sound was O'Malley, praying earnestly in his Irish brogue. I gave orders to clean and resupply the guns in case the enemy should come right back and bomb us again, as he often did in raids of this kind. This job took several minutes, but when it was over and I turned around, there was O'Malley, still on his knees.

I said, "Come on, Father, get up. The thing's over for now."

O'Malley shook his head. "I don't know, Don," he replied, "I don't know. It's you I'm praying for. You should have heard yourself when the Japs were dropping their bombs. There I was, down on my knees praying for the immortal souls of you and your men, and with every other word out of your mouth you were tearing yourself down with the Lord."

In one of the more pleasant coincidences of my life, I met Father O'Malley again in Los Angeles in April 1987. He came to hear me speak, and we talked over old times afterward.

In the autumn of 1944, after the recapture of Guam, I was sent back to Kauai, in the Hawaiian Islands, to train replacements for the invasions of Iwo Jima and Okinawa. By now Ann and I had been apart for more than two years, but my applications for leave were refused. Her letters were very sad, and so I made her this promise: "Be in San Francisco on July 1, 1945, and I'll be there to meet you." I had a strong feeling that I would keep this date. Ann immediately wrote to thirty hotels in the San Francisco area, and one of them actually offered her a reservation—a minor wartime miracle that encouraged us to believe that my hunch was right.

However, as the last week in June began, I was still on Okinawa, where I had gone ashore on D day plus 10. Then, on June 29, eight days after organized enemy resistance ended on the island (the battle was officially declared over on July 2), I was ordered to report to Marine Headquarters on Hawaii. I flew to Honolulu by way of Guam and reported to Major General Henry Paige, the commander of Marine antiaircraft artillery in the Pacific and formerly my superior in Iceland. I drew curious glances from the starched and polished Headquarters staff. The mud of Okinawa was still on my shoes, I was still wearing sidearms, I hadn't shaved or bathed in two days, and my last clean set of khakis were considerably less so after forty-eight hours in transit. I weighed 125 pounds, down 35 pounds from my normal 160. After hearing my report, General Paige told me that I could go home on leave.

It was June 30. Had I been able to hitch a ride on an aircraft, I would have made it to San Francisco on July 1, but all planes were filled with wounded men from Okinawa. I found a berth on a jeep carrier and sailed through the Golden Gate on the Fourth of July. Ann was waiting for me. Photographs taken that evening in the Top of the Mark suggest that I made a valiant effort to keep the promises I had made to many comrades who had asked me to have a drink for them in that famous bar.

By now I was a major. In just under three years I had taken part in the battles of Guadalcanal, New Georgia, North Solomons, Guam, and Okinawa. I expected to be sent back to the

Pacific for the invasion of Japan. The enemy had not surrendered, and from what I had seen of him along the Shuri Line in Okinawa, I did not think that he would do so. One hundred and ten thousand Japanese had died rather than surrender on Okinawa. We were being told that they would fight to the last man in defense of the home islands, and that there might be as many as a quarter of a million Americans killed in Japan. Nothing the Marines had so far learned about Japanese fighting spirit caused them to question these estimates.

A month after my return to the United States, the atomic bomb fell on Hiroshima and Nagasaki, and Japan sued for peace. Having witnessed death by fire on a smaller scale over a period of years, I understood the horror of the bombing. Nevertheless, these events filled me with joy when they were announced, and I will not pretend otherwise today.

Many of my friends died in the war. The memory of them was bright then and has hardly faded since. It is friendship, and something beyond friendship, that binds the Marine Corps together. Even after the passage of all these years it is very difficult for me to forgive the enemy who killed those young Americans or to forget the hatred and the ferocity that existed on both sides of the conflict. I have heard it said that men who go into battle against each other in their youth often become friends in their old age. This opportunity for reconciliation has never presented itself to me. Every Japanese of my own age whom I have met since the end of the war seems to have fought against the Chinese in China or the British in Malaya or the French in Indochina, never against the Americans in the islands of the Pacific. Remembering the scorched and blood-soaked islands where U.S. Marines and Japanese infantry engaged each other in combat, I am not surprised that this should be so.

After our reunion in San Francisco, Ann and I traveled by train across the country to Washington. We arrived at Union Station on July 10. There we were met by Ann's mother. Accompanying Mrs. Buchanan was a small blue-eyed girl with blond ringlets, my daughter Donna Ann, who had been born during the Battle of New Georgia.

Donna Ann was wearing a beautiful dress. She curtsied and said, "Hello, Daddy."

She was two years, three months, and two days old, and this was the first time she had ever seen me or I had ever seen her. When I remember the war, it is this last moment that I remember first.

· 7 ·

Lessons of Experience

The Marine Corps invited me to remain on active duty after the war as a regular officer, but Ann and I had had enough of separation. In the last days of 1945 I resigned my commission and went on terminal leave. This lasted until mid-March 1946, so that my military pay kept coming in while I hunted for a civilian job. Ann and Donna Ann had been living with Ann's mother on Bancroft Place, and I joined them after being relieved of my last assignment, as commanding officer of the Officer Candidate School at Camp Lejeune, North Carolina. I had been in the Marines for five and a half years.

My dream of being a lawyer had survived the war, but Ann and I decided that attending Harvard Law School for three years on the GI Bill of Rights was not a practical choice. We were expecting a second child. We wanted a home of our own. And we both felt that we had waited long enough for our life together to begin. Like other couples in our circumstances, we longed to put the war behind us and lead the normal, uncomplicated, peaceable American existence we had dreamed about and described to each other in our letters.

Three companies expressed an interest in hiring me—Mobil Oil Corporation, the Muzak Corporation of America, and the New York brokerage house of Merrill Lynch, Pierce, Fenner and Beane. I knew nothing about oil, music, or the stock market. In fact I possessed no qualifications for any occupation apart from a college education and the experience of training and leading men in combat. It was this lack of credentials and experience, rather than any natural bent for Wall Street, that led me to choose Merrill Lynch. The company had a training program for newly hired employees, and I figured that I needed all the help I could get in learning a trade. Nevertheless, the decision surprised my parents: my thrifty grandfather Regan had lost some money when a Cambridge bank failed in 1933, an experience that blackened the name of investment in our family for a long time after.

The course lasted six months. My fellow recruits were very bright young men, nearly all of whom had held commissions in the armed forces. The Merrill Lynch partner in charge of the school was another returning veteran, Alph Beane, son of the Beane of Merrill Lynch, Pierce, Fenner and Beane. Alph was an expansive, likeable fellow, but his career at Merrill Lynch did not live up to his own expectations. In early 1958 he left the firm and requested that the family name be removed from the logo; Win Smith's surname was substituted and the firm became Merrill Lynch, Pierce, Fenner and Smith.

The mysteries of the stock market and high finance were explained to us by a genial professor of finance from New York University named Birl Shultz. Shultz, tweedy, patient, encyclopedic in his knowledge of Wall Street and its workings, was a worldly Mr. Chips. He had a soft spot for ex-Marines because his own son George had been a Marine officer in the Pacific. George Shultz became a distinguished academic, public servant, and corporate executive; he appears in this book as President Reagan's second Secretary of State.

Doc Shultz had the gift of making the arcane obvious. Because I had imagined that it was abstract, I expected to be mystified by the stock market. Instead, I was fascinated by it because I saw that it was based on the interplay of the two profound but simple forces that make the world go round: money and human nature. The stock market may be complex, but it is not mysterious. Yet neither does it behave according to rational standards. It cannot possibly do so, because its daily and even its hourly movements are determined by the effect of thousands of decisions made by hundreds of thousands of human beings who have invested money in stocks. At any given moment the market is the sum of their wisdom or their folly, and it is always in a state of tension because money, in all its many levels of symbolism, is at risk.

That is why it is unwise, even irrational, to "play the market." The rational investor, finding himself inside the maze that is the stock market, will apply good sense to his situation, realizing that the most inviting path is not always the best way forward. He will think in terms of individual investments, and he will think in terms of the future, buying stock on the basis of two fundamental criteria: the soundness of the corporation in which he is investing and the relevance of that corporation's products to future trends in the national economy. If, for example, the United States ratified a treaty with the Soviet Union banning nuclear missiles at the same time that Congress passed a bill creating a system of government insurance against the cost of catastrophic illness, the sensible investor would put his money into the best-managed health-care and drug companies he could find. He would not buy stock in companies that manufacture missile components.

The academic subjects taught as part of the Merrill Lynch training course appealed to me because their practical application was obvious. There was no geometry here—just simple arithmetic and the plain objective of turning sums of money into larger sums of money. Though I had never taken an accounting course in my life, I won a prize in this subject. For the third time since leaving Harvard six years before, I felt the exhilaration of having made the right choice in life—first the Marines, then Ann, and now my lifework. At the time I felt very fortunate to have stumbled into exactly what I was best suited to do; I still feel the same, and the exhilaration never flagged.

At the end of the training course I asked to be assigned to the Washington office of Merrill Lynch even though another trainee, Carmen Saccardi, had already been chosen to go there. The manager of this office was George Garrett, a longtime partner in the firm who was afterward appointed American ambassador to Ireland. Although I did not know it at the time, Garrett did not want me. One inexperienced trainee in his office was enough, he told Alph Beane, who pleaded my case. "I'll give this fellow Regan six months, but if he doesn't do well, you get him back." Had I known how Garrett felt at the time, I'm not sure that I would have been as optimistic about the future as in fact I was.

Garrett's good opinion was a prize worth winning. He was an aloof, old-style, penny-watching manager who was as slow to praise good work as he was certain to reward it. He knew how to lay down a marker for his subordinates. Thinking that membership would be an advantage in business as well as a pleasure, I joined the Army and Navy Club soon after my arrival in Washington. Would it be all right, I asked Garrett, to apply to the firm for reimbursement of the cost of a customer's luncheon at the club— not my own, of course, just the customer's? Garrett recoiled in his swivel chair, glared at me over the top of his glasses, and barked, "Young man, as far as I'm concerned, your entire salary is an expense! Does that answer your question?" It did; I never asked George Garrett for another dime.

Thanks in no small part to a burning desire to show George Garrett that I could do the job, I threw myself into the work, calling on prospects and clients at night and on weekends as far away as Frederick, Maryland, some twenty-five miles from downtown Washington. Garrett tested my mettle by asking me to handle the account of Under Secretary of State William Clayton, who was in France attending an international conference. It was a very important account and Clayton normally handled it personally. While he was away, a sell-off occurred. I reported it to Clayton's office as a temporary setback and recommended riding it out. In a day or two the market recovered, vindicating my judgment. When Clayton came back from overseas, he told Garrett that he wanted me to continue to handle his account.

The hours were long. Ann worked right along with me. Our second child, Donald Thomas Regan, Jr., called Tom, had been born on May 8, 1946, while I was attending the training class in New York. Many a night we sat up late at the kitchen table, stuffing envelopes with brochures while the children slept. I was fascinated by the job. Garrett must have noticed, because he let me stay.

Eighteen months later I was one of ten account executives out of the thousand employed by Merrill Lynch chosen for a new sales-promotion team. Merrill Lynch sent this squad of go-getters into every branch office across the nation to teach new sales techniques and present new products. But it meant that Ann and I had to sell our first home on Greentree Road in Bethesda, Maryland, and move to New York. This was the first of seventeen such moves in my thirty-five years with Merrill Lynch. Our third and fourth children, Richard William, named for his grandfathers, and Diane Gordon, named for Ann's family, were born in Englewood Hospital while we were living in Ridgewood, New Jersey, in the late 1940s and early 1950s.

It was a great opportunity to meet nearly everyone in the firm and observe their methods, and like my job in Washington, it turned out to be fun. At one point I thought that I had put my foot in my mouth and might not get it out again. A very senior partner was delivering a very long lecture on sales techniques. Along with many of my fellow juniors, I grew bored and restless. They held their peace. I raised my hand, was recognized, and said, "What firm, what securities, what customers are we talking about? I don't recognize reality in anything you've said—that's not life as it's lived in Merrill Lynch's branches today."

A heated argument followed. My father had taught me never to back down when I thought I was right, so I didn't. Unbeknownst to me, the managing partners of the firm, Charlie Merrill and Win Smith, the genial New Englander who ran the firm on a day-to-day basis, had slipped into the room and were witnesses to the whole shouting match. Merrill, who had himself fought a good many older men to a standstill when he first came to Wall Street, later mentioned this incident to his son-in-law, Robert A. Magowan, the partner in charge of sales. "That Regan is a fresh SOB," Merrill reportedly remarked. "But, by God, I admire his guts in speaking up when he thinks something isn't right."

After the sales-promotion team finished its work, Bob Mago-wan asked me to stay on in New York as his assistant. When asked for the secret of success, Bob always replied, "Decisiveness. I decided to marry the boss's daughter, and I recommend that you make the same decision if you can." In fact he was a sales-man and manager of great natural talent and broad experience, possessed of a quick wit and a sure sense of judgment. Working with him was one of the turning points in my life.

While combing my files for material for this book I came upon a memorandum from Magowan to the Washington office. It is dated July 23, 1948. "The Sales-Promotion Team . . . is one of the most constructive things the firm has ever done, and we were lucky enough to recruit a grand bunch of guys for the assign-ment," Bob wrote. "It won't surprise you, I'm sure, to hear that Don Regan is one of the best. . . . I think he is destined to go far with this firm." These words pleased me as much nearly forty years after they were written as on the first day that I read them. Bob Magowan was a mentor and a friend and a teacher to me, the sort of man who sees a young man's strengths and lets him use them. More than once in later years, when faced with a de-cision that involved a younger man's future, I asked myself what Bob Magowan would have done in the same situation. The mem-ory of his example never failed to suggest a wise solution.

As I went to work for Bob, the first of the postwar bull mar-kets was just taking shape, and it was a great opportunity to learn about the behavior of the market in a period of expansion and the ways in which a great brokerage house responds to its cus-tomers' needs in such a period.

Bob Magowan liked creativity and I tried to give it to him. Under the tutelage of a talented Yugoslav immigrant named Mil-ija ("Ruby") Rubezanin, I worked on the development of a new line of publications that explained the stock market in simple terms to customers and prospects. The motto of Charlie Merrill, one of the founders of the firm, was *Take the mystery out of finance.* Tell-ing customers the "secrets" of investment was regarded at that time as a daring idea. Not everyone agreed that it was a good idea: if customers could make their own decisions, what use was a broker? Like Merrill I thought that sharing knowledge was a good way to forge bonds of trust between the firm and its customers, and believed that knowledgeable people would be attracted to Merrill Lynch as customers.

Apparently the public agreed. Sales rose; profits increased. The pamphlets and brochures became a hallmark of Merrill Lynch. The lesson was an old one: many heads are often better than one. Most of the credit for the breakthrough belongs to Ruby Rubezanin, a ruthless editor and tireless worker. Love of detail was already very strong in me when I encountered Ruby, but his passion for the right word, the clear sentence, the correctly placed comma opened up a new dimension of diligence.

From time to time I have told myself that I am too interested in detail, and many who have worked with me would heartily agree. But in fact details cannot always be left to others. The big picture is always a work of pointillism, and the wise manager will stay close enough to the canvas to see all the dots. If he fails to do so, he may be subject to unpleasant surprises. In 1951 Merrill Lynch uncovered a scandal in its trading department. Some of the traders were accepting kickbacks from outside over-the-counter dealers who were used to execute some of Merrill's buy and sell orders. The partner in charge of this department, who had been ill, retired, and his deputy was reassigned. The head trader and seven or eight other traders were fired.

To my surprise, I was asked to take over the department and run it. The trading department handled all of Merrill Lynch's transactions in over-the-counter common stocks, preferred stocks, and bonds and all foreign transactions—roughly 10 percent of the total volume traded on the New York markets. More than a hundred people were employed by the trading department. I was thirty-two years old and had been in the brokerage business for only five years. My inner doubts about my ability to do the job must have shown.

Charlie Merrill, who had of course approved my appointment, wrote me a letter from Canefield, his house in Barbados. I reproduce the entire letter here because it reveals so much about Merrill and about the way in which the firm he founded reflected his personality:

Dear Don:

While it will be difficult for me to associate [*sic*] our Trading Department without Johnny Wark, I am very pleased that his mantle will fall on your shoulders. I know as well as you do how little you know about the technical workings of the over-the-counter market, but that is a situation that can be remedied with each passing day if you give to the job the same devotion you have given to the other tasks that have been assigned to you up until now.

I hope you will remember a remark I made to you and the other boys on that Sales-Promotion Team a few years ago to the effect that there was no job in the firm that an alert, able, ambitious young man of thirty could not fill. You need not be discouraged by your lack of years, for God will take care of that in due time.

I wish you great success in your new and very important job.

I seized the opportunity the firm had offered me with a mixture of gratitude and trepidation and immediately set about reorganizing the troubled department.

As soon as new people were in place, working under new procedures that made it less likely that the same problem would recur, I began looking for ways to sell more securities. I saw an opportunity for growth for the firm, and profits for its customers, in an expansion of over-the-counter transactions in unlisted securities. With the help and companionship of a brilliant and seasoned trader named Stan Waldron and an equally gifted research expert named Alan Gulliver, I took this message out to the branch offices. The three of us traveled the country two or three weeks out of the month, explaining the concept. We discovered new wells of enthusiasm; sales went up. And in the mid-1950s, when the stock market began to rise, over-the-counter stocks rose rapidly in value.

At the end of 1953, as my thirty-fifth birthday approached, the firm invited me to become a general partner. This was a thrilling moment for Ann and me—but we did not have the ten thousand dollars in capital required of partners. Another godsend (shades of the Harvard loan fund) saved the day. Charlie Merrill made me a personal loan for the portion I could not raise from my own resources.

The fact that I was the youngest man ever to be made a general partner caused a certain amount of discontent. Over brandy one night in the library of his summer house in Southampton, Charlie Merrill repeated his advice not to worry about criticism based on youth. "Hell, there isn't a job in this firm that a man your age can't handle if he applies himself," he said. "I know—I did it myself when I was younger than you."

Merrill was that rarest of men, a legend who truly deserved to be a legend. After leaving Amherst College, he came to Wall Street and then, in 1915, founded Merrill Lynch in partnership with Eddie Lynch, a transplanted Marylander. There is no comma between the names now because the printer made a mistake in a batch of stationery and the partners afterward refused to put one in out of superstition. The firm was a success from the first day. The partners, imaginative and audacious and not particularly respectful of the advice of their elders, were known in their heyday as "the boy bandits of Wall Street." Merrill regarded the phrase as a handsome compliment. He broke new ground in Wall Street and realized enormous profits for his customers and himself in the teens and twenties by bringing relatively unknown chain-store companies to public ownership. It was Merrill who managed the first stock offerings of Kresge, Good Luck (later known as J.C. Penney), Melville (Thom McAn Shoes), First National, and Kroger. He also founded Safeway. In March 1929, seven months before the Great Crash, he sold most of his stocks and persuaded Eddie Lynch to do the same.

The two men went separate ways thereafter. Merrill returned to Wall Street in 1940 and reinstituted Merrill Lynch, Pierce, Fenner and Beane. When I first met Merrill he was about sixty, a small handsome man with pure white hair. He was several times married and seldom romantically idle between marriages. Ordinarily he was soft-spoken, humorous, generous, and gentle. When angered by a mistake or a foolish word, he was capable of exploding in pyrotechnic wrath, cursing imbeciles, idiots, incompetents, and his partners all in the same breath. Even after he became a patriarch, Merrill never forgot that it was the audacious young Charlie Merrill who made the firm what it later became. He liked young people and enjoyed being a witness to their success, particularly if he had given them the chance to succeed. I think he liked me because I talked back to him. Whatever his reasons, I am grateful for his friendship.

Thanks to the chances Charlie Merrill and Bob Magowan and Win Smith gave me, my career at Merrill Lynch continued to prosper. In ·1955 we were transferred to Philadelphia, where I took over the branch office. Our memories of Philadelphia are very happy ones. It was good to be away from the bustle of Wall Street and the hectic pace of New York. Philadelphia was a civil place where no one elbowed you in a crowd and few people needed a pint of gin at luncheon in order to get through the day until the cocktail hour.

Life was everything Ann and I had hoped it would be. By now we could afford a nice home with a swimming pool in a pleasant neighborhood. It was an easy commute from home to office along the Main Line. My experience in New York had taught me to avoid gin and late hours, and I was usually home by six. Ann and I were able to sit down and talk to each other by daylight. Sometimes we'd have a swim before dinner. After dinner I would work for a couple of hours in the study, and then we would have the evening before us. One of my neighbors was a golfer, and on summer evenings he and I would knock a golf ball back and forth across the fence. The children went to good schools and the house was open to their friends. We made friends in those years who are still our friends. On the page, these details of middle class life may seem ordinary and quiet, and of course that's what they were. That is why we were so happy.

The Philadelphia office ranked tenth or eleventh among the hundred or so Merrill Lynch field offices when I arrived. It ranked third when I left. In 1960 we returned to New York. I became a senior vice president of the firm and then an executive vice president. In 1968 I was named president of Merrill Lynch.

This, too, was a controversial appointment. I was not yet fifty

years old. My critics in the firm and in the Street still thought
that I was too young for the job, too brash, and too liable to
make waves. George Leness, who was chairman of the board at
the time, resisted my appointment because, as he later told me,
he wanted Merrill Lynch to remain as it was. There was little
appetite for change among the older generation in Wall Street.
My seniors had lived through the Crash of '29 and the long financial exile of the Great Depression. Some were still haunted
by dark memories of past disasters. They greeted the rebirth of
the bull market with mixed emotions. They understood the opportunities created by growth, but they were worried by the
changes that they saw taking place in the economy, in society,
and consequently in the climate of business. Could prosperity
last?

In those days Wall Street was still a private club with a public
charter, a cartel masquerading as a capitalist competitive system.
It fixed its own commissions with the blessing of the Securities
and Exchange Commission in Washington. It made its own rules
as to who would be admitted to the exchange and who would be
excluded. It supervised all details of the operations of a member
brokerage firm, including censorship of every word used by the
firm in newspaper, radio, or television advertising. It chose which
specialist could handle which stock and allowed no competing
specialists. It conducted millions of dollars of business every day
by word of mouth on the floor of the exchange, creating a paper
trail that eventually choked the exchange, bringing on the failure
of innumerable member firms. The other face of autocracy is
noblesse oblige, and Wall Street saw to it that the customers of
failed members lost no money as a result of the debacle.

I chafed under this benevolent despotism and believed that it
was an obstacle to growth, progress, and what I will call a de-
mocratized market that would draw on the capital and the ingenuity of the largest possible pool of investors. Centralization is
the enemy of diversity and competition. By now I had seen enough
of capitalism to believe in it. That meant that I welcomed competition, for if you say you are a capitalist, then the next thing
you must say is, "I compete." Restraints on competition, beyond

the basic, indispensable measures to protect the rights, the welfare, and the wealth of individuals, are bad for a capitalist economy (or any other kind, judging by the results obtained in the so-called planned economies). It was competition, stimulated by opportunity, that was bringing about change in the marketplace. I had been saying that change could not be prevented; either we would change of our own free will or change would be forced upon us by events or by the government. This was not a message that everyone wanted to hear. But years later I was gratified when George Leness told me he had been mistaken in opposing my appointment as president of Merrill Lynch—I'd been good for the firm and good for Wall Street.

My years on Wall Street were years in which the American economy, and life in the world at large, was transformed. Twentieth-century technology, which had its origins in the industrial revolution of the previous century, was superseded by a technological revolution that is now bringing the economy of the twenty-first century into being. Whole new industries were created, of which the electronics industry was among the most notable. Japan rose out of the ashes of World War II and, by bringing the old technology to a very high state of efficiency, became the greatest economic competitor the United States had seen since its emergence as a world power. The empires of the West ceased to exist and the Third World was born. The United States continued to symbolize political freedom and economic opportunity in the minds of the world's people. Marxism-Leninism failed as an economic system first in the Soviet bloc and then in the Third World. The gross national product of the United States grew more than tenfold, from $212 billion in 1946 to $2.7 trillion in 1980.

Wall Street was transformed by these events along with the rest of the country, but it did not always make the necessary adjustments to change. In 1968–69, just as I was taking over as president of Merrill Lynch, the Street was dizzy with prosperity. Greed replaced good judgment. Brokerage firms took on more business than they could handle—and choked on the paperwork the new business generated. A paper-intensive industry simply could not keep up with an electronic pace of growth. Computers, and people to operate them, did not yet exist in sufficient numbers to rescue the situation—and if they had existed, few would have understood that they represented a solution to the problem. Many firms failed simply because they could not keep up with their paperwork. A crisis in the market ensued.

At the end of 1970, James Thompson retired as chairman of the board of Merrill Lynch and I was elected to replace him. The stock market was in the doldrums after the collapse of the bull market described above. I did not doubt that the market would rebound, but in the meantime we were faced with the problem of making the firm grow in a period of recession. It was possible to do this by taking the firm in new directions. It was clear, as I have said, that a new world was coming into existence. Merrill Lynch was already one of the most successful brokerage houses that had ever existed. Assuming continued good management, its brokerage activities would expand as a natural result of this established strength. But growth would be limited if we limited our field of action.

I believed that the future of the firm lay in expansion into activities that were not traditionally associated with the brokerage business. In the eyes of some, this was a heretical opinion.

We had already acquired a commercial real-estate firm, Hubbard Westerfield & Co., and had begun selling mutual funds, a product Charlie Merrill had refused to offer to the firm's customers because of the disastrous failures suffered by such funds in the Great Crash and its aftermath. In 1970 Merrill Lynch took over Goodbody & Co., a major Wall Street brokerage with many offices that was on the brink of failure. The merger created management problems that toughened the firm and brought in many new and excellent people, together with a lot of new customers.

The following year we took Merrill Lynch public. This, too, smacked of heresy. Public ownership of a member of the New York Stock Exchange had traditionally been opposed by many members of the Exchange. On June 23, 1971, 4 million shares of Merrill Lynch common stock were offered to the public at $28 per share. The offering sold out, raising $112 million in capital. Merrill Lynch common stock was worth $39.75 a share when I resigned as chairman 9½ years later, and net income had risen from $71 million a year to about $200 million.

Public ownership gave the firm a permanent capital base and an entirely different managerial atmosphere. We established a nationwide real-estate network (1987 sales: $674.1 billion) and expanded into the insurance business through the purchase of the Family Life Insurance Company of Seattle. I wanted to buy Thomas Cook & Co. in order to get into the travel business, and especially the lucrative traveler's checks business, but the directors of this distinguished British firm would not sell it to an American purchaser.

Merrill Lynch's most startling venture was the establishment in 1975 of the Cash Management Account (CMA), an all-encompassing method of handling and managing family finances. The CMA pays interest on deposited funds. Checks can be issued on it and credit card purchases can be charged against it. Securities of all kinds can be bought and sold through the account, and the customer can activate loans to himself by writing checks on a margin account at broker's loan rates, which are lower than the prime interest rate.

This brilliant concept, which broke down barriers between brokerage and banking, was initiated by Thomas L. Christie, a leading Merrill Lynch investment banker whom I had asked to develop new ideas in collaboration with the California think-tank, Stanford Research. Like most innovative ideas, it met with resistance. Did it comply with the provisions of the Glass-Steagall Act of 1933, which prohibited commercial banks from underwriting securities?

I saw no conflict. A bank, by definition, is an institution that makes commercial loans. Merrill Lynch had no interest in making commercial loans; it was interested in providing a financial service for its customers in support of their investment activities. We tested the concept in the Pacific Northwest and in Utah. It won immediate public acceptance but encountered some initial objections from the authorities, which had to be overcome. Today there are more than 1.3 million Merrill Lynch Cash Management Accounts.

By 1980 I had been working at Merrill Lynch for just under thirty-five years. In that year, my last as chairman of the board, the firm paid me more than $1 million in salary and other compensation. My private fortune had grown over the years with the fortunes of Merrill Lynch. Ann and I owned a house in Florida and another in Virginia besides our principal residence in Colts Neck, New Jersey. The children were grown and living their own lives, and we were discovering the joys of being grandparents. Ann suggested that I think about early retirement. I agreed that I would consider it. I was sixty-one years old, but I felt about the same in most ways as I had in 1946. Although I had never worked anywhere else, I had never been bored at Merrill Lynch and I still woke up every morning eager to get to the office.

Yet my mind was not always on business. "The life which is unexamined," Plato tells us, "is not worth living." My own life could only have been lived in America, and all examination of it begins with that fact. If I had been born in Ireland, I might, with luck, have become a parish priest or a schoolteacher. Because the Regans and the Ahearns and the Ryans and the Flynns crossed the Atlantic Ocean, the world was open to me. I am the beneficiary of a long line of people, ancestors and strangers, who believed in the future. My family staked its very existence on it when they left the old country behind. It was the future of the Catholic faith and the United States of America that the Sisters of Notre Dame de Nemours had in mind when they filled little boys' heads with useful facts and taught them the difference between right and wrong with a rattan blackboard pointer. Mr. Buckley's scholarships to Harvard were a blind investment in the future. The young Marines with whom I served in the war never questioned that the future of the United States was worth dying for. In the many neighborhoods of my childhood, at Cambridge Latin School, at Harvard, in the Marines, at Merrill Lynch, my fellow Americans took me as they found me and judged me by what I did. The most fortunate event of my life, my marriage to Ann Buchanan, was made possible because we were introduced by a kind woman who was a virtual stranger to me.

I had reached a time and place in life where I was very conscious of the origins of my good fortune. Although I have never been one to deny my own accomplishments, I am very conscious that others have provided my opportunities. There is no such thing as a self-made man. Some of my benefactors have been described in these chapters. Many more have gone unnamed. I was conscious that I owed them a great debt—and that I owed an even greater debt to my country, which had imbued them with the altruism that had made my career possible. As my career in business came to an end I was searching for some way to repay the debt.

Government had always interested me greatly because I saw the effects of its policies and actions on Wall Street in terms of dollars and cents. Forty years after listening to Wendell Willkie's remarks in Harvard Square, I still thought that there was too much government intrusion in the private sector, and that this intrusion was sapping the nation's energy. No doubt the inflexibility of my opinion had something to do with my having become a crusty capitalist who refused to change his mind, but it had a great deal more to do with the fact that the Washington establishment had turned FDR's reforms into a stultifying orthodoxy.

The idea of running for public office never entered my mind; others have rightly pointed out that I do not possess the politician's temperament. My involvement in political activity was marginal. I donated my own money to Republican candidates, studied the issues in the press, and voted in every election. Once in a while I would talk politics with those I knew—Bill Casey, Bill Rogers—who were players in Washington. Beyond that I was uninvolved, although I did serve for three years as an unpaid member of the board of directors of the Securities Insurance Protection Corporation, a quasi-governmental body that was set up after the Wall Street debacle of 1969–70 to insure brokerage accounts under a federal program similar to the Federal Deposit Insurance Corporation (FDIC) underwriting of bank accounts.

In 1976, when Gerald R. Ford was running for President, I supported him. It seemed to me that he had done well in difficult circumstances and deserved the chance to continue. Ford's opponent in the Republican primaries, Ronald Reagan, came to

New York and I was invited to meet him at a small luncheon for Wall Streeters. I accepted out of curiosity. In common with many other imperceptive people, I did not take Reagan very seriously as a Presidential candidate. I knew little about him apart from the facts that he had been a movie actor and, later, Governor of California and was associated with the conservative wing of our party.

When we were introduced before sitting down at the table, Reagan immediately seized on the similarity in our names. He grinned delightedly and snapped his fingers. "That gives me an idea for a lead-in story for my speech," he said. "Do you mind if I use it?"

This is the story he told: A man who doesn't know Reagan is asked to introduce him at a luncheon shortly after Reagan was elected governor in 1966. The man doesn't know how to pronounce the new governor's name and can't find anyone who knows for sure whether its' *Ray*gan or *Ree*gan. The worried man goes for a walk in Beverly Hills and meets a comedian he knows, who is walking his dog.

"I've got a problem," the man says to the comedian. "I've got to introduce this new governor at a meeting tomorrow and I don't know how to pronounce his name. Is it *Ray*gan or *Ree*gan?"

"It's *Ray*gan," the comedian replies.

"Are you sure? I don't want to mispronounce the new governor's name."

"Believe me," the comedian replies, "it's *Ray*gan. I've known the guy for years."

"Gee, thanks—now I can sleep," says the neighbor. "And by the way, that's a nice dog you've got there. What breed is it?"

"It's a bagel," the comedian replies.

The·joke, and Reagan's amiability, are my only memories of this first meeting.

I encountered him again in the spring of 1980, when he was campaigning for the Republican Presidential nomination. Bill Rogers, whom I had brought onto the board of Merrill Lynch after he resigned as Richard Nixon's Secretary of State, suggested that I do something for Reagan because he believed Reagan was going to win the nomination. "He's the type of guy who deserves our support," Bill said. I thought a lot of Bill Rogers, and so I agreed to do what I could. Soon afterward Helene Van Damm, a Reagan loyalist who rose from a secretary's job to become ambassador to Austria, helped with the arrangements for a cocktail party fund-raiser for Reagan at the Sky Club. About two hundred people came and paid five hundred dollars apiece.

Despite the similarity in our names, Reagan had difficulty remembering me, but he covered his loss of memory gracefully by asking me about the stock market. He seemed to agree with what I said to him—that high interest rates and inflation were approaching dangerous levels. Once again I was impressed by his geniality.

In September, after he had been nominated at the Republican convention, Reagan came to New York again. Bill Casey, who was Reagan's campaign manager, suggested that I help raise a pot for the Republican cause. Together with John Whitehead, who was then an executive of Goldman, Sachs and later became Deputy Secretary of State, I organized a bigger fund-raiser for Reagan—a thousand-dollars-a-plate dinner. Reagan spoke for fifteen minutes and took fifteen minutes of questions. Afterward we discussed the economy in passing. He said nothing remarkable, but he seemed to have had sound economic advice.

On November 4, I voted for Reagan, and when Jimmy Carter conceded the election even before the polls closed in California, I rejoiced. Interest rates were at 21 percent, the official rate of inflation was 13 percent, and it was obvious that the country was in serious economic trouble.

Just before the election, a Wall Streeter who was on the inside of the Reagan camp called me from California. He told me that my name was on a short list of candidates for the post of Secretary of the Treasury in the Reagan Cabinet. My informant was a reliable man with excellent sources in the Kitchen Cabinet, so I did not doubt the truth of his report. At the same time I didn't take it very seriously. Why would President-elect Reagan appoint a man he had met only twice to a post as important as Treasury?

One of the other names on the list was that of William E. Simon, who had been Secretary of the Treasury under Nixon and Ford.

"That's a nice compliment," I said. "But I don't see how I have a chance."

"Don't be so sure," my informant said. "You'd better start thinking what you'd do if you were asked to take the job."

I discussed this conversation with Ann.

"What *would* you do?" she asked.

"Well, it would be pretty hard to say no to the President-elect of the United States if he asked me to serve," I replied.

Ann gave me a look in which the wisdom and skepticism of forty years of marriage were distilled. "Why not just take early retirement, instead?" she asked.

"This is the type of thing you do for early retirement," I said. I pointed out that recent Secretaries of the Treasury had served only a couple of years. Two or three years before, we had bought a house on the Potomac just south of Mount Vernon and were already going there for weekends. We both enjoyed Washington, a town that held so many happy memories for us both. A couple of years at Treasury, I said, and then retirement. Maybe that wouldn't be so bad. . . .

I subsequently learned that my name had moved to the top of the list after Bill Simon withdrew his own name from consideration. Bill Casey brought my name forward. The appointment was agreed upon in a conference telephone call with the President-elect in which Meese, Casey, Jim Baker, and several others were involved.

I tried to put the matter out of my mind, but reports kept coming in that I was under consideration. Friends told me that Reagan wanted to appoint his Cabinet on an objective basis; his chief headhunter, a Californian named Pendleton James, had been instructed to find the best-qualified man for every post, regardless of past political services.

Finally Pen James himself called and invited me to luncheon at the University Club in Washington. He was accompanied by Ed Meese. The two of them grilled me on my economic philosophy, my management ideas, and my opinion of Ronald Reagan.

I told them exactly what I thought. They listened and, at the end of an hour, shook my hand and wished me well. After that, silence descended. I told Ann that my bluntness had probably guaranteed that I would be able to please her by taking early retirement.

Then, on the evening of Wednesday, December 3, while Ann and I were chatting before dinner in the sitting room of our house in Colts Neck, New Jersey, the phone rang. Ann answered and handed me the receiver.

"Ronald Reagan on the telephone," she said.

I took the instrument and, out of long habit, said, "Hello—Regan."

Gosh, said Ronald Reagan in his whispery tenor, I guess I'm going to have to get used to that pronunciation.

"It must be the same family tree—just a different spelling," I replied. I congratulated him on his victory.

Let me tell you why I'm calling, Reagan said.

"Yes?"

I'd like you to be my Secretary of the Treasury.

I said, "Thank you very much. I accept."

A surprised silence ensued at Reagan's end of the line. After a moment he said, Don't you want to think it over?

"Mr. President, what is there to think over?" I replied. "How could any American say no when asked to serve by the President-elect? If you've selected me, it's my duty to say yes."

Well, Reagan said after another pause. Thank you very much. You'll be hearing from somebody, and I'll see you in Washington.

I said, "Fine, Mr. President. Good luck with the rest of your Cabinet."

I hung up. Ann had been sipping her iced tea while I was on the telephone.

"What was that all about?" she asked.

I said, "I'm the new Secretary of the Treasury."

Ann said, "Damn!"

· 8 ·

The Guesswork Presidency

March 11, 1981

To this day I have never had so much as 1 minute alone with Ronald Reagan! Never has he, or anyone else, sat down in private to explain to me what is expected of me, what goals he would like to see me accomplish, what results he wants. Since I am accustomed to management by objective, where people have *in writing* what is expected, and explicit standards are set, this has been most disconcerting. How can one do a job if the job is not defined? I have been struggling to do what I consider the job to be, and let others tell me if I'm wrong, or not doing the right thing. (So far no one has said!) This . . . is dangerous.

This excerpt from a note I wrote to myself in a spiral notebook late in the second month of the Reagan Administration is interesting as a commentary on the nature of the fortieth Presidency, and as a prophecy of things to come in my own life in Washington. In the four years that I served as Secretary of the Treasury I never saw President Reagan alone and never discussed economic philosophy or fiscal and monetary policy with him one-on-one. From first day to last at Treasury, I was flying by the seat of my pants. The President never told me what he believed or what he wanted to accomplish in the field of economics. I had to figure these things out like any other American, by studying his speeches and reading the newspapers.

In our telephone conversation on December 3 the President had said, "I'll see you in Washington." To my surprise, that was what he meant—literally. Between my appointment and Inauguration Day there was no summons to California or Blair House, no private meeting in which the President-elect revealed his economic objectives and gave me my instructions as his chief spokesman on economic policy. After I accepted the job, he simply hung up and vanished. From time to time I heard from Ed Meese or Meese's assistant, Craig Fuller. They seldom quoted the President or referred to his wishes. I found this disembodied relationship bizarre.

In 1981 I had not yet begun to understand that this was the way Ronald Reagan did business—that his public persona *was* his real persona. For a while I struggled against a certain anxiety that this method of running the world's greatest economy might wreck the new Presidency. Happily, I was wrong. In fact Reagan's openness created an atmosphere of confidence and political dynamism that produced the longest period of economic recovery and the highest levels of employment in the history of the United States. The President himself had very little to do with the invention and the implementation of the policies and mechanisms that encouraged this remarkable increase in the nation's wealth and general well-being. He was content to exercise the symbolic powers of his office—and his astonishing skill in doing so was of course the very thing that made success possible.

After a short time I realized that there was no good reason why the President should call his Secretary of the Treasury into his presence and tell him confidentially that he had meant what he said about federal spending and fiscal and monetary policy in his campaign speeches and his other public utterances. Although other appointees to the Cabinet had asked for assurances concerning the boundaries of their authority or their right of access to the President, I had taken my job without conditions. I had always created my own conditions of employment; I thought that I could do so again. But where to start? What were the rules?

The President seemed to believe that his public statements were all the guidance his private advisers required. Ronald Reagan's campaign promises *were* his policy. To him, in his extreme simplicity of character and belief, this was obvious. It has never been obvious to the political sophisticates who have supposed that Reagan's political motives are suspect and his achievements are accidental. But I believe it is the truth.

In the beginning the truth was less obvious to me than it is now, but before long I decided that my job as Secretary of the Treasury was to find ways to carry out the President's promises. Once I had grasped that principle, I understood that I was free to interpret his words and implement his intentions in my field of policy and action according to my best judgment. Theodore Roosevelt believed that the President could conduct his office in any way that was not specifically prohibited by the Constitution. Reagan, who laid down no rules and articulated no missions, conferred a Rooseveltian latitude on his subordinates. This liberated the inventiveness and the competitiveness of his lieutenants—along with many less desirable qualities.

At first it was difficult to believe that such a management policy could be intentional. Mixed results were inevitable; disaster was possible—even probable. I had spent my life planning, defining, and identifying objectives, and assigning and assuming responsibilities. My whole method of management was based on a system that left as little as possible to chance. Now I found myself in an environment in which there seemed to be no center, no structure, no agreed policy. I struggled to understand a reality that was far removed from what I had always imagined life in a high government post to be. This was not an easy process.

Before I could begin work I had to be confirmed by the Senate. That process is less majestic when experienced from the inside than it appears to be on the surface. The Washington equivalent of Diogenes' lamp had been blown out by the storms of accusation associated with Watergate and its aftermath. "The town" (as Washingtonians call the capital's politico-journalistic establishment) seemed to be looking for rascals, not honest men. Estimates of my net financial worth and inventories of the temptations of a Wall Street career appeared in the press. Some seemed to believe as a matter of ideological dogma that these temptations were irresistible. Doubts were expressed that a man who had spent thirty-five years in Wall Street could be squeaky-clean enough to be confirmed as a Cabinet officer. In other press reports it was suggested that I was not a friend of Wall Street. Even today I don't know which of these stories were planted by my friends and which by my enemies, or if they were just journalistic smoke rings. In any case, it was a shock to realize that appointment to a position of great public trust aroused mistrust of the appointee on such a massive scale.

I understood, and had always accepted, that in a democracy a public man renounces his right to privacy, but I had not realized how time-consuming it is to have one's virtue certified by the bureaucracy. Between Christmas and Inauguration Day, I spent days filling out forms designed to help those who were investigating me to discover a reason why I might not be fit to serve. Perhaps some historiographer will one day tell us what effect the background investigation has had in reducing the proportion of scoundrels in appointive office. Will there be fewer in the year 2000 than there were in 1900 or 1800? Will the next President's computerized files provide a better basis for judgment than the gossip and instinct on which, say, Abraham Lincoln relied?

It required the efforts of three lawyers, including Bill Rogers, who had been through the process several times himself (though never, as he kept saying, in such excruciating detail) to list every dollar of income I had ever earned, every share of stock and other asset I owned, every association I had ever had, every house I had ever lived in, every trip abroad I had ever made, and much else besides. My very efficient secretary of twenty years, Mrs. Betty Lehrman, a keeper of meticulous records, worked for more than three weeks at the job of collating and typing up all this information. I put all my assets into a blind trust after they had been examined by a man who bore the Orwellian title of "the President's Conflict of Interest Counsel" and for the next six years lived in a state of total ignorance concerning my own wealth.

Although I had an office at Treasury and some contact with the transition team, the lion's share of what remained of my time was spent on Capitol Hill. Shepherded by the affable Pat O'Donnell, I called on influential senators and congressmen. Doubt existed in the mind of some of the more conservative Republicans about my fitness to serve—not because anyone suggested that I lacked the qualifications necessary to be Secretary of the Treasury, but because I had been accused of making political gifts to Democrats.

The charge was accurate. As chairman of Merrill Lynch, a public corporation that was not affiliated to either party, I had organized (in conjunction with other Wall Streeters) three fundraisers for Senator Daniel Patrick Moynihan of New York after he had been elected and was attempting to pay his campaign debts. I had also introduced potential contributors to Representative Robert Eckhardt of Texas when he was chairman of a House subcommittee dealing with securities, and to Representative Al Uhlman of Oregon when he was chairman of the House Ways and Means Committee. Some right-wingers were disturbed by these activities, which looked to them like apostasy.

A number of people, including Pendleton James, who was now in charge of personnel operations for the incoming Administration, suggested that I could placate my critics by appointing Lewis Lehrman, a prominent New York conservative, as Deputy Secretary of the Treasury. Although Lehrman was a capable, even a brilliant, man, I declined. I knew that he and I would clash because he would not be content to take a backseat. I wanted an administrator, not a person with policy objectives of his own, as my number two at Treasury.

In the end, with the help of good words from several friendly Republican senators and congressmen—Howard Baker, Bob Dole, Bob Michel, Barber Conable, and especially Representative Jack Kemp of New York—and the benefit of a frank confirmation hearing, I managed to overcome the suspicion of party irregularity and was confirmed by the Senate by a vote of 98−0 on January 21, the day after Ronald Reagan was inaugurated. I was pleased by this result and encouraged by the cordiality, intelligence, and cooperative spirit I had encountered on the Hill.

Inauguration Day itself had been a series of anticlimaxes.

Members of the Cabinet were seated far from the podium, behind the Supreme Court justices, senators and congressmen, and a very large contingent of the Reagans' friends. January 20 fell on a Tuesday in 1981. It was a cold day, the view was poor, and the President's words were distorted by loudspeakers and carried away by the wind. Afterward we all attended the traditional luncheon in the Capitol. Then we were loaded into unmarked limousines and transported down Pennsylvania Avenue at forty-five miles an hour. Seen through the tinted windows of the car, the crowd was a blur. If the mother of any member of the Cabinet was among the onlookers, she certainly was not able to recognize her distinguished child as he sped by in his government Cadillac. At the end of this ride we were deposited in the reviewing stand in front of the White House. There we all sat for about an hour, until the President's motorcade arrived. Then we were shown into the White House.

Because the Secretary of Labor-designate, Ray Donovan, had not yet been confirmed by the Senate, the Cabinet could not be sworn in as a group on Inauguration Day. Two days after the Inauguration we were ushered one by one into the Green Room, where a man to whom I was casually introduced administered the oath of office. (I later learned that he was Bob Linder, a White House administrative aide.) Strobe lights flashed, preserving the moment, while I repeated the solemn words of the oath with Ann at my side and my father and mother and the rest of my family in my thoughts.

As soon as the ceremony ended, Ann and I and our family were guided to the Blue Room to have another photograph taken with the President. All the other new Cabinet members also passed through this same handshake, smile, and flash. It was the first time I had seen Ronald Reagan in the flesh since I walked him to the elevator after his cocktail party in New York. He complimented me on my family's good looks, and we bantered about the Reagans and the Regans again. After his long campaign and the tiring round of Inaugural events, the President looked very fit and ruddy, and up close gave the impression of being far younger than his age: he would be seventy on February 6. I must have commented on this, because he told a story about his early days in Hollywood, and how he had convinced his studio that he had no need to wear makeup before the cameras because of his high natural Irish coloring. We mingled with the other Cabinet families and I have a kaleidoscopic memory of being introduced to a great many California friends of the Reagans.

Ann and I had been furnished with a schedule of Inaugural events—balls, luncheons, receptions—that we were expected to attend or host. We knew very few of the guests at the functions at which we served as hosts for the President. I thought these were strange doings but ascribed them to what many were calling the "laid-back California style." Most of these functions were very pleasant. The party faithful attending them were delighted to be present at a Republican triumph, and the atmosphere of affection and warm good humor that invariably surrounds Ronald Reagan was palpable. His supporters were glad for the great victory that few had been willing to predict even on the eve of the election. After greeting the guests at one of these parties, the President and the First Lady danced together all alone until Ronald Reagan gestured for Ann and me to join them. Ann dislikes being the center of attention in public and is wary of dancing anyway because of her arthritis, but I led her onto the floor, where the Reagans and the Regans spryly danced to the strains of old favorites. It was a moment of high good feeling.

On January 21, a Wednesday, I reported for duty. My first days at Treasury were not uneventful. The forty-four American hostages who had been held by the Iranians for the last 444 days of the Carter Administration had been released during the Inaugural luncheon. As part of the diplomatic deal, the United States had agreed to unfreeze certain Iranian assets that had been seized by our government. The Treasury was charged with the job of untangling the resulting puzzles of credit, debt, and ownership, and disbursing the funds. This process generated lively meetings and many opportunities to adjudicate disputes involving large sums of money.

The Treasury literally had no money to spare—and the Carter Administration's policy of administering financial first aid to failed corporations was one of the reasons why. A huge cash outlay of $2.1 billion to the Penn Central Railroad, added to the mushrooming cost of federal entitlement programs and other schemes tied to the inflation rate, then officially set at 13 percent, had eaten up the government's cash cushion.

Early in 1981, Treasury gave formal approval to a $400-million loan guarantee, the last of a series, for the Chrysler Corporation that had been promised earlier in January by the outgoing Carter Administration. In May, Lee Iacocca, the chairman of Chrysler, asked that his company be allowed to retain a Gulfstream II aircraft that it had promised to get rid of as part of an austerity program imposed by the Carter Administration; he said that flying by commercial jet or renting small planes to visit remote plant sites was wasteful of his time and that of his executives. Lee also asked that Treasury reduce the guarantee fee it was charging Chrysler from 1 percent to ½ percent; this would have meant a loss of $2 million to the taxpayers.

I said no to both requests, telling Iacocca that the Reagan Administration expected Chrysler to honor its deal with the American people. I had never believed that corporate jets were a necessity—as chairman of Merrill Lynch I had usually flown on regular commercial flights and had never suffered undue inconvenience. The firm did not acquire a corporate jet until after I left.

"Those planes are just for show, Lee, and you know it," I said.

A colorful discussion ensued. Iacocca did not modify his demands. I did not change my mind.

As he rose to leave, Iacocca said, "Regan, you're a nasty son of a bitch."

I replied that he was mistaken—I wasn't nasty.

(A couple of years later, after Chrysler had recovered its corporate health and was paying back the balance of the $900 million in loans that the government had guaranteed on its behalf, Iacocca made another attempt to get his way. As part of the deal with Chrysler, the U.S. government had been granted warrants to buy 14.4 million shares of Chrysler stock while the price was low—though higher than the market price at the time. As Chrysler prospered, partly as a result of the infusion of capital underwritten by the taxpayers, Iacocca took the position that this was "too much reward" for Treasury and asked that the government give Chrysler back the warrants. This would have meant a loss of $311 million to the American people. Again I said no. I could hear every word of protest and reproach that Iacocca uttered, though I held the telephone a foot away from my ear. In 1982, Iacocca had tried to buy back the Chrysler warrants at two dollars each. Treasury finally sold the warrants in 1983 for $311 million.)

Between the election and Inauguration, the lame duck Ninety-fifth Congress had raised the federal debt ceiling to $930 billion. Congress, controlled by Democrats in both houses, knew that the debt would go through the authorized ceiling by February or March 1981 and the new Republican Administration would have to ask for an increase in the ceiling in its early days in office. In mid-January G. William Miller, the outgoing Secretary of the Treasury, told me that the federal government might run out of money by February 15—three weeks after Inauguration Day.

My first action on January 21 was to order a survey of the cash situation. I was told that the government might have enough money to operate through February 18, but not beyond. Congress traditionally adjourns for Lincoln's Birthday, and would be out of session this year from February 6 to February 16. This meant that Congress would have to act before it adjourned eleven working days hence. As part of the discovery of facts in this situation I learned that the Secretary of the Treasury is responsible by law if any money is spent in excess of the debt ceiling. This may seem to the reader to be an amusing quirk in the law; that was not the way I looked at it as Secretary of the Treasury.

The Democrats may have lost the election, but they preserved their political canniness. They had hoped that the Republican Administration, after lambasting the size of the national debt during the campaign, would have to ask that the debt ceiling be raised to a trillion dollars. Some in the Administration recommended that we do this, arguing that it would break the psychological barrier and make it easier to obtain later increases in the ceiling. I told them I'd be damned if I'd hang somebody else's trillion-dollar albatross around the President's neck in his first few weeks in office. Psychological barriers were not the question. The question was, How much do we need? The experts at Treasury estimated that a ceiling of $980 billion would carry us through fiscal year 1981, which ended on September 30. We settled for $985 billion.

Everyone knew that the alternative to raising the ceiling was acute embarrassment for the President, who would be unable to pay the government's bills. Government operations would cease. Social Security checks would bounce, the armed forces and the civil service would go unpaid; the whole scenario would create a picture of impotence. Nevertheless it was no easy matter to persuade conservative Republicans, who had always refused as a matter of principle (and political point-making) to vote for increases in the debt ceiling, to do so as a matter of solidarity with a conservative President. Speaker O'Neill and Senator Robert Byrd of West Virginia, the Democratic leader of the Senate, played straight politics with the issue, withholding any support from the Democratic side of the aisle until every obtainable Republican vote was committed.

In two weeks of frantic behind-the-scenes activity, we prevailed. We had valiant support on the Hill from the Republican leadership, headed by Howard Baker in the Senate and Bob Michel in the House. The President performed like a champion, inviting delegations from the Hill into the Oval Office for sessions in which he twisted arms, traded horses, and—a key element—sympathized with transparent sincerity with conservatives who had to vote against their instincts in order to vote with their party and their President.

Despite predictions that I'd never be able to play the political game, and despite some doubts of my own on this score, I enjoyed the whole experience tremendously. Senators and congressmen are engaging people, with whom it is fun to bargain and match wits and lay up debits and credits against the political future. The Treasury's liaison with Congress, Assistant Secretary

Dennis Thomas, was invaluable as the department's point man and my teacher and adviser on the arcane lore and ceremonies of Capitol Hill. Ann McLaughlin, afterward Secretary of Labor, tutored me in the mysterious ways of the Washington press corps, but even her expert advice could not prepare me for what awaited me at the White House.

I was not invited to the White House ceremony at which the President signed this first important bill of his Administration. That particular anticlimax stung a little, but it was a passing detail in a panorama of much more important problems. The economy was in shambles—growing unemployment (7.5 percent), high rates of interest that stifled growth (20 percent), and the worst inflation since 1947 (13 percent). An erratic monetary policy had sent the prime interest rate skyrocketing and had debauched the purchasing power of the dollar. Confidence and national pride were very low. Jimmy Carter himself had described the national mood as "malaise."

It had been maddening to watch the country slide downhill. I had come to Washington in the expectation of being part of a team that would seize these problems, analyze them, and solve them. Though I am not given to daydreams, I had envisaged a meeting in the Oval Office in which the President laid out the problem, listened to ideas, assigned responsibilities, and told us all to get cracking. Instead, in the transition period, Ed Meese had asked me to serve as cochairman of a committee in which others were doing all the talking—and, in my opinion, talking about the wrong subjects.

The other cochairman of the President's Economic Policy Coordinating Committee was David Stockman, the Director of the Office of Management and Budget (OMB). Stockman was young, bespectacled, articulate, and opinionated to the point of zealotry. A two-term congressman from Michigan, he brought along a staff who shared his opinions and his ambition to make OMB the center of economic policy and action in the Reagan Administration. During the transition period, when we first met, Stockman was still a member of Congress, having been reelected in November. His staff was still on the government payroll, and in gathering information still had access to many resources of the Congress.

The President's Economic Policy Coordinating Committee met almost every day from January 2 until February 18—weekdays, weekends, and holidays. The objective was to deliver an economic policy statement to the Congress. Stockman provided the working papers, distributing these documents at the beginning of each meeting and then talking about them until the meeting was nearly over so that there seldom was time to ask questions. Because the papers were never distributed in advance, and because it was very difficult to interrupt the stream of Washington jargon that issued from the glib, quick-minded, chain-smoking, impatient Stockman, very few ideas except Stockman's were ever expressed. Everyone was singing from his sheet of music. This seemed to suit the White House staff. Stockman had the trust and confidence of Meese, who had become the Counselor to the President, and of James Baker III, the Chief of Staff. Stockman understood the budget; they didn't. As a result, they tended to give him his head.

Stockman and his people, working in phalanx, overwhelmed the rest of the members with statistics, rapid-fire argument, and a brassy confidence in their own expertise that would have gotten them fired for an excess of zeal from any group except the government or graduate school. Few others, as I have noted, were seeing the President on a regular basis. Reagan didn't understand the budget, either, and his aides were bringing Stockman in to explain it to him. This permitted Stockman to quote the President or refer to the President's wishes. The Cabinet officer who protested against cuts in one of his programs, no matter how logical or humanitarian his case, found himself looking like a selfish protector of turf who cared nothing about the reform of the federal spending program.

By Inauguration Day, Stockman was already regarded by the press as a *Wunderkind*. In private as in public he was the most visible, and certainly the most audible, figure in the Administration after the President. His missionary fervor, and that of his aides, may be explained in part by the fact that they were all

congressional types who, after years of frustration and exasperation, had been given the opportunity to impose congressional
ideas about the nature of the budget, the economy, and the political realities that flowed therefrom upon the Executive Branch.
Because no one else had yet hired, much less indoctrinated, a
staff, the committee's discussions were devoted almost entirely to
the budget—what to slash, whom to outwit and outmaneuver,
how to stimulate activity in the private sector by manipulating
government spending. Blizzards of statistics, few of them precise
and fewer still germane to the general economic situation, blocked
all alternative routes of discussion.

Stockman was possessed of one simple idea. He believed that
the federal budget should run the economy and thereby shape
social policy. This was a philosophical position designed to be
executed by bureaucratic means. His plan of action was corre-
spondingly simple: by controlling the flow of money into the
Cabinet departments, the Director of the Office of Management
and Budget would starve certain programs (for instance, welfare)
and feed others that were more productive in economic terms. If
spending were cut in the right places, inflation and interest rates
would fall, employment would rise, and prosperity would follow.

It seemed to me that this was a profoundly negative approach
to reform and that we would have a problem on our hands if
these ideas became the basis of national economic policy. Stockman had things backward. What the country needed—and what
Reagan had promised it—was not more centralization, but less.
Surely, I said to the group, we wanted to discuss the economy
first, adopt a policy to avert recession and institute growth, and
then decide what the budget would be on the basis of economic
factors. I remarked that the thing they called the federal budget
was not a budget at all, but merely a plan for spending.

Stockman concerned himself with only one aspect of economic policy—fiscal policy. What about the other rein on the
horse, monetary policy? I suggested that we ought not to be talking about spending in isolation from management of the process.
Nor should we be speaking in visionary terms about deep cuts in
spending. As a practical matter, though waste should and could

be reduced, federal spending would continue to increase. The key to the situation was to hold the increase within bounds, controlling it in such a way that it grew at a slower rate than revenues. The increase in revenues should be financed not by new and higher taxes, but by *lower* tax rates that would produce more money for the government by stimulating higher earnings by corporations and workers in an atmosphere of ready capital. Among the alternatives was a huge budget deficit that would have the government financing its debt by sucking up funds from the money supply that the private sector needed to pay for plant and research in order to create jobs.

How could we have a rational spending policy if we did not yet know what our policy for raising revenue was going to be? Why should the federal government not have a capital budget, like every business and every family in America, in which its possessions are calculated as a part of its wealth and its debts are amortized over a period of time? Few people pay cash for a house in which they intend to live for thirty years. Why should the government pay cash for an aircraft carrier that would be operational for the same period of time?

This was heresy. Stockman and his followers looked down the table at me in condescension and disbelief. They suggested that I had not been in Washington long enough to understand the realities. The budget was the only game in town. In that belief, they were correct. But on my last day in public office as on the first, I was still insisting that this was a malady to be cured, not a benefice to be thankful for.

The fatal flaw in Stockman's approach was a practical, not a theoretical, one. The budget is not controlled by the Executive Branch but by the Congress. What goes up the Hill in the form of the President's budget has little meaning. What comes down the Hill represents the fiscal reality of the U.S. government, and it is invariably a command to spend according to the whim and the myriad political debts of Congress. It may be that I was too new in town in January 1981 to articulate this obvious point. But I am surprised that Stockman, who had been through four budget processes as a congressman, did not understand it.

There was something else the matter with Stockman's approach: He was promoting much of his own policy and following his own agenda, which was not necessarily that of the President. It was Ronald Reagan, not David Stockman or anyone else, whom the voters had elected. In my rusticity I thought that this egoism was arrogant and antidemocratic and likely to undermine the authenticity of Reagan's Presidency. Although my records do not show that I ever made this point before the entire group, it would have been out of character for me to hold my peace on such a resonant question.

By and large, Stockman and his loyalists ignored me after I began to oppose their ideas. It would be more accurate to say that they brushed me off. This introduced a human factor as well as a philosophical one into the situation. It had been a very long time since I had been treated like the new kid in town, and I will readily admit that I did not like it. While these events were still in progress I wrote the following words in my spiral notebook:

> Left in the backwash [unable] to do anything except try
> to learn the ropes, assemble staff, and try not to be left
> too far behind. . . . I realized why it was happening, but
> I couldn't console myself because up to this point I was
> the guy who . . . had all the answers, made things hap-
> pen. Now I was a passenger on someone else's boat, though
> I had the title of captain.

If it were possible to draw up a psychological geography of those bewildering early days in Washington, then the confrontations in the President's Economic Policy Coordinating Committee would represent the point on the map at which I started looking for a separate path out of the woods.

I decided not to let the meetings end when they officially adjourned. I took Stockman's papers home and gave them to my staff for analysis. Gradually I began to have a better understanding of what Stockman was trying to do. I instructed my staff to discover the precise agenda of meetings before they took place so that I could arrive at the conference table armed with questions, arguments, and above all, alternatives. Stockman was angered by this process, but I persisted in it because I did not think that the President would be well served by a Secretary of the Treasury who failed to make all his experience, knowledge, and judgment available to him.

No human being likes to admit that he is in the dark on important questions. This tendency is stronger in Washington, where knowledgeability is power, than in any other place I have ever worked. A circle of high government personages, on hearing an unfamiliar term or a new idea, will generally nod sagaciously as if this subject is something they'd been discussing since they climbed out of the cradle. Nobody wants to ask a dumb question ("What exactly is a Laffer curve?") in the presence of a dozen people who bear resounding titles, even though most of the dozen don't know the answer either. This is especially true where the wishes, policies, and casual remarks of a President are concerned. Few will openly concede that they are not in the confidence of the Chief Executive, that they do not know his mind or support his goals.

My basic position was simple. Ronald Reagan had been elected by the American people to carry out the ideas and programs he had discussed in his campaign. My job was to identify these promises and do my best to translate them into policy and programs. Resorting to an old habit, I went in search of the basic data. If the President would not come to Treasury, then Treasury would go to the President. I called for all of Reagan's speeches and interviews in which he referred to economic matters. I read the economic portions of the Republican platform with great care. I reviewed the economic theories on which the President's remarks were said to have been based and discussed them with my staff. Reviewing my notes at the end of this process, I saw that there was a remarkable consistency in the President's public utterances.

It was clear, first of all, that he was influenced by the economic theories of Professor Milton Friedman, the Nobel laureate from the University of Chicago. Friedman is a strong believer in monetarism, which holds that the level of economic activity is most directly affected by the money supply, or, in institutional terms, by the Federal Reserve. Friedman also believes—in my view, correctly—that erratic monetary policy by the Federal Reserve is perhaps the greatest threat to economic stability and growth. Friedman is a true believer in free markets, that is, markets free of government regulation and interference. Ronald Reagan sympathized with these ideas.

The President was, moreover, a believer in the supply-side theory of economics, a system of ideas derived from many sources, including Adam Smith. The theory holds that the economy will be stimulated to grow by incentives that increase the supply of goods through encouraging business to produce and the individual to save more money. The theoretical results of a policy based on this idea, provided that government spending is held down, would include a reduction in inflation and an increase in the creation of capital which would expand government revenues without the necessity of increasing taxes. A certain tension, but no essential conflict, exists between the more passionate advocates of Friedman's monetarism and those who embrace supply-side economics.*

The mixture of the two, with some other elements added in, was what the press called "Reaganomics." In a famous phrase, George Bush, when he was opposing Reagan in the 1980 Republican primaries, had termed this philosophy "voodoo economics." The Democrats, who had based their policy on stimulating increases in demand and creating employment through government programs as prescribed by the economic theories of John Maynard Keynes, were aghast. They may not have understood supply-side economics (few at that time did), but they did understand that Ronald Reagan was proposing to revolve the economic turntable of the nation by 180 degrees.

The President, as an extension of his ideas, was also in sympathy with two organic pieces of legislation. The first of these

*Based on the theories of Professor Robert Mundell of Columbia University as popularized by his more famous disciple, Arthur Laffer of the University of Southern California. Interestingly, neither Mundell nor Laffer nor any of the other well-known proponents of the theory joined the Administration.

was the Kemp-Roth Bill, introduced by Representative Jack Kemp and Senator William V. Roth, Jr., Republican of Delaware. This bill, drafted by a team of supply-siders that included professional economists and congressional staffers, called for a 30-percent tax cut for all taxpayers in three increments of 10 percent each over three consecutive years. The second was a proposal calling for the rapid depreciation, for tax purposes, of plant and equipment as a means of modernizing American industry and making it more efficient.

If these were the things the President wanted, I was ready to help him get them. I ordered my priorities, and chose my staff at Treasury, with the idea of carrying out the President's campaign promises. At the time, it was suggested in the press that conservative appointees had been foisted on me by the White House and the right wing of the party. This is the opposite of the truth. As the reader has seen, it was hardly the President's style to insist on any appointee. None of his top aides—Jim Baker, Ed Meese, Mike Deaver—ever suggested by word or gesture that I should favor one candidate over another. Neither did any member of the transition team or anyone else. In the Lehrman case, strong arguments were made for his appointment, but no one tried to overturn my decision once it was made.

Many excellent candidates were suggested by Pen James, whose job it was to recommend candidates, and some were suggested by the White House staff, whose collective wish likewise seemed to consist of sending me the best people available. Nearly all were qualified, but the choices were mine. I hired the people I wanted on the basis of their qualifications and what I believed to be their will to carry out the President's program without trying to insinuate their own ideas and objectives into the process.

With the salaries the government pays its top people, there is little incentive to accept a Presidential appointment beyond patriotism and a desire to contribute to history—and to share in the power and the glory. As Secretary of the Treasury I earned less in a year than I had earned in a month as chairman of Merrill Lynch, but I had already put my children through college and maximized my savings and investments. The sacrifice made by a younger person who leaves a good job in the private sector to accept a post as under secretary ($55,000 in 1981) or assistant secretary ($52,000) is much more likely to be keenly felt when tuition bills and mortgage payments come rolling in. Most Americans, of course, do not regard a salary of over $50,000 a year as poverty, and I suppose that there is some truth in the argument that underpaying public servants helps to keep them in touch with the ordinary problems of life. Ironically, office secretaries on the federal payroll earned about half again as much as those who worked at Merrill Lynch.

Nevertheless, good people came forward. As Deputy Secretary I chose R. Timothy McNamar, a no-nonsense businessman from California who had been executive vice president of Beneficial Standard, an insurance company based in Los Angeles. He held an M.B.A. from the Tuck School of Business at Dartmouth and a law degree from Michigan. At age forty-two, Tim ran the 26 miles 385 yards of the marathon in an average of under three hours. Endurance and speed were important qualifications in the man who would be responsible for the administration of a federal department employing twenty-five thousand men and women. In 1981, Treasury, the billpayer of the federal government, was disbursing an average of almost $3 billion in public funds every business day.

Two under secretaries handled the major policy issues—Monetary Affairs and Economic and Tax Policy. These two posts, and the two assistant secretaryships that supported each, required appointees who had the ability, the experience, and the fortitude to carry out the reforms that Ronald Reagan had discussed.

For the Economic and Tax Policy post we found the man we wanted in Norman Ture, a highly respected economist and expert on taxes who held a doctorate from the University of Chicago. Norman was a supply-sider, one of the few prominent adherents to that philosophy to find his way into the Administration. Even the Keynesians respected his formidable intellectual gifts.

For Monetary Affairs I wanted a monetarist who had the experience, the intellectual weight, and the conviction to hold his own with the experts of the Federal Reserve. He must share the supply-side belief in the slow, steady, certain growth of the money supply and be able to represent this view forcefully at the Fed. I found this combination of brilliance, personality, and philosophy in Beryl Sprinkel, a disciple of Milton Friedman's who was chief economist and executive vice president of the Harris Trust Co. of Chicago.

There was plenty more brainpower and intestinal fortitude down the line, and when the staff was finally complete I felt that Treasury would be able to hold its own philosophically and on the battlements with any other entity in the Administration.

My job was to establish an atmosphere of frank give-and-take with the President that would permit him to know about and approve the policies and actions Treasury proposed to undertake. I would have preferred to speak my mind in private, but as I have said, I never saw the President in private. Therefore I had to make my points in the presence of the sizable group that crowded into the Oval Office or any other room in which the President happened to be receiving one of his advisers. It was difficult in these circumstances to break through the soporific language and formal manners that are habitual in the presence of a President. Early in the Administration, however, I managed to break through to Ronald Reagan, the man, on a matter that touched his ready sympathy for individual Americans and their problems.

As Treasurer of the United States I had chosen a remarkable young woman, Angela Buchanan—called "Bay" because one of her older brothers had been unable to pronounce the word *baby*. Bay had done a fine job as treasurer of the Reagan campaign. Instead of letting her talent vegetate in what had been a largely ceremonial post, I gave her responsibility for the manufacture of all U.S. coins and currency by placing the Mint and the Bureau of Engraving and Printing under her management.

The Treasurer was also responsible for selling Series E savings bonds, and this was the issue I raised with the President. The ancestors of Series E were the Liberty Bonds and Victory

Bonds of the two world wars, and patriotism had always been an important motivation for people who bought them. At a time when six-month certificates of deposit were yielding 18 percent annually, these U.S. government bonds paid interest of 5 percent on a capital sum invested for twenty-five years. The inequity of the situation exasperated me and I put the bonds on the agenda for discussion with the President.

"Mr. President," I said, "I don't know how you expect me to sell these goddamn things when I know in my heart that the buyer is getting ripped off. The government doesn't put out a prospectus on Series E bonds, but if it did, we'd all deserve to go to jail. Five percent with a thirteen-percent rate of inflation? It's a fraud and we're perpetrating it on the very people who trust us most and know the least about money."

Suddenly the President was fully alert.

I can't believe what I'm hearing, he said. We can't do that to people. I take it you want to change the situation?

"I certainly do."

Then go to it, the President said.

Eventually with the very able assistance of James Robinson, the enterprising head of American Express, as chairman of the Savings Bond campaign, we introduced a new issue of savings bonds that yielded as much as 8 percent. By then the rate of inflation was down to 4 percent and I had no trouble recommending the bonds as a good investment for anyone.

That was the first hammer-and-nails discussion I had with the President. It was far from being the last.

· 9 ·

The Attempt on the President's Life

On Monday, March 30, 1981, as President Reagan was getting into his car after delivering a speech at the Washington Hilton Hotel, a young man armed with a .22-caliber revolver fired several shots in an attempt to assassinate him. One bullet struck the President in the chest. Another inflicted a head wound on his press secretary, James S. Brady, and Timothy J. McCarthy, a Secret Service agent, was shot in the abdomen when he placed his body between the President and his assailant. A Washington police officer, Thomas K. Delahanty, was also wounded.

Four days later, working with a ballpoint pen and a spiral notebook in the study of my home near Mount Vernon, I wrote down my recollections of those shocking events and of the hours that followed in the Situation Room of the White House. At the time I was fatigued by the stress of work and emotion and took no particular care to write a polished narrative. My intention was to record all the details I could remember while they were still vivid in my mind. When I reread these rough notes more than six years later, I decided to reproduce them in their original form, except for a few changes designed to clarify meaning and eliminate redundancies and irrelevant material. Nothing that bears directly on the situation has been omitted.

About 2:27 P.M. Secret Service agent George Adams hurried into my office at Treasury. Speaking in a whisper, he told me that shots had been fired at the President outside the Washington Hilton. Adams urged me to go to the White House at once.

Accompanied by Adams, I left immediately, and in the car kept asking for more information as Adams monitored a Secret Service radio channel. Adams told me that the President was being taken to George Washington Hospital. There were other wounded. I asked if the Secret Service knew who did the shooting. Adams had no information about that as yet.

I arrived at the White House at 2:31 and told my driver to stand by. On the way inside, Adams told me for the first time that the President had been wounded. I immediately went to Jim Baker's office. Most of the senior staff of the White House were gathered in Baker's office. Both Baker and Ed Meese were on the telephone to Mike Deaver, who was with the Presidential party at the hospital.

I told some Secret Service agents who were standing outside Baker's office to keep me posted on any developments, and also told the agents accompanying me to make sure that I got prompt information.

Except for Ed Meese, I was the first Cabinet officer on the scene, but made no attempt to assume authority. After some hectic moments Al Haig [Alexander M. Haig, Jr., the Secretary of State] came in. In a very short conference, Baker and Meese decided to go to the hospital. I volunteered to get them a car and Secret Service clearance. Agent Rick Riley, the head of the Secretary of the Treasury's Secret Service detail, had joined Adams outside Baker's office. He got my driver and car and provided a very fast trip to the hospital for Baker and Meese.

Dick Allen [Richard V. Allen, the National Security Advisor] suggested that we go to the Situation Room. Haig agreed, so down we went. The staff followed. No formal orders or procedures were established. Questions were raised regarding executive authority, the "football" [the briefcase containing secret codes for the President's use in case of nuclear attack], and the Vice President's whereabouts. Haig put in a call to the Vice President.

At this point most questions and statements were being directed to Haig, who was number one in Cabinet rank in the room.

There were probably fifteen or twenty people in the Situation Room, which is not very large. People had arrived there quickly. Cap Weinberger [Caspar W. Weinberger, the Secretary of Defense] came in, followed by Bill Smith [William French Smith, the Attorney General], and Bill Casey. An early arrival was Drew Lewis [the Secretary of Transportation], who immediately sat at the table—where there are only about ten chairs. For most of the time I was seated between Allen and Smith, across from Haig or Weinberger. Admiral Daniel J. Murphy [the Vice President's Chief of Staff] sat in, representing the Vice President.

I ordered my two Secret Service agents to set up a line to Secret Service Intelligence to keep me posted. They gave me the first information the Situation Room got on the assailant. They correctly identified him as John W. Hinckley, Jr., a resident of Colorado, and said that he carried two ID cards, one from Texas Tech University in Lubbock and another from an institution in Denver. He also had cards from two psychiatrists, one in Texas and the other in Colorado. The Secret Service had found no criminal record for this individual, nor was he in their file of possible suspects. I ordered the Secret Service to keep probing to see if there was a conspiracy.

Haig, [David R.] Gergen [the White House Communications Director], and others tried to keep a line open to the hospital. This proved to be difficult. From time to time, however, we did get reports of the President's condition. As far as I know, none of us at any time thought that the wound was fatal, although we were all concerned about the President's ability to recuperate quickly.

A lot of our information, particularly as it related to the shooting, came from the TV set in the Situation Room. It was tuned to ABC—Frank Reynolds most of the time—although later in the day we were told that the coverage from CBS was better.

Dick Allen, who was very calm, proved to be a master at keeping the record. He had a small tape recorder in front of him to catch words, and a legal pad on which he recorded actions, always with a time reference. A secretary sat behind him.

[White House Counsel Fred] Fielding, Allen, Smith, and several staffers set about determining and interpreting the line of Presidential succession, and so forth. No one stood up to announce these findings, and I was not sure they had found a satisfactory answer. I had my own duties to attend to and was frequently in and out of the room to talk to the Secret Service agents.

The Secret Service gave me the first information on the weapon used by Hinckley. It was a German-made, Florida-assembled .22 pistol—very cheap, a Saturday night special. It had been sold to Hinckley by a Dallas pawnshop. The bullets were long-nose .22s, designed for a .22 rifle and very lethal when used in a revolver. I was told that the President's wound was probably from a ricochet.

During the earlier moments, when the room was full of hustle and bustle, reports on the President's condition were fragmentary. We were getting some word from the hospital, some from Baker, and some from the TV. Everyone was confused. Weinberger reported he had stepped up the alert status of the strategic forces. I'm not sure of the official designation, but it sounded as though he had gone from a normal state of alert to one where he had the crews leave their ready rooms and man their planes. Haig was quick to question this, asking very sharp and demanding questions. Weinberger remained calm but, judging by his tone of voice, was very annoyed at Haig's questioning his actions.

White House press types were saying that we were besieged by reporters asking about the President's health. We decided that all medical bulletins would come from the hospital. Dave Gergen tried to answer press questions. He did a good job. Then a short while later we saw on TV a White House press spokesman—Speakes, I believe. [He was being asked who was in charge of the government; his answers were hesitant.] We were amazed. There were cries of "Get that guy off!" and "Why is he saying that?" and "Who authorized that?"

Haig was livid. He jumped up and left the room. Dick Allen slipped out of another door. A few moments later the rest of us saw Haig, with Allen at his side, on TV from the White House press room, saying he was in charge, and so forth.*

I said to Weinberger, "What's this all about? Is he mad?" Weinberger said, "I can't believe this. He's wrong; he doesn't have any such authority." No one else commented except Casey, who said, "He's all wrong—this is unbelievable." Gergen looked shocked. He asked me how it had happened. I said I couldn't account for it; I guess Al took it on himself.

We had by then established contact with the Vice President [who was airborne on *Air Force Two*.] Bush said he'd be back about 6:30. Haig talked to him; so did I. Murphy sent him coded messages when we found that we were not on a secure line when talking to *Air Force Two*.

When Haig returned to the Situation Room he and Weinberger again began a discussion of the state of readiness of our forces. Weinberger chided Haig for what he called his misstatements on TV as to who was in charge. Haig told him to check his Constitution. Cap replied that he knew that in the absence of the President *he* was in command from a military point of view.

The rest of us said nothing, either from embarrassment or, in my case, from ignorance. We Cabinet members had never been instructed on the chain of command under various circumstances, and as we had not been brought into NSC meetings, we knew nothing of battle plans, and so on.

An unfortunate message came to me from the Secret Service, and it caused confusion and consternation. At the end of a message describing the President's condition, someone had added the words "Brady died." I announced this sad news to a stunned group. Allen asked for a moment of silent prayer. Apparently someone relayed this information to the group at the hospital and we got word back that it was not true.

The Secret Service agents said that they had picked up the news from an FBI agent in the outer office as they were on the

---

*Folklore and my own memory notwithstanding, Haig never said that he was "in charge." His actual words were, "As of now I am in control here, in the White House, pending return of the Vice President and in close touch with him. If something came up, I would check with him, of course."

way in to me with the other message. I ordered them to check and double-check. Meanwhile TV broke the same erroneous story—only to have to retract it later.

Time passed quickly and at 6 P.M. or thereabouts word came that the Vice President would not come directly to the White House by helicopter but would go from Andrews Air Force Base to his residence and then motor down to the White House. This was designed to avoid any appearance of haste or emergency. Jim Baker arrived. We waited for the Vice President. I asked Cap if he had heard anything new. He said no, but he would get up to speed with a new report just before the Vice President arrived.

Meanwhile, at Treasury, emergency measures had been put into effect. Under Secretary for Monetary Affairs Beryl Sprinkel contacted the Fed[eral Reserve Board]. He decided to request limited support of the dollar, which was falling against the deutschemark. With stabilization from the Fed it bottomed at 2.06. This drop of five points cost Treasury about $70 million in swaps— that is, buying dollars and selling deutschemarks.

The Vice President arrived with Ed Meese, who had met him when he landed to fill him in on the details. George asked for a condition report: 1) on the President; 2) on the other wounded; 3) on the assailant; 4) on the international scene. Questions were raised, on the Vice President's orders, as to who among the thirty or so present in the Situation Room had "codeword" clearance. It was determined that all Cabinet members had such clearance. Besides Haig, Weinberger, Casey, Smith, Lewis, and me, two other Cabinet officers were present—Jack Block [John R. Block, the Secretary of Agriculture] and Mac Baldrige [Malcolm Baldrige, the Secretary of Commerce].

After the reports were given and it was determined that there were no international complications and no domestic conspiracy, it was decided that the U.S. government would carry on business as usual. The Vice President would go on TV from the White House to reassure the nation and to demonstrate that he was in charge. The Russians were making no new moves, so it was decided not to talk to them, but only to indicate through the embassy that this was a tragic incident perpetrated by a single individual.

I was scheduled to appear on "Good Morning America," the ABC television show, the following morning. I checked with the Vice President and Jim Baker, and it was decided that it would be a good idea for me to appear in order to show that all was calm. If the financial markets needed soothing, I could do that.

At Treasury, my staff was gathered to hear what had happened and what was to be done the next day. I left Treasury at about 10 P.M. to go to my daughter's house, where my wife had been waiting for me since hearing the news.

The reader will have realized that the men at the heart of the government did not possess much more information than the ordinary citizen about a situation that involved the life of the President and might have involved the safety of the nation. Even less did the men gathered in the Situation Room know what action they were authorized to take or expected to take. Together, they represented a considerable depository of experience, ability, even wisdom. But the Administration had been in place for only seventy days. These men were new to their jobs and new to each other. They performed remarkably well under the circumstances, but in the absence of a framework of authority and procedure, they could do little besides react to events about which they had only limited information.

Some of that information was flawed. After the fact, we understood that the threat to the President's survival had been far graver than we realized—a fact that was obscured by the urgency of the surgical measures that were being taken to save his life and, ironically, by the President's astounding gallantry. He made jokes to reassure the nation after receiving a wound that would have extinguished the altruistic spirit of a lesser man. The bullet fired by Hinckley lodged less than an inch from the President's heart, and it was not an ordinary lead bullet as we believed at the time, but an explosive round that somehow failed to detonate.

Confusion over facts must be expected in connection with an act of random violence. But the absence of system, the ignorance of precedent, the boyish squabbling over procedure and precedence was astonishing to me. Whatever else may have been said about Al Haig's unscheduled television appearance, his instincts were correct: somebody should have been in charge while the President was under anesthesia and the Vice President was flying toward Washington in an airplane. There should have been no question about that person's identity or his powers. I kept wondering at what point some alert staffer would remember that a doomsday book, in which guidelines and contingencies had been outlined, was locked up in a safe in somebody's office and would trot upstairs to fetch it. No such guide to policy, law, and behavior in a time of extreme danger to the state was ever produced; as far as I know, none existed.

Fortunately, no desperate emergency arose. The President recovered from his wound stronger than ever in his leadership and in the affection in which the American people held him. No more sobering episode can be imagined than an attempt on the life of a President. It teaches many lessons, and the most important ones it taught me were that the Administration only existed in the person of Ronald Reagan and the grandeur of the office the people had bestowed on him—and that I owed him every ounce of energy and knowledge I possessed in what promised to be a difficult struggle to organize his ideas into a systematic program.

· 10 ·

A Secretary's Taxes:
A Parable

By the end of the Administration's first year in office the early hopes of David Stockman—that economic and social revolution could be achieved through radical cuts in federal spending—had run aground. The Cabinet departments and other agencies had resisted the Office of Management and Budget's efforts to manage their programs and dictate their priorities by manipulating their budgets, and in so doing had found effective allies on Capitol Hill. Congress had continued largely to ignore the budgets sent to it by the Executive Branch and to appropriate funds at a faster rate than taxes were being collected. This created huge budget deficits ($128 billion for fiscal year 1982) and the specter of even larger ones in the future. At the same time, the governors of the Federal Reserve System, headed by Paul A. Volcker, had instituted a policy of tight money that produced high interest rates designed to cure the runaway inflation created by the fiscal and monetary looseness of the Carter years.

This bizarre combination of fiscal stimulus and monetary restraint had created one of the most serious recessions of modern times. Although it was apparent as early as June 1981 that a long-term economic decline was in the making, there was no agreement within the Administration on how to bring it to an end. The Administration's power to do so was limited. Congress had not, and almost certainly would not, reduce the rate of spending. Volcker, possessed of an almost messianic desire to drive inflation out of the economy, pursued restrictive policies that created large, unpredictable swings in the money supply. Thus Congress was stomping on the accelerator of the economy while Volcker was simultaneously slamming on the brakes. The Administration, given the scary job of holding the steering wheel of the skidding jalopy, was sorely tempted to throw up its hands and cover its eyes.

Congress, responding to its own political priorities and to the emotional and intellectual legacy of the New Deal, continued to appropriate more in non-defense spending than the Administration said it needed—almost $100 billion more between 1982 and 1986. The rise in the cost of defense, though it was absolutely necessary after an era of neglect that included Republican as well as Democratic administrations, was truly staggering. Congress did not resist the temptation to demonstrate that it was ready to defend the poor against the pillagings of the military-industrial complex.

As for monetary policy, nobody argued with Paul Volcker's desire to drive inflation out of the economy. Certainly the Administration could not control it, because the Federal Reserve is, and ought to be, independent of the Executive; still, we did try to influence monetary policy. At a weekly breakfast, held on Thursdays at Treasury and the Federal Reserve alternately, I argued with Volcker for a steady, predictable monetary policy that would assure an adequate and dependable supply of money for the private sector. Volcker is a brilliant and dedicated man, and there is no doubt that his actions did, indeed, cauterize inflation, but the burn cost the patient the use of his right arm for nearly two years. The combined public effect of Volcker's two outstanding qualities as a manager—which were Delphic mysteriousness and a bureaucratic fascination with tinkering—created an atmosphere of fitful government activity and uncertainty in the market that, in my opinion, prolonged the slump well past the point of necessity.

Sometimes I thought that he liked correcting his bankers for the sake of correcting. "Get back inside! Quiet! That's two pennies off your allowance!" his voice seemed to be floating through the nursery door. "Paul, you're a nanny!" I used to say to him after he had given the bankers another spoonful of medicine. Volcker would smile in his amiable way and tell me I didn't really mean it; but I did. In fairness, it must be said that the bankers liked him; so did the press, perhaps because of his enigmatic qualities, perhaps because Volcker was the only figure in Washington who could stand up with impunity to Ronald Reagan's popularity. Whatever the reason, Volcker enjoyed a remarkably good press—a fact that did not escape the notice of the public relations experts in the White House.

The situation got steadily worse. By February 1982, the prime rate stood at 16.75 percent, unemployment was at 8.4 percent, and the gross national product was shrinking at an annual rate of 0.1 percent. There was not enough money in the economy to pay the government's enormous bills (Treasury was disbursing $10 billion a month in interest on loans) and also finance a recovery by the private sector.

David Stockman raised the flag of impasse. He argued, with the unanimous backing of the White House staff and the President's Council of Economic Advisors, that further cuts in spending could not be achieved without an increase in taxes. In support of this position Stockman and his allies wheeled out the guns of Realpolitik. Congress was demanding new taxes as the price of reform and blaming its demand for new money on the deficit; for example, the Senate Finance Committee chairman, Bob Dole, a Republican, warned publicly that new taxes would be unavoidable if the economy did not improve in three months' time. Senators and congressmen, particularly conservative Republicans to whom budget deficits were anathema, were saying far stronger things in private. In other words, Capitol Hill, which in fiscal year 1982 had mandated spending $128 billion more than Treasury was receiving in taxes and other revenues, claimed it wanted more money so that it could balance the books and start over again with a clean slate.

This Orwellian argument did not make sense to me in practical terms or in terms of the President's promises to bring government spending under control and cut taxes. This was not just a matter of acquiescing to an increase in taxes—it meant retreating from the three-year, 25-percent cut (actually, for arithmetical reasons, 22½ percent) in income taxes that had been enacted into law in 1981 with great fanfare. It meant sacrificing not only the tangible benefits of this measure, but also its symbolic meaning.

Suppose the President could somehow renege on his promise to reduce taxes without inflicting mortal damage on his political credibility, what then? I was convinced that an increase in taxes, coupled to a monetary policy that was already starving business of capital, would make our economic troubles worse. An economy could not expand if it was burdened by new taxes at the moment when it was already all but overwhelmed by high interest rates that devastated profits and eliminated millions of jobs.

In my judgment, having 8 or 9 million unemployed was worse than having a deficit of $128 billion. Besides, OMB seemed to be unable to predict the size of the deficit with reliable accuracy: in one case, the error was $50 billion in less than forty-five days. The deficit could be reduced and confidence could be restored if a slow, steady increase in the money supply was accompanied by a controlled rate of federal spending. New taxes would send a signal that neither of these things was going to happen. I told the President that the best tax policy would be no new taxes at all and the next best would be the lowest possible increase in taxes. It was better to borrow money to finance the deficit while the economy recovered and people went back to work than to impose taxes that would cripple the recovery or prevent it altogether. I never have believed, and never will believe, that increasing taxes is a cure for recession.

I did and do believe that deficits did not matter in the short run *if in the long run the economy generates sufficient revenues to pay off the deficits, and the rate of growth of government spending is controlled in such a way that it is consistently less than the real growth of the economy.* The question concerning the budget was never how to reduce it, but how to keep it in rational proportion to income by regulating its growth. But if spending were not controlled, nothing could control the deficits—certainly not new taxes, and not even, as we have seen, the longest sustained period of economic growth in American history.

In my bullish way, I believed that the economy would recover and advance if given the chance. In February 1981, testifying before the House Budget Committee on the day after the President described his tax and economic program to the nation, I had predicted a drop in inflation in the next five years from 11 percent to 4 percent, a 4- to 5-percent annual growth in the gross national product beginning in 1982, and the creation of 11.8 million new jobs. At the time these figures were dismissed as visionary propaganda—a "rosy scenario," in the vocabulary of Congress and the press. In fact the economy outperformed my predictions in all areas but one—employment. Between 1981 and 1986 we added only 9.3 million new jobs. But inflation dropped to 1.9 percent in 1986 and between 1983 and 1986 the GNP grew at an average rate of 4.1 percent.

In this same testimony I made the radical statement that the Administration's forecast was not a conventional prognosis based on an econometric model that assumed no change in the behavior of the people. Rather, I said, "the . . . scenario is based on an internally consistent set of policies which, if enacted, will produce an economic climate in which people's expectations and behavior will change in response to these policies to produce the results summarized in the scenario." In other words, people would work harder and more creatively if the burden of a discriminatory tax system was lifted from their shoulders, and business would expand if it was able to borrow money at rates of interest that made it possible to turn a fair profit. The Reagan Administration intended to change the way the government did business with the people in a fundamental fashion.

Every opinion I had ever heard the President express in public and in meetings with his advisers made me think that he agreed with me in these matters, and especially on tax policy, but mine was nevertheless a lonely voice. Elsewhere within the White House and outside it in the Congress and in the press, he heard a rising clamor for new taxes as the only antidote to fiscal disaster. This was the Keynesian solution, and it was natural that it should be favored in a town dotted with real and metaphorical temples to Keynes. The pressure was too great to resist in an election year. In January 1982 the Administration proposed a combination of measures, including a new withholding tax on dividend and interest payments, designed to raise $86.6 billion in new revenues.

In the early months of 1982 it became apparent that it was going to be unusually difficult to achieve a budget compromise. Stockman, Baker, Weidenbaum, and Darman were urging the President to strike a bargain with Congress as a signal to the financial world and the international community that the United States was serious about its budget deficit and was going to get it under control.

Finally the President authorized Jim Baker to open negotiations with Congress. The discussions were to be held in the strictest of confidence—no leaks to the press! Bob Michel, the Republican leader in the House, had gotten the impression that Tip O'Neill was prepared to compromise on domestic spending in return for an increase in taxes. On March 19, a Friday, Baker called O'Neill and arranged to meet him privately the next day at O'Neill's home. O'Neill immediately suggested bringing three committee chairmen—Dick Bolling of Missouri (Rules); Dan Rostenkowski of Illinois (Ways and Means), and Jim Jones of Oklahoma (Budget)—into the discussions. The following Monday, March 22nd, Jim Baker got together with Jim Jones and came away with the impression that a compromise was possible. When Rostenkowski, who had been in Hawaii, returned to Washington on March 25, Baker took him in to see the President for a private discussion before Reagan had met with any other Democratic leader.

The next day Baker met at his home with Jim Jones, Dave Stockman, and Dick Darman in an effort to get Stockman and Jones together on hard figures for the budget so that Congress and the Administration wouldn't be arguing past each other on the budget effect of issues. On March 24, the Baker group met with Bolling. I was left out of these discussions—nobody wanted a hard-nosed tax-cutter sitting in on meetings designed to give Congress what it wanted: a rise in taxes. My own view of the matter was that O'Neill had baited a trap with a promise of spending cuts but that his real purpose was to take back the tax cuts we had achieved the year before.

Oddly enough, it was Nancy Reagan who brought me into the process—through a back door. Mrs. Reagan's stepbrother, Dr. Richard Davis, had a friend connected to the savings and loan business who was worried about the health of the thrift industry. He wrote a letter on the subject that found its way to Mrs. Reagan. Mrs. Reagan had quizzed me over the telephone on the questions raised by her brother's friend, and subsequently asked me to answer the letter. I did so by telephoning her brother and giving him my general views, and then forgot about the matter.

One Friday afternoon Nancy Reagan phoned me at Treasury to ask why I hadn't answered the letter. I told her about my telephone call to her brother. She wanted to know what I had said to Dr. Davis, and my answer led to a general discussion of the economy. I told Mrs. Reagan that we needed to make budget cuts, including cuts in defense appropriations and entitlements, in order to avoid having to raise taxes. Otherwise the deficit could get out of hand.

The First Lady agreed, saying that she was upset with the Defense Department and Cap Weinberger. In her opinion, Cap was greedy for funds and had no idea how this was hurting the economy. Embarrassed, I reminded Mrs. Reagan that Weinberger was a former director of the Office of Management and Budget and was well aware of the economic effects of defense spending, but he now had to be a strong advocate of defense; the military was in woeful shape.

We chatted on. Mrs. Reagan asked about the mood of Wall Street. I told her that both the bond and the stock markets were waiting for action on the part of the federal government; neither one would take off until we did something to reassure investors. She said she knew that if Ronnie didn't act soon, the Republicans were in danger of losing a lot of seats in the 1982 congressional elections. I agreed with that and said that we would have to have much lower rates of interest by the fall of 1982 if the electorate were to trust us for two more years with the leadership in the Senate.

"You should tell Ronnie that—quickly," Mrs. Reagan said. "I'll have Mike Deaver put you on the schedule to see him."

Again I was surprised. The President's wife was going to tell the Deputy Chief of Staff to put the Secretary of the Treasury on the President's schedule so the Secretary of the Treasury could tell the President of his views on the economy?

That—or something like it—is what happened. The next day, Saturday, at around 11 A.M., the White House operator called: the President wanted to talk to me from Camp David.

Hi, Don, the President said. Is this a good time to talk?

I said, "Couldn't be better, Mr. President. I'm downstairs in my den, trying to stay out of the way. My wife is having twelve ladies for lunch."

The President told me that Jim Baker, Ed Meese, and Mike Deaver had urged him privately on Friday before he left for Camp David to consider whether or not he should start getting used to the idea of a budget compromise with Congress—in other, plainer words, he had better make up his mind to accept new taxes as the cost of cuts in spending.

His aides had told him, the President said, that the situation was serious and time was of the essence. He asked for my views.

I told him that the first quarter of 1982 was turning out to be much worse than we originally predicted because high interest rates foreclosed any chance of recovery in the first quarter of the year.

I told him about a breakfast I had had the past week with Paul Volcker. Volcker had assured me that he would try to be accommodating to the Administration—he would ease money to bring interest rates down if he could see some movement by us on the deficits. Otherwise, Volcker thought, a fall in interest rates could reignite inflation. The sooner we moved, the sooner rates would come down. I thought we should move now on defense, entitlements, discretionary cuts, and also raise some revenue. I suggested a $75 billion package in 1983, which would increase in succeeding years. I estimated this would bring deficits below $100 billion, say into the high 80's, in 1983, and even lower in later years.

I told the President that inflation would be around 4½ percent for the current quarter. If the Consumer Price Index were also below 5 percent for five months or so, it would be logical not to have Social Security cost of living adjustments (COLAs) in the 8-to-9-percent range, as Congress was planning.

The President laughed in surprise. He said, Now I *know* we're cousins. I had this same thought just yesterday.

His reply tickled me. I wasn't used to being related to Presidents. I said, "Look. Let's keep the Administration out of this. Let Howard Baker be the one to suggest to the Congress that we not give an 8 or 9 percent raise when the cost of living index will be below that. We don't want to get our fingers in that. It's too sticky."

He replied, That's a good suggestion. I'll talk to Jim Baker about talking to Howard.

We talked on for a long time, covering nearly every aspect of economic and tax policy. Our views were remarkably similar on nearly every point, and every coincidence seemed to buoy Reagan up.

The President was determined that no deal be made that would take back the tax cuts for individuals that had been enacted the year before.

I worked hard to get that program, he said; I compromised once. I wanted 10-10-10, but I agreed to 5-10-10. I promised these tax cuts in my campaign and I'm not going to go back on my word.

I said, "Look, your staff is so scared of you that none of them dares bring up these issues with you. Congress is afraid of your popularity—and they're also afraid that you'll claim victory if they compromise. I think that we should give the country the signal sooner, rather than later. And the sooner we do, the sooner real interest rates will start to fall because Volcker will feel free to go to work."

Which way do you think we should go? he asked.

"Negotiate with the Democrats on the Hill," I replied. "But watch your back and stick to your guns."

The President seemed reassured by our chat. I had the impression that he did not often talk to anyone who gave him facts and figures that supported the policies he believed to be right.

Don, he said, the Prime Minister of Ireland was in for lunch last week and he gave me a beautiful map of Ireland. I'm going to have them take a picture of that map for you. I want you to know where our common ancestors came from.

Early the following week, Jim Baker briefed me on his conversation with O'Neill and the other House Democrats and told me that the President had authorized him to set up a small group on budget strategy consisting of himself, Dave Stockman, perhaps Dick Darman, and me. We were going to tell no one about this group, and if necessary I should lie to my staff about my whereabouts when I attended these meetings. It was essential to keep them secret.

I told Baker that I wasn't surprised that the President authorized the meetings because I had urged that course of action on him.

Baker pounced on this information. "When did you talk to the President?" he asked.

I told him about the phone call from Camp David.

Baker clearly was miffed. "The President," he said in a chilly tone, "hasn't gotten around to telling me about that conversation."

The first meetings took place on Thursday, March 25th at 5 in the downstairs den of Jim Baker's home. Bob Michel and Trent Lott, the Republican Whip, represented the Republicans on the Hill. Jones, Rostenkowski, and Bolling represented the Democratic side of the House. Bolling added, emphatically, that he represented Tip O'Neill. From the outset Bolling was the real leader and strong man of their group; both Rostenkowski and Jones deferred to him.

Ominous signs appeared immediately. Instead of starting off discussing cuts, we started off by discussing revenues. Rostenkowski said that there was strong sentiment in the House for postponing the third year of the tax cuts, or even eliminating it. I said that Ronald Reagan could never accept that. We discussed every kind of cut in spending and many kinds of revenue measures. It was clear that this group was composed of practical people who wanted to arrive at workable solutions. We agreed to meet on Tuesday, March 30, again at Jim Baker's home—this time for breakfast. The rule of absolute discretion was reaffirmed.

Many meetings followed. Step by step, the group was expanded to include the Vice President; Ken Duberstein of the White House staff; Senators Dole, Laxalt, Hollings, Russell Long of Louisiana, and Pete V. Domenici, Republican of New Mexico; and Republican Congressmen Delbert L. Latta of Ohio and Barber B. Conable of New York. We began calling ourselves the Gang of Seventeen.

Because the group was too large to be accommodated conveniently—and discreetly—in anybody's home, we moved the site of the meetings to the Indian Treaty Room in the Executive Office Building. The acoustics in this vaulted and galleried chamber are such that even the softest voice produces a noticeable echo. There were few soft voices among us, and our discussions sometimes produced such a reverberating babble that people sitting at one end of the conference table could not understand what people at the other end were saying. The sound effects intensified personality traits that always become more vivid in negotiations: the bombastic members seemed steadily more bombastic as the hours passed, the sarcastic more sarcastic, the dogmatic more dogmatic.

Nevertheless we persisted. We met at Blair House, in the family theater in the White House, in the Roosevelt Room, at the Vice President's residence. Innumerable sets of numbers were discussed, innumerable formulas were proposed, but no obvious compromise emerged. We could not even agree on the size of the deficit. Stockman, whose estimates as usual changed dramatically, thought that it would be much higher than the people from the House found possible to believe. The senators and congressmen seemed unable to believe that current patterns of spending would produce deficits of $233 billion in only three more years—let alone the much higher figures that Stockman was intoning. Although there was good will on both sides, the fundamental difference between the parties never went away: the Administration wanted to cut spending in domestic programs and control it more closely in defense programs; Congress wanted to increase revenues and slash defense spending so as to maintain high levels of domestic spending. We thought that Congress was running up the bills with no thought for the consequences; they thought that the Administration was letting untold billions in revenues slip through its fingers as a result of its unprecedented tax cuts.

The whole process provided an example of circles within circles, with the President, the First Lady, and the Secretary of the Treasury forming a circle to work within the Chief of Staff's circle, which had been formed to work within the Speaker's circle, which was obliged to work within the circles of the Senate leadership and the Republican leadership of the House. No single, unified circle ever emerged from these separate entities.

At one point, after exhaustive discussions, we reached a consensus that provided for $250 billion in spending cuts over a three-year period, coupled to $115 billion in tax increases—or roughly two dollars in spending cuts for one dollar in taxes. This huge reduction in spending brought us nowhere near to a balanced budget.

My goal was a three-to-one ratio: three dollars in spending cuts for every one dollar in new taxes. I urged that we rethink spending proposals. But the discussion centered, as it had from the beginning, on tax increases. In their belief that taxes, and nothing else, could cure the deficit and restore the economy, the delegation from the Hill had the sympathy, if not the allegiance, of the White House staff. The latter thought that they were defending the President's best interests. I knew that the President did not agree, and did what I could to defend his philosophy and program. Very grudgingly, new reductions in spending were agreed upon. Gradually the ratio between spending cuts and tax increases became more favorable. I began to think that we had a chance of achieving the three-to-one ratio.

At about this time I had to go up to New York to make a speech. A blizzard had closed the airports, so I traveled on the Amtrak Metroliner. On arrival at Penn Station I was told by a Secret Service man that the President was trying to reach me. In a matter of minutes, we were on the phone together. The President was surprised to learn that I was in Manhattan—he just wanted to chat and when he put in the call had assumed I was across the street in my office at Treasury. We passed the time of day about interest rates, employment, and unemployment. He mentioned a story he had read or heard about a small bank in Indiana that had reduced its interest rates on car loans in order to help local automobile sales.

Hundreds of cars are being sold in that community, the President said. Couldn't we get all the banks to do the same thing?

I said, "No, Mr. President, not now. But if we cut the deficit as we're trying to do in the Gang of Seventeen, we can lean on Paul Volcker and the bankers to get interest rates down. If we show fiscal discipline, they can help us with monetary policy."

Would Volcker really stick to a deal like that? the President asked. What's his state of mind?

"Volcker has assured me that if we got together with the Democrats and cut the deficit, he'd have plenty of elbow room to ease money gradually without scaring the business community about the return of inflation."

I described the wearisome process that the Gang of Seventeen was going through.

What have you come up with so far? Reagan asked.

"I think it can be quite a package, Mr. President," I replied. "But Jim Baker's going to tell you about it, so don't tell him what I've told you. We're discussing $300 billion or more in cuts and $115 billion in tax increases. That would mean $415 billion, or more, in deficit reductions over three years. If we can pull that off, it will startle Wall Street and the world and we'll be on our way to a sound economy."

Can we do it? he asked.

"That's not really the question, Mr. President," I replied. "The question is, Can we do it without violating your principles or breaking the promises you've made to the American people."

Well, he said, I suppose I'll have to sit down with Tip O'Neill at some point and try to iron it out.

"That's true. But don't do it until we bring you the whole package, if we ever do. That's when you'll be able to tell what's possible and what's acceptable."

Is there anything I can do now? he asked.

"I'd advise you to be conciliatory toward Congress on other matters and keep your own counsel on this subject," I replied. I knew that he and Mrs. Reagan were planning to spend Easter in Barbados at the home of Claudette Colbert. I said, "Just lie on the warm sands, Mr. President, and let us negotiate."

Okay, I'll do that, the President said.

The package was never delivered. The Gang of Seventeen produced no agreement because the Democrats held out for elimination of the third year of tax cuts. Finally the House and Senate passed a Budget Resolution calling for $3 in spending cuts for every $1 in new taxes, a formula that would have reduced the deficit by about $100 billion in the first year and even more dramatically thereafter. The West Wing circle regarded this as a triumph, and if the agreement had been honored, it would have been.

In fact, Tip O'Neill's trap had snapped shut. His men had agreed on spending cuts they never believed in as a means of getting the Administration to agree to an increase in taxes. The Tax Equity and Fiscal Reform Act, in which this agreement was supposed to be enshrined, never accomplished its purpose, and after all the smoke, mirrors, and bookkeeping tricks cleared away, it was discovered that the taxes had been voted but the spending cuts had never been enacted.

The perfidy and wiliness of Tip O'Neill and his cohorts on the Hill was too much for the well-meaning but economically unsophisticated West Wingers. The President was snookered into a deal that gave Congress—and, incidentally, Baker and Stockman—what they wanted all along: more taxes. It did not surprise me that spending—and the deficit—increased as a result.

The Administration's budget for fiscal year 1983, as proposed to Congress, called for expenditures of $757.6 billion against expected revenues of $666.1 billion, creating a deficit of $91.5 billion. Congress actually approved outlays of $808 billion, or $50.4 billion more than the President had requested. Actual revenue was $600.6 billion, a shortfall of $65.5 billion, producing an actual deficit of $208 billion.

The evangelical campaign to banish waste, fraud, and abuse from federal programs no longer dominated our conversations about the economy. Stockman began to tell the President, whose own enthusiasm for sweating the fat out of government never waned, that reforms in the way money was spent by the Executive Branch might save $10 billion a year, but if the combined 1982–83 deficit was $191 billion, where was the other $181 billion going to come from? Although he may have been somewhat late in coming to an obvious conclusion, Stockman was right about the limits that reality placed on the OMB's capacity to reform spending habits that serviced the interests of powerful political constituencies.

The budget sent by the President to Congress called for cuts of almost $26 billion in social programs. In fact Congress increased such spending by more than that. It was one thing, in the privacy of a meeting of like-minded reformers, to identify programs that were ill-conceived or wastefully managed and to propose ways to make them more cost-effective. It was another matter to explain those shortcomings in a politically acceptable way, and yet another to organize a constituency to bring about change. The scale of defense spending, coupled to the historic tension and suspicion between the two political parties, doomed the effort from the start. In fact the reform of the welfare system would have benefited the poor by making it more efficient and driving out large numbers of the unneedy who were cheating the disadvantaged of money that rightfully belonged to them.

Few Presidents started out in life poorer than Ronald Reagan, and I doubt that any of his predecessors cherished a more genuine sympathy for the down-and-out. He resented those who robbed the poor by freeloading on the system as only a person who knows the meaning of poverty can. He believed in what Stockman had called the "safety net" of social programs and wanted to preserve it. His opponents did not wish to believe these truths about the President, and the tactics and vocabulary of Reagan's principal spokesmen on budgetary matters were not designed to change their minds. Through little fault of Ronald Reagan's, the brave early approach to budget reform turned out to be all sizzle and no steak.

All this is not to suggest that the reduction of waste in the everyday operations of the government is not worthwhile, or that no result had been achieved. Ten billion dollars, the amount Stockman estimated might be saved annually by better management, is a lot of money. The Grace Commission, a task force of some two hundred businessmen headed by Peter Grace, of W. R. Grace & Co., had come to Washington in the early days of the Administration with a mandate from President Reagan to study government operations to make them more efficient. The Grace Commission suggested many innovations, and if a majority of these had been put into effect, the government would indeed have been leaner and more effective. Unfortunately, many of the big-ticket items, such as reforming the federal retirement system, required legislative remedies. Congress would not make these changes.

Some of the commission's suggestions delighted the President. He liked to recount instances of savings from his days as Governor of California. A particular favorite involved a California agency that had been buying an unusually large number of file cabinets because they had been running out of space. It was found that the file clerks had been cramming legal-size paper into letter-size drawers. The agency switched to smaller paper and cut down on the number of file cabinets it needed.

Now that's the kind of thing I'm talking about! the President would exclaim, charmed by the simplicity of this solution.

But the incentive to put the more far-reaching of the commission's recommendations into effect was weak. Some required changes in the law that the Administration was reluctant to expend the energy and political capital to enact. Others interfered with countervailing recommendations by OMB and fell victim to territorial jealousy and bureaucratic maneuver.

It was not the civil service that resisted change and improvement; most men and women who worked for the federal government were eager to do things more efficiently. My own experience at Treasury had taught me that it was possible to eliminate waste from government practice by the simplest innovations. We saved $10 million a year by replacing antiquated punch-card checks with a computerized system that wrote and recorded the electronic "stubs" of paper checks. Hundreds of millions in interest payments were saved by requiring all government agencies to deposit payments made to the government in interest-bearing accounts on the day they were received, instead of letting these billions of public money lie about in desk drawers and in-baskets. Under the able leadership of Assistant Secretary Carole Dineen, a former New York banker, Treasury pursued an aggressive policy of cash management and effected many other savings—perhaps as much as $4.3 billion over 6 years—by improving technology and working procedures.

The career employees who run the day-to-day operations of Treasury not only accepted these changes, they welcomed them and suggested many ways of improving the operations and cost-effectiveness of the department. Those men and women are among the most dedicated, hardworking, and—given the tools and the incentive and direction—the most efficient I have ever encountered.

By the beginning of 1982, when the battle over the Administration's economic policy was beginning in earnest, I had gotten to know Ronald Reagan a little better. After the initial period in which most of my impressions of the President and his objectives were formed at second hand and most of my tasks as Secretary of the Treasury were assigned by Ed Meese, I began to suggest that a more orderly process was needed for discussing economic policy directly with the President. The practice of operating through lieutenants, capable and conscientious though they were, created an irksome atmosphere. It was difficult, not to say impossible, to convince White House aides that any matter was important enough to be brought directly to the President for a decision. "Bring that up in the Cabinet Council on Economic Affairs [CCEA]," the Presidential aides would say in a kindly way. "See if they understand what you're trying to do and see if they agree." I would do so, but this was not usually a method that was capable of producing decision and action. As chairman of the CCEA, I was usually able to bring the members to an eventual consensus on a given question. In the absence of a consensus or a choice of options, the President could not be petitioned for a decision.

This baffling system, in which the President seldom spoke, while his advisers proposed measures that contradicted his ideas and promises, created uncertainty in a situation that cried out for action. I thought that I understood the President's philosophy. But how did he want it carried out, if at all? Casual exchanges in Cabinet meetings and other large gatherings were not enough to give the necessary guidance, especially at a time when the economy was in distress.

The President himself sent out no strong signals. He listened, encouraged, deferred. But it was a rare meeting in which he made a decision or issued orders. Reagan's personality and his infectious likability are founded on a natural diffidence. He hesitates to ask questions or confess to a lack of knowledge in the presence of strangers—and thanks to the way his staff operated, nearly everyone was a stranger to this shy President except the members of his innermost circle. (That was not the only reason. To an unusual degree, Reagan is loath to cause inconvenience or embarrassment. After I became his Chief of Staff there was a minor fire, caused by a clogged chimney. Guards scurried everywhere, searching for the source of the smoke. Finally they traced it to the President's study in the West Wing. The President happened to be working in the study at the time. Although he heard the disturbance and noticed the smoke, he stayed at his desk, reading his documents with smarting eyes, until the guards asked if he wouldn't like to move to another room while they put out the fire and the place was aired out. He hadn't wanted to bother anybody.)

Although in those days I did not know as much about the President's habits and personality as I later learned, I told Ed Meese that I did not think that the President was being well served by the way in which economic advice was being presented to him. I suggested that we set up regular briefings in the Oval Office in the presence of the smallest possible number of people so as to permit an atmosphere of give-and-take. I took it for granted that

I would deliver the briefing, and made sure that Meese understood this. Though I had not insisted on assurances that I would be the Administration's chief economic spokesman and the President's principal adviser on tax and fiscal policy, that was precisely what I was by logic and long-established custom. By temperament it would have been impossible for me to accept a lesser role.

Besides, my main purpose in proposing these encounters was to hear the President's ideas at first hand. By meeting with him for a frank exchange every six weeks or so I thought that I would be better able to judge his state of mind and the state of his knowledge. Was he getting the data he needed? Did he understand it completely? There was nothing condescending in these questions. Later in our relationship, when the President would apologize for asking a basic—sometimes even a startling basic— question about an arcane subject, I would joke that the President of the United States was not supposed to know everything: if he did, he'd be editor of the *Encyclopaedia Britannica*.

The ultimate objective was to provide policy options that expressed the President's convictions. In my opinion the policy team that had been assembled at Treasury was as good as any in the government in terms of education, experience, and creativity— and, not least, in terms of its philosophical compatibility with the President. The results achieved by this circle of intelligent and dedicated men and women once the President began acting on their counsel turned my confidence into pride.

It is remarkable how well these appointees have done in subsequent years. Two, Ann McLaughlin and Beryl Sprinkel, presently hold Cabinet rank. Another, Manley Johnson, is vice chairman of the Federal Reserve Board. Still others have gone on to success in the private sector, most notably Buck Chapoton, who has become one of Washington's premier tax attorneys. Others include Paul Craig Roberts, a distinguished supply-side economist, Roger Mehle, Tom Healy, and Marc Leland. One, Ron Pearlman, was even hired by Democrats—Danny Rostenkowski and Lloyd Bentsen—to be the new staff director of the Joint Committee on Taxation.

Even on the basis of our limited personal contacts, Reagan and I had developed an easy rapport. The similarity in our names continued to intrigue him. After he became President, genealogists the world over took an interest in his lineage. These investigations established, to the President's satisfaction at least, that the Regans and the Reagans were the same family. He had an ancestor named Thomas Regan; Thomas is my middle name, after my grandfather Regan who was one of a long line of Thomas Regans. The President's ancestors came from County Limerick, next door to my family's ancestral County Cork. Even the spelling of our names would have been the same, the President joked, if that English customs officer on the dock in Liverpool at the time of the potato famine had had a better ear for his Grandfather Regan's [sic] Irish brogue. One researcher traced the blood back to Brian Boru, King of Ireland (940–1014). The President loved tales of our fierce mutual ancestor, if indeed that's what he was, sweeping down on the Danish strangers and routing them; and he would regale me with tidbits of legend and history and make me presents of genealogical charts and chapters of books about the family. Here, Don, he would call across the Cabinet table before a meeting started, I've got something new on the family. It may be, too, that the President felt comfortable with me for another reason. Though he displays no special fondness for people with old money, he numbers many self-made millionaires among his friends; I was fortunate enough to be a member of that breed.

Then, too, I shared his fundamental opinions on economics, and here, also, the reasons were rooted in common experience. In my early and middle years on Wall Street, beginning in 1954 when I first earned more than the maximum allowed in lower tax brackets, I found myself in the 91-percent tax bracket. That meant that on the margin I could keep nine cents on every dollar I made in any given year above a certain amount. The other ninety-one cents went to the U.S. government. This rankled, but I kept on working just as hard because I liked the intangible benefits of my profession almost as much as I liked the money. As a movie actor in the 1950s, Ronald Reagan was in the same situation. Unwilling to work for nine cents on the dollar, he solved his dilemma by limiting himself to making two movies a year. This took up about half his time. For the other six months he hung around his country club in order to be seen by producers who might wish to cast him in a movie. Playing golf and swapping anecdotes with some of the famous Hollywood comedians of the time, he laid up the foundation stock of his enormous inventory of funny stories and jokes. We talked about the frustration each of us had felt in being penalized for success. It had made us both determined to do something about punitive taxation if we were ever in a position to act.

The President was fond of reminding people that he had majored in economics in college. His grasp of basic economic theory as it had been taught in his time (Eureka College, class of '32) was excellent, and he had kept abreast of later theory. He had no trouble understanding the leading ideas of the day, or in making reasonable judgments about the effects produced by policies based on Keynesian theory, of which he was deeply suspicious. He had an advantage over academic economists in that his knowledge was not entirely theoretical.

For eight years he had been governor of California, a state with a larger economy and a more complex budget than most independent nations, and while in Sacramento he had learned a great deal about the realities of fiscal policy. As a result of all these experiences, he had developed strong ideas and even stronger instincts. I thought that both were generally sound, and when the occasion arose I told him so, advising him to stick to his guns and all would be well in the end.

The Oval Office briefings, which began in late 1981, did not eliminate competition for the President's ear. I never intended that they should; all I wanted was a chance to compete on equal terms in the presence of the Chief Executive. Others attending these sessions were Meese; Baker; sometimes Deaver; Stockman; Murray Weidenbaum, chairman of the Council of Economic Advisors (and later his successor, Martin Feldstein); Malcolm Baldrige, Secretary of Commerce; Larry Speakes; and anyone else Meese and Baker gave permission to attend.

It is fair to say that the idea that I was the President's chief economic adviser was not unanimously accepted in these meetings. Nevertheless, as we sat in a semicircle by the fireplace, facing the President, I occupied the chair that commanded eye contact with Reagan. This chair was mine by virtue of my rank in the Cabinet—it was reserved for the highest-ranking person present. When the Vice President attended, or the Secretary of State, I was obliged to move to the couch. In matters of protocol and tradition, little things mean a lot.

The Oval Office and proximity to the President's person imposed a certain decorum, but acerbic flare-ups occurred. The others, especially Stockman and Weidenbaum (and later, even more fervently, Feldstein), were preoccupied with the deficit, while I was focused on the means of stimulating an economic recovery. To this end I played on three main themes: fiscal controls; monetary policy; and tax policy. There was no essential difference of opinion on fiscal policy; everyone wanted to control spending, although preferences varied on methodology. My view that Volcker should be encouraged to loosen monetary policy in a cautious way, and my very strong opinion that a tax cut would produce more revenue than a tax increase, won little support from my colleagues. They were afraid that a tax cut would produce a jump in inflation and that this, in turn, would frighten Volcker into tightening monetary policy even more. Over and over again we stressed that the Fed should give us a slow, steady growth in the money supply. Instead, in 1981–82, the Fed gave us an erratic decline.

The President listened to both sides and, to outward appearances, chose neither. I kept advising him to hold course, avoiding new taxes and trying to get more money into the hands of the private sector at rates of interest that would permit business to make the profits that would create jobs. I said that if he did this, everything would come out right in the end. Others did not agree. They wanted some sort of contingency tax to reduce the 1983 deficit.

The debate about tax policy continued outside the meetings. Decades of legislative and administrative tinkering had turned a complex subject into a labyrinth of the arcane. To illustrate this point to the President I asked Roscoe Egger, the Commissioner of the Internal Revenue Service, how much shelf space an accountant or tax lawyer just starting out in business would need for a basic, no-frills library of reference books. After a couple of days of research, Egger came back with the answer: one foot of shelf for the tax code plus three volumes of regulations; four feet for sixteen volumes of reference materials published by private tax services; thirteen and a half feet for cases heard in the tax courts; thirty feet for cases decided in higher courts; twelve feet for revenue rulings; and two and a half feet for Internal Revenue Service manuals. Total shelf space required: sixty-three feet. The cost of installing the shelves, like the cost of the books, was tax-deductible.

The tax system was complicated, inequitable, expensive to administrate, and so filled with loopholes that it was entirely unnecessary to cheat on taxes in order to avoid them. Some individuals earned millions of dollars in a given year, reported every penny of this income and, by taking advantage of tax shelters and other provisions provided by law, paid no federal income tax at all. The inequity was even more glaring in the case of corporations. The underground economy alone, conducted in cash and unrecorded transactions, probably cost the Treasury at least $90 billion a year in unpaid taxes on an estimated $500 billion in unreported earnings.

A tax code that institutionalized sharp practice and the avoidance (a euphemism meaning "legal evasion") of taxes at the expense of the ordinary, honest taxpayer was bad for the country. I wanted to throw it out and start over again. Two proposals for comprehensive tax reform already existed—Blueprints for Basic Tax Reform, commissioned in 1977 by Bill Simon when he was Secretary of the Treasury, and a more limited plan put forward by Senator Bill Bradley, Democrat of New Jersey, and Representative Richard A. Gephardt, Democrat of Missouri. Both were moribund.

Toward the end of 1983, as we prepared for the President's State of the Union message, I talked to Baker, Feldstein, and

Stockman about tax reform. According to my notes I said, "What we need is not more taxes [familiar theme], but a simplified tax system—one that produces more work, more goods, and . . . more tax dollars in a rising and growing economy." I urged a major push for tax simplification in the coming year. They were less enthusiastic about this proposal than I, and spoke again about the necessity of new taxes to reduce the deficit.

Did the President want to reform the tax system or not? I had the impression, based on observation of his body language rather than any words he had spoken in private, that he wanted to hold the line against new taxes—if only his advisers would let him do so. I raised the question with the President during an Oval Office briefing.

On the theory, I suppose, that it relaxed the participants and established an atmosphere of fellow feeling, President Reagan liked to start every meeting off with a story or a joke. So, as a way of introducing the subject, I asked him a question about his old employer, the General Electric Company: "What does General Electric have in common with Boeing, General Dynamics, and fifty-seven other big corporations?"

Reagan's interest was immediately aroused. He had fond memories of his days as a television host and traveling goodwill ambassador for GE, and a large number of anecdotes and stories about this experience.

I don't know, he said, leaning forward in his chair and smiling. What *do* they have in common?

"Let me tell you, Mr. President," I replied. "What these outfits have in common is that not one of them pays a penny in taxes to the United States government."

What? the President said.

His shock was genuine. A dumbfounded silence settled over his economic advisers. What unconventional idea was I trying to plant in the President's mind now?

"Believe it or not, Mr. President," I continued, "your secretary paid more federal taxes last year than all of those giant companies put together."

The President flushed, a sure sign of surprise and discomfort.

I just can't believe that, he said.

"I don't blame you for doubting it," I replied. "But it's the truth. I checked the figures with Roscoe Egger at IRS, and he tells me there's no doubt about it. It's perfectly legal, but it's wrong, Mr. President, when a hardworking secretary pays more to support her government than sixty of the richest corporations in the land. The time has come to do something fundamental about the tax system. It's too complicated, it's grotesquely unfair, and it's a drag on the economy because it discourages competition."

By now the President's cheeks were carmine and there was a spark of resolution in his eye.

He said, I agree, Don, I just didn't realize that things had gotten that far out of line.

I interpreted his words as an instruction to go full steam ahead with a proposal to overhaul the entire federal tax structure so as to purge it of inequities, plug its loopholes, and lower the rates for individual taxpayers. Kathy Osborne's tax situation was not merely symbolic—it was typical. In 1981 personal income taxes amounted to nearly 10 percent of the GNP and half of government revenues. Including deductions for Social Security, it averaged about 25 percent of personal income; corporate income taxes equaled about 2 percent of the GNP. A myriad of tax dodges gave certain individual taxpayers gross advantages over their neighbors. Whole industries, such as oil and gas, real estate, and agriculture, benefited from tax laws that favored their interests and gave them enormous competitive advantages. Most of these tax breaks had been justified on grounds that they were in the national interest. The accumulated weight of the inefficiency and selfishness they had created had become a burden on the economy and an affront to economic and social justice. It was also, in the opinion of many, an invitation to corruption. Under the current system it was hardly necessary to cheat in order to avoid paying taxes, yet in 1981 individuals and businesses illegally evaded payment of at least $90 billion.

The tax system was like a football field on which some of the players stood in deep holes, others were positioned on top of heaps of sand, others rode donkeys or elephants, while a fortunate few floated overhead in balloons—and some even hid behind bushes planted on the yard markers, carrying concealed weapons. Hardly anybody was playing the healthy old rough-and-tumble game of free enterprise according to the original rules. I thought that the economy should be a level playing field on which everyone could compete on equal terms according to ability. The President's aim, as I understood it, was the same. He wanted to achieve a tax system from which unfair advantage and incentives to outwit the tax collector would be removed to the maximum extent possible.

Few in Washington believed that such a thing could be achieved since it went against the force of human nature; the President held a different view of human nature, and so did I. Fair treatment liberates creative energy. If that isn't the lesson of American history, I don't know what is.

It was now late December 1983. A study of existing proposals to reform the tax system had been going on at Treasury for some months, and Buck Chapoton, the Assistant Secretary for Tax Policy, had reported on our progress in testimony before the Senate Finance Committee in September. He reported our conclusion that none of the plans proposed so far would bring about true reform. The most popular perennial, a uniform tax rate, would result in people with annual incomes above $50,000 paying less in taxes, while those with earnings in the middle and lower range would pay $32 billion more. Doubling the value of exemptions would produce an *increase* in taxes for nearly eight out of ten taxpayers.

And so it went, with arithmetic defeating wishful thinking at every turn. It was clear that abuses could not be eliminated by imposing new ways of collecting taxes on the existing system because the system itself was the problem. You could not control the growth of this aggressive weed that was taking over the land by snipping off new shoots or pruning back old branches. Such methods only made the roots stronger. The whole organism had to be pulled out by the roots.

During the Christmas holidays I thought about objectives and strategy. We wanted two things: radical simplification within a uniform framework that applied the same standards of taxation to all taxpayers. The strategy of getting the plan accepted by the President and then enacted into law had to be designed so as to overcome three main obstacles: the opposition within the Administration to a cut in tax rates; the cynicism in the politico-journalistic establishment which held to the view that true tax reform was unattainable; and the nervousness and caution that were normal in an election year.

To deal with the first, I decided to press on with my arguments. I had also decided that Treasury should have the least harmful tax package possible ready in case the President should decide, after all, to go with the majority of his advisers. As for cynicism and timidity, these could only be overcome by showing that the impossible could be achieved. Election year provided an excellent opportunity to debate the issue—and the President's State of the Union message, scheduled for delivery on January 25, was the obvious occasion for the firing of the opening gun.

On January 2, 1984, a national holiday, I called a staff meeting at Treasury to discuss these issues. Those present were Manley Johnson, Assistant Secretary for Economic Policy; Buck Chapoton, the Assistant Secretary for Tax Policy, and his deputies, Charlie McClure and Ron Pearlman; Ann McLaughlin, Assistant Secretary for Public Affairs; her deputy, Marlin Fitzwater; Bruce Thompson and Mimi Feller from legislative affairs; and Chris Hicks, my executive assistant. Gathered in the Secretary's conference room on the third floor of the empty, silent building, we began with a discussion of ways to raise revenue as a means of reducing the deficit. In effect, I was asking the staff to act as a collective devil's advocate for my opponents' case. I did not expect that my mind would be changed, but I wanted to have the least harmful solution possible at hand in case the President, against my hope and expectation, went with the tax-raisers.

Suggestions included new taxes on such items as energy, cigarettes, and telephone calls. We called our list of tax possibilities "cats and dogs," and estimated that it could bring as much as $190 billion in new revenues into Treasury over the five-year period ending in 1989. Coupled to feasible cuts in spending amounting to $209 billion over the same period, these cats and dogs (including an increase in revenues of $50 billion produced by reform of the tax code) could result in a reduction of $400 billion in the accumulated deficit.

Our real objective was to produce the outlines of a comprehensive plan for tax simplification and reform that the President could describe in his State of the Union address. This was a vital step, because once the President expressed his intentions in this most important of all Presidential speeches, the plan would become scripture.

While the elements of the plan were being hammered out in staff meetings at Treasury, I made the rounds of other camps. At the Republican National Committee, I told the chairman, Frank Fahrenkopf, that Treasury wanted to be as helpful as possible. The Secretary of the Treasury is the highest-ranking member of the Cabinet who customarily makes political speeches, and I volunteered my services. (During the 1984 campaign I took part in forty fund-raisers that brought $1.5 million into the Republican coffers, including an appearance in Texas in which my remarks were interrupted by the trumpeting of an elephant, followed by the braying of a donkey. "I thought I heard the call of an elephant," I said, "but I guess there's a jackass in the crowd." It turned out that the Texans had staged a race between the two animals before I arrived, with all bets being paid to the party's war chest. The donkey won. So much for straw polls.) The chairman of the Platform Committee, Trent Lott, agreed that Treasury should have a hand in writing the plank on tax policy; I did not want tax reform to be blindsided from right or left by enthusiastic delegates to the Republican National Convention.

Although President Reagan had been sympathetic to a flat tax rate, he gave up on it when he saw that it would bring hardship to poorer taxpayers. He agreed that a fundamental simplification of the tax system was the way to go. But he was still worried about the deficit, and so was I. Cutting taxes through reform was only half the apple, I told the President; the other half was a reduction in spending. The President agreed.

Others were less determined. Congress had given no indication that it would cut spending in an election year, and Stockman told us that no further cuts in the budget were possible. The pressure for an increase in taxes continued from all quarters. I proposed a 3-percent across-the-board cut in all budget items except defense, Social Security, and Medicare. I was told that this was impossible to achieve. The President made no specific recommendations for cutting expenditures.

The package of cats and dogs that Treasury had put together in response to White House pressure had been accepted by the President. It would have cut three times as much from the budget as the reductions that had so far been approved. This lack of resolve on the part of the White House was very upsetting. On January 5, at a meeting on legislative strategy, the question of a tax increase was put to the vote. I held out against an increase, and lost in the vote, seven to one. I told the others—Baker; Meese; Stockman; B. Oglesby, the White House legislative liaison; Feldstein, and Richard Darman, Baker's assistant—that I would resign before I'd support a tax increase in the absence of cuts in spending that meant something. The others wanted to send Congress a proposal for a contingency tax that would be so difficult to trigger that it would never go into effect. According to my notes, I said, "That will never fly. We've got to send the Hill something that's realistic." Meese wondered if we shouldn't send Congress a supplemental budget in a month or so, cutting $112 billion and raising $112 billion in new taxes. I said no. But once again I was the only one uttering that word.

Over and over again I made the point that tax simplification plus economic growth would stimulate revenues. The others said that this was an irresponsible statement. Dick Wirthlin said that it would be a mistake not to ask for a tax increase. His polls showed that 40 percent of the American people were in favor of raising taxes. As it happened, the stock market had started off the year with a remarkable day in which 160 million shares were traded—the largest one-day volume in history up to that time.

"You have your polls and I have mine," I said to the others. "My poll says that one hundred and sixty million shares say that investors are not as worried about the deficit as you people are.

They think we're going to have a good economy. But if you raise taxes, you're going to kill the economy—and maybe our chances in November, too. I'm not a politician, but I have a feeling in my heart that if we hold the line on spending and let the tax cuts do their work, you'll see a remarkable improvement in the economy."

They were not moved. "I'm not changing my mind on tax increases," I said. "I'll go to the President over this!" And with that, I stormed out of the meeting.

On Monday, January 9, the Revenue Working Group, supplemented by the presence of two members of the Cabinet who were thought to favor tax increases, George Shultz and Malcolm Baldrige, met with the President at a working luncheon. The proposal on the table was a 3-percent cut in spending tied to a matching tax increase. This would be rationalized by telling the American people that the President was really a tax-cutter, but was raising taxes in order to get the Congress to cut spending as a means of reducing the deficit.

"If he's a tax-cutter, why is he raising taxes?" I asked. "Why doesn't he just order the Cabinet departments to cut 3 percent from their budgets?" I thought the American people would ask themselves the same question in the polling booths.

Dick Darman raised the question of a "deficit commission." I opposed that, too.

Soon afterward I heard that someone else was proposing a deficit commission made up of former Secretaries of the Treasury and other wise men. It sounded to me like a way to avoid the problem until after the election and make the President look weak. Senator Mac Mattingly, Republican of Georgia, called to inquire about this plan after it was rumored in the press.

"If the President agrees to set up such a commission, the country will have one more ex-Secretary of the Treasury than it's got right now," I said. "It would show me that the President is very weak, that he's for tax increases, and that he's going against everything he's stood for. He'll have my resignation the minute he approves it."

Later that day I received a call from Bob Dole, who said that he thought that the President should stand strong. He could get forty-five senators to vote for a 3-percent cut if the defense budget was included, but Social Security excluded.

I continued to battle against the idea of a special commission. The President's Economic Policy Advisory Board supported my position at a meeting on January 11 with the President. The President listened in his usual cheery way, then suddenly leaned over and spoke to me.

I've been thinking about where we ought to stand on this, he said, and I want to tell you I'm with you all the way.

We were seated side by side. I grinned and gave him the A-OK sign. That same day I sent the President a memorandum. It read in part:

> The following is my understanding of your decision on taxes for the State of the Union address and in the upcoming budget proposals. . . . *Major Tax Simplification and Reform*: As a separate and distinct item, you will direct the Secretary of the Treasury to present, by December 1984 . . . legislation that will . . . simplify the tax code so that the average person can understand it and fewer wasteful efforts will be taken to develop "tax deals" that do not promote economic growth. [This legislation will also] ensure more equal treatment of people and families in equal economic circumstances . . . reduce marginal rates to improve economic incentives without raising middle-income families' share of the tax burden . . . remove disincentives to savings . . . provide careful transition roles to avoid harm to taxpayers' business and investment plans.

No occasion is so resonant of the noble history of the American government, or so vibrant with the cynicism of its day-to-day political concerns, as a State of the Union message. It takes place in the chamber of the House of Representatives, with the members of both houses of Congress present, together with the justices of the Supreme Court in their black robes, the Cabinet, and other dignitaries. Distinguished visitors, the press, the wives of the dignitaries, and other personages watch from the galleries. To be present in an official capacity is truly to feel a strong pride in nation and self. If you have contributed in some significant way to the President's remarks, then the sense of being borne along on the river of American history is even more powerful. When the President came to the section of his address in which he talked about tax policy and our plan for simplifying the tax code, I was moved by his plain words:

> To talk of meeting the present situation by increasing taxes is a Band-Aid solution which does nothing to cure an illness that's been coming on for half a century, to say nothing of the fact that it poses a real threat to economic recovery. . . . It would be amoral to make those who are paying taxes pay more to compensate for those who are not paying their share. . . . There is a better way. Let us go forward with an historic reform for fairness, simplicity, and incentives for growth. I am asking Secretary of the Treasury Don Regan for a plan for action to simplify the entire tax code so all taxpayers, big and small, are treated more fairly. I have asked that specific recommendations . . . be presented to me by December 1984.

A wave of laughter rippled through the well of the House. From my seat just below the rostrum where the President stood, I could see the faces of many congressmen and senators. Their features shone with mirth. They shot knowing glances at one another. They were laughing at the President and at me. I suppose that some of them thought that the President's proposal was an election-year gambit designed to get votes. Even as my blood rose, I realized that most of them were laughing because, like the men in the White House, they thought that true tax reform was a pipe dream. They may even have believed that the President thought so too, or else that he was a true naïf—for who else would believe that a measure that engaged the most selfish concerns of the most powerful interests in the nation could be accomplished by the deadline he had set, only eleven months in the future?

The laughter swelled to a louder pitch. My anger rose.

I said to myself, Just wait. I'll show you guys.

· 11 ·

Paying for Civilization

Counting weekends and holidays, the President had given Treasury 310 days to revolutionize the American tax system. I told my staff that that was plenty of time. *Revolutionize* was the operative word: we did not aim to plug loopholes and plaster over tax breaks, but to tear down the ramparts of the old tax system, level the ground, and start over again.

After we had met the deadline and delivered our proposal for tax reform to the President, a columnist of the *Washington Post* wrote that it had been carefully engineered to arouse the sympathy and support of middle-income and working-class Americans who resented the unfairness of the system and who would benefit from the lowering of individual tax rates. The columnist was absolutely right. It was obvious from the start that the only way to achieve true tax reform was to overwhelm the old guard with our boldness. The structure of inequity and inefficiency that had been built up over decades could not be dismantled piecemeal. It could only be smashed by a single blow.

At our first formal meeting at Treasury on February 13, 1984, I told the staff to be bold: to think in terms of compromise was to doom our effort. Our job was to make the tax system fairer and simpler and more economically efficient. We could not do that job if we played by the Washington rule of limiting ourselves to proposing the minimum that Congress and the special interests and the White House staff and others in the Administration might be willing to accept. It had been a long time since anyone in America had believed as wholeheartedly as Oliver Wendell Holmes that "taxes are what we pay for a civilized society." Our task was to replace a tax system that had made cynics out of nearly everybody it touched with a new system that would be so simple in its operation and so obvious in its purposes that taxpaying could once again be regarded as an unquestionable act of citizenship.

I realize that this sounds visionary, but in fact it was practical: my goal was to lower tax rates for everyone by eliminating the special privileges enjoyed by the few. A tax system in which everyone plays by the same rules, and in which the taxpayer is guaranteed that he can keep more of what he earns, provides incentives for harder work, greater efficiency, and higher productivity. This generates more earnings and consequently more revenue for the government. In other words, the same share of a bigger total makes for a fuller Treasury.

The Stockman-Feldstein-Baker-Darman faction and Congress would certainly keep up the pressure for a tax increase, and it was always possible that the President would be forced to yield to them. In case that happened, I told my staff to explore the possibilities of a value-added tax (VAT) and other forms of sales tax. This class of taxes is a great favorite of politicians and certain economists because it raises large amounts of money in relatively invisible ways. The arguments against it are well known: it is inequitable because the poor pay the same percentage of tax on what they purchase as the rich, and it tends to create a big, expensive bureaucracy to watch over it, a development that tends to perpetuate VAT, since it is almost always represented as a short-term solution to a shortfall in revenue. It is also inflationary. The VAT can be made somewhat more equitable by exempting necessities such as food, clothing, and medicine and concentrating on items that are more likely to be purchased by the well-to-do, but its fundamental social clumsiness cannot be cured altogether. Oddly enough, it seems to be the tax of choice of socialist governments, and is a common expedient in Western Europe.

The Treasury did not regard the value-added tax in any guise as an instrument of tax reform, or as a substitute for, or supplement to, the income tax. But its virtues as a method of easily raising large sums were obvious to everyone in Congress and the Administration who was arguing for a tax increase. Treasury would continue to argue against any increase in taxes, but if we lost the argument, and if the President yielded on tax increases as a means of reducing the deficit, then I wanted Treasury to be ready with a plan that would do the least possible economic damage.

Our aim, I repeated, was to reform the income tax *without raising taxes or lowering revenues*. In the jargon, this concept was expressed as "revenue-neutral reform." Of course we had been discussing tax reform and awaiting our opportunity to carry it out for three years, so we were hardly starting from scratch. The thinkers at Treasury had produced three main lines of approach.

The first was a consumed-income tax. Under this system, the taxpayer would deduct all the money he had saved or invested (but nothing else) from his income and pay taxes on the remainder at a fixed rate. This form of income tax has the obvious advantage of offering mighty incentives for savings and investment, and for that reason it has had many advocates among economists. But even economists acknowledge that the practical difficulties of administering such a plan are staggering.

The second was an income tax that included an adjustment for inflation, and the third was an income tax that did not take inflation into account. The question of whether a flat tax or a graduated tax should be used was embedded in all three choices.

I instructed the staff to marshal arguments for the three alternatives by March 15 so that I could decide which path to follow. They had absolute freedom of thought, speech, and action; political considerations were irrelevant. They were to disregard every factor except fairness, simplicity, and efficiency.

"Nothing is sacred," I told them. "The objective is to produce a level playing field on which all taxpayers are equal. Look at everything: the family unit, itemized deductions, fringe benefits, tax rates, tax credits."

Ever since the enactment of the income tax in 1913, taxes had been collected only on earnings actually in hand. If two neighbors have identical salaries of $20,000 a year, but neighbor A receives $4,000 worth of free but untaxed medical insurance, retirement benefits, and other fringes from his employer while neighbor B has to purchase the same benefits out of what he earns, it is clear that A is making $24,000 a year while B is making only $20,000. Yet both would pay taxes on $20,000. On a grander scale, actual statistics show that 60 percent of the $35 billion in "losses" reported from tax shelters in 1983 were claimed by taxpayers who earned more than $250,000 each. This is wrong and inequitable, and when the same concept is extended to entire industries, the results range from the absurd to the near-piratical. For most of my career on Wall Street I chafed under laws and regulations that gave the banking industry tax breaks that brokerage firms were denied under identical circumstances. After thirty years of trying I concluded that it was impossible to change the situation. Where the tax structure was concerned, justice and logic availeth nought.

It is no wonder that the popular saying equates death with taxes. The two were not only inevitable but almost equally incomprehensible. Why did the government take one person's money and not another's? Where did taxes go and why did they never come back in visible form? Such efforts as had so far been made at tax reform had been, in a sense, an effort to give back what had been taken away. That was certainly true of the tax cuts that were enacted in 1981: we may have said that we were reducing rates, but what in fact we were doing was giving back to individuals and corporations some of the unfair taxes that had been collected mainly as a result of inflation. A worker needed to earn $30,000 or more in 1980 to purchase the same goods and services that $20,000 would have bought in 1975. If he was lucky enough to dig up the extra $10,000, he had to pay taxes on the increase. The extra taxes, generated directly by inflation that was caused by deficit spending and loose money policy, created a huge windfall in unexpected taxes for the federal government. In Washington parlance this was called a "fiscal dividend." It gave Congress more money to spend, and little incentive to cut tax rates.

Looking at ourselves was part of the process, too. We would

examine the way the Internal Revenue Service conducted its affairs. How could tax forms be simplified? How could tax collection be simplified? How could the methods and purposes of the IRS be demystified so that every taxpayer could understand what the tax collector wanted and why he wanted it?

We knew that Treasury was losing billions through noncompliance with the tax laws. At least $90 billion in taxes due on personal and corporate income went unreported every year. The government did not know why; it was time to ask basic questions. Were tax rates too high? Was the cash economy a magnet for tax evaders? Was there more going on in the economy than was being captured by statistics? Were some people just naturally dishonest? These inquiries, I said, should be carried out as test of the validity of our underlying belief that higher tax rates produced higher levels of cheating.

In this connection I did not spare the staff my anecdote about my own feelings when I found myself in the 91-percent bracket on marginal earnings. And I returned again to Executive scripture, quoting the President's words in a speech delivered on July 19, 1982: "Will Rogers once said, 'I see a great deal of talk from Washington about lowering the taxes. I hope they get them lowered down enough so people can afford to pay them. . . .' We can close loopholes. We can broaden the tax base. . . . *We should go further in reducing tax rates and making the whole system fair and simple for everyone*." [Emphasis added.]

That, in the plain words of the man who had been elected by the American people, was our charter. I was determined that we would take it seriously and make the rest of Washington do the same. I was determined, too, that we would meet the President's deadline:

On March 15 we would decide which kind of income tax system to pursue.

By June 15 we would have a detailed analysis of the tax base, with particular attention being paid to deductions and credits. We would also have an analysis of special rules for special industries: oil and gas, real estate, banking, and all the others who had benefited from tax breaks.

By October 15 the complete tax reform package would be ready in outline form. And by November 15, we would go to the President with our final recommendations.

In response to a question from an interviewer on ABC's "Good Morning America" I had said that every Secretary of the Treasury must dream of reforming the tax system. The months between the State of the Union message and Election Day were, in that sense, a dream come true. The give-and-take of meetings in which first-class minds grappled with a problem that had generally been regarded as insoluble was extremely satisfying in itself. The knowledge that the result of this good-humored but fiercely pursued intellectual exercise might influence the economic course of the nation for generations to come answered the question of why one entered into public service. It really is possible to make a difference. There is no exhilaration like the exhilaration of working all out in the public interest, and I think that all of us who were engaged in the process felt this keenly at the time and will remember it long afterward.

Of course, tax reform was not all that we were doing at Treasury during this period. An Economic Summit in London reaffirmed the commitment of the Western powers to policies that would continue to encourage the economic recovery that was occurring in all the major nations. I attended the World Bank/International Monetary Fund meetings in Washington, and traveled to China for meetings to prepare for the President's visit. Third World debt, as well as our own budget deficit, was always with us. There were times during 1984 when the recovery looked very weak; we had to jawbone both the Federal Reserve and Congress to keep things on the right track.

The daily routine of the Treasury Department with its broad responsibilities and its large and very active staff was filled with interesting and difficult problems. From the Dallas convention in August until election day on November 6, the President was engaged in a campaign for reelection that occupied much of his attention and nearly the entire attention of the White House staff.

He was on the road every week, stumping on his own behalf and that of other Republican candidates. My own much more limited political activity took up a surprising amount of time, sometimes in a bizarre fashion: Republican fund-raisers auctioned off a game of golf, and two sporting party regulars from Denver paid $2,000 apiece to play eighteen holes with me as the third member of a foursome at Burning Tree Golf Club.

Nevertheless the process of tax reform went forward. We had decided, after lively argument, to develop a tax reform plan based on an income tax indexed to inflation, so that people would never again be taxed on earnings that had been wiped out or devalued by inflation.

Few stones remained unturned. Every provision of the tax code was examined on its merits. On point after point, large and small, we ruled against tax breaks that could not be justified on the basis of real need. Our method cut so deep, and assaulted such entrenched elements and practices, that very basic questions were brought to me for resolution. On one occasion, at the end of a long session in which sacred cows had been falling like ten-pins, I was asked to decide whether such things as heating oil and free rent of the parsonage, provided to a clergyman as part of his stipend, should be taxed as income. The logic of equal treatment that we had imposed on every similar question dictated the answer. "Tax it as income," I ruled, adding, "we've mugged everybody else—why should the clergy escape?"

In the end we made the March 15 deadline and eventually produced a simplified system that neither soaked the rich nor threw the burden of taxes onto the poor.

The old fourteen-tax-bracket system that ranged from 11 to 50 percent was replaced by a simple three-bracket system, with rates set at 15, 25, and 35 percent. The personal exemption for all taxpayers and dependents was increased to $2,000 from $1,090. Marginal tax rates were reduced by about 20 percent and individual tax liabilities by an average of 8½ percent.

Seventy-eight percent of all taxpayers would experience either a tax decrease or no change in their tax bills. Of all taxpayers facing higher taxes, half would experience a tax increase of less than 1 percent. Families with incomes below the poverty level ($11,800 for a family of four) were virtually exempted from taxation. Tax liabilities of families with incomes below $15,000 were reduced by 16.6 percent, double the average decrease.

Our proposals repealed or consolidated sixty-five provisions in the tax code, eliminated the need for at least sixteen tax forms, shortened the 1040 form by ten lines, reduced the number of individuals who itemized their deductions from 36 percent to fewer than 25 percent, and raised the possibility of a computer-based program that would eliminate tax filing altogether for the taxpayer who did not itemize deductions and was willing to trust the IRS to figure out his taxes on the basis of the data on wages and withholding already in its files.

Medical expenses, casualty losses, and the interest on home mortgages remained deductible, along with interest on consumer items and interest on second homes, but only up to $5,000 in excess of investment income.

The deduction for individual retirement accounts (IRAs) was increased from $2,000 to $2,500, and the IRA for spouses working in the home was increased to $2,500 as well.

We retained a deduction for charitable contributions in excess of 2 percent of adjusted gross income, but did away with the special exclusion for group term life insurance and the special treatment of cafeteria plans, as well as that for other employer-provided fringe benefits such as educational benefits, legal services, and dependent care. This was like shooting Santa Claus. But small companies couldn't provide such services, and individuals who were self-employed weren't allowed them.

Itemized deductions for all state and local taxes were eliminated. These deductions were claimed on only a minority of tax returns and disproportionately benefited higher-income individuals who worked in high-tax states and localities. And in another very controversial move, we recommended curtailing the use of business deductions for personal expenses, saying that deductions for entertainment should be denied, and deductions for business meals should be limited.

The corporate tax rate was cut to 33 percent, two percentage points below the top individual rate. Capital gains, like individual income, were adjusted for inflation, but then taxed as ordinary income. The investment tax credit for business was eliminated, but some relief was provided from the double taxation of dividends in which both the corporation and the stockholder paid taxes on the same dividend. We proposed that some interest on bonds issued by state and local governments for private purposes should be taxed, on grounds that they detracted from the fairness of the tax system and distorted capital flows.

Special tax preferences for the energy and financial sectors were phased out, including the oil-depletion allowance, which would henceforth be based on cost depletion rather than percentage depreciation, while the elimination of the windfall-profits tax on energy was brought forward to 1988. We also sought to make the rules for taxing all financial institutions uniform.

Though we simplified the tax system to the limits of our ingenuity in the time available, our report to the President, including all of its tables, was 262 pages long, not counting the 536 pages of two supplemental volumes. I reflected, as I placed this weighty document in his hands on November 26, 1984, that our simplified plan was still far too long, but it was a hell of a lot shorter than the sixty-three feet of bookshelves required to accommodate the existing tax code and its concordances.

I asked the President if he had ever made as much as a million dollars a year before he became President.

He was surprised by what must have seemed an irrelevant personal question.

Not that much, by a long shot, the President replied.

"Six figures, then?"

The President nodded.

"Okay—how much did you pay in taxes?"

By now the President saw a story coming. He named a figure that amounted to about half of his earnings.

"*Sucker!*" I said. "With the right lawyer and the right accountant and the right tax shelters, you needn't have paid a penny in taxes even if you made more than a million dollars a year—and it would have been perfectly legal and proper. The tax system we have now is designed to make the avoidance of taxes easy for the rich and has the effect of making it almost impossible for people who work for wages and salaries to do the same. As someone who has made a lot of money and benefited from the system, I can tell you it's a great thing for people with high incomes and good tax advisers. But as your Secretary of the Treasury, I'm telling you that it ain't fair and that it is undermining the morale of taxpayers and crippling the economy. Too many people are getting away with too much. You asked for a plan to change all that, and that's what I've brought you today."

In my letter of transmittal to the President I made the same points somewhat more formally.

After this would come the political deluge. If the President acted on his principles, I was sanguine about the outcome. In taxation as in defense policy, the best politics is no politics. Treasury's job was to produce a tax system that treated everyone alike and collected enough money to run the government. I was under no illusion that we had produced an irresistible document, but I knew that we were giving the President a powerful lever; if he stood his ground he might very well move this particular world. Let the opponents of reform fight for their special constituencies. The President, to paraphrase Harry S Truman, has only one constituency—the people. If any President ever understood that truth in his bones, Ronald Reagan did. Whether the White House apparatus understood this, even after a victory at the polls in which Reagan had carried forty-nine of the fifty states and virtually doubled his winning margin in the popular vote, was questionable.

The meeting in which we explained the tax package to the President lasted for an hour and forty minutes—the longest encounter by far I had had with him to date. It was obvious that Ronald Reagan liked what he heard. Manley Johnson, the Assistant Secretary of the Treasury for Economic Policy, had told us that his studies of the new tax plan had shown that it would be more effective than the existing tax system in stimulating economic growth. I believed that Johnson was correct, but it was impossible to be certain of this result, and others would certainly dispute our conclusions. I advised the President to stand back for a while and listen to the arguments on the other side.

"Don't embrace the whole plan right away," I said. "Be cool—watch what happens. This plan steps on a lot of toes, but I think we've given you what you wanted—a tax system that's simpler and fairer and doesn't raise taxes. If it turns out that we're wrong, that what we've proposed will ruin certain industries or undermine the economy, then you must be prepared to scrap the whole idea and preserve your authority and credibility so that you can start over again."

The President grinned and nodded. That's a good idea, Don, he said wryly.

In his discussions of the Treasury plan, the President followed my advice to the letter. On November 27, the day after he received the plan, he told the Cabinet that he would wait for reactions to Treasury's proposals before deciding what to send to Congress. On the same day he issued a public statement saying that his Administration would "listen to the comments and suggestions of all Americans, especially those from Congress." On November 29 he invited the Republican leadership of the House and Senate to the White House to discuss the Treasury study.

The critics were already at the moat. *U.S. News & World Report* wrote as follows: "Within hours of its unveiling, the Treasury plan drew criticism from big business, big labor, oil, real estate, and many other industries as well as charities, mayors, and a myriad of other groups with stakes in the current tax code." *Time* quoted an aide to Democratic Senator William Proxmire as saying, "Among those who have expressed opposition to the tax plan are organized labor, banks, the life insurance industry, charities, colleges, state and local governments, aerospace companies, chemical companies, metal fabricating firms, railroads, airlines, utilities, real-estate groups, oil companies, restaurants and hotels, credit-card companies, stock exchanges, and credit unions."

The chairman of the Senate Finance Committee, Robert Packwood, Republican of Oregon, was quoted as saying, "I sort of like the tax code the way it is." Democratic Senator Pat Moynihan said that the plan would be ruinous to New York and added,

"I'm on the Finance Committee to see that it doesn't happen."
But Representative Charles Rangel, a Democrat whose district in
upper Manhattan includes Harlem and other neighborhoods in
which many poor people live, said, "It's the greatest thing to come
along. . . . I've been pleading for four years to get the working
poor out of the tax system, and this plan does it." *Newsweek* columnist Robert J. Samuelson was quoted as saying, "If you sim-
plify the tax code [Congress] lose[s] power, and that's why
Packwood doesn't like it." Samuelson noted the political appeal
inherent in a plan in which individuals—who vote—receive a
tax cut averaging 8½ percent while corporations get a tax increase. Governor Bruce Babbitt of Arizona, a dutiful liberal, told
his fellow Democrats that they should abandon the "lazy orthodoxy of the past and adopt the Treasury plan. . . . It is a superb
proposal . . . so good that the President won't have the courage
to endorse it." Ralph Nader praised the plan. The Chamber of
Commerce denounced it. This juxtaposition of reactions caused
me to wonder whether I had missed some oddity in my own plan
that was obvious to others.

Time commented that the Treasury plan, "if enacted . . . would
put Ronald Reagan's mark on the U.S. economy and on American society for a generation or more." Robert McIntire of the
liberal Citizens for Tax Justice was quoted in *The New Republic* to
the effect that the plan might boost the rate of U.S. economic
growth by 2 or 3 percent yearly. John Makin of the conservative
American Enterprise Institute was quoted in the same magazine
as saying that the plan could produce efficiency gains of $1 bil-
lion a year by encouraging investors to invest their money more
efficiently.

The reaction of the White House staff in the face of this uproar was predictable if exasperating: the ship of state began to
leak like a sieve. On the morning after I presented the plan to
the President (and before I had given my own verbal summary
to the press) the substance of that confidential briefing, issuing
from anonymous Presidential aides, appeared on the front pages
of the *Wall Street Journal*, the *New York Times*, and the *Washington
Post*. Even the *Baltimore Sun* was able to discuss my program in

detail before I revealed it in a press conference. Unnamed White House sources were quoted as saying that the President had decided to distance himself from the plan. Maybe these shadowy leakers did not know about my advice to the President, but their hint that Reagan lacked enthusiasm for the Treasury plan did not make it any easier to gain Republican support for our proposals, and it also cut the moral ground from under the President's feet.

On Wednesday, November 28, on "Good Morning America," I was asked about the President's purported ambivalence and seized the opportunity to quote myself on what I had actually said to him. I said, "I told him to back off. I said, 'Look, it's Treasury's proposal. We put it out to get it on the table. Let's have a discussion. By the time of the State of the Union message in January, you'll be able to come out with a plan for simplification.'"

Whether the truth sounded like the truth was by now a real question. On the morning of November 26, *before* I briefed the President, the columnists Evans and Novak, referring to "worried White House aides," wrote that "Treasury's tax plan would launch a second term by alienating some of his staunchest supporters and exciting nobody. . . . The White House is now faced with a need for radical surgery in a product so long in the making that it could further roil disturbed waters between Treasury Secretary Donald T. Regan and the President's men [*sic*]. Anything less could mean legislative disaster for the freshly reelected Reagan."

The White House staff, from its Chief on down, was surprised, not to say taken aback, by what Treasury had produced. I don't think they expected anything like the plan we came up with, and the more they studied it, the more they realized the far-reaching effects true tax reform would have on the economy, the electorate, and society in general. Great risks were involved in pushing the plan, and risk-taking is not the language of image-makers. In winning reelection the President had just won the greatest gamble an American can take; his advisers naturally thought in terms of resting on their laurels. The President had not run on a promise of tax reform but on a wave of good feeling that his advisers believed, with some justice, was a product of their manipulation of the media. Why should they subject the President and themselves to the bruising public battle that tax reform was certain to be? Their hearts simply weren't in it.

Mine was. And so was the President's. But how effectively he would be able to act on his principles and his instincts was unclear. The men around him were experts in indirect action, more accustomed to avoiding issues than to advising the President when to say yes and when to say no. The good fight for tax reform, like so many issues before it, was degenerating into a squabble in the media rather than becoming a grand debate on the future of our nation led by the President. Once more a question that involved the most profound interests of the nation would find its answer in the war of words and the struggle for advantage that was now taking place in the press, in the Congress, and in that cacophonous electronic cloakroom that is made up of television images, telephone conversations, and computerized polls.

This was happening not by design, but because there was no design for leadership. There was no inventory of national priorities, no philosophical consensus on which policy was based, no system for carrying a problem that subordinates could not solve to the President for final decision, no provision for the confidentiality without which no friendship, no marriage, no business, and certainly no Presidency can function. It seemed to me, after four years of living in an environment in which policy seemed to be made on the basis of a belief in public opinion that amounted to superstition, that the Presidency was in need of sound management advice. Willy-nilly, Ronald Reagan had achieved great things in four years. What might he do if his office were better organized and his ideas were more systematically transformed into policy?

I had not conceived of myself as the Lone Reaganite, rescuing the President's ideas from the captivity of yesterday's headlines and translating them into policy and programs. But I had often reflected that the Administration might be more efficient if its members acknowledged that the President was the inspiration for its actions and the source of its power. Its objective was, or ought to have been, to act on the promises, express and implied, that Ronald Reagan had made to the American people.

Gradually the thought had formed in my mind that it might be possible to manage the Executive Branch with that objective clearly in mind. It might be possible, if you could get a grip on the apparatus, to change the way this government did business in a fundamental way. The Treasury plan for tax reform was proof that management by objective was an attainable goal in government. We had set out to cut the Gordian knot, and judging by the way the Washington system was reacting, we had succeeded. But now the fate of our plan had passed into other hands. If all that we had accomplished went aglimmering as a result, what was the point of all the creative work that Treasury had done?

On November 15 something had happened at a Cabinet meeting to crystallize my misgivings about the way in which the President's business was being handled. The Treasury Report had been compiled and was about to be presented to the President without any of its provisions being leaked to the press until the very last days. This was regarded by some of my Cabinet colleagues as a minor miracle, and George Shultz suggested that I bring up the question of leaks at the Cabinet meeting. I did so, making a strong case to the President for discipline in relations with the press—and for strong disciplinary action against leakers, particularly White House staffers.

The next day, the substance of my remarks on my assigned topic—economics—appeared in a story by the *Washington Post*'s White House reporter as the result of what I took to be a leak by the White House staff. I was infuriated by this treacherous insult to the President and to me, and at 7:50 A.M., with the *Post* still in my hand, I called Jim Baker and gave him the full benefit of my reaction in Marine Corps terminology. The conversation ended with my shouting something a lot stronger than Go to the devil, Jim Baker! and slamming down the receiver.

As soon as I had hung up I dictated a letter of resignation to the President and sent Chris Hicks to the White House to deliver it. The aide to whom Chris handed this communication, the

President's personal assistant, Dave Fischer, was reluctant to forward it, without sending it through channels. Inasmuch as Dick Darman, the Baker aide in charge of paper flow, was among the usual suspects where leaks to the *Post* were concerned, Chris insisted that the letter be delivered by Fischer.

However, the letter did find its way to the Oval Office, and later in the morning I received a call from the President.

I got your letter, he said, and I'm calling to tell you that I can't accept your resignation. In fact I'm tearing it up right now and burning it in the fireplace.

"I appreciate that, Mr. President," I replied. "But I meant what I wrote. This atmosphere of leaks and mistrust is simply intolerable, and I want to go."

Well, you can't go, Don, and that's final, the President replied. You're the only friend I have around here. If you go, I'll have to get my hat and go with you.

The man is not yet born who could resist words like these from the President of the United States. But my misgivings were still very close to the surface a few moments later, when Jim Baker called to ask if he could drop in "just for a chat." It was obvious that he wanted to explain the leak and smooth things over. I asked him to stay for lunch. My anger cooled, and I was glad enough to have the opportunity of talking to Baker. He seemed tired, distracted. He dropped into a chair, sighed loudly, shook his head, gave a wry smile. I asked him what was bothering him.

He spoke the several names of the Lord one after the other, and then described some of his behind-the-scenes experiences with the leading figures of American politics and government. The Administration was fighting the annual battle of the budget in a Presidential election year, the President was constantly on the campaign trail, a dozen issues were being promoted by a hundred advocates, and the press was hostile, hungry, and confused. Wolves were all around the White House, and even inside it. As Chief of Staff, he was in the thick of everything, responsible for mistakes he never made.

I said, "You know what the trouble with you is, Baker? You're tired."

Jim gave me an ironical look: How did I know?

"You're right," he said. "I really am tired. I've got to get away from this."

"You'll never do that," I said with a laugh. "You're a political junkie; you're hooked."

But Baker would not be kidded. We talked more about the strains and tensions of his impossible job. He kept insisting that it had worn him out, that he needed a change.

Finally I said, "You know what we should do, Jim? We should swap jobs."

Our conversation had been half-serious, half-joking. I tossed out these words without thinking. But Baker bobbed his head like a man who has been hit with an idea.

"Do you mean that?" he asked.

I thought for a moment. "I guess I do," I said.

We sat in silence for a moment. Baker rose to his feet. He now looked much less tired and harried.

"Watch out—I may take you up on that," he said.

"Okay," I replied. "When you're ready to talk, I'll be here."

It was as simple as that.

PART THREE

In the White House

· 12 ·

"Let Reagan Be Reagan"

Mike Deaver later claimed that he broke the news of the Baker-Regan job swap to Ronald Reagan with the words, "Mr. President, I've brought you a playmate of your own age." If Deaver uttered this witticism on the day in question I don't remember it. But it is certainly true that the atmosphere in the Oval Office was relaxed, even lighthearted, when Jim Baker and Deaver and I called on the President just after New Year's, 1985, to tell him what we had in mind.

Near the end of November, Baker had called me to ask if I remembered our conversation about the job swap. I said that I did. Was I still thinking in the same way? I suggested that we get together and talk about it. On November 30, Baker called on me in my office at Treasury. Over lunch in the conference room, he came right to the point: would the President accept our plan if we decided to go ahead with it?

"How would we approach The Man on this?" Baker asked.

"Hell, I'll talk to him," I replied.

Baker passed over that suggestion. He asked a series of very intelligent questions about Treasury. The job interested him; it was only slightly less prestigious (if much less visible to the media) than Secretary of State, the Cabinet post I guessed he might have preferred, and the forthcoming struggle with Congress over tax reform would give him a chance to use his strong talents as a legislative negotiator in an important cause that was bound to create a lot of press coverage. I do not mean to suggest by the foregoing remark that Baker was primarily interested in personal publicity, but he understood very clearly that celebrity and effectiveness are inseparable handmaidens in Washington.

We swapped insights on our respective jobs for half an hour or so. At the end of our conversation we had achieved a meeting of the minds without committing ourselves to a course of action. I asked for a few days to think the matter over. So far, I had not discussed the swap with anyone but my wife, and I assumed that Baker had not done so, either. Now he suggested bringing another person into our confidence.

"We'll have to get Mike Deaver involved," Baker said. "We could never do this without telling Mike."

"Fine," I said.

On December 18 the three of us met at Baker's house for luncheon. It was a discreet gathering, designed to avoid arousing the curiosity of the White House press corps. On the telephone, Baker and I had agreed that a quiet lunch at Jim's home (Deaver lived nearby) would excite less attention than my walking into the gossipy inferno of the White House. It was only natural, we told each other conspiratorially, that the three of us should meet to discuss the economy and tax reform and other such issues in the wake of the election.

At this time I hardly knew Mike Deaver. For four years, on encountering me in the White House, he had greeted me with the brief nod that he bestowed on nearly all outsiders (according to the pecking-order charts kept by lofty White House aides, even Cabinet officers are outsiders). It was the same when we met elsewhere. Deaver and I did not travel in the same social circles: Ann and I tended to have small dinners with old friends and neighbors, while the Deavers frequented the tables of famous journalists and powerful politicians. Like most human beings, great and ordinary, Mike had no particular interest in people who did not know the people he knew. We were, moreover, interested in different subjects. On the occasions when Deaver had sat in on Presidential meetings that involved economic issues, I had been struck by his easy manner with the President and by his evident boredom with issues. When fiscal and monetary policy were discussed, Deaver's eyes visibly glazed over. There was, of course, no reason for him to be interested in the substance of policy. His job was to sell the product once it was invented and ready to be marketed. Deaver was in charge of the Reagans' public image, and judging by the results he had achieved, he deserved his reputation as a public relations expert.

At our luncheon at Jim Baker's house, Deaver was alert, interested, and cordial. Baker and I took him through the history of our conversations on the subject, leaving nothing out, and described our reasons for believing that the swap was a good idea. Deaver, eating sparingly (I later learned that he preferred health food), listened to our words with the polite air of a man who had already heard what he was now being told and had made up his mind how to react. I supposed that Baker had sketched in the details beforehand. In my innocence the thought that Deaver had cleared the plan with the First Lady before discussing it with me, or even with the President, did not occur to me.

"Yup," Deaver said at last in a decisive tone. "It's a good idea." He listed his reasons: the beginning of the second term was the natural time for a change of Chiefs of Staff; I had been loyal to the President; I had no discernible personal agenda; nobody had to worry about my running for public office à la Al Haig. In Deaver's view, even my age was in my favor: my sixty-sixth birthday was less than a month ahead.

"This would be your terminal job, Don," Deaver observed, turning a memorable phrase. "Let's go to the President with it."

These were important words, and Baker's satisfaction on hearing them was obvious. It was evident even to a newcomer like me that it was a good thing to have Deaver aboard. He had not become the Reagans' closest retainer by letting himself be perceived as a bearer of bad tidings. Evidently he felt that he would be telling the President something that the President would want to hear in describing the proposed trade of his Chief of Staff and Secretary of the Treasury. That, at least, is the way I interpreted the facts at the time.

Christmas was almost upon us, so we decided that we would

not talk to the President before he and Mrs. Reagan departed for Palm Springs, where they were scheduled to spend the New Year's holiday. In my unfamiliarity with Reagan's ways, I had imagined that the President would want time and solitude to think over an exchange of men and responsibilities that had no precedent in the history of the Presidency. However, Baker would schedule a meeting for us later in the Oval Office.

Ronald Reagan, as I was shortly to learn through experience, observes his schedule religiously. He is never late for an appointment, seldom so carried away by a discussion that it runs overtime. It often occurred to me later on that this remarkable personal discipline had something to do with his life as an actor: he was used to making movies, an activity in which every word and gesture were scripted. In Hollywood, time was money, and punctuality and preparation were the hallmarks of the professional. As President, Ronald Reagan acted on the work habits of a lifetime: he regarded his daily schedule as being something like a shooting script in which characters came and went, scenes were rehearsed and acted out, and the plot was advanced one day at a time, and not always in sequence. The Chief of Staff was a sort of producer, making certain that the star had what he needed to do his best; the staff was like the crew, invisible behind the lights, watching the performance their behind-the-scenes efforts had made possible. . . . I won't carry the analogy further. Reagan's performance was almost always flawless. If he was scheduled to receive a visitor at ten o'clock, he would finish whatever else he was doing at 9:58, clear off his desk, clear his mind of whatever had gone before, and prepare himself for the next scene. There was no element of falsity in this. Nearly all politicians, and many other people besides, are actors by nature. Reagan just happened to be a trained professional to whom the mechanics of the craft had become second nature through a lifetime of practice.

These insights would come to me later, but even on that first morning of my new and closer relationship with the President I felt it in the air. A composed, smiling Reagan was waiting for us when Baker, Deaver, and I walked into the Oval Office on January 7, 1985. He expressed no surprise at the unusual sight of the three of us together without the customary retinue of aides and dignitaries crowding along behind.

After an exchange of pleasantries about our respective vacations, Deaver broached the subject of the job swap to the President. Omitting preliminaries, he said, "Mr. President, Don has something he wants to discuss with you that he's talked to Jim and me about. We think it's very interesting and we'd like to know what you think about it."

Naturally Deaver gave the impression that whatever I was going to say was strictly my idea. That was fair enough. After all, the exchange *was* my idea, and besides, Deaver and Jim Baker would have to go on working for "The Man" no matter what the outcome of this interview. If Reagan rejected this novel scheme, it was better that they not be too closely associated with it.

Reagan replied without hesitation.

I could see that something was up with you three, he said. Let's have it.

There was a twinkle in the Presidential eye; Deaver—bald, small, and bustling—projected a sort of cheeky familiarity in the President's presence and Reagan seemed to enjoy his irreverence. All this was new to me, of course; I had seen very little of the President as he was now—at home and relaxed with the men who were closest to him.

I explained what Baker and I had in mind. Reagan listened without any sign of surprise. He seemed equable, relaxed—almost incurious. This seemed odd under the circumstances. The change I was describing was significant in itself, but it was only the latest in a series of changes that involved the President's closest aides. Deaver had ideas about leaving, but I do not know whether he had at this point told Reagan about his intention to resign as Deputy Chief of Staff (a title that in no way described the truly pervasive influence and power that Deaver exercised in the White House), and Ed Meese was soon to become Attorney General. Now Baker, the last of the three advisers who had been at Reagan's side all during his two successful campaigns for the Presidency and his first term in office, wanted to go elsewhere. Any Chief of Staff who came after this triumvirate would be taking over duties formerly carried out by all three men. It was a demanding situation, and one in which the President could not afford a mistake.

To a degree, I was an unfamiliar quantity, although by now the President knew my work and my ideas, and I had the impression that he was comfortable with both. Certainly my belief in his aims and in his ability to achieve them was very strong. But Treasury was one thing and the White House, with its swirling political currents and the stark visibility of nearly all its actions, was another. It was also true that Reagan and I hardly knew each other as men. In the President's place I would have put many questions to the applicant: How will you be different from Jim Baker? How will you handle Congress? What do you know about defense and foreign affairs? Who will you bring with you and who will you want to get rid of? What practices will you want to change? How will you handle the press? Why do you want this job?

Reagan made no inquiries. I did not know what to make of his passivity.

"Well, Mr. President," I said after a moment. "Maybe you'd like to think about all this."

Reagan waved away the suggestion. Tell me a little more, he said.

Thinking that he wanted to know where this unusual idea had come from, I summarized its history, mentioning Baker's fatigue, my sense that I had completed my mission at Treasury, and our mutual desire for a new challenge. With due sensitivity to the presence of the man I was going to replace, I told the President about my thoughts in regard to reorganizing the management of the Executive Branch. Cordial but silent, Reagan listened.

"You know me well enough after four years to know what I stand for," I said finally. "And I think that you and I see things alike."

Reagan nodded affably. He looked at Baker and Deaver as if to check the expressions on their faces, but asked them no questions, either. Baker and Deaver were even quieter than the President; they offered no comment or advice. Finally the President broke the silence.

This thing does make sense, he said. Yes, yes—I'll go for it.

I looked at my watch. Less than thirty minutes had passed since the meeting began. The President's easy acceptance of this wholly novel idea of switching his Chief of Staff and his Secretary of the Treasury, and of the consequent changes in his own daily life and in his Administration, surprised me. He seemed to be absorbing a *fait accompli* rather than making a decision. One might have thought that the matter had already been settled by some absent party. Perhaps, I thought, the President should be encouraged to take a little more time.

"There's no need to decide this question right this minute, Mr. President," I said. "Take your time; really think it over. This is a serious move. And if you decide against it, my nose won't be out of joint."

I appreciate that, Don, the President said with the bright courtesy that is typical of him. But I don't see why we shouldn't just go ahead with it.

In the brief discussion that followed, it was decided that the President and Baker and I would give the matter more thought, including personnel to go or stay. But, unless one of us changed his mind, the President would make the announcement himself as soon as possible. There were grins all around: all of us knew what a stir this would make. Before we parted, Baker, Deaver, and I spent a few minutes together in Baker's office, talking over the details. We agreed to say nothing about this to anyone except our wives.

That evening, while I drank my glass of white wine and Ann had her orange juice, my wife and I discussed the encounter in the Oval Office and the mixed future it opened up before us. Ann had already given me her opinion of the project in the form of the obvious question: Why, at my age, did I want to subject myself to the demanding and essentially thankless job of Chief of Staff, when the house in Florida, our grandchildren, the golf course, and personal peace and freedom were mine for the taking? I explained my goal—to bring a semblance of managerial order to the affairs of the Presidency. Ann pointed out that I was not the first businessman who had come to Washington with this quixotic notion in his head. I answered that not many others had been offered the opportunity to manage the day-to-day operations of the Presidency itself. I thought that I had a chance to make a difference—maybe even change the way the government did business once and for all.

Ann, born and raised in Washington, was skeptical. I outlined my reasons for optimism: the voters had given Reagan an overwhelming victory at the polls and a matchless opportunity to complete his agenda, but the golden moment would not last. It seemed to me that he would have to accomplish his domestic goals—tax reform, budget reform—before the next congressional elections. I told Ann that these were the issues on which I was qualified to help him the most. Soon, if history repeated itself, Reagan would be a lame-duck President whose domestic accomplishments would largely be behind him. Like most of his modern predecessors, his interest would shift and be absorbed by foreign affairs in the last two years of his second term. When that happened it would be time for me to leave.

"It will just be for a couple of years and then I'll be out," I told Ann. "The President can bring in a caretaker for the last two years."

Ann reminded me that I had said the same thing about my probable length of service on becoming Secretary of the Treasury—and here we were, four years later, still in Washington. This time events would make a better prophet of me.

Ann and I had spent a happy Christmas with members of our family. During the holidays I had had time to think over what I might do if the President liked the idea and wanted to go ahead with it. Apparently, Baker had done the same.

So, despite Ann's entirely sensible reservations about the enterprise, Baker and I quickly agreed on a rough timetable. "I'll take him through the State of the Union, and then we'll make the switch around the first of February," Baker said. "Meanwhile we can help each other to learn the ropes—you can start coming over to the White House and attending more meetings, and I'll start spending more of my time at Treasury." The announcement came on Tuesday, January 8, and as we had hoped, it caught everyone by surprise.

In fact, I began work as Chief of Staff at 7:20 A.M. on Monday, February 4, 1985—two days before the President delivered his State of the Union address. He was not happy with the draft of the speech, and said so in my first meeting with him as Chief of Staff. The President welcomed me very cordially and asked me to sit in the chair on his right alongside his desk; thereafter I never sat anywhere else except when the Vice President or the Secretary of State were present. The President had been working on the speech for several days, crossing out sentences and writing in new ones and making suggestions for the speech writers. He had gone over the final draft the night before. Plainly he was not yet satisfied with its tone or substance.

It's too much like my Inaugural address, the President complained, and it doesn't spell out what we're going to do over the next four years.

He wanted a more forward-looking speech, one with bite and substance.

Speeches were Deaver's province. "We'll staff it out, Mr. President," he said. "But I doubt that there can be any more changes on substance."

To my surprise, the President accepted this, deciding to go along with only minor changes, as Deaver had suggested.

We moved on to other matters, discussing the state visit by King Fahd of Saudi Arabia the next week, and talked about the "voluntary restraints" (VRA) on imports of Japanese cars. The President was under the impression that the Japanese had in fact volunteered to limit imports. I bluntly told him that this was not so: there had been a lot of winking, nodding, and prodding of the Japanese by members of his Administration to produce the VRA. The President did not think that VRA was needed, but he foresaw a big push by the auto industry for more protection. I told him that General Motors had just reported earnings of $4½ billion for 1984; the industry as a whole would probably earn between $8 and $9 billion for the year. With those earnings coming on top of record earnings for 1983, there was no way we could justify being saddled with a VRA. The President agreed.

Owing largely to the President's sunny and open personality, these first exchanges seemed natural and relaxed. By now, too, Baker and I had been visiting back and forth for several weeks. I had accustomed myself to the idea of working in the White House at the right hand of the President, so that the experience of being driven through the southwest gate that first morning in an official car was less spine-tingling than it might have been if I had arrived fresh from the outside world.

Still, it would be a strange American who did not feel the presence of history and the power of patriotism almost as a physical sensation on entering the White House in the circumstances that brought me there. Other impulses, less worthy perhaps but equally human, were present also: this house is, after all, the center of power in our epoch, and even for a person of my age, there is a certain exhilaration in knowing that you have become the right-hand man of the President of the United States and an eyewitness to the making of history. Every schoolchild is taught that such an outcome is possible in any American life, but that does not altogether eliminate what can only be called the thrill of being the one person in a population of almost 240 million who actually gets the job.

Yet it is a sobering experience to realize that you have been entrusted with managing the time of the most powerful man in the world. A President has no more than eight years (and he may be granted half that time or even less) to keep the promises he has made to the people. Therefore it is true of the President as it is true of few other men that he hasn't a minute to waste. Every meeting, every conversation, every ceremony must have a purpose, and it must take place in the time allotted to it. What a President might fail to do for lack of time can have profound consequences. Long after I got used to the daily reality of being Chief of Staff I would find myself waking with a start to the strangeness of my situation. No doubt that sensation occurs in every life, and it had happened before in my own. But this was not the same as moving to a new neighborhood in childhood, or Harvard, or the Marines, or Wall Street. Now, when I remembered where I was, I would say to myself, My God, Regan—who are you to be telling the President of the United States how to spend his day?

The job of Chief of Staff provides many correctives to *hubris*, and I will try to provide a fairly complete inventory of these before coming to the end of this book. The West Wing of the White House, where the President and his staff do their work, belongs on the list. It is populated by the shades of people who have risen to great heights, but also fallen in failure and even disgrace. The West Wing is a cramped, shadowy place of small offices and narrow corridors—plainer by far than most other such places in the world.

The office occupied by the Chief of Staff is located on the southwest corner of the West Wing. The Oval Office occupies the southeast corner, with only a small staff office in between. Location—the supreme value in real estate—and some excellent paintings of Western scenes on loan from the National Gallery of Art, were pretty much all that the space allotted to me had in its favor. My offices at Treasury and Merrill Lynch had been palatial by comparison, and a whole lot sunnier. Heavy drapes, trimmed in ribbon, covered the windows. These looked out on shrubs screening the South Lawn on one side and the Executive Office Building on the other, but such light as they admitted seemed to be absorbed by a huge built-in desk and bookcase made of dark wood. The desk faced the wall, so that the occupant sat with his back to the room. Bare wires, originally installed for a vanished communications system of the Nixon era, dangled from holes in the desk. Overstuffed wingback chairs and a matching sofa, upholstered in bold stripes, were placed in front of the fireplace on a worn gold rug. A conference table stood behind the desk chair. The total effect was dusty and cluttered. I was told that H. R. ("Bob") Haldeman, Nixon's first Chief of Staff, had chosen the desk, and the decor seemed to match. None of his successors had bothered to change it. It would have been unwise for me to follow my instincts and order immediate renovations ("REGAN DEMANDS PLUSH WHITE HOUSE OFFICE"). But as soon as I could tactfully do so, I had the place redecorated and refurnished mostly at my expense. To my surprise, Pat Buchanan claimed Haldeman's great somber desk when I was through with it and installed it in his own office elsewhere in the West Wing. Despite their shortcomings, offices in the West Wing were hungrily coveted. One high-ranking official, relegated to a beautiful and spacious vaulted office in the Executive Office Building, pleaded with me with tears in his eyes for space, any space, in the West Wing.

The President had given me freedom to organize the White House as I thought best. I had asked him at the outset which he preferred—a continuation of the present system or a reorganization based on the way of doing business I had developed in ten years at the head of Merrill Lynch and four years as Secretary of the Treasury. Some changes were inevitable. Where formerly he had had four principal advisers—Baker, Meese, and Deaver on the domestic side and McFarlane for foreign affairs, he would now have only two. McFarlane would remain, his duties and powers unchanged, reporting directly to the President, and with the right (accorded to only six people under Baker)* to walk unannounced into the President's office. All duties formerly exercised by Baker, Meese, and Deaver devolved on me—personnel, the coordination of information, the choice of issues, the flow of paper, and the schedule that controlled the President's travel and other movements and determined who would see him and who would not.

Reagan told me to handle this many-sided job any way I wished. But he made one proviso:

Just be sure that I hear both sides of every issue, the President said. And if there are more than two sides, I want to hear

*The six were Baker, Meese, Deaver, McFarlane, Dave Fischer (the President's personal assistant), and Kathy Osborne (the President's secretary). In practice, McFarlane checked with Baker before entering the Oval Office. In my time as Chief of Staff, access was limited to McFarlane, Jim Kuhn (who replaced Fischer), Kathy Osborne, and myself. The Vice President obviously had the privilege of calling on the President whenever he wished.

all of them. I don't mind making decisions as long as I know what everybody thinks.

The President and I never sat down to discuss the organization of the White House staff. I got the impression that he expected me to keep most of the staff, replacing only the people who departed with Baker or on their own. The exodus was gradual—Craig Fuller, then Deaver, Stockman, and later Fred Fielding, the Counsel, Jack Svahn, and Larry Speakes. I replaced them one by one and told the President of my choices. He never demurred until the end.

Some of my ideas for change were far-reaching. In the first Administration, Ed Meese had organized the Cabinet into seven "Cabinet Councils" to deal with various aspects of domestic and foreign policy. As a Cabinet officer I had found the system cumbersome and redundant, and I envisaged reducing the number dealing with domestic affairs to two—a Domestic Policy Council, headed by Meese, and an Economic Policy Council, headed by the Secretary of the Treasury, who of course was the outgoing Chief of Staff, Jim Baker. These two men were familiar with nearly every detail of the whole range of issues and were particularly sensitive to the President's thinking. The National Security Council constituted a de facto policy council on foreign affairs, and I left it undisturbed except to recommend to the President that he approve Jim Baker's request that the Secretary of the Treasury, the Attorney General, and the Chief of Staff be added as members.

Issues for the policy councils would be researched by the Office of Policy Development (OPD). Only Cabinet members and essential staff would be permitted to attend meetings. The formulation of policy requires an atmosphere of confidentiality. How else can you expect people to say what they really think? The deliberations of these bodies were designed to produce recommendations for the President. It was his practice to speak to the issue after it had been placed before him by his advisers.

The Executive Office of the President is a large establishment, employing about sixteen hundred people in fourteen separate agencies; the budget authority for this permanent establishment was $116 million in fiscal 1985. Hundreds more people are seconded from other federal departments and agencies; Secret Service agents on detail from Treasury are the best known of the supernumeraries, but others come from the military services, the CIA, the Department of the Interior, and elsewhere. Their agencies pay their salaries and certain other costs; many millions of dollars are involved. Few of these people can be quartered in the West Wing. Many, including the entire staff of the National Security Council except the Advisor himself and his immediate staff, are accommodated in the Executive Office Building, a huge granite structure in the French Second Empire style that formerly housed the entire State, War, and Navy Departments. The EOB offices, designed by French architects and completed in 1888, can be splendid indeed. The building contains two miles of marbled corridors, and to give one example of many, David Stockman's accommodations were fit for a Director of OMB in a movie about Napoleon III. This wasn't Stockman's fault—there just wasn't room for him in the West Wing.

There were, however, some vacant offices in the West Wing. I had decided to reduce the number of Assistants to the President from seventeen to eleven. To a certain extent, this reduction would be accomplished by natural attrition. Jim Baker had taken his aide, Richard Darman, with him to Treasury. Others had announced plans to move on, either to improve their financial positions or to return to jobs from which they had taken leave of absence. Still others were uncertain about their future but eager to remain. Because high-level appointees had the right to choose their own staffs, sometimes numbering thirty or forty people, once they had moved on, a certain number of their remaining staff members were bound to be disappointed. Some were just burned out by four years of service to the President. Several excellent people came with me from Treasury—Al Kingon as Cabinet Secretary; David Chew, as the person in charge of all Presidential paperwork; Chris Hicks, in charge of Administration; and Tom Dawson as my Executive Assistant. The new Director of Communications was Pat Buchanan. I persuaded Max Friedersdorf to handle relations with Congress. Dennis Thomas arrived in July as my de facto number two with the title of Assistant to the President without portfolio.

As an antidote to the leaks to the media that had plagued the White House in the first term, I asked them all to cultivate a passion for anonymity; and with the exception of Buchanan, the Thomas Paine of the Right, they complied so effectively that the press began calling them "the mice." But they were not shy and mild in their dealings with me or with each other. I have always believed that subordinates have two inalienable rights: freedom of speech and credit for their accomplishments. It was reported in the press that I demanded that my staff call me "Chief" and rise in respectful silence when I entered the room. In fact, they called me "you" and went right on with whatever they were doing (debating, usually) when I joined them. At the 8 A.M. staff meeting I usually had to rap on the table to get their attention. They were chosen for their absolute loyalty and devotion to the President and for their brains and ability. Their average work week was seventy hours, divided into days that began at 7 A.M. and usually ended at 6:30 P.M. or later, weekends included. Their highest salary was $75,100 a year—$20.63 an hour.

It is true that I imposed a new system on these people. The discipline I wanted for the White House was not a discipline of manners, but a discipline of procedure. We had to know what we were going to do and when we were going to do it. Otherwise, the staff—and the President it existed to serve—would be overwhelmed by the whirlwind of events, ceremonies, crises, petitions, attacks, issues, and surprises that make up a Presidential day. My second day on the job, as reconstructed from my raw notes, will give the reader some idea of the kaleidoscopic nature of the enterprise.

7:30: Breakfast with Deaver, Kingon, and Craig Fuller over eggs and bacon served at my conference table by a member of the White House mess crew. Discussed the day's schedule: where the President was already committed, where he would have photo ops, what might happen. Moved on to the State of the Union message. President still is not happy with the talk, but he seems resigned to it.

8:15: Staff meeting. Discussed events of the day: testimony on the Hill by Stockman, Weinberger; Meese confirmation as Attorney General coming up.

8:30: Quick meeting with Speakes and others on the story of the day, photo ops for the President, and where else news could be expected.

9:00: The President. He brought along a copy of *Jet* magazine showing coverage of blacks and their participation in the Inauguration. Discussed at some length the possibility of encouraging blacks to think well of Reagan despite what their leaders were telling them, and of trying to work with younger, more affluent groups in order to encourage their participation in the Republican party. Discussed the day's schedule. At 9:30 Bud McFarlane came in. The only item he had for the President was the visit, scheduled for 10:40 this morning, of the new French Foreign Minister.

After McFarlane left, Mike Deaver, Ben Elliott (the chief speechwriter), and I sat down with the President and went over his radio talk for Saturday. Subject: the budget. The President wants to give a series of talks on the budget; he feels that people know too little about it. Gave him quite a bit of material.

10:30–11:00: Met with people on the White House staff who wanted to discuss their personal situations and their future. Fred Fielding alerted me to a potentially embarrassing situation concerning a dispute over payment of the marriage counselor's bills in a divorce case involving a member of the Cabinet. Told Fred to investigate further and get back to me. It looks like I'll get the bad news pretty quickly in this job. Read the State of the Union message for the first time; edited it, inserting some of the points the President had said he wanted to make.

11:00–12:00: NSC meeting to discuss the forthcoming visit of King Fahd on the Monday and Tuesday of next week. Jim Baker attended in his capacity as Secretary of the Treasury—the first holder of that office to be a member of the NSC. The Chief of Staff and the Attorney

General are now members, rather than observers, also for the first time. This double appointment, designed to give the President the benefit of the advice of his top aide and his chief economic and legal adviser in questions of foreign policy, was one of the elements in the agreement concerning the exchange of posts by Baker and me.

12:00 – 12:30: Briefing by the staff on questions that might be raised by the press later today when I announce the appointments of Pat Buchanan, Max Friedersdorf, and Ed Rollins as Assistants to the President.

12:30 – 12:50: In press room to announce appointments. Questions dealt mainly with Buchanan.

12:50: Had a sandwich and iced tea on the run. Joined the President at 1:00 with a group of small businessmen who had grown into big businessmen through the use of venture capital.

1:30: Photo opportunity for the President in which he signed the Economic Message to the Congress.

2:00: Cabinet meeting. Gave the Cabinet a quick overview of the President's main themes in the State of the Union message. Warned them that they were the only ones who knew these details, so if I saw them in the paper in the morning, I would know that someone in that group in the Cabinet Room had leaked it. Bill Niskanen described his *Economic Report* and what was in it. Joe Wright talked about his *Management Report* that will be due to the Congress in a few days. The President made a few remarks about the State of the Union.

Got blindsided by Baldrige. Had talked to him earlier in the day regarding the State of the Union message. He wanted to get in an item indicating that the President will favor a merger of the Special Trade Representative and the Department of Commerce. Commerce would then rid itself of the Bureau of the Census and the National Oceanic and Atmospheric Administration so as to become a small, streamlined Cabinet department dedicated to trade promotion. I'm not too sure about this, but Baldrige seems to think everyone is for it. He persuaded the President to endorse the idea last year.

3:00–3:30: Met with Stockman, Secretary of Agriculture Jack Block, and others on the farm credit situation. Told Agriculture it was their job to get this out to the press; we were keeping the President away from it. Short-range loans to farmers for spring planting were not to exceed the budget limit of $700 million. Any farmer producing any kind of crop—maple syrup, apples, dairy products—is eligible for this money, which was originally intended for wheat and corn and soybean growers of the Midwest. Refused to allow Jack Block to bring in a group of Farm Bureau people to talk to the President on Friday. Said we would have him talk to these farm groups after he returned from California. Reason for keeping the President away from this is that I think it is a no-win situation in which the President can be damaged because there literally is no way to help these farmers. Four hundred thousand businesses go broke every year. If farming is a business, why should the government support them any more than it supports an electronics company or a parts store? If the proprietor makes a wrong judgment, has too much inventory, borrows too much, and gets caught, that's his fault. If farmers do the same things—gamble, buy more land at inflated prices as they did during the seventies and early eighties and then are unable to farm it properly in order to make a profit during a period of disinflation and receding commodity prices—why shouldn't they suffer the same consequences?

Met with Roger Porter [the Deputy Assistant to the President who handled the Cabinet Council on Economic Affairs], who told me that he has been offered a tenured professorship at Harvard in the Kennedy School of Government. Urged him to accept. He will have time available until the summer, and I think we can use him in planning some of the Cabinet Council changes, as well as setting up a long-range policy-planning unit in the White House. Am aghast at the lack of planning in the White

House for periods longer than a week or two. My own idea is that we could probably have the political people looking forward to '85, and on into '86, to the elections of that year. We should have the communications people thinking in terms of how the President can articulate what the future might be. At the same time, we should have the policy people thinking about what's going to happen in those years under certain economic conditions. The Council of Economic Advisors, which I intend to revive, should be the vehicle for describing what the economy might be like in that period so that we anticipate problems, rather than being victimized by the unforeseen.

Met with John Herrington of Personnel.

Mac Baldrige came in with Bud McFarlane to complain about the leak of a very sensitive document [dealing with trade talks in Moscow] to Clyde Farnsworth of the *New York Times*. The *Times* story will certainly embarrass the Soviets, because their representative was talking about the emigration of Jews from Russia in return for trade concessions. This endangers our relations with the Russians. Don't understand why anyone wanted to leak this particular document. McFarlane will ask the Attorney General to have the FBI investigate. [The investigation produced no result.]

At the conclusion of the day, wrapped up with the staff, going over what we will be doing tomorrow and how things were played today. Read all the way home in the back of the car.

The President's time—how to use it to the best advantage of the man and his program—was constantly in my thoughts even before I moved over to the White House. During the transition period, when I was alone in front of the shaving mirror in the morning, or at my desk at the end of the working day, or riding home in the back of the car, I would ask myself the basic questions: What does the President want to do in his second term? How can I help him do it?

As in the first term, the answers to these fundamental questions were set out in the Republican platform and in the statements made by the President during the election campaign. Few referred to these records. Like Edgar Allan Poe's purloined letter, the documents in which politicians record their intentions assume a strange invisibility even though they lie about in plain sight. This is not my view of the way things should be. Although the job of drafting the platform had fallen to others, especially to Drew Lewis and Trent Lott, I had contributed to the sections dealing with economic and fiscal policy. The platform was a sober and realistic document, a statement of the party's collective wisdom after four years in power. It had been approved by the President; his own words as a candidate had been consistent with its provisions. Therefore it was the charter of the second Reagan Administration.

After an electoral triumph, especially a victory on the scale achieved by Ronald Reagan in 1984, there is always talk among the President's followers of a "mandate," as if this were some disembodied power that had been entrusted to the person elected by the voters. But what the word actually means (*Webster's* again) is "an authoritative command, order, or injunction : a clear instruction, authorization, or direction." The question is: to do what?

In Reagan's case, I thought, the answer was twofold. First, the people had given him an authorization to go on running the government and leading the country for four more years in the same style as the first four years. Second, they had given him a clear instruction, underwritten by 54,455,075 popular votes and 525 of 538 electoral votes, to carry out the programs he had advocated during the campaign. In foreign affairs, this meant peace based on a strong defense, and in domestic affairs, tax reform and budget reform.

In short, the American people wanted Reagan to be Reagan. It was my job, as I saw it, to make that possible.

· 13 ·

Journalism and Dysjournalism

Letting Reagan be Reagan was no simple matter. His greatest strength—the manifest affection and trust of the voters—was also his most debilitating weakness. Reagan's enemies genuinely believed that his actions as President would destroy his popularity by revealing his true purposes, and his chamberlains often seemed to believe that the other side was right about this. This was a truly staggering misjudgment. The reality was that Reagan's ideas were shared by a large majority of the American people, who had voted for him because they clearly understood what he was saying to them. No American President of the television age has combined the common touch with the unique ability to be everywhere at once in electronic form so successfully as Ronald Reagan. To a degree, this triumph was forced on Reagan by the times in which he lived—times for which he was superbly equipped by his physical appearance, his personality, and his long experience in front of the camera. (He made his first movie in 1937.)

Some of Reagan's opponents have suggested that his mastery of television constituted an unfair advantage—that the people who watched him on the screen and then voted for him were deceived by imagery. This is nonsense. All political candidates are men of the moment, and all capitalize on their greatest strength. The qualities that endear statesmen to history—Lincoln's rusticity, Churchill's bullheadedness, Truman's common sense—are very often the same ones that infuriate their contemporaries. Reagan's opponents despised him for his optimism. Elderly liberals who denounced his popularity as a sham and a delusion in the 1980s sounded uncannily like elderly conservatives who said the same thing about Franklin D. Roosevelt in the 1930s. Both groups of skeptics failed to realize that the country had changed, bringing a new political reality into existence: the strange new figure at the center of events was the product of this new reality, not its creator. Great leaders are seldom anticipated or understood by the conventional wisdom of their own time.

Both the liberals and the conservatives perceived Reagan as a man of the Right, and for their own different purposes pushed him in that direction. Only the people perceived him for what he was—the occupant of the authentic center. That center had moved appreciably to the right in the forty years since the death of FDR—a period in which Republicans had won six of ten Presidential elections and no Democrat elected President in his own right had won reelection to the office.

Even some of the people closest to Reagan saw the image instead of the man. If Reagan's enemies thought that the American people had made a mistake in electing him President, Reagan's own managers seemed to have trouble believing that his *ideas*, and the revival of patriotism and national self-confidence that came out of those ideas, were the secret of his success.

Clearly these were antidemocratic reactions, but there was nothing so very surprising about them: it had been a long time since the vocabulary of national self-assurance had rallied a decisive constituency in American life. How could a philosophy of government that flew in the face of liberal pessimism win votes? Especially in Washington—where the most influential elements of the bureaucracy, the press, and the Congress constituted a stern priesthood of liberal orthodoxy—it was natural to believe that even a President who had won his office by a landslide had to "go along to get along," like one of the late Mr. Sam Rayburn's obsequious freshman congressmen.

Reagan's advisers, accepting this dubious proposition, never insisted on carrying out his program. If Reagan was opposed to tax increases on philosophical grounds, his advisers were for them on tactical grounds; if he saw the need for increases in defense spending as a means of restoring American influence in the world, they favored cuts in the defense budget for the purpose of placating his opponents in Congress. The list was long. Reagan was continuously being pressured to compromise in ways that preserved the influence and the policies of the defeated opposition.

Of all the inherent duties of an American President, the duty to say no on matters of principle is among the most important. In the Reagan White House the word was seldom uttered, and then usually only at the last possible moment. Reagan's record on legislative vetoes—only thirty-nine in the first four years, as compared to sixty-six by Ford in barely two years—is an index of the Administration's reluctance to stand the ground it had won in its greatest electoral victories.

In my opinion this failure of political will stemmed, in significant measure, from a superficial belief on the part of some of Reagan's people that his agenda was unfashionable. Mike Deaver has written in his memoirs that he exerted great effort to move Reagan's thinking and behavior to the left on policy matters, and that in doing so he was acting on behalf of Nancy Reagan. Although I personally never knew Deaver to express an opinion on a policy matter, there may be truth in this assertion. It certainly appeared to me that some members of the President's official household admired the President's enemies and wanted to be like them. This self-effacing tendency expressed itself in many ways, including the cultivation of the Democratic social elite: invitations from such famous hostesses as Katharine Graham, the publisher of the *Washington Post*, were greatly valued by the First Lady, as were her many conversations with Robert Strauss, a former Democratic national chairman and a leading member of the Washington power structure. Rich liberals were, by common consent, the aristocracy of the nation's capital. Republican Presidents of the late twentieth century—Eisenhower, Nixon, Ford— had all been men of humble background and no inherited wealth. So was Ronald Reagan, who had the added disadvantage of having been a movie actor who was never a superstar. In Reagan's Washington, Republicans were the new rich, the outsiders, people who were invited into the great houses of local society only as curiosities.

This fascination with image produced a strange effect. Ronald Reagan seemed to be regarded by certain members of his inner circle not as the powerful and utterly original leader that he was, but as a sort of supreme anchorman whose public persona was the most important element of the Presidency. According to the rules of this school of political management, controversy was to be avoided at nearly any cost: every Presidential action must produce a positive public effect. In practice, this meant stimulating a positive effect in the media, with the result that the press, not the people, became the President's primary constituency.

As Secretary of the Treasury I had, of course, been aware of the power of the press in Washington. But I did not fully understand how closely the interests of the media and those of the Administration were intertwined until I became Chief of Staff. To say that I was surprised by this state of affairs would be an understatement. I was shocked by the extent to which the press determined the everyday activities, and even the philosophical tenor, of the Presidency. This is not to say that I did not know that the press plays an important role in the life of a democracy beyond its function as a watchdog of official morality. Publicity is a modern form of pomp, and if it were possible to govern without display, there would be no ruins in Rome or jewels in the Tower of London. But unless I have misread the histories of the great empires of the past, a preoccupation with outward style at the expense of inner conviction is not a favorable sign in the life of a superpower.

In my early days at the White House I was given the valuable opportunity of observing the style of management that had applied in Reagan's first term. Mike Deaver remained in his office (the one closest to the Oval Office) for about three months and in that period continued to handle scheduling and imagery. As a result of my later experiences with him I developed reservations about Deaver, but I have no complaint about the way he worked with me during this transition period. His fundamental style, which is that of a man who advances himself by doing favors for others, was not one that I admire, but he was very useful to the Reagans and seemed to be more secure in his relationship with them than any other person on the staff. He treated the White House like the residence of an indulgent aunt and uncle, bringing his friends home to play tennis and eat in the mess. Apparently he saw nothing wrong in using the trappings of the Executive Mansion to impress his friends—but neither then nor afterward did he ever ask me for a favor for himself or any third person. Altogether, Deaver was affable and accommodating in his dealings with me—and of course he was the leading expert on the temperament and methods of the First Lady.

For about a month, while he awaited confirmation as Attorney General, Ed Meese was also on hand. Both men sat in on all my meetings with the President. They were devoted to Reagan and determined to preserve him from harm and embarrassment. They accepted that this often meant dissuading him from acting on his bedrock convictions because of the political costs involved.

The whole effort of the staff, and especially of the work that Deaver did, was designed to make life easier for the Reagans. They relied on Deaver to do this and gave him a remarkably free hand in arranging the details of their lives. He anticipated most problems and dealt with the ones that slipped through the system. This is a legitimate objective founded on strong historical precedents: an unhappy monarch is a dangerous monarch. If this is carried too far, of course, you can end up with a Louis XIV, who required an entire roomful of people to dress him, with only the dauphin permitted to handle the royal shirt. Reagan was far too sensible to let personal service degenerate into servility, but the opinion of his assistants that he should be preserved from conflict and from his own accommodating instincts did combine to insulate him from the hubbub of life.

It was Deaver's job to advise the President on image, and image was what he talked about nearly all the time. It was Deaver who identified the story of the day at the eight o'clock staff meeting and coordinated the plans for dealing with it, Deaver who created and approved photo opportunities, Deaver who alerted the President to the snares being laid by the press that day. Deaver was a master of his craft. He saw—designed—each Presidential action as a one-minute or two-minute spot on the evening network news, or a picture on page one of the *Washington Post* or the *New York Times*, and conceived every Presidential appearance in terms of camera angles.

If the President was scheduled to make a ceremonial appearance in the Rose Garden, he could be sure that he and the recipients of whatever greeting or award was involved would be looking into the sun so that the cameras would have the light behind them. In the morning, when the sun was over the Treasury, this meant that the President stood on the steps right outside the Oval Office; in the afternoon he would stand on the long side of the colonnade. His position was always chosen with the idea of keeping him as far away as possible from the reporters who hovered at the edge of these events with the intention of shouting questions. Every moment of every public appearance was scheduled, every word was scripted, every place where Reagan was expected to stand was chalked with toe marks. The President was always being prepared for a performance, and this had the inevitable effect of preserving him from confrontation and the genuine interplay of opinion, question, and argument that form the basis of decision.

The President accepted these arrangements with what seemed to me to be practically superhuman good nature. *Second nature* might be the better term: he had been doing this kind of thing— learning his lines, composing his facial expression, hitting his toe marks—for half a century. They constituted no inconvenience to him. As Deaver (later Bill Henkel or Jim Kuhn, Reagan's personal assistant) rehearsed him for an appearance he would say: "You'll go out the door and down the steps. The podium is ten steps to the right and the audience will be in a semicircle with the cameras at the right-hand end of the half-moon; when you finish speaking take two steps back but don't leave the podium, because they're going to present you with a patchwork quilt. . . ."

Larry Speakes would caution him that the press would be there and he should watch out for questions on X or Y. Reagan would smile and nod: Yup, yup, that's fine, all right; thanks fellows.

Deaver, (and later, I) would slap him on the back and out he'd go. The scripted part of his performance was always flawless. But after it was over, as he walked back toward the White House, he often broke out of the role and into his own original character, answering questions that he should have ignored, making news that his advisers had hoped he would not make. He couldn't help himself. It was not in Ronald Reagan to say, To hell with you, buster—that's a tricky question and I'm not going to answer it. If leather-lunged Sam Donaldson bellowed a question across the Rose Garden, the President's natural politeness compelled him to answer it.

When that happened, Deaver, Speakes, and the others would shake their heads in affectionate bafflement and scurry to contain what they regarded as "the damage." This did not seem to me to be right. What did the inconvenience of an offhand reply really matter? It had been demonstrated often enough that these glimpses of Reagan's fallibility on small matters did him no harm with the people. They knew where he stood on the great issues and did not expect him to know everything: he was the leader of the Free World, not a student taking an oral exam administered by journalists.

The President is possessed of a philosophical agenda based on a lifetime of experience and thought. He is a formidable reader and a talented conversationalist with a gift for listening. It was precisely this gift that led to many of his gaffes and misstatements in encounters with the press: Ronald Reagan remembered nearly everything that was said to him. If someone told him (to use a wholly fictitious example) that there had been 35,987 hairs in Stalin's mustache, this fact would go into the Presidential memory bank, possibly to emerge weeks or months later in the middle of a press conference. It never seemed to occur to him that anyone would give him incorrect information. His mind was a trove of facts and anecdotes, something like the morgue of one of his favorite magazines, *Reader's Digest*, and it was impossible to guess when or why he might access any one of these millions of bytes of data.

Reagan started nearly every meeting with a story, no matter whether the participants were people he saw every day or the hereditary ruler of a remote kingdom who had never before laid eyes on an American President; he thought that laughter brought people closer together and dispelled the anxiety that they feel in the presence of the mighty, and of course he was right. The President knew more funny stories, ranging from jokes innocent enough for a Sunday-school class to the raunchiest locker-room humor, than anyone I had ever met. If you told Reagan an Irish joke, he'd come back with a better Irish joke, and could do the same in every category. Deaver had a new joke or bit of amusing gossip for him every morning as the first order of business—a practice I carried on with support from the Vice President (one of whose sons acted as a scout for new stories) after Deaver departed.

Reagan shunned the abstract, the theoretical, the cold and impersonal approach to problems. His love of stories was connected to this same tendency to see everything in human terms. Although even some of his intimates scoffed (ever so discreetly) at his bottomless fund of anecdotes about it, Reagan's experience as governor of California constituted a unique body of executive and political experience. He had a formidable gift for debate when he was allowed to debate in a spontaneous way. His problems in these matters, as in the first debate with Walter Mondale in 1984, nearly always resulted from his being overprogrammed. His briefers, forgetting that a President has a cast of thousands to remember facts for him, had crammed his mind with so many bits of information that he tried to rely on data instead of explaining the issue and defending his policy. I had seen him defend his ideas and critique the proposals of other heads of state with the best of them at six international economic summits, and it was not uncommon for him to render courageous decisions on domestic economic questions in the face of nearly unanimous advice and pressure to do the opposite.

In such moments Reagan was himself; I thought that there

should be many more such moments in the second term. No leader can abandon compromise altogether, but the time had come for a more insistent approach to the President's agenda. His staff could prepare the way for this. But only the President himself could make the case for his program. He could not do this without creating controversy, without startling the press from time to time.

Severe risk was involved in any abrupt change in the way in which we dealt with journalists. The men and women who covered the White House had become used to a routine that provided them with unprecedented benefits, and I knew that they would not give it up without complaint. The Reagan White House had understood from the beginning that the press was not its natural ally. The President's aides were essentially the same people who had gone through his campaign for the Presidency, and they were aware that very few journalists sympathized with Reagan's policies or were attracted by his personality. The President's men set out, therefore, to make the best of the situation — if the Reagan White House could not hope for love, it would settle for dependency. The triumvirate of Baker, Meese, and Deaver decided to control what it could not prevent, and in an action filled with meaning for the future, instituted a policy of leaking information to journalists on a systematic basis. In effect, White House aides were assigned to tell reporters the innermost secrets of the Administration.

This new open channel for leaks was in addition to the existing, and probably natural, leaching of secret and confidential material into the media. In the normal course of business, the government sloughs off a great deal of information that is supposed to be held in confidence. This happens to some extent because of the skill and persistence of journalists. A good reporter, given a mere hint of the existence of a story, will pursue it to the end. It is the business of journalists, after all, to discover hidden facts and publish them. Everyone knows this, and it is disingenuous to blame journalists for leaks or call them irresponsible when they publish what has been smuggled to them by untrustworthy government officials. The press has little obligation to protect the government from itself. Many would argue (without convincing me) that its obligation in a free society is just the opposite.

Government servants often, even usually, have their own purposes in revealing secrets to journalists: they want to kill a proposal by exposing its details prematurely, or they want to attract support from the Congress or the public by the same method, or they want to head off a rival who has a conflicting view. Vanity plays a role of overwhelming importance on both sides: the journalist publishes leaks and dines out on his revelations for essentially the same reason that officials violate their oaths of confidentiality—in order to be perceived as members of a know-all insiders' elite. The fact that the media are by nature profoundly profit-oriented operations (General Electric owns NBC, ABC is the property of Capital Cities, CBS is related to Loew's, and all the great newspapers and newsmagazines are aggressive marketers) is irrelevant—or, in the case of front-line reporters who generally do what they do in the genuine belief that they are the keepers of the nation's conscience, effectively sublimated. Nevertheless the truth remains that a thirty-second commercial spot on the top-rated network evening news show costs the advertiser $55,000. The same amount of time on the third-ranked network news costs only $45,000. Since there are about twelve thirty-second spots in the typical network news half hour, the difference between being first and last is something like $120,000 a day. Similar considerations apply to newspapers (the Washington Post Company earned $187 million in 1987), and these provide a strong incentive to compete for the news.

As a practical matter it is impossible to control the leakage of information in a large democratic society in which many people in the government have access to its innermost deliberations. Indiscretion is built into the system. If the President confides in two or three members of his Cabinet in the belief that they must know his mind on a certain subject, those Cabinet members will confide in their closest aides for the same reason, and then the aides will tell *their* assistants, too. One of the motives in all this confiding is the natural human urge in people to let others know that they know what "only" the President knows. But if they tell a journalist, they tell the world how important they are. The potential for corruption is obvious in a practice that involves secret relationships, stealthy methods, deception of colleagues and superiors, and rewards in the form of career advancement and even fame as a result of commerce in a property (that is, national secrets) that belongs not to those who buy and sell it, but to the American people.

In the past, an honor system prevented this contagion of broken trust. Among civilians this quaint institution is now remembered only by older men—such as President Reagan—with nostalgia. He could never understand breaches of confidence, and the fact that he often read secrets in the daily press before he read them in his top secret daily briefing never failed to amaze him. Usually the origin of the leaks and the motives behind them were easy enough to trace. When, in May 1985, the *Washington Post* discussed some of the sensitive aspects of the Administration's Nicaragua policy in a story headlined "Buchanan Seen Hurting President," it was possible to suspect that Bud McFarlane had been chatting with the reporter Lou Cannon about the differences between them in regard to support for the Contras. Cannon came away with the impression that McFarlane's recommendations helped the President while Buchanan's were likely to hurt him, and shared this insight with the *Post*'s readers—who, fortuitously for McFarlane, included the President and the First Lady.

Beyond the category of leaks described above exists a second category: the officially sanctioned leak calculated to produce a specific effect. This technique was not unknown in earlier Administrations—the Kennedys in particular had shown that it was possible to make an ally of the press by offering it a limited silent partnership in the making of policy—but it was raised to the level of an art form under Baker, Meese, and Deaver. In Reagan's case, of course, there was no possibility of turning reporters who detested his party and his policies into collaborators. Instead, they seemed to imagine that what they were doing in accepting handouts of sensitive information was a form of investigative reporting in which the suspects provided the evidence against themselves. This point of view was not totally lacking in realism.

The triumvirate and their closest aides (Dick Darman and David Gergen for Baker; Craig Fuller, Jack Svahn, and Ken Cribb for Meese; Deaver for himself and the First Lady, sometimes in concert with Stu Spencer or her press staff) cultivated selected reporters. These became a sort of pitching staff, with the starting assignment rotating. Lou Cannon of the *Washington Post* might be given an exclusive one day, Steve Weisman of the *New York Times* or Paul Blustein, then of the *Wall Street Journal,* the next, Bill Plante of CBS the next. (When Deaver left the White House, Plante was one of the main speakers at his farewell party in the Rose Garden.)

The leaked material covered a wide range of issues both foreign and domestic, and in general was accurate as far as it went. Reporters sometimes wove in details derived from other sources, and the rest of the press uncovered additional data in the stories they wrote to follow up on the scoops of the media stars. This resulted in a remarkably free flow of unsourced information out of the White House and into the public domain. Paradoxically, these secret arrangements created what was probably the most open government in history.

Issues were not the only matters discussed. Each member of the triumvirate was interested in maintaining his reputation as a close adviser to the President, and his aides were strongly motivated to see that their boss was given his due. This sometimes led to negative references to the other two members. And when the entire apparatus concentrated on a single rival, as in the case of Al Haig in 1983, the concentrated dose of negative publicity was usually fatal.

This organized feeding of the media produced predictable results. As in the children's book about the little boy who fed his pet fish too generously, the creature grew bigger; and the bigger it grew, the hungrier it became. In the spring of 1985, shortly after the changeover, my executive assistant, Tom Dawson, was invited to lunch at the Biltmore Hotel in Santa Barbara by a group of White House reporters. He accepted and asked another member of the staff, who had received a similar invitation, to accompany him. Among Tom's hosts was David Hoffman of the *Washington Post.* After an interlude of general conversation, Hoffman came to the point in the form of "advice" to a newcomer: Play ball with us and we'll play ball with you. This proposition did not surprise Tom, a very bright young man who had grown up in Washington, but the example of playing ball that Hoffman gave him did. The *Post* reporter suggested that Tom and the rest of the new members of the White House staff would do well to be treated like Jim Baker, "who got good press," and not like Bill Casey, who had generally been the subject of unflattering coverage. The reason? "Jim Baker talked to us; we liked him; we understood him." But Casey did not play ball. Consequently, when the "Debategate" controversy (centering on accusations that some of President Carter's confidential briefing material had been pilfered and provided to the Reagan campaign staff for use in the candidates' debate) broke in 1981, "We went easy on Baker and gave him the benefit of the doubt. But we were tough on Casey."

(This episode had a remarkably symmetrical sequel. Two years later, at the height of the Iran-Contra affair, the *Post* published a story containing the startling but utterly false charge that I had influenced President Reagan to change his testimony to the Tower Board because it contradicted my own subsequent testimony. The inaccuracy of this charge, which was based on the stated premise that the President had initially testified before I did when the opposite was actually the case, could easily have been checked by a single telephone call to the staff of the Tower Board. When the *Post*'s piece appeared, Tom Dawson phoned Lou Cannon, who had signed it along with Bob Woodward, and asked for an explanation. Cannon replied, "Maybe if you guys had played ball with us, things like this wouldn't have happened.")

Tom's conversation with David Hoffman sounded like plain blackmail to him, and he decided to talk it over with an old White House hand in whom he confided. Before Tom could describe what had happened, however, this man told *him* what Hoffman had said to him. The *Post* reporter had seen him the night before and brought out the fact that he had tried to teach Tom the ropes. The old hand had expressed surprise to Hoffman that he had used Casey as an example to Tom, who had been Casey's assistant at the State Department and was an admirer of his former boss. But Hoffman had given the impression that he was quite untroubled by the possibility that what he had done was improper or even in bad taste. After all, he had only been telling Tom the facts of life. (In early 1987, when Peter Wallison asked Hoffman why the *Post* would not print the White House version of events in regard to the Iran-Contra affair, Hoffman replied that our side of the story would not be covered in his newspaper until the President agreed to hold a news conference.)

Even though I had to admit, surveying the techniques involved and the results obtained, that this policy of deliberate leaks was an interesting example of management by objective, I thought that it ought to come to a halt. For one thing, I lacked the temperament for it, and for another I did not think that it constituted an efficient use of the staff's time. In my experience, people who tried to attain their ends by covert means came to unfortunate ends. In Wall Street I had been trained to keep secrets: people engaged in the brokerage business go to jail for tipping stocks or otherwise sharing insider information. At Treasury there was reason for discretion in nearly all our operations because much of what the department did—dealing with the issue of government securities and making recommendations to the Fed that might affect interest rates—had the potential for disturbing the integrity of the market if the intentions became public knowledge.

Of course, I knew that I could never go back to the discreet silence of former years, but I was determined that the second term of the Reagan Presidency would be more closely focused on action than on appearance. What the press had the right to know and the need to know—and in my view that included everything that did not breach the confidences that were necessary to the accomplishment of policy goals or savage the reputations of honest men and women—the press would openly be told. After Deaver left, I asked Pat Buchanan and Larry Speakes to sit in on most decision-making meetings so that their briefings of the press would be based on firsthand knowledge of the President's business. (This applied only to domestic matters, inasmuch as the National Security Advisor and his staff did not report to me and were strictly McFarlane's responsibility. Bud managed his own press relations, both overt and covert. Even so, the press was never able to separate the NSC staff and the domestic White House staff in its mind or in its words.)

So that the flow of news would come only from the proper quarter—the White House Press Office—at one point I laid down the rule that no member of the senior staff could talk to the press unless a member of the White House Press Office staff was present. I myself always observed this rule. As time went by, others on the staff routinely ignored it, though never in my presence and never with my consent or connivance. I also instituted a rule against accepting hospitality from the press. Tom Dawson's experience in Santa Barbara had suggested to me that breaking bread with the media and breaking confidences went together. Experience had amply confirmed my intuition in this regard by the time I left the White House. Ironically, the Office of Government Ethics barred such meetings in a ruling handed down after I left the White House.

Early in my tenure as Chief of Staff, an appalling public relations disaster occurred, and it demonstrated how little control even the cleverest men can exert on events that engage the deep emotions and memories of mankind. The debacle sprang from the best possible intentions: the President had wanted to make a gesture that would help to heal the wounds of World War II, he wanted to affirm the friendship of the United States for a democratic West Germany that was its staunch ally, and he wanted to do a favor for a man he greatly liked and trusted, Chancellor Helmut Kohl.

The commitment in question was already on the President's calendar when I arrived at the White House. At Kohl's personal request during a visit to Washington in November 1984, the

President had agreed to visit a military cemetery at Bitburg, nea
the Luxembourg frontier in the Rhineland-Palatinate, the distric
that Kohl represented in the Bundestag. A U.S. Air Force bas‹
was located nearby. The visit would take place in connection witl
the annual Economic Summit, scheduled to be held in Bonn ir
the first week of May 1985, just before the fortieth anniversar)
of V-E day. Kohl had already met with President François Mit
terrand of France at the World War I cemetery at Verdun; the
gesture had been well received by the French and the Germans,
whose soldiers were buried there.

Even forty years after the end of World War II, Reagan's gesture was fraught with political risk. Obviously the President was
aware that many in America and elsewhere had never forgiven
Germany for the crimes of the Nazi regime. But he took the
entirely laudable and typically generous view that there was no
such thing as collective guilt involving the whole German nation,
and that the sacrifice of the young soldiers who died on both
sides of the conflict had carried their memory beyond politics.

The President also wanted to oblige Kohl. Personal considerations play a larger role in the actions of the powerful than is
generally imagined. During Reagan's first term, the leaders of
the seven most important industrial nations—Canada, France,
Germany, Great Britain, Italy, Japan, and the United States—
had become personal friends. Reagan, with his extraordinary knack
for bringing people together, was largely responsible for this. Only
a few weeks after his inauguration, at the first Economic Summit
he attended at Montebello in Canada, the President was unset-
tled by the atmosphere of stiff formality. After a short time, he
looked around the table and said, I'm not really used to this—
being addressed as 'Mr. President,' or calling others by their titles. Can't we get on a first-name basis? I'm Ron. After a surprised silence, his colleagues took the suggestion, the atmosphere
lightened, and the seeds of a new relationship were sown. Thereafter it was Pierre and François, Helmut and Margaret, Giovanni
and Zenko-san and Ron.

New as he was to his own high position, Reagan had instinc-
tively understood that he and his fellow leaders were a unique

group; only a head of government, existing half in the limelight and half in isolation, can truly understand the life of another. Of course, ideological and policy differences persisted. (Dammit, Pierre! How can you object to that? Reagan barked at Pierre Elliott Trudeau of Canada at the London summit, rapping peremptorily on the table with his reading glasses after Trudeau had taken exception to the phrase "peace and freedom for peoples everywhere"; Trudeau had felt that the phrase was an indirect slam at the Soviet Union.) But on the whole the leaders were nearly as easy with each other as old school chums—in fact, they began to call the group photograph that was always taken at the end of the session "the class picture." It was amusing to see them give special support to any one of their number who happened to be up for reelection—placing the candidate at the center of nearly every picture, making certain that he or she was given generous credit in the communiqué and other public statements and appearances. Ideology did not enter into this ritual: they were standing behind one of their own.

That is not to say that Reagan was not content to see socialists replaced by conservatives in the natural course of events. Margaret Thatcher had welcomed him enthusiastically into the group at least in part because he shared her political views. In my opinion, the close friendship between the two owes much to the early battles that they fought side by side against such voluble socialists and social democrats as Trudeau, Mitterrand of France, and Helmut Schmidt of West Germany. In time Trudeau was replaced by Brian Mulroney, Mitterrand was joined by the conservative French Prime Minister Jacques Chirac, the pragmatic Bruno Craxi became Premier of Italy, and Helmut Kohl supplanted Helmut Schmidt as the Chancellor of West Germany. Of all the Europeans, Schmidt had certainly devoted the greatest amount of time to denouncing Reagan's economic policy, and it may have been that the warm spot the President developed in his heart for Kohl had something to do with the fact that the Germans stopped nagging him about taxes and interest rates after the Christian Democrats regained power. Whatever subconscious factors may have existed in addition to the normal political urge to see a like-minded ally remain in power, Reagan wanted his friend Helmut Kohl to remain as Chancellor of West Germany.

When the decision to visit Bitburg was announced on April 11, it immediately drew criticism, especially from Jewish groups. But the President resisted all pleas to change his plans. It had forcefully been suggested that he visit the site of a concentration camp to show that the atrocities committed against Jews and others by the Nazis had not been forgotten or forgiven by the United States. The First Lady opposed this idea on grounds that it was bad imagery and instructed Deaver that there were to be no concentration camps included on her husband's itinerary. The President himself had said at his press conference the month before that he would not visit a concentration camp because he did not wish to impose guilt feelings on a new generation of Germans. This reluctance to visit the scenes of the Holocaust was connected to Helmut Kohl's very strong feeling that the German nation should be treated by the United States as the loyal friend that it had been for the last forty years instead of a defeated enemy that had been guilty of war crimes. Kohl, an enormous man who towers over most people, had made this point in the Oval Office with tears in his eyes when he invited the President to Bitburg. The youthful German soldiers buried there, he said in effect, were also victims of the Nazi regime, which had sacrificed their lives in an unworthy cause. This phrase implanted itself in Reagan's memory and emerged in his exchanges with the press.

Then, on April 12, 1985, it was revealed in the media that forty-seven members of the Waffen SS, combat units of Adolf Hitler's murderous elite guard, were buried in the Bitburg cemetery among two thousand members of the regular German armed forces. The Germans had not previously brought this fact to our attention.

"How the hell did *that* happen?" I asked Mike Deaver, who had led the advance team that surveyed the ground that was going to be covered by the President in Germany.

Deaver replied that the cemetery had been covered by snow when he and his team visited it in February: the SS tombstones therefore were not visible. Moreover, Deaver said, our embassy in Bonn had assured him in response to a specific question that there were no Nazi graves in the Bitburg cemetery.

Deaver was mortified by his mistake and immediately admitted it to the President and gave him a detailed assessment of the damage already done and that likely to follow. Deaver began suggesting ways to soften the impact by adding new events to the itinerary that might placate the opposition. His ideas were excellent. At a later time, when Deaver was preparing his defense against the felony charges that rose out of his lobbying activities, I saw statements in the newspapers to the effect that Deaver's judgment had been impaired by alcoholism at about the time of the Bitburg incident. It was said that he was consuming a quart of Scotch whisky a day and masking his breath with mints while he went about his duties in the White House. It is true that he chewed mints from time to time, but I never saw the slightest sign in Deaver's behavior that he was drinking to excess; in fact I was then under the impression that he was a teetotaler. Watching him explain the Bitburg situation to the President, I would have said that he was one of the soberest men in Washington.

Thereafter, hardly a day passed in which Bitburg was not the most absorbing issue on the President's schedule. Media coverage was massive. The White House withheld no detail of its own knowledge of the situation from the press, and I talked to a number of reporters in an attempt to explain the President's reasons for his actions. A poll showed that a narrow majority of Americans sampled disapproved of the visit. The Jewish response was one of outrage. Elie Wiesel, the author and activist who would win the Nobel Peace Prize in 1986 for his work on behalf of the victims of the Holocaust, came to the White House to be awarded the Congressional Gold Medal by the President and (after assuring me that he would do no such thing) delivered a moving appeal during the televised ceremony. "You were not aware of the presence of SS graves," said Wiesel, himself a former prisoner in a Nazi concentration camp. "But now we are all aware. May I, Mr. President, if it's possible at all, implore you to do something else, to find another way, another site. That place, Mr. President, is not your place. Your place is with the victims of the SS." Prominent Republicans, including Bob Dole, advised the President publicly to cancel the trip. So did fifty-three senators in a joint letter to the President.

Press opinion was nearly unanimous: the President had been put in an impossible position by an almost inconceivable blunder, and I was probably responsible for it even though it happened before I came on the scene. A *New York Times* writer, quoting a Democratic political consultant to Mayor Ed Koch of New York City as his authority, took the position that Jim Baker would never have permitted such a debacle. The *Washington Post* quoted worried Republican political advisers as saying that Bitburg had had no noticeable effect on fund-raising, but might have. In a separate story, the *Post* reported that "Mr. Regan is being criticized on the ground that he did not anticipate the political fallout of the dispute." Columnist Joseph Kraft, remarking that "Deaver has not been himself for some time now," wrote that the White House staff, "including . . . Donald Regan . . . also has egg on its face." *U.S. News & World Report* reported that "Inside information . . . indicated that staff work greatly aggravated the problem, as did a shift in operating style that occurred when Donald Regan, an able administrator but not a seasoned politician, replaced James Baker on February 4." Clearly there were not enough fingers to plug up all the holes in the dike.

Although statements appeared in the press to the effect that the President had been advised the controversy would "blow over in twenty-four hours," I recall no one uttering any such inanity. Everybody knew at once how serious the situation was. We explained it painstakingly to the press, leaving out no detail.

But the President would not be moved from his determination to keep his promise to Kohl. It was Kohl himself who had chosen Bitburg. In Bonn, he and other Christian Democrats were bringing strong pressure on the American ambassador, Arthur Burns, and Burns was reporting this through State Department channels. The Chancellor telephoned Reagan, and in another emotional conversation lasting some twenty minutes, pleaded with him not to abandon his plans. To do so, Kohl told him, would cost him his Chancellorship.

This strengthened the President's determination to carry out the visit as intended. Although I admired his courage—he certainly was not sacrificing principle for image in this case—I had an obligation to play devil's advocate, and so I took the other side, telling him that nearly all sections of American opinion were against him and arguing that the original purpose of the visit, reconciliation, had been lost in the storm of protest. The press had published reports that some of the SS troops buried at Bitburg had been members of the Second Waffen SS Panzer Division, which had massacred 642 French civilians in the village of Oradour-sur-Glane in June 1944.

The President was aware of these facts, but he saw a larger issue: his credibility as a leader who kept his word and stood by his friends and allies despite high political costs. Richard Nixon and Henry Kissinger had urged him to stick to his purpose. The President talked about the vacillations of Jimmy Carter, and the way in which indecision had crippled the Carter Presidency and led to its humiliation abroad and its defeat in the United States.

I don't want people to see me as that kind of President, Reagan said. No, Don—I'm not going to change. We've got to face this out and do what we said we'd do. I've given Helmut my word, and now he's come back to me and pleaded with me not to break my word. I know this is an emotional situation, I know it's going to hurt a lot of my friends who are Jewish, but I have to go.

"Then stick with your instincts and go," I said. "Your gut feelings have gotten you this far; trust them. Emotions will cool in time and your reasons will be understood. But if you yield, you risk your whole second term because Congress and the press will be left with the impression that you can be swayed, that your mind can be changed on a matter of principle. You can't afford that."

This was the first tough Presidential decision to which I had been an eyewitness as Chief of Staff. In my view Reagan had come through with flying colors. He had reasoned and reacted as a President—choosing the future over the past and the long-term interests of the nation over the passions of the moment.

I urged Mike Deaver to find a way for the President to keep

his promise to Kohl, yet reach out to the people who had been offended. Deaver arranged for the President to visit the site of Bergen-Belsen, the camp in which Anne Frank and tens of thousands of others had died, and in consultation with the First Lady, brought in Ken Khachigian to write a speech to be delivered there.

The President made no speech at Bitburg. He and Kohl, escorted by American General Matthew B. Ridgway and General Johannes Steinhoff of the German Air Force, who had opposed each other on the battlefields of World War II, marched solemnly among the stone crosses and paused by the two wreaths that had already been placed at the main monument. A trumpeter played the mournful "Ich Hatt' Einen Kameraden," then the President and the Chancellor departed.

That morning Reagan and Kohl had visited the grave of Konrad Adenauer on a hilltop above the Rhine, and there, too, an atmosphere of solemnity prevailed that called to mind the tragic history of Germany.

At Bergen-Belsen the President, accompanied by his wife, passed among the roll of the dead, the burial mounds. No one who saw his face could have doubted the depth of his feeling. In his speech, delivered from an outdoor site that overlooked the burial mounds in which the camp's victims had been interred, he said: "Death cannot rule forever. . . . We are here today to confirm that horror cannot outlast hope. . . . Therefore, even out of this overwhelming sadness, there must be some purpose. And there is. . . . Such memories take us where God intended His children to go—toward learning, toward healing, and above all, toward redemption."

Few American Presidents can have passed through a day of such unrelieved mourning in time of peace. The symbols and memories of untimely death lay all around from morning till night. Reagan went through the ceremonies like a President, shoulders squared, features composed, every gesture correct. It was clear that he felt that he was carrying out a difficult and historic duty.

It was a cold, damp day. As we walked to the car after the President's speech at Bergen-Belsen I made small talk about the weather, hoping to divert his thoughts. He shuddered.

It's given me quite a chill, he said.

· 14 ·

The Random Factor

Because of the distractions caused by Bitburg and the President's hospitalization, and the delays involved in assembling a staff and merging its talents and missions into a unified routine, it was mid-August before I was able to give the President a formal paper recommending a course of action for the future. The document, based on discussions by the senior White House staff, focused on three critical objectives: maintenance of the economic recovery, foreign policy, and the legislative agenda.

This was a plan for an activist Presidency. If he accepted its recommendations, Reagan would use his veto and his popularity aggressively to attack excessive congressional spending and thereby seize control of the deficit, defend free trade, and promote the adoption of a comprehensive farm policy. He would personally lead the fight for tax reform. In foreign policy (a section of the report drafted by Bud McFarlane and his staff at NSC), he would meet the new Soviet leader, Mikhail S. Gorbachev, at a summit in Geneva, deliver a major speech before the United Nations General Assembly on the UN's fortieth anniversary, lead the effort to revive the peace process in the Middle East by encouraging Jordan and Israel to engage in bilateral negotiations, encourage liberalization in South Africa, and insist on a policy in Central America that buttressed democracy in the region, drove the last of the Communist guerrillas out of El Salvador, and kept up the pressure on the Sandinistas and their Cuban and Soviet mentors by continuing support for the Contras.

The policies and actions outlined in the document were logical extensions of existing policy. They were not designed to impose a program of action on the President, but to give him a summary of his options and a list of recommendations for action. The latter were divided into three categories: short-range (through October 15), medium-range (through the end of 1985), and long-range (through the end of 1986). Some of the actions contemplated—such as the veto of any farm bill that exceeded a ceiling on spending to be determined through consultations with Congress, the fight against protectionism, and support of the Contras—involved profound consequences. Others, including the proposal that the President personally lead the fight for tax reform, made significant claims on his time and political capital.

To borrow from the vocabulary of corporate practice, I was presenting a plan of action to the chief executive officer of the firm. According to the methods under which I had always operated, objectives were hammered out through discussion by the people who would have to carry them out, this consensus was reduced to writing, and the result was submitted to the man in charge. He then told you what he liked about the plan and what he did not like. You revised on the basis of his criticisms until you had a paper that he was willing to approve. Once he had signed off, debate ceased and you went to work to carry out the final plan.

This paper represented the first stage of this process. It was not a plan of action but an outline of goals. I expected that the President would read it, decide on his priorities, and call for more detailed suggestions. After that he could be expected to call in his department heads and give them their marching orders: cut the budget or increase it, fight for this policy on taxes and spending, concentrate on these bills before Congress, meet these objectives in research and development, develop a program to increase exports by X percent, make the following points to the Russians and offer the following reassurances to our allies, and explain it all to the public on the basis of these considerations.

Instead, Ronald Reagan read the paper while he was at the ranch and handed it back to me on his return without spoken or written comment.

"What did you think of it?" I asked.

It's good, the President replied, nodding in approval. It's really good, Don.

I waited for him to say more. He did not. He had no questions to ask, no objections to raise, no instructions to issue. I realized that the policy that would determine the course of the world's most powerful nation for the next two years and deeply influence the fate of the Republican party in the 1986 midterm elections had been adopted without amendment. It seemed, also, that I had been authorized as Chief of Staff to make the necessary arrangements to carry out the policy. It was taken for granted that the President would do whatever was asked of him to make the effort a success. We went on to the next item on the agenda.

I confess that I was surprised that this weighty matter was decided so quickly and with so little ceremony. In a way, of course, it was flattering: it is always gratifying to anticipate the boss's wishes with acceptable accuracy. Still, I was uneasy. Did the President really want us to do all these things with no more discussion than this? I decided that this must be the case, since always in the past, if he did not say no, the answer was yes. By now I understood that the President did not share my love of detail and my enthusiasm for planning. I knew that he was not an aggressive manager. Perhaps I should have quizzed him on tax policy or Central America or our approach to trade negotiations; certainly my instincts and the practice of a lifetime nudged me in that direction. But I held my tongue. It is one thing brashly to speak your mind to an ordinary mortal and another to say "Wait a minute!" to the President of the United States. The mystery of the office is a potent inhibitor. The President, you feel, has his reasons.

Another President would almost certainly have had his own ideas on the mechanics of policy, but Reagan did not trouble himself with such minutiae. His preoccupation was with what might be called "the outer Presidency." He was content to let others cope with the inner details of running the Administration. In this he was the antithesis of most recent Presidents. Kennedy might call up a minor bureaucrat to check on a detail; Johnson might twist a senator's arm; Nixon might discuss the tiniest details of China policy with his staff; Carter might micromanage a commando raid in the Iranian desert from his desk in the Oval Office. But Reagan chose his aides and then followed their advice almost without question. He trusted his lieutenants to act on his intentions, rather than on his spoken instructions, and though he sometimes asked what some of his less visible Cabinet officers were doing with their departments, he seldom spontaneously called for a detailed status report. The degree of trust involved in this method of leadership must be unprecedented in modern American history. Sometimes—as was inevitable given that many of his closest aides, including almost all of the Cabinet, were virtual strangers to him—this trust was betrayed in shocking fashion. When that happened Reagan seldom criticized, seldom complained, never scolded. Not even the Iran-Contra debacle could provoke him into harsh words, much less subordinates who had let him down.

Never—absolutely never in my experience—did President Reagan really lose his temper or utter a rude or unkind word. Never did he issue a direct order, although I, at least, sometimes devoutly wished that he would. He listened, acquiesced, played his role, and waited for the next act to be written. From the point of view of my own experience and nature, this was an altogether baffling way of doing things. But my own style was not the case in point. Reagan's method had worked well enough to make him President of the United States, and well enough for the nation under his leadership to transform its mood from pessimism to optimism, its economy from stagnation to steady growth, and its position in the world from weakness to strength. Common sense suggested that the President knew something that the rest of us did not know. It was my clear duty to do things his way.

Still, some means had to be found to fill in the blanks. Logic suggested that we bring the substance of the policy memorandum before the Cabinet at its next meeting and assign the job of developing programs to carry it out to the two new policy councils. The President amiably agreed, and a couple of days later, on Tuesday, September 3, we did so. Cabinet members carried the assignment back to their departments, and soon the whole town was busy carrying out the Presidential wishes, or seeking ways to circumvent them, or dissecting and denouncing them in the media. None of this surprised Reagan in the least or elicited much comment from him. He understood better than anyone around him that in the Presidency, as in the movies, small gestures by the leading man could produce large effects.

The White House press office told the media nearly everything the President knew, and within a fortnight the press was reporting, in the words of a headline in the *Christian Science Monitor,* that "Reagan [is] 'rarin' to go.'" The writer, Charlotte Saikowski, was quoting the President, who had said at a speech in Independence, Missouri, "I'm back an' rarin' to go." The *Monitor*'s reporter asked, "Will the President capitalize on his immense public popularity to exert strong leadership on tax reform, the budget deficit, and foreign policy? Or will he be content simply to remain popular and let his Presidency acquire the image of declining power that has beset many Presidents in their second term?" A White House official was quoted as answering this rhetorical question for the *Monitor* by saying, "The President will be trying to move the country and . . . is not resting on his oars. So we have the opportunity to break the historical pattern." The President himself was quoted as saying that he would examine each spending bill "with my veto pen hovering over every line."

The rest of the media reflected this view of an activist President keenly pursuing a policy he deeply believed in. This was, of course, the fact. Reagan was engaged in a struggle with Congress over deficit spending, over the debt ceiling (up $850 billion since he was elected and due to be raised to $2 trillion), over the farm bill, over international trade, over sanctions against South Africa, and over aid to the Nicaraguan freedom fighters. These confrontations generated political heat, but few were prepared to blame Reagan for any unpleasantness. "Irritation with the White House is aimed less at the President than at Donald Regan, the new White House Chief of Staff," wrote the *Monitor* in the story quoted above. "'Most recognize that it's not the President but his new staff,' says one GOP congressional aide. 'Don Regan has failed to understand what has to be done and how to work with the Senate.' " This was a theme I would hear repeated in imaginative variation in the year and a half as Chief of Staff that lay still ahead of me. During an interview I told Jack Nelson of the *Los Angeles Times* to judge me on what happened, not on what people were saying. At the time the criticism in the press seemed irrelevant because it was so naïve. Later I would be reminded that inaccuracy and misinterpretation are among the greatest of all Washington relevancies.

My mind was on my work, and I had never been more fully occupied. My day began well before seven in the morning with reading in the backseat of the government Mercury that carried me from home to the office. There, after a brief conference with my aides, I sat down to a working breakfast. Most days I lunched alone at my desk on a bowl of soup while reading correspondence and scribbling replies. Although everyone who works in the White House is a member of the President's personal staff and is there to serve him and nobody else—the Chief of Staff has no real staff of his own—I was the link between the President and the rest of the staff. The President's assistants came to see me in a steady stream all day long when I was not occupied with the President himself. They called me on the phone or sent me memoranda or experts or journalists. This was an enjoyably stimulating process. Their business was urgent because it was the President's business, their ideas were excellent, and their work was of the highest caliber. Sometimes, at the end of a day that had flown by largely because I was in such good company, I would remark, "I haven't had time to go to the bathroom!" Then the young people who worked with me would laugh unsympathetically, evidently pleased to have preserved me from boredom. I also had a more easily satisfied visitor; the President's likable but clumsy dog, Lucky, dropped by my office early every morning for a doughnut before galloping thunderously back to the residence.

The President lived at a somewhat more leisurely pace, as was the intended result of the frenetic activity of his aides. He carried on his day-to-day routine as usual, giving his cheery good-morning wave to Kathy Osborne, feeding acorns to the squirrels outside the Oval Office (one morning, looking over Reagan's shoulder, I saw a large Norway rat scouting for food beyond the windows and alerted the exterminators, who soon trapped the rodent), and conscientiously attending to his daily tasks. When he went upstairs to the family quarters around four o'clock, he took a thick folder of homework with him—briefing papers, communications from foreign and domestic leaders, decision-making documents to be read and signed. He never failed to deal with every single item, whether it amounted to five pages or five hundred. His first act every morning was to deliver his completed homework to Kathy Osborne or to me for filing or dispatch. Reagan's discipline and study habits were unique—but once he had completed an assignment he seemed to lose interest in it. Only occasionally did he talk about what he had read the night before.

I did nothing to disturb the rhythm of the Presidential day. Obviously Reagan's routine suited him; it would be hard to imagine anyone enjoying a job more than Ronald Reagan enjoyed being President of the United States. He seemed to like everything about it. His daily schedule was the centerpiece of his life. The scrupulous way in which he observed it, checking off each event with a pencil after it ended and preparing himself for the next, gave his life a regularity and a tangible measure of accomplishment that evidently was deeply pleasing to him. He seemed to feel that his schedule set him free: more than almost any other person in the world, he knew exactly what to expect all day long, every day.

He was, of course, immune to interruption except in dire emergency or in case of an important congressional vote. He seldom interrupted others unless his schedule reminded him that a member of the staff was having a birthday. Then he would wander down the hall to the office of the celebrant and present him or her with a funny hat or a tee shirt bearing a jocular message. These gifts were chosen by others, and sometimes Reagan barely knew the person to whom he was giving them, but his pleasure in these contacts was genuine. He always had a joke, of course, and his visits certainly meant a lot to the staff. Any sign of ordinary humanity in the great is endearing, and Reagan was nothing if not transparently human. On one occasion, when he was somehow given the wrong date for one man's birthday and called to offer congratulations, nobody had the heart to tell him about the mistake. But the Reagans as a couple were somewhat less cordial to those who helped them live their lives, and in my time I was never able to get them to render a personal word of thanks to the hardworking people—such as the remarkable White House telephone operators and the volunteers who handled the mail and phone calls—to whom even the briefest "thanks and well done" would have meant much.

Reagan's natural courtesy prevented him from changing his own schedule. I cannot remember a single case in which he changed a time or canceled an appointment or even complained about an item on his schedule. Never did he decide on the spur of the moment that he wanted to wipe his calendar clean and, say, work on a speech. To do so would have caused an upheaval and wasted the work of the dozens of people who prepared the way for any Presidential activity. Never did he complain about an appointment or protest that he did not want to see someone who had been granted an interview. He seemed to be genuinely horrified at the prospect of causing embarrassment or disappointment or inconvenience to another person. If he promised that he would do something, he did it.

The one chore for which Reagan displayed no enthusiasm whatever was the annual presentation of the National Thanksgiving Turkey; the President always groaned when he saw this event on his schedule, and more than once suggested that the Vice President stand in for him. "Oh, no you don't!" I would reply, "you've got to have your picture taken with the turkey, Mr. President—it's tradition." He would sigh and go through with the photo opportunity, but he hated it and it required all his skill as an actor to conceal this from the cameras.

Reagan remembers the words and mannerisms of strangers for years after he encounters them, and this, too, may have more to do with his actorly study habits than with any natural gregariousness. His reminiscences are populated with singular characters he had run into along the campaign trail, or on the mashed-potato circuit for GE, or in his days as an actor. Nearly everyone likes him in return. With his ready humor and his strong hand-shake, he is a man's man, and women admire him for the same qualities as well as for his handsome presence.

Although he is truly uxorious, he tends to be more animated in the presence of women, to whom he is unfailingly gallant. He genuinely enjoys the company of the opposite sex. In Cabinet meetings Reagan was generally animated; he loved the give-and-take of policy discussions in the Cabinet councils, when he had a chance to pronounce on the broad general principles that primarily interested him. But the presence of Ambassador Jeane Kirkpatrick or Secretary of Transportation Elizabeth Dole at a Cabinet meeting always made for a heightened Presidential mood; he was more amusing, more talkative, more of a participant than a presence. It is devoutly believed by those who travel with the President that Pan American World Airways assigns its prettiest stewardesses to the plane carrying the White House press. This happy circumstance did not escape the President's notice. When *Air Force One* landed, the President always looked for the Pan Am stewardesses from the press plane and gave them a fatherly wave. They waved back enthusiastically, pretty young women in their uniforms smiling at the most famous man in the world. It was a moment everyone looked forward to on Presidential jour-neys.

On the other hand, Reagan was habitually shy and withdrawn in personal meetings with people he did not know well, especially if the visitor happened to be present as an expert. In such circumstances jokes were usually omitted and the President would listen intently but seldom speak. He was reluctant, even, to meet with some of his speech writers because they were comparative strangers to him. Sometimes, when the subject was esoteric, Reagan would be particularly passive, and as we grew to know each other better I would occasionally ask him why after the meeting was over. It would usually turn out that he had hesitated to ask questions because he did not wish to seem uninformed in the presence of people he did not know well.

Reagan loved the mail and there was plenty of it. On a typical day in 1985, more than 4,500 letters addressed to the President of the United States were delivered to the White House. A few of these, identifiable by a special code on the envelope, came from the President's old friends, such as the members of the Kitchen Cabinet, and these were delivered to his secretary unopened. All the rest were opened and sorted. All but the few that came from lunatics received a reply. Those requesting help with a problem involving the federal government were sent to the agency most able to deal with matter if the White House could not respond adequately from its own resources. Anne Higgins, head of this very important operation, regularly provided the President with a tally of letters dealing with issues—how many for tax reform, how many against. These figures went into the Presidential memory bank, and in his meetings with senators and congressmen and others, Reagan habitually quoted from letters from citizens who supported his position on a given issue.

Every couple of weeks, Anne also provided a selection of these letters, including five or six from people who had written to the President to share their troubles or their happiness. He read these letters at night, and in the morning he would sometimes tell me about a father who had written to describe how he had been reunited with his family, or about a mother who had worked hard all her life to educate her children, or about a child who had been stricken by disease and was fighting gallantly against death or discouragement. Such letters moved him, and he almost always wrote personal replies, offering solace or congratulations as the case suggested. Often he wrote in longhand—but these versions were typed before they were mailed. Reagan's heart was easily touched: a newspaper story about an afflicted child often stimulated him to send a check or write a letter, or both—or inspired him to instruct me or someone else to look into the case and see if there was anything an agency of the federal government could do to help. His emotions were engaged by the fact that some people wrote to him as President and poured out their hearts as if he were a sort of father of last resort. Reagan placed a high value on the goodwill and approval of the common peo-

First briefing for President on the new budget. In Oval Office, January 28, 1981. Attending: David Stockman, O.M.B.; Donald Regan, Secretary of the Treasury; Murray Weidenbaum, Chairman, Council of Economic Advisors; Marty Anderson, Office of Policy Development.

Greater New York "Take Stock in America 1982" savings bonds luncheon, the Plaza Hotel. Left to right: Donald T. Regan, Secretary of the Treasury; Angela M. Buchanan, Treasurer of the United States and National Director of the U.S. Savings Bonds Division; F. Ross Johnson, President and Chief Operating Officer, Nabisco Brands, Inc.; James D. Robinson III, Chairman, American Express Company. December 1, 1981.

Briefing session, U.S. Embassy, Paris, before Versailles Summit.
June 4, 1982. Left to right: Ed Harper, Presidential Assistant;
Beryl Sprinkel, then Under Secretary of Treasury, now CEA
Chairman; Donald T. Regan, Secretary of the Treasury;
President Ronald Reagan; Al Haig, Secretary of State.

Donald T. Regan being sworn in as Chief of Staff to the President
of the United States by Dan Marks, Deputy Executive Clerk of
the White House. In Mr. Regan's office, February 4, 1985.

First day as Chief of Staff to the President. Edwin Meese, Counsellor to the President; Mr. Regan; the President; Michael Deaver, Assistant to the President and Deputy Chief of Staff. The Oval Office, February 4, 1985.

President Reagan in meeting with National Security Council after hijacked TWA Flight 847 was flown from Algiers to Beirut. From left: General John Vessey, Chair of Joint Chiefs of Staff; Caspar Weinberger, Secretary of Defense; Vice President Bush; the President; George Shultz, Secretary of State; William Casey, CIA Director; and Mr. Regan. The Situation Room, the White House, June 16, 1985.

Helmut Kohl's remarks at Bergen-Belsen concentration camp. Left: Donald T. Regan; center: the Reagans; right: George Shultz. May 5, 1985.

The President, Vice President Bush, and Mr. Regan. Bethesda Naval Hospital, July 17, 1985.

President Reagan and Mr. Regan
during Summit meeting with
General Secretary Gorbachev
on the driveway of Maison
De Saussure, Geneva.
November 19, 1985.

President and Mrs. Reagan visit the "pool house" at Villa Fleur d'Eau as part of preparation for Geneva Gorbachev meeting two days before "spontaneous" meeting between Reagan and Gorbachev on the first day of the Summit. Left to right: Bill Henkel, Ronald Reagan, Nancy Reagan, Larry Speakes (partially obscured), and Don Regan. November 17, 1985.

President Reagan, Don Regan, Jim Kuhn, and Bill Henkel debate whether or not the President should take off his overcoat prior to greeting General Secretary Gorbachev. Left to right: Bud McFarlane, Grey Terry, Bill Henkel, Donald T. Regan, Ronald Reagan, Jim Kuhn. November 19, 1985.

Geneva Summit: Larry Speakes and Don Regan; on couch, President Reagan and Soviet leader Mikhail Gorbachev; Mr. Shevardnadze and Secretary Shultz. November 20, 1985.

Mr. Regan's 1985 birthday party. Vice President Bush, President Reagan, and Mr. Regan in the Roosevelt Room at the White House. December 20, 1985.

Golfing over the New Year's holiday at Sunnylands, the Annenberg estate, Palm Springs, California. December 31, 1985.

Don Regan, Jim Baker, and the President at Treasury Department campaigning for enactment of tax reform. Scene shows Jim Baker returning to Don Regan one of Regan's shirts allegedly found in Treasury Secretary's bathroom after the job swap. February 5, 1986.

Signing ceremony for tax reform legislation, South Lawn of the White House. Looking on: Robert Byrd, Jack Kemp, Jim Baker, Don Regan, Dick Gephardt, Bob Dole, Dan Rostenkowski. October 22, 1986.

President and Regan on campaign trail in the back of the Presidential limousine, Idaho. October 31, 1986.

At Hovde House for meeting with General Secretary Gorbachev at Reykjavík. President Reagan, Secretary Shultz, Mr. Regan, Admiral Poindexter, SS Agent Ray Shaddix, and Bill Henkel. October 11, 1986.

ple, and these tokens of their affection and support were important to him.

The morning meeting, commencing always at nine o'clock on the dot unless the President happened to be a few minutes early—a lapse for which he always apologized because it caused me to hurry down the corridor on being told that he was approaching the Oval Office—was always cheerful. The Oval Office is a sunny room with many windows and pleasant views. Except in the hottest months, a fire burned in the fireplace and a fresh potted plant brightened the room (cut flowers make Reagan sniffle). After the exchange of jokes, the President would "give me what he had." Often this consisted of a series of questions: someone may have told him something at a dinner that interested him and he wanted more information, or he may have read something or heard something on television that piqued his curiosity. Before the meeting he would read the White House news summary at breakfast. This is a digest of the day's stories in the leading newspapers and a summary of network coverage, together with a smattering of commentary by the columnists and commentators. He would also scan a number of newspapers and watch all three network news shows. He read the *Washington Times* with greater attention than the *Washington Post* and the *New York Times*, but regarded the *Los Angeles Times* as his hometown paper. One of the differences between Reagan and his Vice President emerged from these morning discussions: Reagan generally recited passages from the conservative *Washington Times*, while Bush usually quoted the *New York Times*. This is a big difference.

Reagan was an avid reader of the conservative monthly *Human Events*, and frequently quoted from it at length. The writings of Warren Brookes, one of the leading contributors to this publication and to the *Washington Times*, deeply impressed the President. He had been reading this man's work for years, and Brookes's ideas were woven into the President's philosophy. Reagan received his copy of *Human Events* so swiftly that I used to josh him that the first copy off the press must be beamed to him by satellite. I began to read this publication, which had not hitherto been on my required reading list, as a means of holding my own with the enthusiasms it generated in the President, but I was never able to get my copy before he got his, so he was always a day ahead of me. This pleased him and irked me as we both liked to be the first to read the items. The press was not Reagan's only source of ideas. Many of his questions were originated by friends; he paid close attention to the advice of people he had known for years. In this, as in so many other matters, the personal dimension was the one in which he preferred to operate.

Reagan resorted to the personal touch as a matter of instinct and long practice. In his days on the road for GE, he explained to me, he had developed the habit of answering his mail in longhand. He still preferred the pen to any other instrument. I kept a computer terminal in my office. One day at my suggestion he dropped in to look it over. I explained its advantages and offered to get him one, waxing enthusiastic about the capability it would give him to call up all sorts of facts and data—even to tap out messages.

Not me! he replied, eyeing the blinking screen with suspicion. I was born into the age of pencil and pen and I'm too old now to change over to one of those things.

When working on the budget or some other task that involved arithmetic, he would scribble the sums with a pencil, covering sheets of scrap paper with columns of addition, subtraction, multiplication, and long division. I gave him several pocket calculators, and while he always feigned delight and sometimes even punched up a few functions to please me, he never actually used the devices.

When the issue engaged the President's convictions or touched on a situation to which he attached special importance, he was likely to sit down and pen a letter to another head of state. He was possessive of letters from his partners at the annual Economic Summit, and insisted that these be sent to him before they were read by anyone else. Normally he answered such letters at once, often in his own hand. Letters from other heads of government, particularly unfriendly ones, passed through the NSC and/or the State Department for analysis and a draft reply before the President saw them. Usually he let himself be guided by the advice of his experts in foreign policy, but in his early days in office, I am told, he sometimes dashed off an answer without benefit of such counsel. This practice dismayed certain professional diplomats at the State Department who were unused to the idea of a President answering his own mail, but Reagan was not deterred. In such letters he sounded very much himself—direct, sincere, kind, and eager to dispel any possible misunderstanding.

Reagan was a master of the Presidential signature as souvenir. In signing a piece of legislation or some other important document, he would use a different pen for each letter of his name so that he could hand out twelve historic pens to the twelve most important senators, congressmen, and other personages whom he had invited to witness the ceremony. The President liked the *Reader's Digest* story of a woman who watched him perform this feat and cried, "Ah! He finally found one that had ink in it!"

He was equally at ease on the telephone. On the occasions when he called senators and congressmen to lobby for their votes on important legislation, he projected an impression of sympathy even over the wires. The person at the other end of the line was left in no doubt that Reagan believed in his sincerity and his good intentions. The President never bullied, never threatened, never cajoled. It was always: Let me explain why I'm for this bill, and I hope that we can count on your vote. He would listen to the reply, making meticulous notes as he went. If the senator or the congressman had some sort of problem with a provision of the bill, Reagan would assure him that he would look into the matter, and he never failed to do so—usually by handing his notes to me and asking for a follow-up.

Only Tip O'Neill seemed to be immune to Reagan's gift for conciliation. Although photographs taken after their meetings suggested a sort of underlying Irish cameraderie between the two men, the reality was that they were hammer and anvil. O'Neill seemed determined to dislike Reagan and disagree with him, and sparks flew as a result.

Reagan complained, I don't know what the hell's the matter with the man; I just can't seem to reach him.

The Busby Papers, a perspicacious newsletter published by Horace Busby & Associates, offered a possible explanation in its issue of May 31, 1985:

For four years Speaker O'Neill has held most of his [Democratic] majority in service to . . . his party's promise that Mr. Reagan would be a one-termer. When the 1984 returns came in, it was as if a great door had clanged shut on yesterday's liberalism. Besieged by an aroused public opinion, old loyalties are faltering. The younger Democrats intending to be the party's next leaders are distancing themselves from the past.

O'Neill's antipathy to Reagan, founded perhaps on bafflement that this Irish Republican had won the victories and the public approval that Irish Democrats better deserved, affected nearly every issue. But the one that roused the Speaker's passions to the boiling point was Central America. O'Neill seemed to believe absolutely that those Central Americans who were aligned with the United States—the government of El Salvador, the Nicaraguan freedom fighters—were evil and corrupt and that those on the other side were very much more virtuous than the President's intelligence reports and nearly every other unbiased source suggested they were. This fixed idea of O'Neill's colored every discussion between the two men. Often it boiled over into something resembling the schoolboy bullying I remembered from recess at Saint Augustine's School in South Boston.

A case in point was a discussion I will call "the Willow Oak Tree Agreement." The President had invited the leaders of Congress to the White House for a drink at the end of the day to discuss the budget. The meeting, one of several of its kind, took place on a terrace just outside the President's study (formerly Mike Deaver's office) adjoining the Oval Office. A willow oak tree grows at the edge of this patio.

The President, who drinks very little alcohol, sipped his favorite cocktail, a weak orange blossom. Some of the others— O'Neill, Wright, Foley, Michel, Gray, and Lott from the House;

Dole, Thurmond, Domenici, Chiles, Long, and Byrd from the Senate—joined him. It was a relaxed occasion, as it was intended to be, in which to discuss differences in a friendly atmosphere. A number of points were raised—Could this item be cut? Could that one be eliminated?—until finally someone suggested that one way to solve the problem would be for the President to raise taxes. The suggestion was in the nature of a gentle needling—everyone present knew how Reagan felt on this question.

The President said, Come on, fellows. You know I'm not going to raise taxes.

As the senior member of the House, O'Neill sat on the President's immediate left. His face flushed. With his meaty hand he delivered a karate chop to the table, rattling the glasses.

"All right, goddamnit!" he shouted. "If that's the way it's going to be, then everything is off the table with me, too!"

Silence fell. Was this the Speaker of the House of Representatives yelling at the President of the United States in the latter's own house?

Reagan's face flushed—a little pinker than usual because even a small amount of alcohol causes his naturally ruddy color to rise. The Presidential lips pursed, a sure sign of anger. But he held onto his self-control.

Well, damn it, Tip, he said, I just can't do it.

The embarrassment created by this exchange sent everyone else present scurrying for a way to patch up the differences between the two sides, and out of the suggestions that were made a compromise eventually emerged. This may go to show that there's some good after all in an Irish temper. At the time the point was not obvious.

In the early months of 1985, even before Bitburg, the President had experienced setbacks in Congress. In part because of O'Neill's intransigence on the issue, and in part because of a genuine ambivalence toward U.S. involvement in guerrilla wars (arising out of a complex mixture of factors that included Vietnam and the ideological fissure opened by that war in American life) he failed to get the financial support he had sought for the Contras. Congress had also failed to approve full financing for the

MX missile, regarded by experts in strategic arms as vital in maintaining the balance of strategic nuclear weapons with the Soviet Union. Furthermore, the budget deficit for fiscal year 1986 was estimated at a horrendous $221 billion, and there was little sign that Congress was in a mood to reduce spending in the absence of a tax increase.

The budget submitted by the President for fiscal year 1986, which would commence on October 1, 1985, would have reduced the deficit by some $62 billion, or 28 percent, but that enormous accomplishment was both problematical and in the future. Meanwhile the President's critics in the press and the political opposition were adding up these small embarrassments, including the inevitable drop in the popularity polls that followed his enormous electoral victory (job approval down to 55 percent in May from the high of 70 percent at the time of the second inauguration). It was their intention to suggest that the negative total was greater than the sum of his recent accomplishments. Was he a lame duck only a few months after his reelection? The President did not think so, and neither did I.

We later worked with Senator Phil Gramm of Texas on legislation that would mandate a balanced budget through systematic reduction of the deficit. This law, passed as the Gramm-Rudman-Hollings Act and signed by the President on December 12, 1985, established a schedule of deficit reductions beginning in 1986. In years when the budget fails to meet the goal established by the act, the President is required to propose the necessary cuts. Social Security and many social programs are exempt from reductions, but the intent—and so far, the effect—has been to impose a welcome measure of publicity, if not discipline on the budget process.

What was needed now was a major legislative victory that would change the atmosphere of political resentment and resistance on Capitol Hill. Any such success would make other successes possible. In the strategy sessions that produced the outline of issues I had handed to the President, the staff had searched for something that would permit him to go on the offensive and outflank the Congress by appealing to the broad coalition of Americans who had elected him. All agreed that the issue must be one that affected the everyday existence of men and women in all walks of life. The astute Stu Spencer suggested that the President place his political bets on foreign trade under the slogan "Buy America." Another faction led by Pat Buchanan spoke of the anxiety generated by criminal violence and suggested a war on crime. The OMB people and their allies saw the balanced-budget amendment and an attack on the deficit as a popular and morally resonant issue. Worthy ideas all—but none seemed to me to be the right one at the right time. The balance of trade was worrisome but it would not yield to Presidential jawboning; the prevalence of crime was frightening but it was not primarily a federal issue; and if the first Reagan term had taught us anything, it had taught us that the President alone could not decide the fiscal fate of the nation.

I came down on the side of tax reform. Taxes were everybody's business and they were the key to sane management of the budget. The existing tax system was widely perceived to be incomprehensible in its details and shady in its exceptions, and its replacement by a fair and rational structure that placed all taxpayers on the same footing would certainly be regarded by the people (and, incidentally, by historians, who are always an important presence in a second term) as a great act of Presidential leadership. Admittedly, my judgment was colored by pride of authorship. But I also thought that tax reform was the best horse in the race for three basic reasons: it was an emotional issue that deserved to be an emotional issue; it was an issue that the Democrats could not oppose without abandoning their historic claim to be the protectors of the people; and, above all, it was good for the country.

Not everyone believed that the issue was a winner. Senator Paul Laxalt, Republican of Nevada, a canny political adviser and close friend to whom the President listened with respect, summed up the pros and cons. "[Tax reform] could be the hallmark of his second term, along with arms control, but it also has the potential for great mischief," Laxalt said. "When you open up the whole code, lobbyists from all over the country, and perhaps the world, will be crawling out from under any rock."

The President, however, decided to barnstorm the country,

selling tax reform in a series of speeches. The media would follow in his wake, and though we realized that writing about the same subject day after day would make for a restive press corps, Bill Henkel, who had replaced Mike Deaver as chief event meister, believed that he could keep the correspondents engaged with a variety of backgrounds. The President would go to Williamsburg, Virginia, a place close to his heart. The 1983 Economic Summit had been held there, and the tranquil atmosphere of the recreated colonial village had charmed and delighted the assembled heads of government. Each had been provided with one of the restored houses as a temporary residence, and they had been able to call on each other like neighbors by walking a few steps along the brick sidewalks from one house to another. (I am happy to say that the choice of Williamsburg for the summit was my idea, proposed to Mike Deaver aboard *Air Force One* on the way back to Washington from the 1982 summit at Versailles. Deaver had been worried about topping the French and their magnificent palace. He planned to propose California as the site of the next summit. "We'll dazzle them," he said. "Good luck on that," I replied. "I can just see us all having dinner at the ranch—the heads of government in one place, the foreign ministers in another, and the finance ministers probably sitting on some mountain peak surrounded by ants and wild animals." In the end, Deaver's fixation on a rustic summit in the California mountains yielded to reality—the seven delegations and accompanying press required more than six thousand rooms and suitable meeting facilities—and the summit was in fact held at Williamsburg, an island of tranquillity surrounded by hotels and motels.)

The President was in great form in Williamsburg in 1985, possibly because it held such happy memories for him. The warmth of his delivery and the mellow surroundings had a strange effect on Sam Donaldson of ABC. "Hey, Regan," Sam bellowed in his inimitable basso. "I've just figured it out. I can save a hundred and thirty thousand dollars in taxes under your plan. I'm all for it!" I thanked him for the endorsement, saying, "I knew you'd see the light of day as soon as you got the arithmetic straight."

The rest of the tour was a triumph of the bully pulpit. In a stroke of genius, Henkel and his cohorts had suggested that the remainder of the President's speeches take place in heartland towns—Oshkosh, Wisconsin; Malvern, Pennsylvania; Independence, Missouri; and others. The President was greeted by enthusiastic and affectionate crowds wherever he went, and his speeches developed a revival-style pattern of question and response:

PRESIDENT: Do the people of Oshkosh want our tax
    system to be complicated and unfair?
CROWD: No!
PRESIDENT: Do you want steeply rising tax brackets that
    punish the workingman and hurt the American
    family?
CROWD: No!
PRESIDENT: Do you want dramatic simplification that
    eliminates loopholes and makes our tax system straight-
    forward and fair to all?
CROWD: Yes! [*Cheers. Wild applause.*]

The crowds contained an exceptionally high proportion of young people and their presence energized the President. Many had waited for hours to catch a glimpse of him. To the dismay of the Secret Service, Reagan responded to the crowds, grinning and chatting and shaking hands. At Oshkosh, a group of students from the University of Wisconsin waved anti-Reagan banners and chanted heckling slogans. Several young women in the group stripped to the waist as a way of drawing attention to their cause and started a commotion. Afterward the President asked what had happened. When we explained, he said, I always miss the fun—I had to keep my eyes on the text.

The original proposal for tax reform that my team at Treasury had put together was now called Treasury I. I had told the press when presenting this proposal that it was "written on a word processor," meaning that it was open for improvement. Secretary of the Treasury Jim Baker and members of his staff had produced a modified version called Treasury II after consultations with key Treasury officials and members of Congress. Not every change had been an improvement—the new plan abandoned the key idea of taxing indexed capital gains on the same basis as ordinary income, diluted the reform of the depreciation system, and allowed the oil industry to continue the full deduction of "intangible drilling costs," among other concessions to business. But the revised version was regarded by judges of political reality, such as Baker, as having a better chance of getting through Congress more or less intact. In Baker's words, as quoted in the press, concessions had to be made "to the real world in which we live." Still, tax rates were drastically reduced, the personal deduction was doubled, and standard deductions were raised, so that a husband and wife making $80,000 a year between them would pay around $5,000 less in taxes, and a family of four earning up to $12,798 would pay no federal income taxes at all.

Treasury II was the proposal that the President had sent to Congress and was discussing in his tour of the country. After the President described the plan in a television speech on May 20, 1985, a *New York Post* editorial writer wrote that it was "a far inferior animal [to Treasury I]—less simple, less fair, and less efficient."

The *New York Times*'s Hedrick Smith quoted a "White House adviser" as saying, "The President's major task is to pound home again and again the gains that will be experienced by the average American, and to keep the special interests at bay. To the degree that the bill is cast as being from Main Street and not from Wall Street, it increases the chance of passing." I was the source of that quote, and it encapsulates the advice the President was receiving, and heeding, from me and most of his White House staff.

Dan Rostenkowski said of the President's proposal that "his words and feeling go back to Roosevelt and Truman and Kennedy," but warned that the Democrats "would not rubber-stamp the Reagan program but strive to make it fairer." Other Democrats, including even O'Neill, attached themselves to the proposal. "If the plan is perceived as helping the middle class, there's a lot of grass-roots pressure for it," said Representative Bob Matsui, Democrat of California.

Some Republicans were less enthusiastic. Bob Dole said that the Senate might be busy with other things, such as foreign trade and the farm bill. Republicans on the Senate Finance Committee said that they'd be glad to work with the President on tax reform, but added that they'd have little enthusiasm for such a bill if it did nothing to reduce the deficit. "The idea of getting a bill to the Senate to me is like a child going to Disneyland," Rostenkowski said. The President continued to campaign at the grass roots. On February 6, 1986, in his State of the Union speech, he told the Congress what he had been telling audiences across America: "One thing that tax reform will not be is a tax increase in disguise."

In that the President was correct. When the 1986 Tax Reform Act was finally passed on October 22, 1986, Senator Russell Long, Democrat of Louisiana, called it the most important change in our tax system in fifty years. Treasury I shone through many of its provisions. The maximum rate for individuals was cut from 50 percent to 28 percent. A couple filing a joint return would be paying 15 percent on the first $29,750 of taxable income and in the 28 percent bracket on income above that amount. The standard deduction was increased to $5,000 for joint returns and $3,000 for individuals. The personal exemption was nearly doubled to $2,000 in 1989 and then indexed for inflation. Deduction of interest on mortgages for both first and second homes was retained, but interest on such things as car loans, credit cards, and life insurance policies became nondeductible. Tax shelters were dealt a body blow; the investment tax credit was repealed; deductions for business entertainment and travel were curtailed. For the first time, corporations were made subject to the alternative minimum tax, the same as individuals. The maximum individual rate on long-term capital gains was increased from 20 to 28 percent, the same as ordinary income.

The law that the President signed did not remove every inequity from the system, and in its treatment of business taxation it retained many preferential provisions that Treasury I would have eliminated. True simplification was not achieved. Treasury I had been 798 pages long. The House version of the tax bill was 1,379 pages long, the Senate version 1,580 pages. The law itself was 858 pages long and the conference report accompanying it—which explains the law—totaled 886 pages.

But the law was a great improvement on the old system, and in comparison with what had been thought possible, it was an astounding accomplishment. Much of the credit for this belongs to Senator Bob Packwood, the chairman of the Senate Finance Committee, to Dan Rostenkowski, and to the members of both their committees, who worked long and hard with Jim Baker and his crew from Treasury.

Will the law achieve the economic results intended? As yet nobody knows, but I am no less optimistic now than I was in those heady days at Treasury. There's no doubt in my mind that lower rates of taxation will encourage people to save. A taxpayer in the upper brackets knows that he's going to keep 72 cents of every dollar earned. Even if inflation is high in the future, the government will not gain at the taxpayers' expense. Corporations' earnings will now be the result of what they save after they have sold their product and accounted for their expenses. Under the old code, it was a race to see who could get what sort of tax advantage. If that energy and ingenuity is henceforth channeled into competition for profits from superior products, the advantages to the economy will be considerable.

Of all the issues the President might have chosen to support in the climate of political resentment and resistance that followed the 1984 election, tax reform was the most risky. The victory that he won was a victory for the whole country, but it also had important rewards for the President. His triumphant speaking tour restored his confidence in his own popularity, and if his success did not silence his harshest critics, it raised the possibility that they were wrong about the validity of Reagan's ideas and the vitality of his Presidency in its second term.

This positive outcome was important to the President in a

peculiarly personal way. Even after all their years in public life, he and the First Lady were extraordinarily dependent on the praise of others and sensitive to the slightest criticism. At the end of the trip to Germany, Chancellor Kohl had arranged a final appearance for the President before a German audience. This occurred on a sunny day in May. The setting was lovely—the castle of Halmbach, located on a hilltop, provided a splendid background for Deaver's cameras. A choir of German youngsters sang, concluding with a rendition of "The Star-Spangled Banner."

Reagan was greatly moved. Those clean-cut young people, singing the American national anthem on German soil in the sunlight of a spring day, seemed to affirm all that he had believed and said about reconciliation between our two peoples. Misty-eyed, the President told me as we walked away together after the ceremony that he had seldom felt so elated, so sure that he had done the right thing by coming to Germany in a spirit of friendship and renewal. As we spoke, signs of amity were everywhere, and the mountain road was lined with smiling, waving Germans—except for one scruffy couple who mooned the President's limousine while holding up a sign that read, Reagan Go Home.

"Did you see that? Did you see those awful people?" Mrs. Reagan asked as soon as she emerged from the car. The one negative note of the day, the one hint that the affection and approval in which her husband had been basking was not universal, was the one that captured her attention.

Although the President was not downcast by this trivial incident, he was subject to puzzlement and self-doubt in the absence of public approval. In extreme cases, such as the storm of blame and suspicion that surrounded the Iran-Contra affair, he might be virtually immobilized. Much of Mike Deaver's work, and a great deal of my own after Deaver left, had to do with organizing a psychic atmosphere in which the President was routinely made aware of the good things that were being said about him by people in their letters and in public-opinion polls, by the press, and by other politicians. A good review always bucked him up and a bad one generally saddened him. Once again the facile explanation for this quirk—his past as an actor—is probably the correct one.

Certainly his wife's preoccupation with image had much to do with her realization that he needed praise. This laudable wifely concern led to all sorts of difficulties. The First Lady's intense identification with her husband and his political fortunes was the random factor in the Reagan Presidency. Mrs. Reagan regarded herself as the President's alter ego not only in the conjugal but also in the political and official dimensions, as if the office that had been bestowed upon her husband by the people somehow fell into the category of worldly goods covered by the marriage vows. I realize that this statement may sound flippant, but it accurately reflects my experience.

Mike Deaver, who had been with the Reagans for twenty years, appeared to take this situation for granted, and his function in the White House had as much to do with the mysterious process of managing this shadowy distaff Presidency as with his visible role as the custodian of the Presidential image. It was Deaver who had devised the highly successful campaign to rehabilitate the First Lady's image after the unfortunate first impression made on the public by her fondness for expensive clothes, glittering dinner parties, and other forms of display. Under Deaver's management, Mrs. Reagan made a charming surprise appearance at the most important press party of the Washington year, the Gridiron Dinner, dancing and singing "Second-Hand Rose." This flattered the press and softened its heart, so that when the First Lady's campaign on drugs was announced, it was treated seriously as a benefit to society, rather than as a means of influencing the media to report more favorably on Mrs. Reagan's personality and her activities, and thereby upgrade the public's opinion of her. Although Mrs. Reagan's considerable full-time staff included a press secretary and handled her affairs with great efficiency, it was Deaver who was entrusted with important and sensitive missions. By long habitude he knew how to relieve Mrs. Reagan—at least momentarily—of the worry, irritation, and impatience that seemed to be her constant companions. Like the hero of *How to Succeed in Business Without Really Trying*, Deaver's motto, as I noted in a spare moment, appeared to be "Don't worry about it, dear—I'll take care of it."

Deaver also appeared to act as a messenger between the First Lady and her husband, and sometimes even as a surrogate. If Mrs. Reagan was unable to persuade the President to act on her advice on an official matter, she would put Deaver in play. He was an insidious (*Webster's*: "watching for an opportunity to ensnare : lying in wait . . . having a gradual, cumulative, and usu. hidden effect") manipulator and, as I found to my cost, he devised ways to communicate Mrs. Reagan's demands to the President by planting stories in the press that the President was bound to read, and by creating a climate of exposé with which the President was forced to deal. Sometimes gossip—the suggestion that someone was not doing his job and had lost the President's confidence—was enough to solve the problem without engaging the President directly, with the result that sometimes people left Reagan's service convinced that he wanted them to go when, in fact, he had little or no idea that they were going.

These adroit guerrilla actions usually had the effect of achieving some goal that the First Lady desired: perhaps the resignation of an aide whom she could not control or whom she perceived as a threat to the President's popularity or effectiveness. Not all of the actions of this combination were negative by any means. The First Lady and her agent often stage-managed actions, such as some of the remedial public relations in connection with Bitburg, that had a constructive effect. Moreover, as I tried to remember—though sometimes with difficulty—Mrs. Reagan's actions were motivated by a genuine belief that she was the best judge of her husband's interests.

In my first months as Chief of Staff, I benefited greatly from Deaver's wisdom in these matters. From the viewpoint of his unique knowledge of the First Lady's character and methods, he understood that Mrs. Reagan would place demands on me and my time that I could not foresee. Until I understood the reasons for it, his approach to his job puzzled me slightly. He was, remember, still in charge of the Presidential schedule. The senior staff met every week or two in the Roosevelt Room to suggest appearances and other Presidential activities. Although in theory Deaver was empowered to make any entry he wished on the President's calendar, he never agreed to any trip or outside event on the spot. "Let me play around with this," he would say, "let me see what can be done." Sometimes days or weeks would pass before a decision was made. This caused inconvenience and a certain amount of grumbling—what was taking so long? Deaver was, of course, waiting for approval from the First Lady's Friend, and it is a measure of his discretion and loyalty that few in the White House ever suspected that Mrs. Reagan was even part of the problem—much less that an astrologer in San Francisco was approving the details of the Presidential schedule.

As the time of Deaver's departure drew nearer, I began to deal more frequently with Mrs. Reagan as a matter of necessity. Some of the requests she made seemed so far out of her proper area of competence that I was disposed to ignore them. A case in point was her determination to force the resignation of Secretary of Labor Ray Donovan, who was under investigation by a New York grand jury on charges of which he was subsequently acquitted. It was clearly wrong in these circumstances to drive Donovan out of his job, and I refused to approach the President on this subject or discuss the possibility of resignation with Donovan himself. When the indictment was handed down, Donovan knew what to do: he resigned like the honorable man that he was. I arranged for a final private meeting between Donovan and the President—who steadfastly maintained a belief in Donovan's innocence—and assured him that he would be welcome back in the Administration after he was exonerated. The summons to return to duty was never issued.

Mrs. Reagan's concern in the Donovan case was understandable. Her husband was all but incapable of firing a subordinate, and I suppose that she had become used to supplying the missing determination. Her purpose was to protect the President from embarrassment and to insulate him from associates who might tarnish his reputation; in this she was above reproach. It is certainly true that the people who attach themselves to a President sometimes place their own interests above those of their chief. In

Donovan's case, however, her concerns were misplaced: he was an innocent man caught up in a frivolous prosecution that was widely perceived to be politically motivated.

When, later on, Mrs. Reagan wanted to compel the resignation of Margaret Heckler, the Secretary of Health and Human Services, I agreed that this was the sensible course of action. Mrs. Heckler was having difficulty in managing this huge department which employed 128,000 people and spent $334 billion in fiscal year 1986, or 34 percent of the entire federal budget. A former congresswoman from Massachusetts, she had developed the legislator's habit of compromise and tended to bargain away the President's program in sessions with her former colleagues on Capitol Hill. She was in the midst of a divorce action, a fact that increased Mrs. Reagan's uneasiness.

"We've got to get rid of her," the First Lady told me. "You know Ronnie will never fire her—he can't even talk to a woman in a stern voice. She'll just twist him around her little finger."

I discussed the matter with the President and he agreed that I should handle it. Mrs. Heckler resisted every suggestion that she leave, and complained to her friends on the Hill that she was being cruelly treated by me. It is true that I was frank about our dissatisfaction with her management of HHS, but at the same time I tried without success to placate her by offering her some other, less demanding, job in the Administration. She would not agree. I began to appreciate the benefits enjoyed by Ronald Reagan as a result of his kindly nature and his high position. Finally the ambassadorship to Ireland was offered, and after certain personal arrangements were agreed upon, Mrs. Heckler, born Margaret Mary O'Shaughnessy in the environs of Boston, agreed to accept this highly coveted post.

If the First Lady was not always wrong in her recommendations, the correctness of her exercising what were clearly the prerogatives of the Presidency was less obvious. Deaver's consistent advice was to humor her. When I inclined to resist, he counseled circumspection. "I wouldn't phrase it quite that way," he would advise on reading the draft of a letter or a memorandum that touched on some subject of interest to Mrs. Reagan. ". . . I wouldn't push that . . . I'd be careful on that one." I was left with the impression, which turned out to be entirely accurate, that walking on eggshells was a useful skill to cultivate if you were going to deal with Mrs. Reagan on a day-to-day basis.

The President's view of the situation was never discussed. The fact that he permitted it to exist, and that he never reversed any of the situations created by his wife's intervention, was regarded as sufficient evidence that he was willing to tolerate the state of affairs.

My own instinct was to separate myself from it as much as possible, and with that in mind I proposed giving Deaver's old title, Deputy Chief of Staff, to Dennis Thomas, who had been at Treasury. The idea made Deaver nervous. "I, uh, don't think this will fly with the First Lady," he said. Nevertheless I called Mrs. Reagan on the telephone and told her of my intention.

"There should be somebody on the President's staff you can call on," I explained. "Dennis will be very good at the job."

A silence gathered on the telephone line. Finally Mrs. Reagan said, "I don't think you need a deputy, Don. I think you can handle this yourself."

"Well," I replied, "I thought that somebody should be attentive to your needs in the way that Mike was."

"When I need something, I'll call you directly," the First Lady said. "I don't see any need for an intermediary."

Fateful words.

· 15 ·

With Gorbachev in Geneva

From the first days of his Presidency, Ronald Reagan clearly understood that he had to undertake some great initiative toward world peace in order to be sure of his place in history. With his instinct for simplification and the big story, he also understood that only one such action could achieve the desired result: a treaty with the Russians that would dramatically reduce the number of strategic nuclear missiles deployed by the two superpowers. In his book about foreign policy in the first eighteen months of the Administration, Al Haig, Reagan's first Secretary of State, describes the President's attitude toward arms talks with the Soviets:

> President Reagan was, and is, committed as a matter of principle to reductions in strategic arms, and any perception to the contrary is mistaken. It was he who changed the name of the arms control negotiations from Strategic Arms Limitation Talks (SALT) to Strategic Arms *Reduction* Talks (START). In symbolic as well as real terms, this was an important departure from the past because it implied that the numbers of weapons would be systematically reduced, instead of *limited*, or reduced in selected categories.*

*Haig, Alexander M., Jr., *Caveat* (New York: Macmillan Publishing Company, 1984), p. 222.

Reagan's every action in foreign policy—the dramatic and very costly buildup in U.S. military power; the steadfast support of America's allies in large matters and small; the overt and covert resistance to Soviet adventurism in the small but murderous "wars of liberation" that Moscow sponsored around the world; the public rhetoric of confrontation and the private signals of conciliation directed toward the Soviets; the dogged Geneva arms talks, and, above all, the Strategic Defense Initiative (SDI) for deploying a futuristic missile shield in outer space—had been carried out with the idea of one day sitting down at the negotiating table with the leader of the U.S.S.R. and banning weapons of mass destruction from the planet. Few diplomats believed that such a dramatic breakthrough was possible. But Reagan, who believed that large questions were easier to resolve than small ones, and that the big answer usually contained all the smaller answers within it, probably never doubted it.

I would not say that Reagan knew exactly what he was doing on the conscious level as he worked toward his goal, but I believe that he always had the big answer in mind. In common with most other U.S. Presidents, he knew little about foreign policy when he came into office, and he learned as he went. His lack of expertise was a handicap in that it gave some of his subordinates the idea that they had a duty to save him from himself. The Iran-Contra affair is the most celebrated case of this in action, but there were others: officials in the State Department, for example, seemed to welcome the fall of Ferdinand Marcos in the Philippines in direct contravention of official U.S. policy and the President's wishes.

Such unhappy results were inevitable for a President who seldom stated his aims in private and who relied almost wholly on others to cope with details. Although he was deeply disturbed by the broader implications of these setbacks—the undermining of Marcos was not so very different in its details or in its predictable consequences from the overthrow of the Shah of Iran under the defeated Carter—Reagan seemed to accept them as being among the things that Presidents must live with. In foreign policy as in other matters, he proceeded on the basis of his instincts and a few fundamental convictions: democracy supported by a market economy resulted in a better life for people everywhere than did Marxism-Leninism or other forms of totalitarianism based on planned economies; the moral, economic, and military strength of the United States and its allies was the basis of peace in the world, and the surreal political and economic policies of the Soviet Union were the source of much of the world's misery and discord; despite the conflict between the two systems, no question was so complicated that it could not be reduced to its basic elements and resolved by personal agreement between two men of goodwill who had the power to act in the names of the United States and the Soviet Union.

At last, following the deaths of one aged Soviet leader after another, the sort of man Reagan had been waiting for, Mikhail S. Gorbachev, appeared on the scene. Even more than most of his predecessors, Gorbachev was virtually unknown in the West when he came to power. Reagan had never met him. He was fifty-four years old—young for his job even by American standards—but a real juvenile in terms of the gerontocracy that had ruled the Soviet Union in recent years. It soon became evident that the new Soviet leader had some of the qualities associated with youth. He was energetic, headstrong, and unorthodox—and he had compelling reasons for reducing the ruinously expensive Soviet nuclear arsenal. Foremost among these was his need to consolidate his power. He was looking for a historic achievement on which to found his career at the very moment at which the President of the United States was seeking one on which to end his.

Reagan understood that his opportunity had come, and I encouraged him to seize it. Ordinarily I did not presume to advise the President on the details of foreign policy. Such matters were handled by the Secretary of State and the National Security Advisor. But I do know something about economics and finance, including international monetary affairs; believing that these were the keys to an agreement on nuclear arms, I spoke my mind to the President.

Knowing where I come from, the reader will not be surprised

to learn that I believe that money makes the world go around. In *War and Peace*, Leo Tolstoy writes that the historians of the era just before his own saw history as a series of events expressing the will of God, while scholars of his own time interpreted it as the product of the virtues and faults of historical personages. No doubt both these forces, and many others, are present in history, but history can also be understood as a search for wealth. Alexander the Great may have been seized by an irresistible impulse to lead armies into battle, but the Persian empire that he conquered was the symbol of wealth in his era. The Mongol hordes that swept through old Russia and beyond rode west to take booty and captives. Cortez and Pizarro may have carried the Cross into Mexico and Peru, but Spanish galleons transported gold and silver back to Spain. Even the westward expansion of the United States had its economic motives. And unless I have misread Marx (*Capital*) and misunderstood Lenin ("Political institutions are a superstructure resting on an economic foundation"), the primary goal of the 1917 Revolution was to seize and redistribute the wealth of the Russian empire.

Gorbachev's motives in seeking a reduction in nuclear arms seemed to me to be almost entirely economic. When the possibility of a summit on arms reduction arose, I looked at the Soviet budget. Fifty kopeks in every ruble went to the military. The Russians were spending a staggering 17 percent of their gross national product on defense. Even with the huge increases in defense spending put into place by the Reagan Administration, the United States was only spending between 6½ and 7 percent of the GNP on its military establishment. At least 50 percent of the Soviet budget in one form or another goes to the military defense complex.

The Soviets could not spend more on arms without running the risk of bankrupting the state—or delaying further the delivery of civilian goods and services that had been promised to the Soviet people over the seventy years of unremitting sacrifice since the 1917 Revolution. However, to stay in the arms race, the Russians had to spend a lot more money because President Reagan had committed the United States, with all its wealth and all its technical capacity, to developing SDI, a defensive system that might make the entire Soviet missile force useless. To stay equal, the Soviets had either to build a missile shield of their own or develop a new generation of offensive weapons capable of penetrating it.

This meant that Reagan had been dealt the winning hand: either option facing the Soviets would be enormously expensive. Whether SDI would work, whether it might bankrupt the United States (an unlikely prospect), or whether it was more likely to increase than decrease the fear of nuclear war were irrelevant questions. The logic of deterrence, which is based on each side matching the technological advances and destructive power of the other, dictated that the Soviets must respond to SDI with a new strategic system of their own. We knew that they were already at work on such a system, but a worldwide propaganda onslaught against SDI, and many statements made by the Soviets during diplomatic contacts, left no doubt that the new Soviet leader, like those who had gone before him, was worried about SDI to the point of fixation.

That was why Gorbachev wanted to negotiate—and that is why, in my opinion, President Reagan was holding the trump card. Soviet propaganda often takes the line that Moscow is frightened by American weapons and convinced of America's warlike intentions, and this may very well be so. Certainly the Russians' historical experience with the French and the Germans has made them realize that nations sometimes undergo character change, and nobody can know what some future President of the United States might do with SDI. But in the world as it now exists, the Kremlin is primarily worried about American wealth. After visiting the Soviet Union for the first time, the editor of a leading American magazine said privately that he had been surprised to find that it was "essentially a Third World country with a big army." That statement is an oversimplification, but it contains a kernel of truth. There are all sorts of reasons, ranging from a genuine fear of the West, to the employment situation at home, to unrest in the satellites, why the Russians must keep their enormous military forces at something close to their present level.

As a matter of practical politics, Gorbachev could not stay in power without at least the acquiescence of the Red Army, and he knew that reducing expenditures for conventional weapons was not the way to keep the Red Army happy. The bottom line was that in the Soviet Union, as in every other nation state in history, money talked.

There was another factor. Thinking as a manager, it seemed to me possible that Gorbachev had strong psychological reasons to succeed in his own right and to show the world that communism can succeed as an economic and political system capable of delivering the goods to its people. He is the first man born and raised under communism to become head of the Soviet party and state. All other leaders since the Revolution were born under the Czars. Gorbachev, a child of the system, could see the failures of the system as only an intelligent and ambitious offspring can. He abhorred the mistakes of his elders and did not wish to repeat them. But if he was forced to allocate even more resources from the non-military to the military sector in order to counter a new American threat, the Soviet masses would be worse off under Gorbachev than under previous leaders. That was why he was so frightened of SDI. Unless he found a way to make the United States give it up, nothing would change in the Soviet Union, and the best he could hope for in his relations with the U.S. was another strategic stalemate costing billions if not trillions of rubles.

On the basis of this analysis of the problem, I urged the President to stay strong in dealing with Gorbachev. I told him that if Gorbachev was driven by his economic problems to want a treaty, then no matter what Reagan did, no matter how the first summit ended, Gorbachev would come back to the table until he had an agreement. He might threaten to break off the talks forever, he might speak of last chances, he might rant and rave at the President in private and hurl anathema at the United States in public for theatrical purposes, but he would come back. Faced with the choice between bankruptcy and a fall from power that would deliver the U.S.S.R. back into the hands of the faction that had all but ruined her economically, he would have no choice. The key was SDI. To match it, Gorbachev would have to mortgage the whole future of communism.

I mentioned these ideas to the President one day as we were riding together in the backseat of his car, remarking that Soviet-ologists generally are impressed, to the point of obsession, by the Soviets' military strength, by their intelligence capabilities, and by their political ruthlessness. But few such experts know very much about economics or pay much attention to the relationship between the U.S. economy and the Soviet economy in terms of the balance of power.

Reagan gave me a quizzical look. It's funny that you should bring up their economy, he said. I've been thinking along the same lines. Tell me more.

I did so. After that the President and I talked about the economic aspects of summitry frequently. The amount of time that I spent discussing the negotiations themselves with the President was small compared to that which was devoted to the logistics of the summit. Moving the President and his official household to a foreign country, even for a brief time, is an immensely complicated business; no amount of practice makes perfect because every episode has its own objectives and its own set of problems. Meeting Gorbachev in Geneva was quite different from visiting Kohl at Bitburg or attending an Economic Summit at Versailles. Nevertheless, every contingency had to be anticipated and provided for.

The Geneva summit was, among other things, the first big field test of the new techniques and policies that I had instituted in the White House. Deaver had departed by now to pursue his career as a lobbyist, and the advance work was supervised by Bill Henkel, who had taken over this aspect of Deaver's old empire together with the day-to-day management of the Presidential schedule. Henkel was an experienced hand, having been an advance man in the Nixon, Ford, and Reagan campaigns and Presidencies. He had also worked with Deaver on the Bitburg advance mission and had learned much from the experience.

As might be expected, the First Lady took a close interest in the arrangements. Even while the President was recovering from his cancer surgery at Bethesda Naval Hospital, Mrs. Reagan had been concerned about the house that she and her husband would occupy during the summit. Henkel had located a luxurious house, the Château de Belle Rive, a residence of Prince Sadruddin Aga Khan. The First Lady was not happy with this choice when she learned of it, and called me at home at 11:15 P.M. on a Sunday to tell me that friends had advised her to see about borrowing the lakeside villa occupied by Prince Karim Aga Khan IV, the head of the Isma'ili sect of Shiite Muslims, and his family. As Mrs. Reagan put it, "They say that Kitty's house is much nicer than the other one, and we ought to look into it." As it turned out, the First Lady's friends were correct—the Maison de Saussure, as the second house was called, was more conveniently located than the first and had other desirable features.

Henkel made the change—and that resulted in an unusual problem for the advance team. The Aga Khan's son, Hussein, left a note for the President asking him to feed his goldfish. Reagan did so conscientiously, but on the second morning—the day he was scheduled to meet Gorbachev for the first time—he found one of the fish dead. He wore a glum expression when I came for him that morning. I asked him why.

I've got a problem, the President said, showing me the small dead creature. The fish died.

Henkel was summoned. "We've got to find another goldfish for that boy," I told him. "Your job is on the line, Henkel!"

As the President and I set off for the meeting with Gorbachev, Bill sent one of his men, a big resourceful Irishman named Andrew Littlefair, to find two replacements for the deceased goldfish. Littlefair succeeded, and a somewhat less guilt-stricken President left a note for the little prince, explaining what had happened and expressing the hope that the new goldfish would be an acceptable substitute. All the other fish survived the Presidential feeding.

As usual, Mrs. Reagan insisted on being consulted on the timing of every Presidential appearance and action so that she could consult her Friend in San Francisco about the astrological factor. The large number of details involved must have placed a heavy burden on the poor woman, who was called upon not only to choose auspicious moments for meetings between the two most powerful men on our planet, but also to draw up horoscopes that presumably provided clues to the character and probable behavior of Gorbachev.

In Geneva, Reagan and Gorbachev were supported by large, hardworking staffs of diplomatists. Secretary of State George Shultz and Soviet Foreign Minister Eduard Shevardnadze were the ranking aides in terms of diplomatic protocol. Both were attended by high-ranking members of their diplomatic services, including our ambassador to Moscow, Arthur A. Hartman, and the Soviet ambassador to Washington, Anatoliy F. Dobrynin. McFarlane was there with some of his aides, and so were Max Kampelman and Paul Nitze, members of the U.S. negotiating team at the Geneva arms talks, Assistant Secretary of State Rozanne L. Ridgway, and several members of the White House staff. The Soviets arrived with an equally large and eclectic group, including a KGB major general who was Bill Henkel's opposite number as chief of the advance team.

This made for a crowded room when the delegations got together, and provided the three thousand or so newspeople who had flocked to Geneva with busy work. The press compiled lists that attempted to establish the relative importance of the players and match up the Russians with the Americans in terms of who was who and who did what. At the conference table, Shultz was seated on the President's right with McFarlane in the next chair. I was on the President's left. Evidently these arrangements had caused discontent, but I did not know about this until I appeared on the "Today Show" from Geneva on November 19, and a question from Bryant Gumble told me that McFarlane's relations with NBC remained excellent:

GUMBLE: Given his role in the preparation of this summit, Mr. Regan, it seems odd to many of us that Bud McFarlane won't be seated right next to the President. As Chief of Staff, your proximity to the President is, of course, your right, but can you explain to us the thinking behind that?

REGAN: I don't know that we did any particular thinking about that. Bud'll be next to George; they can confer during the ongoing discussions. . . . If the President needs some advice on anything relating to the domestic economy—things of that nature—I'll be on his left side.

The fact is, being seated on the President's left was awkward for me because I am nearly deaf in my right ear and would have preferred to have my good ear pointed in his direction; protocol decided otherwise. Reagan often urged me to get one of the tiny but powerful hearing aids he wears, sometimes in both ears, but I never could get used to the things.

In the remainder of the interview, Gumble asked a number of good questions about more substantive matters. So did most other reporters with whom I spoke before the meetings began. During the talks, a news blackout eliminated contact with the press except for photo opportunities. This measure was exceedingly frustrating to reporters, but the press in general did an excellent job of covering the summit, nevertheless. In this they had the enthusiastic collaboration of professional media advance teams from both governments. One of the Soviet spokesmen, Georgiy Arbatov, was fluent in English and was justly admired by Western journalists for his sophisticated manner and his formidable skills as a defender of Soviet policy. I don't know how well Arbatov would have done working for an American President, but it did not seem to me at the time that he or the other Soviet sources were taxed to the utmost by questions from American and other Western correspondents on such matters as Afghanistan, Central America, Soviet Jewry, and human rights.

The fact that the Soviets had decided to play by Washington rules, more or less, in their relations with the press at the summit was of course a story in itself. There were sidebars. Someone at the Pentagon leaked a letter from Cap Weinberger to the President urging him to make no arms deals with the Soviets at Geneva. What did the leak mean? Was this some diabolical right-wing plot to sabotage the summit, or just run-of-the-mill American clumsiness? Was this the end of Weinberger? The President defused the one-day sensation when a reporter asked him during a photo opportunity if he was going to fire Weinberger for this indiscretion.

"Do you want a two-word answer or one?" the President asked.

"Two," said the reporter.

"Hell, no," said the President.

In the preliminary stages of the summit the biggest story by far was the Reagan-Gorbachev matchup. The imagination of many U.S. media pundits had been captured by the energy and flair of Gorbachev, and the papers and airways buzzed with speculation that Reagan, the Great Communicator, might be beaten at his own game by this dynamic new Soviet leader. Would the old movie actor lose the television-and-ink battle for the hearts and minds of mankind to this appealing new leading man on the world stage? Would Reagan be overpowered by Gorbachev's toughness and diplomatic savvy and give away the store? The media regarded Gorbachev as the odds-on favorite to dethrone the old champ. I wasn't so sure.

In all fairness, it ought to be said that the news blackout agreed to between us and the Russians left the press with little to do except speculate. Larry Speakes, in announcing that no details of the four scheduled meetings would be provided to the press, said, "The U.S. will comply completely [with the blackout]. Those who talk don't know what's going on, and those who do won't talk. If anyone does brief the press it will not meet with the approval of the President." The blackout had been proposed by the American side, and while it was due, as Speakes pointed out, to the "seriousness of the subjects and the far-reaching implications of the talks," it was also an interesting test of the U.S. delegation's ability to give up leaks for a few days. I hoped that they would feel so much the better for it that they'd keep it up when we got home.

Actually, there was little to leak. The main story was out in the open: Reagan and Gorbachev had decided to meet after six years without a U.S.-Soviet summit; consequently the United States had only limited objectives at Geneva. For all his optimism, the President never expected that he would be able to conclude a satisfactory arms agreement at a first meeting. Little in the on-going negotiations concerning limitations on American and So-viet nuclear missiles targeted on Europe suggested that such a breakthrough was at hand. Rather, the President had three lim-ited objectives: 1. to establish a personal relationship with Gor-bachev; 2. to obtain a commitment from the Soviet leader that their talks on arms reductions would continue; and 3. to agree on the place and approximate time of the next summit. The agenda contained a number of other items, but the points I have listed were the main objectives. As it turned out, they were Gor-bachev's objectives, too. A great deal of ice needed to be broken before any deadlocks could be broken, but Reagan was buoyantly confident that he could at least achieve a breakthrough in his personal relationship with Gorbachev. In the President's constel-lation of factors, that man-to-man contact was far and away the most important.

Because the Soviets had acted as hosts at the previous U.S.-Soviet summit (Carter and Brezhnev in Vienna in 1979), proto-col dictated that the Americans receive them for the opening ses-sion (Tuesday, November 19) and the third session (Wednesday, November 20) of the Geneva summit. The Soviets would host the talks on the second day at their mission on the Avenue de la Paix, near the old League of Nations building. The talks between Reagan and Gorbachev took place at the Villa Fleur d'Eau, an-other large mansion overlooking the lake that we had rented for this purpose.

The day of the first encounter was cloudy and cold. The me-dia were gathered outside the Villa Fleur d'Eau, awaiting the ar-rival of Gorbachev. He was due to step out of his car at precisely 10 A.M. Inside the villa, a cavernous gray-stone house that com-manded broad views of Lake Leman, this was the scene: The President of the United States was trying to make up his mind whether to wear an overcoat when he stepped outside to greet the Soviet leader. His personal assistant, Jim Kuhn, was holding the overcoat. The President was surrounded by his advisers—Shultz, McFarlane, Regan, Henkel. They were divided in their counsel. On the one hand, it was damn cold outside, with a sharp wind blowing down the lake between the cloud-shrouded mountains. On the other hand, the President hated overcoats; as a Californian, he believed that overcoats did not apply to him. Nobody except Kuhn, who is fearless where the President's health and well-being are concerned, wished to appear to be pro-overcoat. The President looked out the window at the scudding clouds, put on the overcoat, then took it off. Should he put it back on?

Before more advice could be offered, a lookout announced, "He's here!"

The seventy-four-year-old President, coatless and hatless, dashed outside, trotted down the stairs of the villa to the driveway, strode to his guest's limousine just as its door opened, and held out his hand in welcome. Gorbachev, twenty years younger than Reagan, emerged from the car. He was wearing a scarf, an overcoat, and a gray fedora hat. Reagan, heedless of the chill wind, grinned and pumped the Russian's hand.

"Welcome, Mr. General Secretary!"

Cameras whirred, reporters scribbled, commentators murmured. In a Reaganesque gesture of spontaneous and unrehearsed graciousness, the old Republican grasped the young Communist by the elbow and *helped him up the steps.*

A moment before, I had been mildly worried that the President might catch pneumonia, but now it was quite clear that everything was going to be all right.

Inside the villa more cameras waited, and as soon as Gorbachev was inside the door, but before he entered their range, he peeled off his coat. He wore no trace of a smile—it was clear that he regretted having worn his overcoat that morning—but his expression changed as he and Reagan walked into the glare of the Klieg lights. Smiling broadly, the two leaders shook hands—an extra-strong handshake, each grasping the other by the elbow and nodding in his pleasure at meeting. Waves of cameramen—I'm told that close to one hundred were present and filming—recorded this scene as Reagan and Gorbachev, like stars on a movie set good-naturedly going through many takes, play-acted their historic first meeting over and over again.

This encounter—strobelights flashing, television lights burning, reporters shouting questions ("Are you going to tell him what he should do about Afghanistan, Mr. President?")—lasted for about twenty minutes. Neither leader lost his smile or his composure for an instant; both knew that a single glower on either of their faces would be reproduced on millions of front pages and television screens all over the world. Gorbachev may have had a small advantage in that Soviet reporters did not shout questions at him in Russian, but of course he had not been through this bedlam as often as Reagan, who could probably go to sleep with Sam Donaldson of ABC bellowing in one ear and Bill Plante of CBS shrieking in the other, if he chose to do so.

After the press photographers came the official photographers from both governments. They took formal portraits of the two leaders side by side in wingback chairs, smiling again. By the time the last picture had been shot, three-quarters of an hour had elapsed. The entire morning session was scheduled to last two hours. Now, in an adjoining room, the staff members who would be present at the plenary session had assembled; Soviets were on one side of the room, Americans on the other. Nods, brief smiles, tentative waves were exchanged before formal introductions were made—the Soviets were presented to Reagan, the Americans to Gorbachev. After being introduced, the officials from the two sides had little choice but to mingle. The atmosphere was something like a 1930s-style college mixer, with everyone dressed in his or her best and eager to make a good impression without getting hooked up with somebody who might turn out to be the wrong sort. The diplomatic types maneuvered their chiefs through the milling company so that Shevardnadze and Shultz stood together not far from the President and the General Secretary. I found myself next to Dobrynin. McFarlane, who had no exact counterpart on the opposite side, stood with Nitze and Max Kampelman. The three of them chatted with some of the Soviet negotiators to the Geneva talks.

Finally we sat down at the table. This piece of furniture had been transported to Geneva by Air Force freighter from the U.S. mission to the United Nations in New York because the advance team had been unable to find a suitable table locally. At this point cameramen from the press pool and the official White House and Kremlin photographers entered with their lights and made still more pictures of this historic *tableau vivant*. At last, at 10:45, we got down to business.

Gorbachev and Reagan sat in the middle of the table on opposite sides, flanked by their aides. We had arranged the seating so that Gorbachev faced the windows that looked out over the lake. As Reagan's guest he was entitled to the best view, but he also had the sun in his eyes if the sun happened to be shining (an unlikely event in Geneva in late November) and he had to contend with whatever distractions the lake offered in the way of sudden storms or the white paddle-wheel boats that carry commuters and tourists to the towns along the shore. There were flowers on the table and a cheery fire burned in a fireplace to Reagan's left. For security reasons the fire was tended by a member of the advance team who carried in the logs himself and wielded the poker.

Little of interest occurred at this first session. Gorbachev delivered his opening remarks and Reagan replied. This took more than twice as long as such an exchange would take between two men who spoke the same language because of the time consumed by the interpreters. Each leader spoke for about fifteen minutes, and so did each leader's personal interpreter. Although Gorbachev made some highly debatable points (and so, from the Russians' point of view, did Reagan), neither man attempted to rebut the other at this stage. The President did not depart from his prepared remarks, and as far as I could tell, neither did Gorbachev. A certain amount of back-and-forth commentary followed the opening statements, with Shultz and Shevardnadze or others sometimes being asked to comment by the two principals. The language was restrained, the atmosphere polite; neither side wanted anything to go wrong before the summit had fairly begun.

At noon we broke for luncheon and the President and his

party motored back to the Maison de Saussure. The adjoining house, called the Villa Palmetta, had been rented as a place for the staff to live and carry on its business. Here, in a makeshift conference room, we debriefed the President after every session—that is, talked over what had been said, critiqued his replies to Gorbachev, and made suggestions for points to be raised at sessions to follow. This room had been inspected for listening devices, but for truly sensitive conversations there was "the Bubble," as the theoretically bug-proof, transparent security chamber at the U.S. Mission was called. Henkel and Speakes were always present at the Villa Palmetta so that they would be aware of every detail. Other members of the delegation who had some special expertise—Shultz's aides or Kenneth Adelman of the Arms Control and Disarmament Agency, for example—would come in as needed to offer facts or advice. Others waited in the anterooms for the President's call.

One member of the press, dressed in a russet down vest, maroon trousers, and what appeared to be a crimson smock, wandered among the waiting staff. His presence in restricted areas had aroused the anxiety of the Soviets. Who, they asked, was this arresting figure dressed in shades of red? They were told not to worry: it was young Ron Reagan, the President's son, who was covering the summit for *Playboy* magazine. At one point, according to the *Washington Times*, Ron suggested to his father that he and Gorbachev go outside and toss a football around. That certainly would have created a unique photo opportunity.

That afternoon at two-thirty Gorbachev arrived at the Villa Fleur d'Eau conspicuously *sans* overcoat and fedora. The negotiations went slowly. Missiles and warheads were counted; our numbers and the Soviet numbers did not agree. The experts haggled while Reagan and Gorbachev sat by in silence.

We had hoped for a moment like this. In Washington after his return from an advance trip to Geneva, Bill Henkel had described the summerhouse near the swimming pool on the grounds of the Villa Fleur d'Eau. It had a fireplace and a cozy atmosphere, and this had given Bill an idea. "There are some great camera angles walking down from the big house," Bill said. "We can have a fire going in the fireplace and the two of them can sit beside the fire and talk, tête à tête."

On its face this was a promising idea, though it had the potential of backfiring if the event looked too contrived. I approved it in principle and told the President about Bill's suggestion and recommended that he take the first opportunity that came up to invite Gorbachev to walk down to the summerhouse. It was about two hundred yards from the main house. I suggested that the President and the First Lady inspect the summerhouse together. They were reluctant to do so, but Henkel persisted, calling on her in her quarters. Fatigued by her journey, Mrs. Reagan was reluctant to give up her nap to inspect the site, but finally agreed to go with Henkel, the President, and me to look it over. The inspection was thorough, and so was the discussion of the site's advantages and disadvantages. Finally Mrs. Reagan said that she liked what she saw.

Yep, the President said, nodding approvingly. This would be a nice place to come if we just wanted to have a one-on-one chat.

We discussed calling the Geneva meeting "the Fireside Summit," a name that appealed to Reagan because it evoked FDR's fireside chats, but it never caught on with the media or the public. Among the many similarities between the two Presidents—their showmanship, their smashing of idols, their great popularity in the land and their lack of it among the politico-journalistic establishment in Washington—the fact that both were great communicators is among the most striking. Roosevelt was to radio what Reagan is to television—the first President to master the medium and be defined by it. Men of my age and Reagan's can still hear Roosevelt's voice merely by closing their eyes, and I suspect that FDR would probably have liked Henkel's idea as much as Reagan did.

In any case, around 3:45 P.M., about an hour into the afternoon meeting, while aides haggled over the particulars of each nation's inventory of warheads and launchers, the moment for the walk seemed to have arrived. The President gave me an inquiring look: Was this the moment? I gave a slight nod. Reagan leaned across the table and spoke directly to Gorbachev.

Well, we seem to have reached a little stalemate here, Reagan said. Why don't we let our experts figure it out? You and I, let's go for a walk, just the two of us . . . get some fresh air, see what this thing is about.

Gorbachev seemed to be surprised by the suggestion. Because of the security situation, Henkel had told his counterpart that the President might invite the General Secretary to visit the summer-house, and Gorbachev's bodyguards had checked out the site. Possibly they had not reported this exchange to Gorbachev. In any case, he hesitated for a moment. His aides scurried about, murmuring in Russian. The gist of their comments seemed to be, "What the hell is *this* all about?"

After a pause, Gorbachev agreed to Reagan's suggestion. Aides fetched his overcoat. He did not put it on until he was sure that Reagan was going to wear *his* overcoat. Reagan shrugged into the despised garment—possibly because his instincts told him that to do so would help repair the overcoat gap he had inadvertently created that morning. The two men, led by Henkel and the KGB major general, surrounded by security men but accompanied within earshot only by their personal interpreters, strolled down to the summerhouse together. I trailed along behind, just to make sure that they got there all right. Inside, the two leaders shed their coats and sat down facing each other in armchairs that had been set out beside the hearth. The official photographers were present, and as Henkel had foreseen, it made a beautiful picture for the front pages of the world's newspapers.

The two men chatted together for fifty-four minutes. No one except Gorbachev and Reagan and their interpreters knew then exactly what was said (the interpreters' notes were of course made part of the official record), but it was obvious when they emerged into the early Swiss twilight that they had gotten along well. It was time for Gorbachev to go, and so Reagan walked him toward his car.

The two men made small talk about their respective coun-tries. Gorbachev told Reagan that he must visit Moscow someday.

Reagan seized the opening. I'd love to do that, the President said cordially. But only if you come to America first. And I'd like to see you there next year.

Gorbachev said "Yes—but then you must come to Moscow the following year."

Reagan agreed.

The President glowed with pride and a sense of accomplishment after this masterstroke of personal diplomacy. He felt that he had stolen a march on his Secretary of State and Chief of Staff and all the other advisers who hovered in the background, and he ribbed us about it for some time afterward. I think that the episode reinforced his basic and abiding belief that two men of goodwill could move the world together if they could only speak as one human being to another.

Mikhail S. Gorbachev was everything that I expected him to be and more. He was quick, decisive, direct, intelligent and studious, and aggressively patriotic. His domination of the Soviets surrounding him was absolute, and it was my impression that this had as much to do with the force of his personality as with the power of his office. When he spoke, the other Russians jumped. There is a tendency in the West to hope that each successive Soviet leader will be the man of reason and goodwill that Marxism promised the world, and Gorbachev's early successes on the Western stage owed much to this fact. Whatever Gorbachev's future actions may tell the world about him, he began his career as General Secretary with the benefit of every doubt.

This atmosphere of positive expectations extended to the highest levels of the Reagan Administration. Nobody hoped more fervently than the President that the man he was going to meet in Geneva would not turn out to be another Stalin or another Khrushchev. And in fact Gorbachev did seem to be a new type. His wife, Raisa, was also quite different in style and appearance from the spouses of earlier Soviet leaders. The way in which they had exploited the world press suggested a sophistication and a casual self-confidence unique in the seventy years or so since Lenin.

The Gorbachevs gave every impression of being fortunate, well-educated, and well-connected members of an elite—and of course that is precisely what they were in terms of their social, educational, and party background. Both were marked early for success, spent their whole lives surrounded by other men and women who had likewise been chosen, and in the end rose by merit and maneuver to the ultimate position in Soviet society. Although they have no exact American equivalent—there is nothing democratic about them and they lack the self-effacing politeness that an egalitarian society instills in its achievers—the Gorbachevs are the kind of people who would be called "upscale" in a profile in the "Style" section of the *Washington Post*. They would be admired for their qualities in any society in the world, and if they had been born in America, would probably have risen to the top as surely as they did in the U.S.S.R.

When the Gorbachevs came to dinner as the President's guests on the first night of the summit, it was clear that the General Secretary had been meticulously briefed on the interests and manners of the Reagans, and that he wanted to be agreeable. He was quietly dressed and composed in manner, and treated all the Americans in the small party—Shultz, McFarlane, Hartman, and myself—with polite interest. He had charm, and he could turn it on and off like an electric light. Clearly he knew that the President liked stories, because he told him a couple of pretty good ones, and insofar as it is possible to judge a joke told through an interpreter, he seemed to know how to tell a story. My impression was that this was an acquired rather than a natural skill. He laughed appreciatively at Reagan's sallies when his interpreter put them into Russian; and when something really tickled him, as some of the President's stories did, he guffawed in outright pleasure. The President was in excellent form.

Nearly everything the two men said early in the evening had something to do with Soviet-American relations, even if only by indirection. The President, speaking in anecdotes as is his way, referred to the accomplishments of earlier Presidents—Roosevelt as a wartime leader when the United States and the U.S.S.R. were allies, Nixon in China, Kennedy's tax cuts which had inspired Reagan's own tax cuts. Reagan sprinkled his conversation with memorable phrases of past Presidents and other famous Americans. Gorbachev was almost wholly impersonal in his own statements. He never referred to any of his predecessors by so much as mentioning their names. He did not quote them—not even Lenin or Marx. This surprised me as I had never before encountered a communist who did not quote these two. He would sometimes nod at one of the Soviets who accompanied him and say, "Shevardnadze may have told Shultz something about that," or "Dobrynin would understand; he knows your country well." But his interest ran to issues rather than personalities, and he seemed to have a technical rather than a narrative style.

This is not to say that he did not have warm moments or a sharp human curiosity. The General Secretary was a man of many moods and he let them show; he was not at all taciturn or poker-faced. When he got excited, you knew he was excited; when he was calm and reposed, that, too, was obvious. When he was interested, his eyes shone and he asked questions in a quick, eager voice.

Both Gorbachev and his wife were spellbound by Reagan's stories about his Hollywood days and his career in the movies. Prompted by the Gorbachevs' questions, the President described the studio system—how movies were produced, how roles were awarded to the actors, how different directors worked, and how various stars behaved in real life. The Gorbachevs devoured every detail. Like any other movie buffs, they were very pleased to be in the company of somebody who had known Jimmy Stewart, John Wayne, and Humphrey Bogart and nearly every other famous movie star personally, and was able to describe what they were really like. Reagan's role in driving communists out of the Screen Actors Guild when he was president of the union did not come up in this conversation.

At one point Gorbachev referred to his grandchildren, saying that he regretted that he did not see more of them, and I told a story about my own grandchildren, who call me "D.T." They had complained that they only saw me on television since I had gone to work in the White House, so I told them that henceforth I would always try to send them a secret signal—a tug on my left earlobe—when I was on camera to show that I was thinking of them. Nobody but the kids and I knew about it, and I never got caught by the eagle-eyed press. Gorbachev laughed. "That's a very good idea—maybe I will have a secret signal, too." When I saw him again at Reykjavík in 1986, his first words to me were,

"Ah, Regan—still touching your nose at your grandchildren on TV?" He had remembered the story even if he had forgotten the exact nature of the secret signal.

It was Raisa Gorbachev for whom Western observers, and especially Nancy Reagan, were unprepared. As the world knows, she is a stylish, handsome woman with an intense and intelligent manner. It was she, far more than her husband, who kept the conversational ball rolling. Even when Mrs. Reagan was the hostess, Mrs. Gorbachev was the chief orchestrator of the dinner party—changing the subject when her husband had been on it long enough, introducing new subjects, entering in on conversations down the table to express an opinion. She did not confine herself, as most other wives of heads of state and government did in such meetings, to cross-chat with Mrs. Reagan on palace housewifery and other harmless subjects. Mrs. Gorbachev was a highly educated woman—a professor of Marxist-Leninist theory. At this dinner party and the later one at the Soviet Mission, she did not hesitate to make use of the opportunities offered to her to educate the President of the United States on the intellectual and philosophical basis of the Soviet policy. It was evident that she was mistress of her subject, an intellectual with a truly impressive grasp of a specialty that she regarded as the key to understanding Soviet society and the world beyond. Reagan listened to Mrs. Gorbachev's extremely detailed and fervently argued opinions with gallant courtesy. Gorbachev, like any husband in his circumstances, kept his peace. Mrs. Reagan, however, chafed under the monologue. After the door had closed behind the Gorbachevs, she said, "Who does that dame think she is?"

Subsequent tension between the two women probably traces from that first prickly encounter—and also from the extraordinary amount of coverage that Mrs. Gorbachev collected in her dashes about Geneva and its environs through the all-but-idle army of the world press. Front-page pictures of the Soviet leader's wife overwhelmed the very effective photographs and television footage taken of the President and the First Lady as they walked, hand in hand as usual, through the garden of the Maison Saussure in a photo opportunity conceived by Mrs. Reagan herself. The Gorbachevs made masterful use of every opportunity for personal coverage. They behaved very much like an American Presidential candidate and his wife out on the campaign trail together. Mrs. Reagan may have been surprised that Russians could be so good at the celebrity business.

To all appearances, the personal relationship that Reagan had hoped to establish with Gorbachev was quick in the making. On the second day of the talks, held at the Soviet Mission, there was a delay caused by another disagreement among the experts over the basic data. While the staffs went their separate ways in search of the information they needed, Reagan and Gorbachev went off by themselves into an alcove with their interpreters and chatted. After nearly an hour and a half the staffs returned. I approached the two leaders and found them seated close together in matching overstuffed chairs of the kind that are found in every communist country and used to be seen in the parlors of my aunts' houses in and around Boston—high-backed, deep, and formal, with lace doilies and antimacassars pinned to the plush upholstery.

Gorbachev and Reagan were drinking Russian tea. They were deep in conversation, relaxed and smiling, like a couple of fellows who had run into each other at the club and discovered that they had a lot in common. They seemed to be comparing notes on life as a head of state—a subject on which they were finding many experiences that matched.

"Mr. President," I said, "I think we're about ready to start. The others are coming back."

Who cares? the President replied. Mikhail and I are having a good time sitting here talking.

"Sorry, Boss," I said. "It's time to go back to work."

Gorbachev looked shocked by my familiarity, then burst into laughter. Possibly this bit of American impertinence from a grayhead like me gave point to some of the stories Reagan had been telling him about what he had to put up with in Washington.

At the negotiating table, however, bonhomie did not apply. It may have been "Ron" and "Mikhail" during the recess, but in the session they were adversaries. Nearly everything was in the air if it was not actually on the table—SDI, Afghanistan, Angola, Central America, and refuseniks, which Reagan raised privately with Gorbachev before the formal meetings began. The atmosphere was always intense, sometimes vehement. Neither man concealed from the other his suspicions, his opinions, his objectives. Their dialogue went beyond the "full and frank exchange" of diplomatic jargon. The issues that are negotiated by heads of government are essentially unresolvable or they would never have reached the highest level. Usually such issues are basic, and therefore so is the language of the negotiators; there is no room for misunderstanding. Reagan and Gorbachev sometimes sounded like taxi drivers after a fender-bender, and in this they were not different from other foreign leaders who had met with Reagan in my presence. Such men are where they are because they are in touch in more than the ordinary way with humanity and its concerns. If they behave like ordinary human beings, it is because they are usually supremely human in their instincts, their perceptions, and their emotions.

Reagan, as I have said, enjoys this brand of give-and-take and is very good at it. He speaks from principle, argues from common sense, and cannot be budged on matters that engage his fundamental beliefs or the basic interests of the United States. Details are of no more concern to him in a setting of this kind than in any other; the purpose of all the staff activity was to make certain that the details were correct and were correctly understood. Gorbachev's technique, as might be expected, was quite different. He, too, took obvious pleasure in argument for its own sake and, no less than Reagan, was stimulated by the highly knowledgeable audience of his countrymen who were present. But he seemed to regard the talks more as a chess game, a contest for small points that would decide a large issue when the final move was made, than as an attempt to achieve a meeting of the minds.

Gorbachev was the more flamboyant of the two. He struck the table with the edge of his hand, pointed a finger at the President, raised his voice, demanded answers. Reagan controlled his voice, his expressions, his gestures; it was a calm and understated performance. The obvious comparison, and a valid one, was that between a stage actor and a movie actor.

The President would make the point that Soviet behavior in Afghanistan, in Angola, in Central America did not encourage the United States to believe that the U.S.S.R. was a peace-loving nation. Who is threatening whom? Gorbachev would reply, and he would go on to describe the potential of SDI for use as an offensive weapon. If this weapon system could shoot down missiles in space, why could it not be used to destroy a city on the ground? How could the Russians know what our intentions were? The two leaders spent a total of about five hours in one-on-one talks in addition to their exchanges in the formal negotiating sessions. Neither won any discernible advantage over the other.

The outcome of the Geneva summit was even more favorable than I had imagined it would be. Agreement was reached on a number of ancillary matters. The Soviets agreed to resolve ten of twenty-five human-rights cases involving separated spouses in marriages between Soviet and American citizens; airline landing rights were restored by each country for the civilian carriers of the other; and the two sides agreed to open consulates in New York and Kiev and came to terms on cultural exchanges. Also, both principals instructed their negotiating teams to proceed at a faster pace on the question of reduction of nuclear missiles in Europe.

All these were worthy achievements, but ambassadors working in obscurity could have made them come to pass. What really mattered was the intangible: Reagan and Gorbachev had discovered that they could talk to each other even if they could not yet agree. On that basis they had decided that they would meet again in Washington and Moscow. In the meantime, they would correspond as man to man, with no insulating layers of diplomats between them. The meeting of the minds, the measure of character, and above all, the decision to go on, could only have been achieved by the President and the General Secretary—and probably not by any others who had ever held their respective offices. Once again, the time had been right for Ronald Reagan, and he had taken advantage of it.

"It is amazing," I said to Shevardnadze, "how quickly things get done when the bosses say, 'Let's do it.' "

One of the last times I saw the two men together in private in Geneva, they were sitting side by side on a sofa in the Soviet Mission, deep in conversation. Henkel and the KGB major general were in another room, working out the details of the public farewell that they had agreed to make the next day. Finally the plan was brought out. I approached and spoke to the President. He could not hear me because I was speaking into his deaf ear and the room was abuzz with other conversations. I leaned closer.

"Mr. President, they're saying that you and the General Secretary should meet tomorrow at ten o'clock in the International Conference Center. Each of you will make a statement to the press and then issue the Joint Declaration."

Gorbachev's interpreter told him what I had said.

The President turned to the Russian. Does that sound all right to you, Mikhail?

"*Da*," said Gorbachev.

It's fine with me, too, Reagan said.

The two men nodded at each other like old friends.

· 16 ·

Completing the Reagan Revolution

During the Geneva summit, Bud McFarlane had told the President the details of a plan to sell eighty HAWK antiaircraft missiles to Iran through the Israelis. It was a complicated operation: the Israelis would deliver the missiles from their own stockpile to a secret destination in Portugal. There they would be loaded aboard three transport planes and flown to Tabriz. As soon as the first plane was airborne, word would be flashed to the Iranians by clandestine means and the Iranians would tell the terrorists who were holding the five U.S. citizens hostage in Lebanon to release them. The plane would not land and no missiles would be delivered until all five Americans had been handed over to the American Embassy in Beirut.

Later on, the United States would give the Israelis eighty new Hawk missiles to replace the ones they had delivered to the Iranians; forty additional Hawks would be given to the Iranians in a separate transaction. In return the Iranians would guarantee that no more American hostages would be taken by terrorists. The swap of the Hawks for the hostages was scheduled to happen on Thursday, November 21, 1985. The transaction was not described in those blunt terms to the President, Shultz, or me. Reagan clung to the belief that he was not paying ransom but merely rewarding an intermediary for services rendered.

Although he listened intently to McFarlane's words, the President asked few questions. He looked straight at McFarlane, occasionally glancing at Shultz or me as if to study our reactions: did we agree or disagree with what McFarlane was saying? Shultz's facial expressions and body language strongly suggested that he believed that he had more important things to discuss with the President, and he commented very sparingly.

McFarlane's conversation with Reagan took place before lunch on the first day of the summit, Tuesday, November 19, in my bedroom on the second floor of the Villa Palmetta. This modest room—normally occupied, judging by the furnishings, by one of the teenage daughters of the family that lived there—had been "swept" for listening devices by our security people. We were crowded into the small space, the President sitting in a barrel-back chair shoved against a wall, Shultz in a smaller chair, and McFarlane and I perched on the edge of twin beds a couple of feet away.

McFarlane's description of the operation was difficult to follow because of the many bizarre elements involved—intermediaries, timing, secret messages, transshipment and verification of weapons, guarantees that the hostages would in fact be released by their captors on the word of people in Tehran and Tabriz who ostensibly had no direct control over their actions, only "influence" and good offices. McFarlane's briefing lasted about twenty minutes, and during it he discussed the cover story. The missiles would be described as oil-drilling equipment in case any questions were asked by customs officials or others about the cargo of the three airplanes bound for Tabriz. This relatively minor fact was discussed with particular attention; I don't know why. Even if the Iran-Contra affair had never become a cause célèbre I would remember this meeting vividly because I had never before experienced anything like it. This was certainly the first time the President had heard the whole scenario. It was not in his character to be especially interested in the nuts and bolts, and he asked no probing questions.

Whether the President absorbed every detail I cannot say. The pattern was not so clear in the verbal briefing he received as it appears to be now on the page, and certain features of the plan later assumed a significance that was not apparent at the time.

The moment could not have been worse, from the point of view of capturing Reagan's full attention. He had just left Gorbachev; he had had no lunch; and many other items dealing with the summit, which was uppermost in his mind, remained to be discussed.

I do not remember that anyone present raised a serious objection to any of the arrangements described by McFarlane. It was obvious that much could go wrong. But this was supposed to be a clandestine operation, and if things went wrong, they would go wrong in secret. That is one of the things that makes secret operations so seductive and so dangerous. I assumed, and I am sure that the President assumed, that McFarlane and his collaborators knew what they were doing. One hostage had recently been released through their connections; why should the others not be recovered by the same means? This was McFarlane's operation. Only the President had the authority to tell McFarlane not to do what he was proposing to do, and the President—once again saying yes by not saying no—did not do that. It would not be surprising if McFarlane gained the impression that he was being given unspoken approval to proceed in the hope of getting our people out of captivity.

We moved on to other more important matters. There is little excuse for the blunder that was finalized that day, but there is no harm, either, in remembering that perspectives were not the same then as later. In that cramped bedroom in the Villa Palmetta, McFarlane was talking about eighty antiaircraft missiles and five unfortunate Americans. At the negotiating table, Reagan and Gorbachev were discussing thousands of nuclear warheads and missiles and the threat they posed to the tens of millions of people who lived in the great cities between the Atlantic and the Urals.

Of course, virtually everything did go wrong with McFarlane's operation. Portugal would not permit the transport planes to land on its territory. With the help of the CIA, other arrangements were made to deliver the missiles, and eighteen were handed over to the Iranians, who were outraged when they discovered that the crates in which they were packed were labeled in Hebrew. The missiles, which were delivered to the Iranians *before* any hostages were released (thus negating the whole basis of the deal), turned out to be the wrong type of Hawk. The Iranians tested one of the missiles by firing it at an Iraqi aircraft flying over Kharg Island and ultimately returned the other seventeen to the Israelis. Most of these details were not known to me, or as far as I know, to the President, until much later.

On December 2, reports appeared in the press that Bud had called on the President in Los Angeles and offered his resignation. The President's response must be described in the tortured language that suits Reagan's style best: the President had not refused to accept it. Whether McFarlane, who had hinted at resignation on other occasions, was surprised by this result, I do not know. He had not discussed his plans with me, and he did not describe his reaction to the President's decision, either. I learned of his resignation through press rumors.

The *New York Times*'s Bernard Weinraub reported that McFarlane's reasons for leaving were twofold: "continuing frictions with the strong-willed White House Chief of Staff, Donald T. Regan, and the security advisor's desire to enter the private sector and earn more money." Deeper into his story, Weinraub wrote, "On a personal level, said several White House officials, Mr. McFarlane resented Mr. Regan's assertive management style and the Chief of Staff's involvement with foreign policy matters. Mr. Regan, on the other hand, attributed several news leaks to Mr. McFarlane and resented his direct access to the President. . . ."

Other reporters, whose source was doubtless just as authentic as Weinraub's, took up the theme of a McFarlane-Regan feud, and very soon it was accepted wisdom. If any such conflict existed, I was not aware of it. It is true that I attributed leaks to McFarlane, and it may well be that he found my style assertive even though I thought it was merely frank. There was little time in the life I was leading for anything but plain speech, especially when the other man was an equal. If I expressed disagreement or disappointment in forceful language and then forgot about it, McFarlane evidently did not. He was a moody man, jealous of his prerogatives and uncertain of his primacy after a lifetime of assistantship. We came from different worlds, had different manners, judged results by different standards, and had nothing in common except that we had both been lieutenant colonels in the Marine Corps. It is no wonder that misunderstandings arose, but they should not have affected our professional relationship.

That relationship had been difficult from the start. In the summer of 1984, while I was still Secretary of the Treasury, I learned that McFarlane had authorized the State Department to discuss U.S. support for Poland's application to join the International Monetary Fund with the fund's managing director without telling me about it. Our subsequent telephone conversation was a study in plain language, but McFarlane held his ground and made no apologies. Poland did not become a member of IMF during my tenure. My first encounter as Chief of Staff with Bud involved office space: he was so eager to have Ed Meese's office (the one with the view of the front lawn previously occupied by Henry Kissinger) that he went directly to the President and applied for it. As the first order of business one morning, Reagan consulted a scrap of paper and told me to be sure McFarlane got the office; it was important to his morale. I was left with the impression that the President thought that he might lose his National Security Advisor unless he had proper quarters—although neither Richard Allen nor William Clark, Reagan's first two Advisors, had had this particular office.

One of the features of this office, as I have mentioned, was its high visibility to the press, and Bud often complained after he moved in that he had been "waylaid" by reporters. But he seemed to enjoy the snare, chatting with his friends from the White House press corps as he walked from his car to his office when he could just as easily have had himself deposited at the same door the rest of us had used in the West Wing basement. He would sometimes walk down to the press room, and his encounters with a female reporter gave rise to postadolescent jokes about the two in Larry Speakes's press briefings. Later on, when the jokes became gossip that spilled over into a national Sunday supplement and therefore became a source of embarrassment to the Presidency, I took Bud out to lunch in Santa Barbara and asked him if there was any truth in these rumors. He assured me that there was not. I dropped the subject, but the gossip persisted.

Certainly I did not resent McFarlane's access to the President or try to limit it. In fact he had greater rights of access in my time than he had enjoyed before. McFarlane had made it a practice to check with Jim Baker before exercising his right to see the President. I placed no such requirement on either McFarlane or Poindexter, and both were free to walk in on Reagan whenever they thought it necessary without telling me before or after the fact. McFarlane was never shy about contacting the President. "Every time the phone rings at three A.M.," the President told reporters in a light moment, "I turn over and say, 'Hi, Bud.' "

My own contacts with McFarlane were limited and structured: the President's daily 9:30 national security briefing, NSC meetings, and special briefings of the President, such as the one in Geneva. Sometimes, especially in my early days as Chief of Staff when the President asked me questions about the details of foreign policy that I could not answer, I tried to overcome my ignorance and the embarrassment it caused by asking McFarlane questions. He would seldom give me the answer I sought, usually saying that I had no need to know. "Why not? After all, I'm the President's Chief of Staff," I would reply. "No, no, no," Bud would say. "There are limits. . . . This is 'black box.' " John Poindexter, as the reader has seen, took a similar view of the matter. In retrospect I wish that I had been less careful of their prerogatives and had exercised control over their activities.

Obviously, the real reasons for McFarlane's resignation are known only to McFarlane. In hindsight it is clear that he left at the moment when the Iran initiative first came unglued, never to be put back together. That fact was not obvious at the time; the keepers of the black box kept assuring the President that all would be well in the end. Some in the West Wing suspected more petty motives. I had heard that McFarlane was upset over a photograph taken by a White House photographer that Larry Speakes had released to the press without consulting me. (There was no reason why Speakes should have consulted me—it was a good picture that was sure to make the papers, and getting pictures into the papers was an important part of Speakes's job.) It showed me whispering to the President while he sat on the sofa with Gorbachev at the Soviet Mission. The occasion was the one I described at the end of the preceding chapter, and I had stuck my head between Reagan's and Gorbachev's so that the President could hear me in a crowded room. It seemed impossible that this photo of a spontaneous moment should cause jealousy and suspicion, but I was assured that this was the case.

In any event, Bud went on December 4, 1985. Fatigue resulting from the strenuous efforts required to mediate between George Shultz and Caspar Weinberger and Bill Casey, all of whom were stubborn defenders of their own turf and their own agendas, may have contributed to his decision along with the failure to recover the hostages, whatever problems he may have had in his mind with me, and with his perfectly understandable desire to improve his financial position after thirty years of continuous military and civilian service to his country.

McFarlane had won his last bureaucratic battle with Shultz, Weinberger, and Casey, persuading the President to appoint his deputy, Poindexter, as his successor. The others had proposed candidates of their own. I had no objection to Poindexter: he was well qualified by experience and background and, with his phlegmatic nature, seemed unlikely to be a source of trouble or embarrassment. So much for appearances. The fact that Poindexter was "up to speed" on Iran and the hostages did not seem to me at the time to be a particularly important consideration. For all its emotional resonance, it was in my mind an issue of minor and passing interest.

The main business for all those who worked for the President was to help him complete the Reagan Revolution. With the progress on tax reform and his success at Geneva, he had shown the nation and the world that he was no lame-duck President whose second term would be devoted to marking time. By those two acts of leadership alone, he had laid the basis for a strong showing for his party in the 1986 midterm elections. If the Republicans could hold their own to take only small losses in the House and Senate, then the momentum could be sustained through the last two years.

To keep my promise to Ann, and for the other reasons I've mentioned, I planned to leave Washington right after the elections. By then, I thought, Ronald Reagan's place in history would be decided. If he achieved the great breakthrough in arms reductions that he dreamed of, then that place might be high on the list of American Presidents. It seemed possible, in light of the fundamental changes he had wrought in the American scene, that when the biases faded away he might be ranked with the greatest President of my lifetime, Harry S Truman. Reagan and Truman were plainly the two most underestimated Presidents since Abraham Lincoln.

All predictions to the contrary notwithstanding, the President had had an excellent year on Capitol Hill in 1985. Under the impetus provided by Gramm-Rudman, the Budget Resolution adopted by Congress and signed by the President contained $68 billion in negotiated spending cuts, far less than the $105 billion in the original Administration-Senate compromise, but more than in the previous three years combined. The Budget Resolution contained no tax increase and no tampering with Social Security. On several key issues, Reagan had won against the odds and against most predictions: Aid was restored to the Contras, though not at the level the President had sought. The defense budget had been tied to real growth in the economy, and levels of spending were sufficient to maintain the strength and readiness of the armed forces. Funding for SDI, the key to any agreement with the Soviets, was almost doubled. The MX missile remained in production.

Reagan had also had a good year in the estimation of the people. His popularity at the end of 1985 stood at 68 percent, lower than his peak figure, but higher—in some cases, much higher—than that of any of his recent predecessors at the beginning of their second terms.

The objective now was to build on the President's successes by mobilizing his popularity behind programs which we knew would stubbornly be resisted by his opponents. Foremost among these was the budget deficit. Fiscal intemperance would drive the deficit up to $221 billion in fiscal year 1986, or about 5 percent of the gross national product. Clearly we had reached the danger point. If the disease was not acknowledged and cured at this stage, even more feverish conditions could result and get out of control. We were confident that tax reform would generate new revenues and have all the other beneficial effects on the economy that we had predicted. But unless tax reform was accompanied by spending restraints, the economy would suffer blows to its vitality from which it might not be able to recover.

The Gramm-Rudman-Hollings Act, signed into law December 12, created a certain amount of pressure for a timelier and more realistic appropriations process. The Balanced Budget Amendment to the Constitution would have done more. The Reagan Administration supported both, but neither addressed the question of fundamental budget reform that would sooner or later have to be confronted and resolved. This would mean line-item vetoes for the President to control the pork barrel, and it would mean amortizing the purchase of equipment, such as $32-billion aircraft carriers and federal buildings, over the life of the asset instead of paying cash up front for everything within a capital budget. It would also mean converting property into cash (what would a developer pay for Governor's Island, which was no longer useful as a coast artillery fort to protect the Hudson and East Rivers from naval attack?), and it will mean, above all, the rational management of the taxpayers' money so that we would never again be in the position of being too poor as a government to help the unfortunate at the same time that we were paying tens of millions of dollars to large agricultural corporations not to grow crops. I did not expect to see this happen in my lifetime, much less by the time Ronald Reagan went back to California in 1989.

The goals of the Administration remained the same: tax *reductions*, not tax increases, spending *restraint*, not spending cuts. We did not ask Congress to cut the budget because we knew that this was impossible politically and impractical in terms of the needs of the country. We asked only that Congress spend slightly less than the government was taking in. Planning was possible because revenues would rise in proportion to the nominal growth of the economy. In that way the economy would pay the country's way through reasonable growth instead of the taxpayer doing so through increases in taxes made necessary by the expenditure of money that did not exist. I don't know why it was so difficult to get this message across, except that many of the people to whom we were sending it did not want to hear it.

Simple belief is often the determining factor in economic matters. When, in 1923, after the reichsmark had plunged in value from its prewar level of four to the U.S. dollar to 2 trillion to the dollar, the German commissioner of the currency, Hjalmar Schacht, introduced a new currency and announced that it would be issued only in small denominations. Schacht told the German people that they must each of them believe that the value of the new money was the same as the old, preinflation reichsmark, or all was lost. The Germans, having no choice, took his advice. Overnight the price of a single egg plunged from 80 billion marks in the debauched currency to a few pfennigs in the new. What worked for the Germans in 1923—common sense— had not yet worked for the Congress in the 1980s, but that was no reason to stop telling members that fiscal discipline was the only alternative to eventual disaster.

The impasse on the deficit notwithstanding, the President had made his issues the nation's issues. In Congress and in the press, in the political arena and in academia, debate centered on economic recovery, tax reform, defense spending, trade policy, and the changing relationship with the U.S.S.R. Other issues—the farm problem, oil prices, weak banks, the malaise in manufacturing—remained on the periphery. In my day-to-day work I urged the President to keep the initiative he had seized, while exhorting the staff and the Cabinet to help him do so by resisting the impulse to be drawn into secondary issues. This was not a time to invent issues, but to unite our forces in dealing with the ones we had. The President had to be out front, leading the fight on the important issues. His energy and influence must not be dissipated by unnecessary controversy. Anything that diverted him from his primary goals was by definition bad.

At this time I had not even conceived of the possibility of a diversion of such overwhelming proportions as the Iran-Contra affair. From my notes of the period, it appears that I thought the worst thing that might happen would be the loss of Republican control of the Senate in the 1986 elections. Even that, I told the staff, would not be a disaster. We would simply change our tactics in order to apply the President's popularity and the force of his ideas by other means. Our goals—peace based on military strength and creative foreign policy, economic growth, tax reform, and fiscal sanity—would never change.

It seemed perfectly possible to meet the objectives we had established. The President had never been stronger and his policies had never been more timely. Tax reform alone was enough to justify his entire second term. But his accomplishments had already gone beyond that. Although his detractors were slow to concede it, Reagan had achieved his objectives at the Geneva summit. The attack on Libya in April 1986, however much it may have shocked liberal opinion here and abroad, had had a chilling effect on state-sponsored terrorism and had demonstrated the President's resolve to the world.

The Tokyo Economic Summit had made an important statement on terrorism, and on his return to Washington Reagan immediately sent a personal report on this aspect of the meeting to Gorbachev. After Geneva, Reagan had established an informal personal correspondence with the Soviet leader. In letters delivered by messenger they exchanged views on the Chernobyl disaster and other matters. This was no small thing, considering that earlier leaders of the two countries had considered it an accomplishment to install a teletype "hot line" so they could speak to each other in the imminent threat of nuclear war. But there were other benefits of the Soviet-U.S. summit: arms talks continued in a somewhat more urgent atmosphere, together with diplomatic contacts in preparation for "Gorbachev II," as the next summit was called in West Wing jargon.

If Presidents think in terms of their place in history, it is because history for them is in the future. They are making decisions whose effects will be felt for years—even generations—to come, and whose full meaning may not be understood for centuries. Ideally, every major action that President Reagan took, every policy that he approved, looked to the future and was consistent with the philosophy on which he had been elected; that was the basis on which his White House was being managed.

An opportunity to exercise far-reaching influence on the future life of the nation presented itself on May 27, when Chief Justice Warren Burger sent word that he wished to see the President. I replied that I would arrange an appointment at any time convenient to him. Suspecting that Burger might have real news for the President—i.e., his decision to resign as Chief Justice—I arranged for my assistant, Tom Dawson, to meet him at the gate and escort him discreetly to the Oval Office.

The only persons present besides Reagan and Burger were Fred Fielding, an old friend of Burger's, and me. The Chief Justice told the President that his eightieth birthday and the two hundredth anniversary of the ratification of the Constitution were approaching, and because he wanted to get ready for both, he had decided to retire. Reagan indicated surprise at this statement but did not attempt to dissuade Burger. After the Chief Justice left I urged the President to keep Burger's decision to resign a deep secret. He agreed and gave instructions that only Ed Meese and Peter Wallison, the White House Counsel, were to be told.

Ronald Reagan fully appreciated the opportunity that Chief Justice Burger's resignation gave him to influence the future role of the Court in American society. The President's adversaries appreciated it even more keenly. Alone of all American institutions, the Court does not rely on the consent of the government in its decisions, and its word is, literally, law. Its power to change the rules by which the nation lives is limited only by the necessity to get five of its nine members to agree on a given constitutional question. Neither camp of American politics wants the other to have a majority. In the left wing of the Democratic party, whose old ability to convince and elect was vanishing, the desire was particularly strong to prevent domination of the Court by those who practiced judicial restraint rather than the judicial activism that had characterized the Court since the New Deal.

This was not an issue on which President Reagan was prepared to compromise. He knew that he would have a fight on his hands if he nominated a conservative, no matter how well qualified the person might be. Reagan had amply demonstrated his political creativity and philosophical consistency in his earlier Supreme Court appointments. Sandra Day O'Connor, the first woman to be named as an Associate Justice, had fulfilled all the hopes that had been placed in her. Reagan knew that not all Presidents had been so fortunate, and remembered the remark attributed to Eisenhower in connection with his appointment of Earl Warren as Chief Justice: "That was the biggest damn-fool mistake I ever made."

The President wanted appointees whose philosophy was fully formed and had already served as the basis for a definitive body of opinion on constitutional matters. The obvious candidate for Chief Justice, William Rehnquist, had already been sitting on the Supreme Court for fourteen years and had compiled a record that left no room for doubt as to his philosophical bent. Rehnquist was also a great scholar and a formidable intellect; no one insisted on this more forcefully than his political enemies. No other candidate was ever seriously considered, and on June 12 the President invited Rehnquist to the White House to offer him the nomination. Like Burger, Rehnquist used a little-known entrance and came and went without being noticed by the press or anyone else.

A search by Ed Meese and Peter Wallison produced two candidates for the vacancy on the bench created by Burger's resignation and Rehnquist's elevation—Robert Bork and Antonin Scalia, both judges on the Federal Court of Appeals for the District of Columbia. Both were brilliant legal scholars who advocated the doctrine of judicial restraint. Both were eminently well qualified by philosophy and record, but Bork, as Solicitor General of the United States in 1973, had fired Special Prosecutor Archibald Cox on instructions from President Nixon. This action, legal and dutiful though it may have been, had earned him the enmity of the large company of doctrinaire liberals in the Congress, the press, and the Democratic party who did not believe that the Watergate scandal should be permitted to fade away.

The President, like everyone else, knew that Senate confirmation of Bork would involve a hard battle, yet he was determined to nominate him and fight it out on the basis of his unassailable qualifications. The only question was timing. Wallison suggested that Bork's name be sent to the Senate on the theory that the Judiciary Committee would be so exhausted by its onslaught on Rehnquist that it would lack the energy to mount a full-scale attack against Bork. Scalia could then be nominated for the next vacancy on the high bench, and the ideological balance of the Supreme Court would be assured for years to come.

I argued, successfully, that waving two red flags before the enraged liberal bloc on the committee would be too much. Meese agreed, after giving Bork high praise. Scalia was nominated, and Wallison's theory held up: after a bitter ideological attack on Rehnquist, the Scalia hearing turned into a love-fest and he was confirmed by a unanimous vote of the Senate. Possibly Bork would not have fared as well, but he could hardly have done worse than he did when his turn finally came in the summer of 1987, after I had left the White House. After one of the most vitriolic confirmation hearings in recent memory—and one in which ideology rather than judicial qualification was established as the criterion for membership on the Supreme Court—Bork failed to win confirmation. So did a subsequent nominee of conservative views, Douglas Ginsburg, who withdrew his name after it was revealed that he had smoked marijuana before being appointed to the bench. A moderate Californian, Federal Appeals Court Judge Anthony M. Kennedy, was finally confirmed by the Senate by a vote of 97−0 on February 3, 1988.

The process of arranging Burger's retirement from the Supreme Court and selecting Rehnquist and Scalia was carried out without a single leak to the media. This would have been remarkable in any circumstances, but the fact that all three managed to meet with the President less than two hundred feet away from the White House press room without being detected— Burger arriving in a shiny black limousine with the seal of the

Supreme Court painted on the doors, and Scalia driving himself in a battered compact car—was an achievement in which I took special satisfaction.

On January 28, 1986, the space shuttle *Challenger* exploded in mid-launch from Cape Canaveral, killing all seven members of the crew. This terrible news was brought to me in the Roosevelt Room, where I was briefing a group of journalists on the State of the Union message at a luncheon arranged by the Office of Media Relations; among those present were the major network anchormen—Tom Brokaw of NBC, Peter Jennings of ABC, Dan Rather of CBS, and Bernard Shaw of CNN. After reading the note that a member of the staff, Kathy Reid, had handed to me, I told the reporters what had happened. After a stunned silence that lasted no more than a fraction of a second, they leaped to their feet and bolted from the room. Brokaw grabbed a phone. Then I heard him shouting, "It's true, and it looks like a major disaster!"

I went to the Oval Office at once, but the President was not there. Immediately on hearing the news from Pat Buchanan he had gone into his hideaway study. Reagan's face was sad as we watched the story unfold on television. Plainly an investigation of the tragedy would be necessary; I told the President as we watched the coverage that no ordinary investigation would be adequate, that he must appoint a blue-ribbon group to probe every aspect of the situation. NASA and its supporters on Capitol Hill, backed by John Poindexter, wished to leave the investigation in the hands of the space agency. On the way back to Washington from Houston after the memorial service for the lost astronauts, the two points of view were put to the President and he opted for an independent commission.

Reagan accepted my suggestion that he ask William P. Rogers, a former Secretary of State and Attorney General, to serve as chairman. He appointed astronaut Sally Ride as one of a list of distinguished and knowledgeable members. The work of the Rogers Commission, completed in less than four months, unequivocally identified the cause of the accident, pointed out weaknesses in NASA procedures, and laid the basis for the safer and more successful space program that is a fitting memorial to the *Challenger* crew.

I was heartened in general by the way things were going in the White House. Management by objective was becoming second nature in the West Wing. The staff was now firmly in the habit of identifying issues, developing them, and bringing them to the President for decision. The two new councils, on Economic and Domestic Policy, worked more swiftly and efficiently under the chairmanship of Jim Baker and Ed Meese than the former system of seven Cabinet councils. The President believed in Cabinet government, and the closer focus that the simpler apparatus provided made it easier for him keep track of the ideas put forward by his Cabinet officers. Members of the Cabinet felt in turn that they were being heard by the President and that the creative energies of their departments were working effectively to formulate the Administration's policy—and to make that policy work. No matter how exalted their station, human beings generally find it difficult to operate unless they know exactly what is expected of them—and, just as important, what they are *not* permitted to do.

The failure to make the latter limits clear was, of course, the Achilles heel that made the Iran-Contra affair and other embarrassing lapses of judgment and deportment possible, if not inevitable. As a practical matter, it is too late for lessons in ethics when you get to the White House. Any Chief of Staff who published such a no-no list, as the press would surely have dubbed it, or encouraged the President he served to do so, would deservedly be laughed out of town. In government, as in the most intimate personal relationships, the glue that holds things together is trust, and the statistic that half the new marriages contracted in the United States end in divorce suggests that Presidents are not the only ones who are subject to disappointed expectations.

My management style was the subject of gossip and commentary from the start, and that, too, was inevitable. The press's picture of me as a sort of Iron Major drilling the troops in the West Wing corridors and making everyone spring to attention when I walked into the room did not jibe with the kindlier image I had of myself, or with the impression I had gained that most of the staff was having the time of its life. But we seldom see ourselves as others see us. As early as the summer of 1985, when I was barely five months in the job, the press began to apply the term "prime minister" to me. Whether this corrosive appellation, with its suggestion that I had either usurped some of the President's powers or that he had weakly delegated them to me, was invented by a clever writer on a dull afternoon, or whether it was planted by some White House *apparatchik* is unimportant. At the time I thought that it was meaningless because it had nothing to do with reality. That sentence may appear to say the same thing twice, but as I would discover, perception had a way of turning into reality in the circles in which I was now traveling. The *Washington Times* summarized the prevailing perception of me in its editions of July 25, 1985, in an article by Jeremiah O'Leary:

> Mr. Regan is . . . tough-minded but with a personality that ranges from tempestuous outbursts to avuncular Irish jollity. Taking over as "prime minister" under President Reagan from the smooth, politics-minded James A. Baker III in a job switch between the two, the contrast has been almost total in its effect on White House staffers, Congress and the Cabinet departments. Mr. Baker got his way with the help of like-minded operatives such as Richard Darman and Michael K. Deaver. Mr. Regan does it with a shillelagh.

In fact the Irish jollity was more of a public relations burden to me than the alleged tempestuous outbursts. Growing up in South Boston is not the best way to learn solemnity and circumlocution, and the sense of the ridiculous that is bred into the bones of my race is pretty hard to control. I made some memorable blunders in interviews as a result of my fondness for the one-liner, offending (according to some) just over half the population of the country by saying in connection with the question of economic sanctions against South Africa that American women might not wish to give up diamonds, platinum, rhodium, and gold, and by remarking before the Geneva summit that women were "not going to understand throw-weights or what is happening in Afghanistan or what is happening in human rights [but would be more interested in] human-interest stuff." Not surprisingly, both Reagan and Gorbachev said publicly that they did not agree with me about this. My comment after the Reykjavík summit that "some of us are like a shovel brigade that follows a parade down Main Street cleaning up" was intended to suggest that the first negative commentary on what was accomplished there had been mistaken, but the simile was too colorful.

The press, which manufactured and merchandised my image along with everyone else's in Washington, could hardly be blamed if they didn't get the portrait exactly right. Journalists barely knew me. My predecessors, and even some of the senior staff in my time at the White House, had chummed with journalists, dining with them in the evening and playing tennis in the cool of the mornings. I abjured these pleasures. Early on, Ann and I attended a dinner in Georgetown at which media stars and high political appointees mixed and discussed the issues and personalities of the day. It was a crowded party. Because of my deafness I have trouble hearing what is said to me in a noisy room. Because of her arthritis, it is painful for my wife to stand during the prolonged cocktail hour that is a feature of most large dinner parties. The desire to meet new people for professional reasons was no longer strong in either of us. We decided on the way home that we would accept no more such invitations. No doubt this contributed to whatever sense of estrangement the press felt as a result of the anti-leak policies I had introduced.

Because I was not in fact a prime minister, but a servant of the Presidency, I did not think it mattered what the press wrote and said about me, and often said so. Substance, not appearance, was my primary mission. And as the second summit in Reykjavík approached, just before the midterm elections, it was clear that the Reagan Administration had a good deal to be proud of where substance was concerned.

· 17 ·

Reykjavík: Disappointment and Triumph

Soviet Foreign Minister Eduard Shevardnadze, seated in a white wingback armchair in the Oval Office, listened stoically while the President of the United States gave him hell over the cynical false arrest of an American journalist in Moscow. Reagan demanded the immediate release of Nicholas Daniloff, the Moscow correspondent of *U.S. News & World Report*, who had been seized by the KGB on trumped-up charges of espionage after a real—and apparently rather important—Soviet intelligence officer was arrested in New York by the Federal Bureau of Investigation and charged with espionage under the laws of the United States.

The Soviets had, in effect, taken an American hostage. Their obvious purpose was to swap an innocent man, Daniloff, for a guilty one, Gennadi Zakharov, a KGB agent using his employment at the United Nations as cover. It was clear that their tactics could easily include a show trial of Daniloff, with all the anguish to him and his family and all the blackguarding of his profession that this would involve. Any exchange of a journalist for a spy would not only throw a shadow over the reputation of the entire community of foreign correspondents, it would put them at risk of capricious arrest by authoritarian regimes everywhere in the world whenever a spy happened to be caught in their home countries. This, in turn, would hamper if not cripple the counterespionage operations by which the United States and other countries of the Free World attempt to protect themselves from the aggressive operations of the Soviet bloc espionage apparatus.

President Reagan responded by having the State Department order an additional twenty-five Soviet diplomats expelled from the United States by October 1. He had already written a personal letter to Gorbachev, giving the Soviet leader his assurance that Daniloff was in no way connected to any U.S. government agency or activity, and demanding the immediate release of the journalist. Gorbachev had replied in a terse and noncommital letter, saying that the Daniloff matter was being investigated and he would let the President know the results. Meanwhile Daniloff remained in jail in Moscow. Nearly a month had passed since his arrest.

When Shevardnadze was ushered into the Oval Office by George Shultz on Friday, September 19, 1986, he was confronted by a very different Ronald Reagan from the genial yarn-spinner he had observed in Geneva. The President's manner was icy. He neither shook hands with the Russian nor greeted him by name, but immediately launched into a scathing denunciation of the Soviet action. How could the United States trust a power that was capable of such a calculated act of false accusation that victimized an innocent American citizen?

Stern and unsmiling, his cheeks flushed, the President told Shevardnadze that Daniloff must be released forthwith and cleared of all charges against him. There would be no quid pro quo. The KGB man, Zakharov, had been charged with espionage and must face American justice. No exchange of the two men would ever take place while Reagan was President.

I have said that Reagan was rarely moved to anger or reproach. On this occasion his emotion was genuine, and I think that Shevardnadze knew it. At first he listened to the tongue-lashing in virtual silence. There was little reason for him to reply because the President already knew that he had nothing new to say. George Shultz, who had also taken an uncompromisingly hard line on the Daniloff matter, had met with Shevardnadze in New York, and had told the President that the Soviet foreign minister had brought no new proposals with him from Moscow. The Russians still wanted to swap Daniloff for Zakharov. Until this changed, every issue between the two superpowers was at a standstill.

In any case, Shevardnadze had not come to see the President with the idea of discussing Daniloff. He was in the Oval Office because he had told Shultz that he wished to deliver a letter from Gorbachev to Reagan. When Shevardnadze produced the letter and handed it to the President, Reagan placed it unopened on the table beside his chair. There it remained unread while the President continued to upbraid Shevardnadze. The session lasted forty-five minutes, a very long time by Presidential standards, and at the end of it Reagan was still furious.

After Shevardnadze left, Reagan read the English translation of the letter that the Soviets had provided.

Gorbachev did not mention the Daniloff case. Instead, he proposed that he and Reagan meet as soon as possible to discuss the complete elimination of Soviet and U.S. intermediate-range nuclear missiles from Europe, without taking into account French and British missiles.

This was a historic breakthrough, the first step toward the treaty on intermediate-range missiles that was signed by Reagan and Gorbachev at the Washington summit two years later. The Geneva negotiations had been working toward reduction of the number of intermediate-range nuclear missiles on both sides.* Now Gorbachev had moderated the Soviet positions on these questions. He also told the President that he favored discussion of the numbers and types of intermediate-range missiles that might be retained by the U.S. and the Soviet Union in Asia and America.

Gorbachev proposed that any work on antiballistic missile systems such as SDI be confined to the laboratory and that the ABM treaty be extended for an additional fifteen years. In return for such an agreement, Gorbachev wrote, the Soviets would be will-

---

*The Soviets had 922 nuclear warheads mounted on intermediate-range ballistic missiles in Europe; the U.S. had 108 such warheads on Pershing II ballistic missiles and 160 on subsonic, air-breathing Cruise missiles. In addition, the Soviets deployed 981 nuclear warheads on short-range ballistic missiles in Europe, as against 72 U.S. Pershing IA short-range missiles.

ing to discuss a significant reduction in strategic nuclear arms, that is, intercontinental ballistic missiles (ICBMs). Finally, he proposed a moratorium on nuclear weapons testing.

In his proposals on SDI and the ABM treaty, Gorbachev was replying to proposals made to him by President Reagan in a personal letter and in a speech on July 25, in which the President had suggested, as a gesture to Soviet nervousness over SDI, that the ABM treaty be extended for a period of five to seven years.

The suggestion for a moratorium on nuclear testing, with its overtones of propaganda, was old and unexciting. But Gorbachev's proposal to separate U.S. missiles in Europe from those under British and French command signified real movement in the negotiations. Until now, the Russians had always insisted that 194 missile-delivered nuclear warheads deployed by France and Great Britain as part of their own nuclear arsenals be included in any agreement. The United States had refused, arguing that it could not negotiate on behalf of other sovereign states. The change was significant not only because it set new goals, but because it also suggested a new Soviet desire to come to an agreement with the Reagan Administration rather than waiting, as some American pundits expected Moscow to do, for a new President to be elected.

Gorbachev wrote that only he and Reagan, talking together, could resolve the questions he raised; Soviet and U.S. negotiators in Geneva could not do so. Shevardnadze later told us that the Soviets thought that the meeting between Reagan and Gorbachev should not take place in the United States or the U.S.S.R., but on neutral ground—in London or Iceland, for example. This meeting would not be considered part of the exchange of visits that the two leaders had agreed on after their fireside chat in Geneva, but rather a sort of minisummit, the warm-up to a visit by Gorbachev to the United States for the first of the "true" paired summits.

The opportunities opened up by Gorbachev's proposals were obvious. Beyond the grand issues of disarmament and reconciliation between the superpowers, Gorbachev's letter was a clear signal that the Daniloff affair would be settled to American satisfaction because the Soviet leader knew that Reagan would never negotiate while this case was unresolved. For his part, Reagan knew that the case had to be resolved in a way that did not undercut Gorbachev's position with the KGB and other important constituencies within the Kremlin. Nevertheless, some of the President's foreign-policy advisers had reservations about Gorbachev's invitation. They reasoned that it would diminish, and possibly even eliminate, the probability of a better-prepared summit in the United States in 1986.

But the decision the President had to make was more subtle and politically complicated than any question of scheduling or agenda. It was clearly impossible for Reagan to refuse to meet Gorbachev on an issue involving world peace, assuming that the Daniloff affair was first settled on terms that satisfied American honor. The President had been speaking out vigorously on disarmament ever since Geneva, and to temporize when he had been offered the chance to negotiate could have incalculable consequences in terms of world opinion and the atmosphere in which future talks would take place. The American midterm elections were little more than a month away. And in the very different way in which political power was won in the U.S.S.R., the political stakes for Gorbachev—who was trying to consolidate his position—were at least as important as those for Reagan.

The President replied to Gorbachev that he would take his proposals under advisement, but no meeting between him and Gorbachev could even be considered until Daniloff was released and all charges against him were dropped. No doubt this was the answer Gorbachev expected and wanted. A period of intense negotiations led by Shultz and Shevardnadze followed. On September 29, Daniloff was released by the Soviets, who made the further gesture of granting an exit visa to physicist Yuri Orlov, a Soviet dissident who had been banished to Siberia after seven years in prison for publicizing Soviet human-rights violations. Orlov's wife, Irina Valitova, was also permitted to leave. Zakharov was delivered into Soviet custody.

The next day, September 30, Reagan announced that he and General Secretary Gorbachev would meet in Iceland on October

11 and 12 to discuss an agenda that included arms reductions, human rights, regional conflicts, and bilateral relations.

This stunning news, coming at a time when Soviet-American relations were portrayed as being at a new low, excited the media. The President's detractors expressed their usual low expectations of his probable performance and of the outcome. "It's a joke," said Zbigniew Brzezinski, who had been President Carter's National Security Advisor. "A summit on two weeks' notice? Without an agenda?" Another former National Security Advisor, Bud McFarlane, told the press that two days wasn't enough time to nail down the details of an agreement. Still another, Henry Kissinger, said that tensions between the superpowers "cannot be removed by the personal relationship between two leaders, and it is not in our interest to create the impression that they can be." One of the most sensible men in the Senate, Alan Simpson, Republican of Wyoming, demurred. "I don't care if they go fly-fishing in Iceland," he said. "It's worthwhile."

The President shared this view. It was true that his schedule had not been designed with a surprise summit meeting in mind. On September 30, the day Reagan announced that he and Gorbachev would meet, he also delivered a major speech before the annual joint meeting of the World Bank and the International Monetary Fund at 11 A.M.; he met in rapid succession with President Virgilio Barco Vargas of Colombia, Finance Minister Noburo Takeshita of Japan, and a group of senators and congressmen to discuss energy policy, and then delivered remarks to a group of Eagles, as those who have contributed at least ten thousand dollars to the Republican Senate and House campaign committees are called.

September 30 was also the last day of fiscal year 1986, and the government would run out of money at midnight unless Congress passed a continuing resolution appropriating funds. The resolution passed both houses before the zero hour and the President signed it. The Senate, meanwhile, was debating a veto of economic sanctions against South Africa, a measure that the Administration opposed on grounds that it would diminish American influence on the South African government and create economic hardship for the very people in South Africa that the sanctions were ostensibly designed to help.

Despite this heavy schedule, the President made his momentous announcement and preparations for the summit went ahead. Over the next ten days, Reagan was briefed and advised in a round of meetings, and every afternoon disappeared into the family quarters bearing the thick briefing books that constituted his "homework."

Final decisions on positions and objectives were reached in sessions involving the President, Shultz, Poindexter, and myself. First, we would discuss human rights in the Soviet Union, including divided families (an issue that had yielded results in Geneva), emigration of Soviet Jews, and the status of dissidents. The President insisted that we work on this issue quietly and discreetly; he felt he could make something happen by talking calmly to Gorbachev and believed that publicity would ruin his chances of success.

Second, we wanted an agreement to concentrate on the reduction of intercontinental ballistic missiles and the START talks. As long as the U.S. and the U.S.S.R. continued to target each other with weapons of mass destruction, the reduction in intermediate ballistic missiles in Europe meant little. Obviously such a reduction would have great symbolic and moral value, but the President's ultimate objective was the speediest possible elimination of strategic nuclear forces.

We were confident that some progress could be made on this and other questions at Reykjavík. We did not, of course, know what was in Gorbachev's mind, or even whether his power to make agreements on behalf of the Soviet Union was absolute. It seemed unlikely, as some of the President's more doctrinaire critics suspected, that he had convened the talks in order to wreck them for propaganda purposes. We believed, for all the reasons I have stated, that the new regime in Moscow genuinely wanted a reduction in arms that would relieve the pressure on the Soviet economy and social system.

The Soviet side sent us the names of people who would be with Gorbachev. George Shultz suggested that he, John Poindex-

ter, and I form the President's first line of support in the negotiations, with Paul Nitze, Ambassador Arthur Hartman, and
Assistant Secretary of State Ridgway standing by as specialists on
whom the President could call when he needed technical support. In one-on-one talks between Reagan and Gorbachev, as at
Geneva, nobody would be present except interpreters and note-
takers.

After extensive consultations with her Friend, Mrs. Reagan
decided that she would not accompany her husband to Iceland.
At first it appeared that Raisa Gorbachev would not be coming
either, but then the Soviet First Lady changed her mind. Mrs.
Reagan decided that she would stick to her original decision. She
did not, she said, wish to give the appearance of competing with
Mrs. Gorbachev in a way that would detract from the seriousness
of the meeting between their two husbands. This was a wise and
commendable decision.

Mrs. Reagan also consulted with her Friend as to the best day
for the Presidential departure, and the astrologer informed us
that Thursday, October 9, was the most auspicious date. We wrote
it into the schedule.

Air Force One took off from Andrews Air Force Base at 9:45
A.M. The President read his briefing material in solitude as the
plane passed over the Atlantic. Despite the four-hour time difference between Washington and Reykjavík, he would be rested
for the meeting on Saturday. The Friday schedule provided for
a maximum of quiet time in which the President could mentally
sort out the enormous amount of information he had absorbed
and decide how he was going to act on it.

I spent part of the first full day in Iceland revisiting the scenes
of my Marine Corps tour on the island. While the presummit
briefings were in progress at the White House I had run across
General P. X. Kelley, the Commandant of the Marine Corps. "Say,
you wouldn't happen to have an old map over at headquarters
that would show where my outfit was in '41, would you?" I asked.
With commendable Marine spirit, Kelley had turned the Marine
historical staff loose on this request and produced an impressive
looseleaf binder filled with maps, charts, and descriptions and
rosters of unit locations in Iceland during my days there.

Bill Henkel's advance team recruited a most distinguished volunteer guide in the person of Giers Hallgrimsson, a former Prime Minister of Iceland. With the Secret Service in tow, Hallgrimsson and I set out with a driver to rediscover the scenes of my youth. Much had changed in forty-five years. High-rise apartment buildings now stood on the heights above the capital where our battery had pitched its tents, and the old Marine Corps maps were of limited help in finding features that had vanished. But finally the driver pointed to a low concrete structure that was half-hidden in the tundra. "That's a machine-gun emplacement," I said, recognizing after all those years for what purpose it had been built. Consulting Kelley's maps, I decided that Marines of my own unit might possibly have dug the hole. The concrete must have been poured by the Army units who replaced us in '42: we Marines, lacking anything as fancy as concrete, had used sandbags. Standing on this quaint relic of World War II, I looked out to sea as I had done so many times as a young lieutenant and remembered the good fellows I had known in this place. The icy gray waters of the Atlantic approaches were as empty now as they had been then.

The views were glorious from Hovde House, the building in Reykjavík where Reagan and Gorbachev were to meet. Its high windows commanded vistas of the harbor, the ocean beyond, and the clean Nordic architecture of the town.

On the first morning, a Saturday, Reagan and Gorbachev greeted each other amiably and with every indication of good feeling. The aftermath of the Daniloff case was still in the air— we still planned to expel the twenty-five Soviet intelligence operatives who had been carrying out their activities under diplomatic cover, and Daniloff himself was present in Reykjavík, covering the summit for his magazine. On the other hand, the U.S. Navy had offered assistance to a Soviet submarine that had caught fire at sea off Bermuda, and the professional courtesy and human concern on both sides had shown once again that the two great adversaries were capable of cooperation.

The first session produced little. Gorbachev read his opening statement, then he and the President retired to a small room and discussed human rights questions quietly together, as Reagan had wished. They sat at a table so that Gorbachev could spread out his notes; Reagan worked mainly from memory. At 11:30, Shevardnadze and Shultz were summoned into the room and the discussions continued while the remainder of the staff waited upstairs.

At 12:30 the President and his party drove back to the chancery of the American Embassy. The Soviets had offered a proposal. Nine people were crowded into a small secure area to examine it so as to be able to summarize it for the President, who was scheduled for a brief rest before luncheon. But Reagan, finding himself alone, surprised us by joining us in our cramped quarters. The Soviet proposition had possibilities. The disarmament experts—Paul Nitze, Ken Adelman, Colonel Robert Linhard of the NSC staff, Assistant Secretary of Defense Richard Pearle, and Max Kampelman—would work through luncheon to come up with a response.

The acute shortage of time was a problem that everyone felt. Shultz made the innovative suggestion that each side designate two teams—one for disarmament questions, the other for all other questions—to go over the issues in detail during the night to try to narrow the differences. The President approved this approach and agreed to propose it to Gorbachev at the afternoon session.

At 3:30, Reagan and Gorbachev returned to the table. The President's opening remarks, with interpretation, consumed a full hour. Gorbachev did not seem pleased by Reagan's surprise suggestion that the staffs stay up all night, if necessary, to prepare the next day's negotiations, but he agreed to it. The meeting broke up at 5:43.

As I said good-bye to him at the door, Gorbachev laughed and gave me a hearty handshake. "Now, we've given you plenty of work for the night, Mr. Chief of Staff," he said jovially. "You have much to do." From the look in his eye and the tone of his voice I surmised that his actual words in Russian might have been saltier than the interpreter let on.

The staffs on both sides began work at 8 P.M. The disarmament group got down to serious business about ten o'clock and broke off at two in the morning in a deadlock. They agreed to meet again at 3 A.M. and continue until 6:20. Marshal Sergei Akhromeyev, head of the Soviet team, was sixty-three years old, while our own Paul Nitze was seventy-nine; neither showed any strain in keeping up with their far younger colleagues, and in fact worked through to late Sunday evening without any sleep at all. It made me proud of my age group. The other team, under Roz Ridgway, dealt with less vexing technical issues, but nevertheless worked without interruption for five and a half hours, made some progress, and agreed to meet again in daylight to resolve differences.

On Saturday evening the President, Shultz, Poindexter, and I dined together at the embassy residence, where Reagan was staying. It was a very informal dinner. The President wore a sweater and was relaxed and in his normal good humor as we discussed the Soviet proposals and our response. We broke up at nine o'clock and the President turned in early. He had a strenuous day before him.

On Sunday morning there was another session between the principals, but it got nowhere. Shultz and Shevardnadze met with the experts from 2 to 3 P.M. The Soviets were now saying they could accept the United States proposal on intermediate missiles; that is, 100 in Europe, 100 in the United States, and 100 in Asia. However, Shevardnadze had another idea: 100 missiles globally for each side—zero in Europe, 100 in the U.S., and 100 in Asia.

This was the "zero option," feared by some geopolitical thinkers as a formula for giving the Soviets, with their overwhelming numerical superiority in conventional forces, a tactical and strategic advantage in Europe. The NATO doctrine for the defense of Western Europe against a conventional Soviet attack had always been based on the use of tactical nuclear weapons against superior ground forces, and many believed that this policy had deterred such a Soviet attack and kept the peace for forty years.

The President thought in more spacious terms. He liked Shevardnadze's proposal immediately because of its symbolism: it called for the total elimination of a whole class of nuclear weapons from at least one region of the world. But he did not respond immediately, so as to give Shultz time to consult with European leaders to see if such an arrangement was acceptable to them.

On the ABM treaty, the Soviets were adamant on a ten-year extension of compliance by both sides. Shultz didn't want to accept that. We countered with a zero-option proposal of our own. This provided for five years of research, testing, and development of antimissile systems such as SDI, but linked such development with a simultaneous 50-percent reduction in strategic nuclear weapons and their total elimination at the end of a second five-year period. This meant that the world would be free of strategic nuclear weapons by the year 1996. Either side could then deploy defenses against missiles.

Gorbachev pounced on the word "deploy." He asked, "Why do we want to deploy an antimissile system if all missiles are eliminated?" The answer was "insurance."

The President was enthusiastic about this imaginative proposal, and going into the final session we knew that the record would show, no matter what the outcome of the summit, that the United States had offered to go to zero—to dismantle all its strategic nuclear weapons. We were calling the Soviets' bluff. If they accepted, nuclear missiles would vanish from the earth.

The key to agreement was SDI; without the insurance policy that it provided, the President could never ask Congress and the American people to trust the Soviets, and no treaty could win ratification. Everyone on both sides knew that. The President had offered to share the system with the Soviets once it was perfected, so that they would have their insurance also.

The summit had been scheduled to end at noon on Sunday, but it went back into session at 3:30 P.M. We presented our proposal. The Soviet response was discouraging. They wanted to limit SDI testing to the laboratory and retain short-range nuclear missiles.

During a break for consultations, the two sides reconvened in separate rooms. Our discussion was animated, urgent, informal, and very tense. The negotiating team split into groups, and experts drifted back and forth. The noise level was high in both languages; all faces were deadly serious. No one sat down.

The President approved a proposal carpentered on the spot: How about eliminating all ballistic missiles by 1996 while testing of SDI continued under ABM rules? The Russians were also talking this over.

At this point the President beckoned me to him.

Don, this is taking too long, he said in a murmur.

He wanted to get started back to Washington—he had planned on having Sunday dinner at home. Now we were talking of staying another night if necessary. Reagan was annoyed and disappointed.

"I don't see how it can last much longer, Mr. President," I said. "But we've got to hang in there—if we can get this package, it'll be worth it."

I was telling the President what he already knew, but sometimes such reinforcement is needed. Reagan sighed and nodded in weary acquiescence. I did not persuade or influence him; he intended all along to stick it out until the end. He had just been letting off a little steam.

Nevertheless his exasperation and weariness were showing. He may have meant them to show. The two leaders had been doing most of the talking, thinking, and worrying over two long days of intensive negotiations.

Some of the press was led to believe after the summit was over that President Reagan had not been a full and energetic participant in the negotiations. That could not have been the impression of anyone possessed of his senses who was present at the sessions in Hovde House. Reagan and Gorbachev spent nine hours and forty-eight minutes in face-to-face negotiations. Moreover, the process of hammering out new U.S. positions amounted to a negotiation within a negotiation. It was a tumultuous, tiring ordeal, with experts clamoring for the President's attention as they advanced their favorite views. Being experts, they seldom agreed and even more seldom budged from dogma. After reconciling their advice into a new proposal, the President would take it to Gorbachev, who had been passing through what I suppose was a similar (though probably more decorous) experience with his own people.

Now, with both leaders on the edge of exhaustion, our final

proposal was ready. The President's determination returned to him. Reagan and Shultz went over the proposal in detail and went back into the final session with Gorbachev and Shevardnadze at 5:32 P.M.

That meeting lasted until 6:30. As was later reported, the two leaders made progress on regional, bilateral, and human rights issues. They also agreed in principle to the Soviet proposal for a reduction in intermediate missiles to zero in Europe, 100 in Asia, and 100 in the United States. They were for eliminating strategic nuclear weapons in two five-year periods while research, testing, and development of SDI continued. Nothing was said about confining such development to the laboratory, as Gorbachev had originally proposed in his letter to Reagan.

What, Reagan asked Gorbachev, had he meant by the reference in his letter to "the elimination of all strategic forces"?

"I meant I would favor eliminating all nuclear weapons," Gorbachev replied.

All nuclear weapons? Reagan said. Well, Mikhail, that's exactly what I've been talking about all along. That's what we have long wanted to do—get rid of all nuclear weapons. That's always been my goal.

"Then why don't we agree on it?" Gorbachev asked.

We should, Reagan said. That's what I've been trying to tell you.

It was a historic moment. The two leaders had brought the world to one of its great turning points. Both understood this very clearly.

Then came the impasse. Mikhail Gorbachev said, "I agree. But this must be done in conjunction with a ten-year extension of the ABM treaty and a ban on the development and testing of SDI outside the laboratory."

Outside the laboratory. Those words negated all that had been agreed upon. As soon as they were uttered, Reagan and Gorbachev were down from the mountaintop and right back where they had started.

Reagan, astonished by this sudden reversal, said, Absolutely not. I am willing to discuss all details, including the timing, of a plan to eliminate all nuclear weapons in conjunction with a plan to reduce conventional forces to a state of balance. But I will not discuss anything that gives you the upper hand by eliminating SDI.

Gorbachev did not reply. After a long silence, Reagan assumed that the Soviet leader had nothing more to say. Thereupon he closed his briefing book and stood up. Gorbachev seemed startled by the President's action and remained in his chair for a moment in puzzlement. Then he rose to his feet also. The summit at Reykjavík was over.

As I came down the main staircase in Hovde House, they emerged into the hall below. I remember their haggard features and the hoarse tone of their voices.

"There is still time, Mr. President," Gorbachev was saying. "We could go back inside to the bargaining table."

Reagan, tight-lipped, replied, I think not.

Their good-byes were stiff and formal. I did not know what had happened between the two men, but it was obvious that neither was happy with the other.

As Gorbachev passed by me, he gave me a hard look. "You should speak to the President, Mr. Chief of Staff," he said.

I replied, "Mr. General Secretary, the two of you have been speaking to each other for two days. Whatever the President has decided is what the President will do."

As Reagan and Gorbachev emerged from the front door, I hurried through a side door and got behind the television cameras to the waiting cars. The dim arctic twilight added to the discouraging atmosphere. In the limousine Reagan was somber, and for the first time since I had know him I felt that I was in the presence of a truly disappointed man.

I leaned over and tapped Ronald Reagan on the knee and said, "Buck up, Mr. President. I don't know what went on in there, but you're going to have to meet with the staff in a few minutes. It won't look well for you to be seen so grim and angry."

Reagan sat in silence for another moment. Then he said, Don, we came so close. It's just such a shame.

He placed his thumb and forefinger less than a half inch apart and added, We were *that* close to an agreement.

His frustration was palpable.

Laboratory, laboratory, laboratory, the President said, repeating the word over and over again. Then he went on: It even got to a personal level, Don. I said to Gorbachev, 'I think we've developed a good relationship. I'm asking you personally to give me this. You've got your ten years; I understand why you need it. But I promised the American people that I wouldn't trade away their future security, which is SDI.' But Gorbachev wouldn't give in even to my personal plea. At one point I even wrote, 'Am I doing the right thing?' on a card and shoved it over to Shultz. He wrote back, 'Stick to it.'

I tried to console Reagan. "Well, Mr. President," I said, "we have to believe that there'll come another day. But for now, we've got a lot to think about."

Reagan nodded, but his gloom did not lift. The limousine took us to the American Embassy. The President managed to be genial and gracious as he thanked the embassy staff and said good-bye, but it was obvious that he did not wish to tarry. As quickly as we could, we reassembled the motorcade and left for Keflavík Airport, where *Air Force One* waited on the runway.

The drive from Reykjavík to the airport took about forty-five minutes. En route, in that space of time, a speech was drafted for the President to deliver to an audience of American servicemen and their families.

It was apparent even while we were still at the embassy that the summit had blown up. But the President had done the only possible thing in refusing to give up SDI. Now his action, and the reason for it, had to be explained to the world. I called Pat Buchanan, David Chew, Dennis Thomas, Tom Dawson, and Larry Speakes together. "Look, we're going to have to put a speech together for the President at Keflavík that reflects some of what has happened today but doesn't reflect any kind of defeat," I told them. "Let's work fast."

I rode to the airport with the President. For much of the way he talked about his disappointment, going over the details of his discussions with Gorbachev. His spirits were so low that I finally tried to cheer him up by telling a joke. The only one I could think of was about horses. The President, true to form, responded with a horse story of his own, describing how a hay barn on his place at Malibu had burned down years before just after he had cut and stored eight hundred bales of hay inside. As he described leading the horses from the barn and fighting the flames, his spirits rose. I told him how, when I had first known Ann as a young girl, she had impressed me with her superb horsemanship, and how, when I came up from Quantico, I had called on her at the stable where she kept her mounts, off Massachusetts Avenue, near Rock Creek Park. Reagan countered with a story of his own about fine riders, movie stunt men, and others whom he had known, and we spent the last ten or fifteen minutes of the journey talking about horses.

By the time the motorcade arrived at Keflavík, the revised speech was ready. We huddled with the President around a table in an anteroom, going over the draft, which had been hastily printed by hand.

Despite the cheering conversation in the car, Reagan was still subdued and pensive. He shuffled the speech cards, changing the order of his remarks, then shuffled them again; his mind was elsewhere. Then the discipline of a lifetime returned, and he began to study his lines. He had only a few minutes to learn them. He was still reading intently when the strains of "Hail to the Chief" came to our ears.

"You're on, Mr. President," Bill Henkel said.

The President looked around the table at each of us in turn, nodded, squared his shoulders, and literally marched the twenty steps to the platform that had been set up on the airport tarmac. He was greeted by wild applause from the little crowd of Americans—good-looking, neatly dressed young men and women holding up their children to see him, waving flags, shouting, and clapping. Their welcome rejuvenated the President. Color returned to his face, his smile came back, and he read his speech in a strong, confident voice. It was a flawless performance.

The press, reacting according to its nature, seized on the dramatic question: What had gone wrong between Gorbachev and Reagan? That something had gone wrong was crystal-clear. Secretary of State George Shultz, a somber man anyway, had seemed funereal in his brief appearances on television immediately after the meetings. As one official put it, "I have never seen Shultz exude through his words, the pace of his comments, and his facial expressions, such disappointment and defeat." It is no wonder that Shultz looked sad and tired; he had been present at one of the most devastating disappointments in history. He had seen total nuclear disarmament in the grasp of his President, then seen it slip away.

However understandable Shultz's dejection was in human terms, we could not permit one man's disappointment to symbolize the summit. As for me, I did not think that America or the hopes of the world had been defeated at Reykjavík. On the contrary, I believed that President Reagan had preserved us from defeat and made a future victory possible by standing firmly on his principles.

I told the press as much in a brief on-camera interview at Keflavík. But it was clear that the tendency already existed to blame the U.S. and the President for what had happened. Aboard *Air Force One*, the President retired to his quarters.

As soon as I left the President, I gathered the staff—Speakes, Buchanan, Thomas, and Poindexter. "This summit must not be seen or portrayed as a defeat," I told them. "We've got to turn any such perception around, starting now."

Poindexter and Speakes went aft to talk to the press pool who were aboard *Air Force One*, spreading the message that the President was disappointed that he had not been able to achieve a breakthrough, but that his firmness would pay dividends for the future. Poindexter talked to the press for an hour and forty minutes and never put a foot wrong. Nevertheless the correspondents in the press pool were skeptical. Their reports from *Air Force One* described Poindexter as being tired, unshaven, and discouraged, and suggested that much had been lost at Reykjavík.

Subsequent coverage heaped blame on Reagan for the breakdown of a summit from which few had been willing to predict useful results before it was held. An interviewer for *USA Today*, summarizing the main line of the President's critics, asked me,

"What do you say to those who say the superpowers came so close, but then walked away because Reagan didn't want to give away his SDI 'toy'?"

I replied, "Jack Kennedy said, 'I'd like to put a man on the moon,' and a lot of people looked at that and said, 'Impossible, that's a toy. It's a dream.' Who are these scientists who are saying we can't do it? How do they know? President Reagan thinks it'll work; the Soviets must think it'll work, or else they wouldn't be trying to kill it."

As the President pointed out, the Soviets had a very good idea of the potential of SDI because they were developing their own strategic defense system in programs that went, in Reagan's words, "well beyond research, even to deployment." In a televised speech on the day after his return from Iceland, the President described the opportunity that had been lost: "This may have been the most sweeping and important arms-reduction proposal in the history of the world. But it wasn't good enough for Mr. Gorbachev. He wanted more. . . . He knew that [insisting that the development of SDI be limited to the laboratory] meant killing SDI altogether, which has been the Soviet goal from the start."

Later, the President repeated that he and Gorbachev had come nearer than anyone else had ever done to abolishing all weapons of mass destruction, and that it had been the Soviet leader whose nerve had failed at the climactic moment. And he added, "Far from being a defeat, Reykjavík was a milepost, a turning point in disarmament negotiations. It will lead to eventual agreements. It is not the end, but a furthering of the process."

Few among the knowing men and women who wrote the news, or provided the "background" that informs the news, believed that Ronald Reagan knew what he was talking about. But as events have proved, he was triumphantly correct.

· 18 ·

The Definition of Chaos

By the time the Iran-Contra affair broke into the news in the first week of November, the perception of Reykjavík as a failure brought on by the amateurism of the American President and his intransigence over SDI had begun to change. This was the direct result of the new policy in media relations that we had been struggling to create at the White House. I told the President that the United States had nothing to gain by speculation and doubt and the publication of slanted assessments by "senior officials" and "knowledgeable sources" and "White House aides who are familiar with the President's thinking." It was time to test the new system. Let the President himself, together with Shultz and Poindexter and Regan and all the other eyewitnesses, tell the real story. Reagan granted blanket approval for all senior officials who had been with him in Reykjavík to discuss the summit with the press *on the record*.

If this onslaught of frankness did not convince or silence the President's detractors, it at least put the American version of events at Reykjavík squarely before the voters in the three weeks between the summit and the midterm elections. Republican losses in the Senate (eight seats, enough to put the Democrats in the majority) and House (five seats) were far less severe than was normal for the party in power in an incumbent President's second term.* This result was heartening not only because it was

*Truman saw the loss of five Senate seats and twenty-nine House seats in 1950. The

good politically, but also because it demonstrated that it was possible, even desirable, for the highest officials in the land to stand up in the light of day and speak frankly and directly to the people through the media. I was under no illusion that the leak, the tip, the clandestine telephone call, and the purloined document had been driven out of the White House like the snakes out of Ireland, never to return. But we had changed the policy once and for all, and the fact that we had done so would shortly save the Presidency.

The Iran-Contra scandal started to break on November 4, only twenty-two days after Reykjavík. The news of the diversion of funds to the Nicaraguan freedom fighters from the arms sales to Iran was released to the press on November 25 by the President himself. The Attorney General of the United States followed him to the podium and told the assembled reporters everything that the investigation had so far discovered about the affair. This policy of total openness was the only one possible in the circumstances. If this seems obvious in retrospect, it was not so obvious at the time to some of those who were most deeply involved, and the old pattern of leaks and secret contacts with favored journalists persisted at the margins of the situation.

At the center, however, we were determined to tell the whole truth from first to last. The success of the campaign to explain Reykjavík was an important factor in the decision to go public with Iran-Contra at once and keep on going public. No other alternative was ever considered or proposed to the President by me. Any other course of action might very well have led to the fall of his Presidency.

On January 6, 1987, I gave the President a memorandum summarizing the staff's recommendations on planning for the year ahead. "With respect to Iran," I wrote, "our focus should now be on *one theme*—getting all the facts out to the American people and setting things right. . . . Success in handling Iran will require an aggressive and coordinated plan to advance all the issues on your agenda."

---

losses for Eisenhower in 1958 were thirteen and forty-seven; for Johnson in 1966, four and forty-seven, and for Ford in 1974 (after Nixon's resignation), five and forty-eight.

Exposing the facts and getting the scandal behind us was of supreme relevancy at the moment. But the moment would pass, while the abiding national issues remained. All predictions to the contrary notwithstanding, it appeared that the deficit for fiscal year 1987 would be reduced by more than 18 percent even without the provisions of the Gramm-Rudman-Hollings Act. We were estimating in early January that the figure would be down to $173 billion from $225 billion in fiscal year 1986. Although Gramm-Rudman-Hollings mandated a further reduction to $108 billion in fiscal year 1988, the initial cut was a significant achievement, not only for its arithmetic but for the new spirit of accommodation between Congress and the Administration that it signified. (As a matter of record, the deficit turned out to be $150.4 billion, a decline of more than $70 billion from fiscal year 1986.)

The President would have a natural opportunity in the State of the Union speech, scheduled for delivery on January 27, to stake out his ground on the budget and the deficit and on other domestic issues, such as catastrophic health insurance, welfare reform, trade, and farm policy. Foreign-policy issues included arms reductions, SDI, defense, relations with the U.S.S.R. (including a meeting with Gorbachev), Third World debt, Middle East policy, and the charged issue of aid to the Contras.

I advised the President that he must choose a few key issues on which to concentrate his energies and pursue them vigorously, as in any other year of his Presidency. This year was one in which his every action and gesture would be seen through the prism of the Iran-Contra affair. "There is a very real need," I wrote, "to 'take the message to the people' and demonstrate that you are not mired down in the Iran fallout by doing more events outside Washington."

The restrained language of that last sentence does not convey the full force of my conviction that the President's inactivity in the storm of prosecutorial criticism that threatened to engulf his Administration was undesirable. I became surer with the passage of every day that he must be more visible, more confiding to the people, and more accessible to the press. Only the President can demonstrate the vitality of his Presidency.

Ronald Reagan understood this, yet he remained in the White House, isolated and remote. As I have described in the early pages of this book, the President's public appearances had always been arranged with the First Lady's approval, and it was impossible to change this through appeals to logic. As Mike Deaver had advised, we had humored Mrs. Reagan. And by humoring her, we had given her control. No one except me, and least of all the President, was disposed to interfere with that.

The frustration of dealing with a situation in which the schedule of the President of the United States was determined by occult prognostications was very great—far greater than any other I had known in nearly forty-five years of working life. I thought that the President should go out to meet the world, and kept telling him so. The First Lady's Friend in San Francisco had predicted on the basis of astrology that harm would come to Reagan if he went out of the White House—or even, on certain days, outdoors. All press conferences were also subject to the Friend's approval.

"Maybe your Friend is wrong," I would suggest. Mrs. Reagan did not think so: her Friend had predicted the Hinckley assassination attempt nearly to the day, had foreseen the explosion of a bomb in the luggage compartment of the TWA plane that was damaged in flight over Greece, and had been right about other things as well, including a premonition of "dire events" in November and December 1987—that is, the Iran-Contra scandal.

Only a very stubborn man could have believed that reason would prevail in a case such as this one. Nevertheless I persisted. My arguments apparently had enough effect to create the belief that my influence with the President had become too great to be tolerated.

The Tower Board's report, the last barrier to my resignation as Chief of Staff, came out on Thursday, February 26, 1987.

"There is no need for slashing of wrists," John Tower, the chairman, told the President when they met at ten o'clock that morning in the Cabinet Room. Tower assured Reagan that the report was straightforward, honest, and free of partisanship. The Board had found no evidence that the President had participated in a cover-up, or authorized one.

Tower and his colleagues on the President's Special Review Board planned to release the report to the press at eleven o'clock, without giving the President, who had appointed them, the opportunity to read it in advance. We had been informed only the night before that the board would proceed in this brusque and unprecedented fashion. I had never heard of anything like this happening before in connection with the report of any Presidential board or commission.

I told David Abshire, who had agreed to this strange procedure without consulting me, that I thought it was unfair and demeaning to the President in addition to being unheard of. The Board expected the President to appear with them before a press conference when they released the report, but he would not be able to answer a single question about it because he would not have read it. In effect, the press would read the report at the same time Reagan did. He would be put in the position of standing by in a state of ignorance while Tower and the others answered questions about some of his most pivotal actions as President. How could he know the accuracy of what was being said? How could he defend himself?

Abshire refused to see my point. It would be better, he said, if the President did not see the report before it was released. In that way, any impression that the President had influenced the report or previewed it would be avoided. Nobody, said Abshire, would be able to say that the President had been given an undue advantage. I was astonished.

"*Undue advantage?*" I said. "He is the President of the United States! He commissioned this report!"

This was my last burst of anger in defense of President Reagan. It availed me not at all. Abshire had been converted.

In the Cabinet Room on Thursday morning, Tower and Ed Muskie and Brent Scowcroft assured the President that they had worked together in a collegial atmosphere and that the report expressed their unanimous view of what had happened in the

Iran-Contra affair.* Tower summarized the report, emphasizing the Board's recommendations to the President.

The President asked about the money realized from the sale of military matériel to Iran. Tower said that a large amount appeared to be missing, but the Board did not know where these funds had gone. Reagan asked about the amounts the Iranians paid for weapons. Tower supplied the figures the Board had compiled.

Peter Wallison asked, "Would you comment on arms and hostages?"

Tower replied that the Board had concluded that arms had been traded for hostages; this had been discussed at all meetings between Oliver North and the Iranians.

The President interrupted. Speaking in an emphatic tone of voice, he said, I'm the one who makes policy in matters like this, and I can definitely tell you that trading arms for hostages was not our policy.

"There's nothing in the report to say that you had determined such a policy, Mr. President," Tower said. "We found that you were not adequately informed by your subordinates."

Scowcroft, referring to the scenario described to the President by McFarlane in Geneva, remarked that a situation in which an aircraft loaded with weapons for Iran waited on the runway pending the release of American hostages could hardly be seen as anything but a swap of arms for hostages. The freighters had been ordered not to take off until they were told by prearranged signal that the hostages were airborne in American custody.

Considering that the discussion lasted for no more than thirty minutes and involved so many people, it covered a remarkable amount of ground. The report itself has been so exhaustively examined that there is no need here to summarize all of its findings. Essentially, the Tower Board recommended no changes in NSC procedures, on grounds that the problem created by Mc-

---

*Besides the President, the Vice President, and myself, those present from the White House staff were Frank Carlucci, the new National Security Advisor; Peter Wallison, the Counsel to the President; and Rhett Dawson and W. Clark McFadden II, the staff director and general counsel, respectively, of the Tower Board.

Farlane, Poindexter, and North had arisen because established procedures had not been followed. Their deception had not been discovered in time or properly discussed and authorized because they had kept inadequate or false records with the purpose of concealing their activities from the President and others.

Vice President Bush asked about Poindexter and North, and was told that their refusal to testify had inconvenienced the Board, but the paper trail was so good that this had made little difference to the result. The Board had considered McFarlane to be a cooperative and credible witness. McFarlane had made his first appearance before the Board without benefit of counsel, but was afterward always accompanied by his assiduous lawyer, Leonard J. Garment, a Washington attorney who had been Counsel to the President in the last Nixon years.

The President asked for opinions as to the likelihood of criminal prosecution of Poindexter and North. W. Clark McFadden II, the Board's general counsel, replied that it was difficult to say whether their activities had violated the Boland Amendment or any law. "We've brought out about as much as can be brought out," Scowcroft said. "There are no great bombshells waiting to go off out there."

Then what do they fear? asked the President, referring to Poindexter and North.

Nobody present could answer the question.

George Bush wanted to know about the allegations that North had been close to the President.

"North grossly exaggerated his position vis-à-vis the President," Tower replied. "We don't know why he did it; probably he was trying to impress the other side."

One of the most important points made by the Board concerned the danger of having the NSC carry out covert actions when it lacked the professional expertise to do so. The amateurism of McFarlane, Poindexter, and North when they attempted to behave like intelligence operatives, combined with their astounding gullibility, had virtually foreordained failure. Operations of this kind should only be undertaken by the intelligence services, and then only under the strictest guidelines. Permitting the NSC to carry out secret operations for which it had neither the trained personnel nor the logistical resources created an intolerably high risk of failure and exposure, with a devastating potential for embarrassment of the President and damage to national security and policy. As Tower told Reagan, "It brings it right into the White House."

How then to control the NSC staff and prevent something like this from ever happening again? Members of the Board said that there should be better note-taking and better record-keeping in the NSC. They suggested that the Chief of Staff could play a role in tightening up procedures, so that complete knowledge of NSC activities would be immediately accessible to the President and anyone with whom he wanted to share it.

Frank Carlucci asked if the Board meant that the National Security Advisor should henceforth report to the President through the Chief of Staff.

Tower, speaking distinctly, said, "No. *Leave it as it is.*" [Emphasis added.]

"Well, you can't have it both ways," Carlucci replied. "The Chief of Staff can't control the paper if he's not in charge."

This exchange confirmed that McFarlane and Poindexter had both operated in complete independence of the Chief of Staff during my time in the White House. It was heartening to hear the reality described by men who had studied the situation in unprecedented detail and concluded that this truth was self-evident. But it was rather late in the day.

I had remained virtually silent throughout this meeting, confining myself to copious note-taking. It was Peter Wallison who asked the Sixty-Four-Dollar Question.

"What about the charges in *Newsweek* and elsewhere that the Chief of Staff was in on the cover-up—is that true?"

John Tower replied, "No."

Tower continued, speaking directly to the President. "We only have one paragraph on Regan in the whole report," he said. "People are going to be disappointed when they see that there's nothing sensational about Don Regan."

As Tower spoke, I had not read the paragraph in question:

More than any other Chief of Staff in recent memory,
[Regan] asserted personal control over the White House
staff and sought to extend this control to the National
Security Advisor. He was personally active in national security affairs and attended almost all of the relevant meetings regarding the Iran initiative. He, as much as anyone,
should have insisted that an orderly process be observed.
In addition, he especially should have ensured that plans
were made for handling any public disclosure of the initiative. He must bear primary responsibility for the chaos
that descended upon the White House when such disclosure did occur.*

Let me speak plainly in response to this paragraph. It is mistaken in its assumptions, defective in its evidence, and wrong in
its conclusions.

The Tower Board never interviewed a single member of the
White House staff besides myself about anything, much less my
methods of management, and never asked me whether I had
"sought to extend [personal] control over the National Security
Advisor." Lacking such control, no Chief of Staff (see Carlucci's
comment on p. 363) could have effectively "insisted that an orderly process be observed" because he would have been giving
orders to a man who did not work for him. The only plan I had
for "handling any public disclosure of the initiative" was to discover and tell the whole truth. As to the responsibility for the
chaos that descended on the White House, that appears to have
been written in the stars, and I am glad to let historians decide
the issue on the basis of all the evidence. It should make a diverting footnote on contemporary manners and the constants of
human behavior under the combined stress of failure and accusation.

With regard to the witnesses and other sources on whom the
Board presumably based its conclusion about my role, I am content to wait until the full process of the law provides an answer

*Report of the President's Special Review Board, pp. IV–11

to the President's question: What do they fear? The President went on to say, in the same conversation in which he asked that question, that he supposed that the lawyers would infer that some bad news was coming, and they would want to protect their clients from it. Leonard Garment, McFarlane's lawyer, has acknowledged that he constructed what may be called a "Washington defense" for his client, creating diversions in the press designed to build sympathy for McFarlane and diminish the appearance of culpability as a means of creating a favorable environment for any eventual trial. In former times witnesses who told all to save themselves were said to have turned "state's witness." Turning "media's witness" is an invention of post-Watergate Washington.

On March 11, 1988, in a plea-bargain arrangement with Independent Counsel Lawrence E. Walsh, McFarlane pleaded guilty to four federal misdemeanors based on charges that he had misled Congress and withheld information from Congress concerning efforts to support the Contras. Five days later, Poindexter, North, Secord, and Hakim were indicted by a federal grand jury on felony charges of conspiracy, theft, and fraud. It was expected that McFarlane would appear as a witness for the prosecution.

In any case, the President's question will likely be answered in due course in the courtroom. Perhaps it will then be more obvious to all why the architects of the Iran-Contra affair and their apologists worked so hard to throw the blame for their actions onto others.

On that morning in the Oval Office when John Tower told me of the existence of the "single paragraph about Regan" in the Tower Board's report, he had smiled wryly at the President, then turned and smiled briefly at me. I did not smile back. By then I knew the difference between good news and bad news.

· 19 ·

A Public Burning

On February 23, the Monday before the release of the Tower Board's report, the President and I had agreed, in the painful conversation in the Oval Office that I have described, that I would resign as Chief of Staff soon after the Tower report was issued. No specific date or time for my departure was discussed. Later that same day, the President had listened to suggestions for dealing with the political consequences of this document from a group of leading Republicans that included Senator Paul Laxalt, Jim Baker, Dick Wirthlin, and Tom C. Korologos, a specialist in congressional relations who had worked in the White House during the Nixon Administration. The atmosphere was strained. Like nearly everyone else, these men had read the stories leaked by Deaver, Stu Spencer, and others predicting my imminent departure as Chief of Staff as a result of my differences with Mrs. Reagan and the fallout of the Iran-Contra affair.

Near the end of this meeting, I told the President's visitors that the questions that were being raised about my future would be answered after the release of the Tower report. Sometime during the following week, I said, the President and I would discuss my future and he would decide what we were going to do and when we were going to do it. The next morning the media, quoting anonymous sources, reported that I would resign soon after the report was issued, and suggested that the President, in the words of the *Washington Times,* "has accepted that the gruff 68-year-old Chief of Staff must go."

Between February 23 and the release of the Tower report, the President and I did not discuss the timing of my departure. He seemed loath to raise the subject and I did not see why I should do so. He knew that I would go or stay at his pleasure, and had only to express his wishes in order for me to sign my letter of resignation and depart. Neither the President nor anyone else had raised the question of a successor, and I had volunteered no suggestions in this regard.

Our days were busy. The President had decided to speak to the nation about the findings of the Iran-Contra report, hold a press conference, and deliver a major foreign-policy speech, all in March. As usual, no dates for these events were set in conversations with President Reagan. I discussed the schedule with Mrs. Reagan, who consulted her Friend and reported that March 4 and March 5, the Reagans' wedding anniversary, were "good days." This raised a familiar problem because the press conference had tentatively been scheduled for March 9, and this date was not among the auspicious ones certified by the Friend. According to a list provided by Mrs. Reagan to Bill Henkel, the Friend had made the following prohibitions based on her reading of the President's horoscope:

Late Dec thru March bad
Jan 16–23 very bad
Jan 20 nothing outside WH—possible attempt
Feb 20–26 be careful
March 7–14 bad period
March 10–14 no outside activity!
March 16 very bad
March 21 no
March 27 no
March 12–19 no trips exposure
March 19–25 no public exposure
April 3 careful
April 11 careful
April 17 careful
April 21–28 stay home

Obviously this list of dangerous or forbidden dates left very little latitude for scheduling. Avoiding any mention of the Friend or the First Lady's communications with her—as I always did in discussions of the schedule with the President—I asked Reagan what he wanted to do about the timing of his television address and press conference. The President repeated that he wanted to schedule his TV appearance for March 4. I pointed out that this would mean rescheduling the press conference because it would be unwise to have a major speech on the Tower report and what was certain to be a highly charged press conference in the same week.

Well, the President replied, my anniversary is March fifth. That's a good day for me, but I don't know what we'd do about the press conference; I guess we'd have to postpone it.

I continued to press for a decision, but the President was lame on this subject; he avoided a commitment. It became clear that there could be no press conference on March 9 and that the President himself was not prepared to suggest an alternative date.

Later that afternoon, Wednesday, February 25, the First Lady called Bill Henkel and told him to reschedule the press conference for March 19. Mrs. Reagan told Henkel that her Friend had identified March 26 as a "good day for travel." The President, therefore, should journey somewhere to make his foreign-policy speech on that date. I told Henkel to make his plans accordingly.

No matter where the President went on March 26, I did not expect to be traveling with him. By then, I supposed, Reagan would have told me when he wanted me to leave and what arrangements he had caused to be made for the dignified departure he had promised when we discussed my resignation on February 23. We'll make sure that you go out in good fashion, the President had said. Naturally I had taken him at his word, and I was heartened by the thought that he would thank me publicly for my service, and that I would have the opportunity publicly to say good-bye to him and to express my gratitude and loyalty for the last time.

On Thursday afternoon, February 26, the day the Tower report was issued, Vice President Bush sent word to me through a secretary that he wished to see me.

"I guess he's the messenger," I said to my associates.

At 1:30 P.M. I went to his office, which was next door to mine.

"I've just had lunch with the President," Bush told me. "He asked me to find out what your plans are . . . about leaving."

My temper flared. "What's the matter—isn't he man enough to ask me that question himself? We agreed in front of ten people on Monday to discuss this matter next week, and I said then that I'd leave the details up to him."

Bush said, "Is that your understanding of your one-on-one meeting with the President?"

"Yes," I replied. "I told the President I'd leave after the Tower report came out and he said okay. Does he want me out today?"

"No," Bush said, "I don't think so."

"If I go now, I'm part of the scandal," I said. "That's what Nancy Reagan and Deaver and Stu Spencer want, but I won't have it that way. I'm determined that I will not have it look as if I'm going out because of the Tower report."

The Vice President sighed. "I know it's rough," he said. "But the President wants it to go smoothly. He mentioned that letter of resignation you showed him last October." This was a reference to my statement to the President, before the Iran-Contra affair was exposed, that I wished to leave the White House after the November elections.

"I don't see how it's going to go smoothly," I said to Bush. "I've been hacked to pieces in the press by these people, and now, after two years as the President's Chief of Staff and four years as his Secretary of the Treasury, I'm being fired like a shoe clerk. I'm bitter, George, and you can tell that to the President."

Bush was embarrassed by my outburst. After a moment he said, "I'll tell the President what you've said." The Vice President then attempted to console me by praising the job I had done in the Administration and expressing his admiration and friendship. In the circumstances I did not thank him for his kindness as I should have done.

Before we parted, he raised a question about the President's schedule. I told him it was in the hands of an astrologer in San Francisco. Bush listened to the history of my dealings with Mrs. Reagan on this question with surprise and consternation on his features. When I was finished, he uttered what was a strong expletive for George Bush.

"Good God," he said, "I had no idea."

He did not ask if the President knew about the Friend. I understood his reluctance perfectly, because this was a question I myself had never asked.

Back in my own office, I discussed my conversation with Bush with Dennis Thomas, Tom Dawson, and Peter Wallison. These members of the staff were worried about what one of them called "character assassination over the weekend." If I did not have a clear understanding as to when I would leave, I might find myself reading of the appointment of a new Chief of Staff over the weekend. It was possible, they warned unanimously, that I might come to work and be turned away by the guards in view of the cameras, or find my office door padlocked. These bizarre possibilities were offered in the most matter-of-fact terms. Two years before, I would have dismissed them as the ravings of hysterical minds. On the basis of my recent experience, and in light of what I had been reading in the newspapers every day, they did not seem to be out of the question. ("THE SUBJECT WAS REGAN: AT PARTY FOR STUART SPENCER, REPUBLICANS SAVOR JOKES," *Washington Post,* February 21, 1987; "CONTRADICTION IN REAGAN'S TESTIMONY ON IRAN IS SAID TIED TO TALK WITH CHIEF OF STAFF REGAN," *Wall Street Journal,* February 19, 1987.)

I went back to see the Vice President and asked if he had seen the President since our talk about fifteen minutes before.

Bush replied, "Yes, I've told him what you told me, and the President seemed relieved."

I wanted to be certain that there was no confusion over the timing of my departure. "Did you tell him that I would be leaving next week—and did he say okay to that?"

"Yes," said Bush.

A weight lifted from my shoulders. "In that case," I said, "the President will have my resignation on Monday morning."

Bush nodded and gave me a sympathetic look. "I don't want you to think that I'm trying to flatter you," he said. "But I think you should know that the President told me just a moment ago that he's going to miss you. He valued your frankness. He said that you always gave him both sides of any question, and if he asked for an opinion you gave it to him straight, directly and openly."

"Then why am I being booted out?" I asked. "Why the haste? What have I done wrong?"

"It's nothing in particular," Bush replied. "It's just been a wearing-away. It's those attacks on you night after night on the tube and the President seeing it after he goes upstairs. He can't stand it. He wants to make a new start."

"I can understand that," I said. "But I wish to hell he'd had the manliness to tell me himself instead of using you as a go-between."

"I feel for you, Don," Bush said. "But that's it."

The next morning, Friday, February 27, the President greeted me and George Bush when we arrived together as usual for the nine o'clock meeting as if it were an ordinary morning.

Reagan gave me a pleasant look and said, George told me of your conversation yesterday. That's fine by me.

I said nothing in reply. The subject was not mentioned again.

For the next thirty minutes, the three of us discussed the Tower report and its reception by the press and the public. Reagan was testy about charges that his aloof style of management had contributed to the fiasco.

The President said that he would explain to the nation in his television address that there had been no swap of arms for hostages. Once again he explained his rationale: the United States had not paid ransom to the kidnappers, but had merely rewarded an intermediary who undertook to arrange for the release of the victims.

My policy was simply to make an overture to Iran, Reagan said. That was mishandled. But I didn't believe I was dealing with terrorists then, and I won't say that I was now.

Reagan was dug in on this position—face flushed, lips pursed, voice strained. "Mr. President," I said, "don't shoot the messenger for what I'm about to tell you, but you can't go on national television and say to the American people what you've just said to us. It just won't wash. No one will believe such a story."

George Bush told the President the same thing in somewhat less frank and direct language.

That morning, during a meeting to discuss the President's foreign-policy speech, Frank Carlucci had told me that he had heard that Howard Baker had already been chosen as my successor. Later in the day at a meeting with the Republican leaders of the Senate and House, the President had said that he thought that they would be pleased with his new Chief of Staff. I did not attend this meeting precisely because I thought that the President might want to discuss my replacement with his visitors. The fact that he had done so in such specific terms clearly indicated that he and those who were advising him had already decided on the new man.

All this, discourteous though it was, seemed normal enough. After all, the President knew that Monday would be my last day; the arrangements had been made. Tom and Dennis advised me to get my version of my resignation on the record. In midafternoon I talked separately to Gerald Boyd of the *New York Times* and Barry Seaman and Dave Beckwith of *Time* about my departure. Earlier, I had made an appointment to have my hair cut, and as the interviews ended around three o'clock I prepared to leave, intending to go straight home from the barber shop.

As I said good-bye to the reporters, I saw that Carlucci was waiting in my outer office. Bob Tuttle, Director of Presidential Personnel, had just called him to say that Cable News Network (CNN) was broadcasting a report that Howard Baker was the new Chief of Staff in the White House. The staff confirmed that this report was accurate.

I dictated a resignation letter to my secretary. It read:

Dear Mr. President:
I hereby resign as Chief of Staff to the President of the United States.

Respectfully yours,
DONALD T. REGAN

I asked Tom Dawson to deliver the letter to the Oval Office, and he went down the hall and handed it to Jim Kuhn. Meanwhile Carlucci was urging me to go see the President or call him on the telephone.

I said, "No, that would be undignified. And I don't trust myself to speak to him. I'm too mad. There's been a deliberate leak, and it's been done to humiliate me."

Carlucci said that I couldn't go without talking to the President. He asked my permission to call Reagan, and rushed out of the room.

A few moments later the telephone rang. It was the President.

Don, I'm terribly sorry about what's happened, he said. I didn't mean for this to happen.

I did not trust myself to reply. After a momentary silence, the President spoke again.

The report was accurate, he said. Howard will be the new Chief of Staff. He's looking forward to talking to you.

"I'm sorry, Mr. President, but I won't be in any more," I said, speaking with great intensity. "This is my last day. I've been your Secretary of the Treasury for four years and your Chief of Staff for two. You don't trust me enough even to tell me who my successor is and make a smooth transfer. I deserved better treatment than this. I'm through. I'm very disappointed."

Don, listen, the President said. I intended to proceed just as we had discussed. My plan was to say that you wanted to resign in November after the elections and had in fact prepared a letter in October. You had told me all this way back then. Then came Iran, and so you stayed on to help in a time of trouble. I planned to let everyone know you had told me more than a week ago that you had made the decision to go after the Tower report was issued and that you are now carrying out that intention.

The President added that he still intended to make that statement.

I hope you'll go along with that, Don, he said.

But I could not do it. I said, "No, Mr. President, it's over. All that's left for me to say is good-bye."

Speaking very softly into the telephone, Ronald Reagan said, I'm sorry.

Although he and I have seen each other at public events, we have never to this day spoken again.

Later the President sent me a letter:

THE WHITE HOUSE
WASHINGTON
February 27, 1987

Dear Don:

In accepting your resignation I want you to know how deeply grateful I am for all that you have done for this Administration and for our country. As Secretary of the Treasury you planted the seeds for the most far-reaching tax reform in our history. As Chief of Staff you worked tirelessly and effectively for the policies and programs we proposed to the Congress.

I know that you stayed on beyond the time you had set for your return to private life, and did so because you felt you could be of help in a time of trouble. You were of help and I thank you. Whether on the deck of your beloved boat or on the fairway, in the words of our forefathers, may the sun shine warm upon your face, the wind be always at your back, and may God hold you in the hollow of His hand.

Sincerely,

In my time with President Reagan, I had seen many such letters, and so I knew that someone else had written it for him.

Afterword
Reflections on Public Service

In the first chapter of Ecclesiastes we are told that "he that in-creaseth knowledge increaseth sorrow." This same chapter be-gins with the famous verse "Vanity of vanities . . . all is vanity."

Some will think that I have added to the sorrows of my party by writing as frankly as I have done about the inside workings of the Reagan Presidency. Others will resent the suggestion that the Washington Establishment is driven by vanity.

They will not convince me that they are right. This memoir reflects my own experience and the conclusions I have drawn from it, and it is my belief that the tendency to process the activ-ities of the government into entertainment constitutes a danger to the democratic process and to the republic itself. The sym-biosis between the press and the Reagan Administration carried a destructive American tendency to trivialize the nation's busi-ness very close to the pathological. Both partners share in the responsibility, but the active partner indubitably was the White House. This was the most damning failure of an Administration that was otherwise a great force for good in America and in the world.

The government of a free country must conduct its business openly to the greatest possible degree. But it cannot design its operations with theatrical effect as the primary objective. To do so creates a voracious appetite for drama with its simplified char-acters, its predictable situations, and above all, its happy or unhappy endings. But finality, as Disraeli said, is not the language of politics. Although it is true, as the activists argue, that government must sometimes make things happen, it is also true that one of its most important functions is to prevent certain things— war being the supreme example—from happening at all. The history of the United States, like that of all other great powers, is filled with questions large and small—the intentions of the framers of the Constitution, slavery and its aftermath, farm price supports, Nicaragua—that have never been answered. It is an illusion to believe that they will be resolved in the near future.

When I joined the Reagan Administration on its first day I knew very little about the new President or what he intended to do. As the reader has seen, my six years of service was a voyage of discovery. On the whole, those years were joyous. I lived through many satisfying moments. The reform of the tax structure was a great accomplishment not only because of what it did to make taxation fairer and more rational in the United States, but also because it showed that the American system still had the will and the power to reform itself in the interest of the people. The lesson that cynicism, special privilege, and orthodoxy cannot withstand the forces of common sense and democratic principle has great meaning for other unwieldy and haphazard structures, such as the welfare system—which, like the old tax system, punishes and represses the people it was designed to help.

It is a great thing to be present at the making of history. In a democracy, the political appointee does well to remember that he is present as a matter of luck and courtesy rather than by any right. It was Ronald Reagan, not any of his advisers or aides, who was elected as the fortieth President. Never for a moment did I doubt that the people were right in their judgment of him. Elsewhere in this book I have compared him to Franklin Roosevelt and to Harry Truman, and while I realize that this must infuriate many admirers of those two great men, I believe that history will find the comparison valid. Like Roosevelt, Reagan changed the political landscape of the United States—and the way in which Americans saw themselves and their country—in a fundamental and probably permanent way. Like Truman, he was perceived by his critics to be unqualified for his office, an accidental President from whom little could be expected.

A generation from now, Reagan's homely understanding of the importance of small things and his sound judgment and good instincts in large issues will be more clearly seen and better understood. If he is remembered, as evidently he wishes to be, as the American President who banished nuclear arms from the world, then he will be a great figure in history indeed, and the very qualities for which he was derided in his own time—instinctive rather than intellectual judgment, simplicity of vision—will be the ones that made greatness possible.

Although the reader can hardly be in any doubt about it at this point in the story, I wish to state that my admiration for Reagan as President remains very great. My judgment of him as a man, in light of my final experience as his Chief of Staff, underwent a certain change, but this is irrelevant. Rulers are not judged as other men, and any man who had seen as much of the world as I had seen when I came to Washington knew better than to put his trust in princes. Whatever frustrations and disappointments I met with in Washington came not from Ronald Reagan but from those who had attached themselves to his person, his name, or his office as a means of advancing their own interests and agendas. In the end these people—many of whom I regarded then, and still regard, as frivolous gossips and sycophants—brought about my departure from the President's service under conditions that caused anguish to my family and destroyed my friendship with the President to whom I had devoted six years of loyal and (as it seemed to me) unselfish service.

This was the bitterest event of my life, and it threw a shadow over all that I had accomplished and the reasons why I had worked to achieve whatever I had achieved in the nearly seventy years that I had been alive. My father and mother taught me to care little for the opinions of others as long as I knew in my heart that I was doing the right thing. This lesson had carried me through difficult periods, but when the campaign of slander was at its height, I was thankful that my parents and my brother and sister were not alive to read these scurrilous lies and see the family name dragged through the mud by malicious strangers. I even wondered if my own children might be tempted to believe that there was some truth in the accusations and feared that I had disgraced them.

After I left the White House I spent a great deal of time trying to understand what had happened to me in those last days, and why. In the end I concluded that the answer was probably very simple: President Reagan and I were too well suited to each other. The psychic and administrative support that I attempted to provide to him as a means of helping him to achieve his own fundamental objectives, rather than supporting the choices that others wished to make for him, created the impression that he was depending too much upon me. The fear arose that I was dominating him, and the press campaign that portrayed me as a martinet who had made himself into an ex officio prime minister fortified the impression. If this was a case of the propagandists believing their own propaganda, it was not the first such case in history.

After I departed, Mrs. Reagan wrote me a note in her own hand on her blue White House stationery, providing a footnote to the circumstances of my last moments in the West Wing. "I . . . did *not* issue a statement 'gleefully'—as they [the press] put it—before Ronnie did when you left," she wrote. "C&N [sic] called Elaine's [Crispin, the First Lady's press secretary] office for a comment. I told her to say I wished you good luck and we were happy to welcome Howard—hardly earth-shattering but they certainly tried to twist it. Elaine called and voiced strong objections."

On the great balance sheet of a human life, the losses are seldom as memorable in the end as the gains. My public service cost me the most acute public discomfort of my life, the friendship of the only man to whom I had ever willingly subordinated myself, and the considerable amount of money that I no doubt would have earned if I had remained in the private sector instead of coming to Washington. Of these three unhappy results, only the loss of the personal feeling I had for Ronald Reagan matters.

After I left office and the motives for blaming me for the acts of others vanished, the truth about Iran-Contra came out. The Joint Committee investigating the scandal cleared my name. By the time I appeared before the assembled senators and congressmen on July 30, 1987, the testimony of others had already established the facts. And these, as I had anticipated, had shown that McFarlane and Poindexter simply had not told the President or me exactly what they and Lieutenant Colonel North were up to. My appearance before the Joint Committee was so cordial, in fact, that I wondered how anyone had gotten the idea that I didn't get along with Congress. But then, of course, I knew how that idea had gained currency.

These words are being written almost exactly a year after the events of February and early March 1987. Looking back, I ask myself if it was worth it. This is a hard question. The losses were hard to take, but the gains were great also. I am a far wiser man now than I was then, knowing much more about the world and a great deal more about myself than I did before. I took part in events that changed the world for the better. Although I know that I will disappear as nearly all chamberlains do when the history of the Reagan years is written, I have the satisfaction of knowing that that history would have been somewhat different if I had not been at the President's side.

I hope that other Americans, young and old, will take themselves to the nation's capital. Much good work is done there by many good people, and on the great balance sheet, the gains to the nation and the person greatly outweigh the losses and the disappointments.

I did what I did because I wanted to go on learning and because I thought that I already knew enough to help the country that had given my forebears a refuge from oppression and poverty and had given me a life that I could not have lived in any other place or time.

Index